Pentecostal Currents in American Protestantism

Pentecostal Currents in American Protestantism

EDITED BY EDITH L. BLUMHOFER,

RUSSELL P. SPITTLER, AND

GRANT A. WACKER

University of Illinois Press

Urbana and Chicago

Manufactured in the United States of America
1 2 3 4 5 C P 5 4 3 2 1

This book is printed on acid-free paper.

Library of Congress Cataloging-in-Publication Data
Pentecostal currents in American Protestantism / edited by Edith L. Blumhofer, Russell P. Spittler, and Grant A. Wacker.
p. cm.
Includes bibliographical references and index.
ISBN 0-252-02450-8 (alk. paper)
ISBN 0-252-06756-8 (pbk. : alk. paper)
1. Pentecostalism—United States.
2. Pentecostal churches—United States.
I. Blumhofer, Edith Waldvogel.
II. Spittler, Russell P.
III. Wacker, Grant A.
BR1644.5.U6 P46 1999
280'.4'0973—ddc21 98-25395
CIP

Contents

Acknowledgments

The editors acknowledge the generous support of the Lilly Endowment, which funded this project through a grant to the Institute for the Study of American Evangelicals (ISAE).

Many scholars participated in consultations and offered stimulating insights during the course of the project. Among them R. Stephen Warner merits special thanks for the two years he spent as a member of the project's advisory committee. Ann Rehfeldt and Mary Noll provided capable technical and research support. Their efforts were invaluable to the preparation of the manuscript.

Some of the studies that the project funded are not included in this collection because they were published elsewhere or fell outside the scope of the present volume. They include fine articles by William Abraham, Courtney Bender, Ian Cotton, Mary Ruth Curlee, Matthew Lawson, Luis Leon, Margaret Poloma, and Wayne Warner. The project also funded a college course and public lectures at Wheaton College; consultations at Princeton University, Gordon Conwell Theological Seminary, and Wheaton College; and a conference at Fuller Theological Seminary. In addition, it supported in part Edith Blumhofer's work on Aimee Semple McPherson, an evangelist who often publicly stood at the intersection of her day's mainstream denominations and the Pentecostal movement. That work resulted in the publication of *Aimee Semple McPherson: Everybody's Sister* (Grand Rapids, Mich.: Eerdmans, 1993).

This book is dedicated to one of the ISAE's advisors, the late George A. Rawlyk. George helped to conceive the project and generously offered wise counsel and friendly encouragement. He is greatly missed.

Introduction

Edith L. Blumhofer

Several years ago the Institute for the Study of American Evangelicals (ISAE) at Wheaton College received a grant from the Lilly Endowment for a project called "Mainstream Protestantism and the Pentecostal and Charismatic Movements." The project addressed questions such as the following: What happens when mainstream Protestantism and Pentecostal movements encounter one another? What are the ways in which they intersect, respond, and realign? The grant funded consultations and research that focused on moments of encounter, beginning with several turn-of-the-century contacts between American Pentecostalism and its surrounding culture. These early encounters established boundaries and expectations that helped to define the religious movement we now call "classical" Pentecostalism. When the charismatic movement emerged in post–World War II America, it crossed those boundaries, indicated the need to rethink the accepted boundaries for Pentecostalism, and prompted reconsideration of expectations. A second focus of the project was thus on encounters between mainstream Protestantism and charismatic movements. The following chapters offer case studies that suggest how religious movements come to be defined in the popular imagination and how those definitions then come to be deconstructed.

The Pentecostal movement emerged at the turn of the century as a protest against dry denominationalism. Its roots in Anglo-American radical evangelicalism ran deep. Its style was separatist and exclusivist, and consequently it inspired the formation of a new denominational family whose distinguishing belief was that all believers should experience a baptism with the Holy Spirit. This baptism, Pentecostals maintained, would always be manifested by speaking in tongues. They referred to speaking in tongues as the "initial physical evidence" of the baptism with the Holy Spirit.

Unlike their fundamentalist cohort, with whom they had much in common, early Pentecostals did not do battle primarily with modernist theology; rather, they sought to reverse the overwhelming trend toward "carnality" in the churches and among church members. Everything from church-sponsored socials to the pervasiveness among Christians of stylish clothing and secular amusements, as well as declining attendance at prayer meetings, verified their conviction that the church had lost spiritual power. "Formal, cold, dead denominational churches" seemed to contrast sharply to the noisy fervor that marked early Pentecostal gatherings. Their faith centered in a series of defining encounters between the individual and God that they regarded as the hallmark of true Christianity. The first encounter—a "know-so" conversion—would lead to others, they believed, most notably a baptism with the Holy Spirit evidenced by speaking in tongues, so that they always yearned for "more" of Jesus. Meanwhile, they offered "the full menu" of biblical Christianity to any and all. They based their claims on a favorite text, Hebrews 13:8: "Jesus Christ, the same yesterday and today and forever." Simple literalism led them to the inevitable conclusion: whatever was recorded as the spiritual experience of the church in the New Testament was intended to be experienced by Christians at all times.

Classical Pentecostalism, then, was primarily a pietistic and only secondarily a theological protest. Its early relationship to other groups on the North American religious scene was typically adversarial. In the first encounters between Pentecostals and the Protestant mainstream, Pentecostals readily defined themselves against the mainstream. General perceptions of the worldliness—and, later, the theological liberalism—of mainstream Protestantism were not the only concerns. These were reinforced by countless testimonies given weekly in Pentecostal missions by people who had been reared in denominational churches but had not "found God" until they came into contact with Pentecostals. Their distaste for the historic denominations made many Pentecostals refuse to acknowledge that their organizations were becoming denominations, too. The Assemblies of God, for example, carefully identified itself as a "fellowship" or a "movement." Avoiding the label *denomination,* with its connotations of spiritual "coldness" or "death," became a central part of early Pentecostal identity.

For charismatics, the situation was different from the outset, at least in key respects. Emerging just after the middle of the century, the charismatic renewal celebrated the presence and work of the Holy Spirit in individual believers, including speaking in tongues and gifts of prophecy and healing. But it contrasted sharply with earlier Pentecostalism in its relationship to the mainstream. Whereas early Pentecostals formed a new denominational family, charismatics constituted a subset of an existing mainstream. Instead of exhibiting the separatism that marked early Pentecostalism, the charismatic impulse had an integrative character. Charismatic service organizations in major denominations were one evidence of this contrasting style. Early Pentecostals often either chose to leave the denominations or were forced out. Many charismatics opted to stay and become agents of renewal in historic communions. They often discovered that charismatic experience simply took the things they shared with others in their denominations and invested them with dramatic personal meaning. Charismatic experience made Catholics "better" Catholics and Methodists "better" Methodists, they insisted, as they drank more deeply than before at the wells of spirituality nurtured by the historic communions.

This behavioral contrast between Pentecostals and charismatics had various roots: theological differences, the changing character of mainstream Christianity, and class distinctions. One must also take into account a notable cultural shift that makes late twentieth-century Christians more inclusive than their forebears. Domesticated tolerance may be more pervasive at the end of the century than it was at the beginning.

The first of the following groups of case studies exhibits ways in which Pentecostalism intersected with mainstream Protestantism. The mode was generally separatist, fueled by the conviction that God always works "outside the camp" with a remnant of true believers wholly dedicated to the fulfillment of God's overarching purpose in history. Those who accepted speaking in tongues as the evidence of the baptism with the Holy Spirit, then, could be expected to abandon "dead denominations" for new affiliations. An apt metaphor from the New Testament reminded them that the new wine of the Spirit mandated new wineskins. And they not only left mainstream congregations; they also denounced them. To be sure, few paid heed, but condemnations of the mainstream had an important place in an emerging Pentecostal rhetoric. Typically adversarial, these "come-outers" tended to be somewhat more evangelistic and missionary minded than the later charismatics who opted to stay within the mainstream. Those who stayed, as the second group of case studies demonstrates, were in some ways more accommodationist, more nurturing of the network of which they were already a part.

Despite their sharp contrasts in style, though, the Pentecostal and charismatic movements also exhibit important continuities. First, both are more pietistic than theological, rooted in the conviction that consciousness of the presence and gifts of the Holy Spirit should mark the individual believer's daily life as well as the church's worship. Second, both manifest a penchant for triumphalism. Advocates of Pentecostal forms of spirituality—whether classical or charismatic—tend to maintain that they possess something that everyone needs; others have not "seen the light" unless they, too, embrace these distinctive forms of Christian experience. Both movements, then, exhibit exclusivist tendencies, informing outsiders of their spiritual incompleteness by actions if not by words: "You lack something if you do not share our viewpoint and experience." Third, both movements manifest a strong puritan bent, nurturing a definite sense of how one should order and discipline one's private life.

The pages that follow offer ten case studies framed by two other chapters, one on Pentecostalism's biblical antecedents and the other on the history of historical treatments of the Pentecostal and charismatic movements. Each addresses the theme of encounter. As case studies, these chapters do not attempt to cover the wide range of ethnic, theological, or class differentiation among American Pentecostals. Rather, they offer suggestions about the shaping of American religious identity and what happens at the confluence of the mainstream and other streams.

In the opening chapter Russell Spittler describes an overvaluation of spirit above body that has plagued spiritualities of the Pentecostal or charismatic sort, both ancient and modern. During project discussions, he maintained that the Pentecostal and charismatic movements have exhibited two styles of intersecting with the Protestant mainstream. Pentecostals generally have intersected by pretending not to, opting for a Johannine model. For these groups, the world is "out there" and evil and includes apostate churches. Charismatics, by contrast, might be considered more Pauline in their approach, engaging in more compromise and adaptation. In both cases, and more than participants recognize, the New Testament offers a way to model how these traditions have expressed themselves.

The first group of case studies explores encounters between Pentecostals and mainstream Protestantism. Grant Wacker offers a backward look to the animosity that marked Pentecostalism's encounter with the Holiness movement. The Pentecostal emphasis on tongues speech resulted in fierce internecine warfare in this religious family dedicated to the realization of John Wesley's ideal of perfect love. Daniel Bays offers an outward look, examining the forms and results of engagement between Pentecostal missionaries and Protestant mission boards in China. Kurt Berends uses two encounters in rural New England to study boundary making and to probe conflict (both literal and metaphorical) over staking out territory on the religious landscape. Douglas Jacobsen reflects on one aspect of the Pentecostal encounter with the modern world of theological studies as he investigates the sources of second-generation Pentecostals' theology.

The second section of case studies turns to encounters between charismatic forms of Christianity and mainstream Protestantism. Corwin E. Smidt, Lyman

A. Kellstedt, John C. Green, and James L. Guth sketch out the contours of the charismatic movement by looking at charismatic political behavior. Marie Griffith examines Women's Aglow Fellowship, an interdenominational prayer fellowship for charismatic women. Albert Schenkel describes how Southern and American Baptists responded to the charismatic renewal. Nancy Eiesland details an encounter in a southern Methodist congregation. Fred Jordan uses evangelist Kathryn Kuhlman's work with the First Presbyterian Church in Pittsburgh as a lens through which to examine encounter at both popular and leadership levels. Helen Turner maintains that, although the charismatic renewal has had little effect on Southern Baptists, a Pentecostal-type worldview thrives in the Southern Baptist Convention and enabled the fundamentalist takeover of the convention.

The concluding chapter reviews the questions and assumptions that have guided historians of Pentecostalism over the past thirty years. Gus Cerillo's historiographical chronicle focuses on the study of classical Pentecostalism, the literature on which has moved through several stages of inquiry since scholars first began studying the movement in the 1960s. He concludes with a brief look at the emerging scholarly interpretation of the charismatic renewal. It will be fascinating to see how the charismatic movement looks through a scholarly lens a few decades from now.

The Pentecostal and charismatic movements affect growing numbers of Americans in denominational and independent congregations, and their vitality in parts of Asia, Africa, and South America have contributed to the transformation of global Christianity. The chapters in this book point to moments in which identities and boundaries have been established or challenged as these movements have taken their place on the American religious scene.

PART 1

Overview of Pentecostal Spirituality

1

Corinthian Spirituality: How a Flawed Anthropology Imperils Authentic Christian Existence

Russell P. Spittler

By whatever name, religion marks most if not all cultures. For two decades at least, the term *spirituality* has flourished as a way to describe religion that is worth something. *Spirituality* refers to what historians have called "lived religion"—the cluster of values, beliefs, and practices that marks the characteristic (at times distinctive) religious lifestyle of a specific religious community, whether ancient or modern, mainstream or marginal.

Corinthian here refers first of all to one pietistic style that overran others in an early Christian church founded by the Apostle Paul around the middle of the first Christian century in the leading city of Corinth in what today is called Greece.

But the term *Corinthian* applies here as well to a generic spirituality whose footprints can be traced widely over the history of the church. Indeed, *Corinthian spirituality* seems particularly apt to designate much, though by no means all, of the religiosity of those twentieth-century siblings, the Pentecostal and charismatic movements.

Nothing esoteric fogs the other terms in the title. *Anthropology* points not to the social science of that name or to any particular one of its methods: it mirrors rather classical Christian theology's traditional name for teaching about the nature of human personhood. And *Christian existence* speaks simply of normal Christian behavior, that is, everyday Christian life that is neither heroic nor heretic but ordinary and usual—taking the gap between the ideal and the real as part of the picture.

Corinthian spirituality, to put it briefly, postulates a misshapen notion of human nature that makes a principled exaggeration of the worth of spirit over body. The term can usefully describe both a major contingent of the apostle's errant congregation at Corinth and an ever-present peril threatening the twentieth-century Pentecostal and charismatic movements.

Corinth is the best attested of the churches in the New Testament.[1] Similarly, the number of persons associated with the charismatic and Pentecostal movements in the course of the twentieth century has come to exceed, surprisingly, the count of global adherents to Protestantism itself.[2] Combined, the Pentecostal and charismatic movements occupy a position second only to the Roman Catholic liturgy among widespread styles of contemporary Christian spirituality.

An assumption that allows this sort of connection between the first and the twentieth century is the continuity of human nature—wryly described by Mark Twain when he said that human nature is widely spread among people.

Can Religious Experience Be Studied?

Can spirituality even be talked about in academic terms? Certainly. The American Academy of Religion, the mother of all such guilds in the Western Hemisphere, raised the question when it convened, at annual meetings between 1984 and 1988, a seminar dealing with recent Christian spirituality. Results were mixed. Bradley C. Hanson, who edited the summarizing volume, admitted the difficulty in fitting spirituality into the academic study of religion and argued for separate faculties and courses for an enterprise that would more appropriately be named *spiritual theology.*[3]

In her lucid and illuminating article in the same volume, however, Sandra M. Schneiders forged a compelling definition: "Spirituality is the field of study which attempts to investigate in an interdisciplinary way spiritual experience as such, i.e., as spiritual and as experience."[4] She went on to make the points that spirituality is, from this perspective, "descriptive-critical rather than prescriptive-normative"; that it is "ecumenical, interreligious, [and] cross-cultural"; and that it is, overall, a "holistic discipline . . . not limited to explorations of the explicitly religious, i.e., so-called *interior life.* The psychological, bodily, historical, social, political, aesthetic, intellectual, and other dimensions of the human subject of spiritual experience are integral to that experience insofar as it is the subject matter of the discipline of spirituality."[5] In other words, spirituality can be viewed as the multichanneled scientific analysis of individual religious experience. This is an academic definition, of course, but a legitimate and useful one.

After all, the twentieth century could be labeled the century of religious experience examined. It opened with Carl Jung's doctoral studies analyzing a teen-age spiritualistic medium who spoke in tongues.[6] At the same time, in 1901–2, William James gave the famed Gifford lectures published under the title *The Varieties of Religious Experience.*[7] These were exactly the years of the Topeka, Kansas, origins of Pentecostalism—from which direct connections can be made to Azusa Street in 1906. By 1909, when the Azusa Street revival that spawned Pentecostalism was in full swing, Sigmund Freud was touring the United States and lecturing on psychoanalysis. Massive research on religious experience over the last hundred years has both paralleled and informed the concurrent growth of psychology into a mature science.

In the last third of the twentieth century, there emerged what Donald L. Gelpi calls "the turn to experience in contemporary theology."[8] Noting that the term *experience* "enjoys a certain pride of place among the weasel words of the English language,"[9] Gelpi documents philosophical interest in experience in Belgian Roman Catholic theologian Edward Schillebeeckx as well as in liberationist, feminist, and process theologians.

As a specialist in the American philosophical tradition, Gelpi cites experience as a conspicuous recurring motif in American speculative thought, including work by Charles Sanders Peirce, William James, Josiah Royce, George Santayana, the later Alfred North Whitehead, and John Dewey. Gelpi himself, over a half-generation ago, wrote *Experiencing God: A Theology of Human Experience,* which remains the most thoroughgoing analysis of charismatic experience from the perspective of North American philosophical theology.[10]

It is not merely in theology that experience gained prominence in the second half of the twentieth century. A marked feature of postmodernity "is the determination to give prominence to experience," suggests Nelson S. T. Thayer in an astute analysis of the cultural context of "spirituality and pastoral care."[11] The philosophical and epistemological fertility of religious experience emerges in such recent works as those by Wayne Proudfoot (*Religious Experience*)[12] and William P. Alston (*Perceiving God: The Epistemology of Religious Experience*).[13]

As the century closed, more evidence for the increasing role of religious experience arose from the Lilly Endowment project tracing Pentecostal currents in the American church. This project has undertaken a three-year study (1991–94) of the effect of decidedly individualized religious experience on mainstream North American Christianity. As for the future, at least one prediction has emerged: by the arrival of the next millennium, religious experience will be available on demand through sophisticated pharmaceutical means.

Whatever else can be said about them, the Pentecostal and charismatic movements have democratized individual religious experience. They did this by holding out as a value an intensely personal religious experience, termed "baptism in the Holy Spirit," which can be known to have occurred by the audible manifestation of speaking in tongues. Glossolalia, it is fair to say, is the religious experience of the twentieth century.

Yes, spirituality can be academically examined. It has been.[14] But the scientific sense of the term *spirituality* is not one that charismatics themselves would readily use. Within these traditions, *spirituality* more often refers to individual piety or personal religiosity. Relevant adjectives in the domain of such usage describe measurement (*deep, mature,* or *advanced*) or quality (*sterling* or *exemplary*). Yet Pentecostals highly rate personal religious experience itself. In an earlier study, I described five implicit values that mark Pentecostal and charismatic spirituality.[15] Chief among these is experience—that is, individual and personal appropriation and expression of religious values in a way that is accompanied with deep religious feelings of joy and gratitude. (It is a mistake to characterize majority Pentecostalism with the language of ecstasy or trance.) The literature of testimony, abundant among Pentecostals and charismatics,[16] profoundly characterizes these movements.

Still useful is Lesslie Newbigin's analysis published in the 1950s, before the public emergence of the charismatic movement. In his book *The Household of God* (written, as he himself later explained, before he knew much about the Pentecostal movement), the then bishop of the Church of South India described three ways of approaching God.[17] Protestants craft orthodoxies inviting assent. "Catholics," where this term denotes not only Roman Catholics but also other highly liturgical Christian groups, devise liturgies enabling obedient and sacramental participation. "Pentecostals" (using the word in a broad sense much like H. P. Van Dusen's term "third force" in a famous article for *Life* magazine[18] published near the same time), on the other hand, reach for God through personal experience. Orthodoxy (believing), sacrament (doing), and experience (feeling)—these provide a taxonomy of approaches to God.

There is a related vocabulary among Pentecostals. One term often used in a mood of warm appreciation is *reality.* It comes in Pentecostal hymnody: few songs evoke such spiritual satisfaction as "It's real, it's real, / Oh, I know it's real." The unspoken antonym, a careful observer would learn, is going through the motions of religion, such as is often thought to happen in liturgical churches, with no heartfelt response or life-affecting outcomes.

Even in the ecclesiastical mainstream, experience looms as a value. One leading East Coast seminary, in a half-page ad in a leading Christian thought magazine, informs potential students that its campus "is more than a place. It's an experience." "We invite you to make the ——— experience your own," the prose says. This is marketing lingo, certainly, but is it only that?

Where is "experience" in the New Testament? One Roman Catholic priest, not a charismatic, said he did not know what such an expression means: he had never had a "religious experience."

Most English-speaking Pentecostals in the formative first half of the twentieth century used the King James Version, in which the word *experience* occurs only once in the New Testament and twice in the Old.[19] None of these passages, nor all of them together, can account for the lofty role of what the word signifies within these movements.

But concepts and ideas can be expressed apart from key words, as experienced users of concordances soon discover. In a recently published Greek-English dictionary intended primarily for translators of the New Testament, the editors take a nontraditional approach to the classification of word meanings, one organized on the basis of ninety-three semantic domains rather than on the most usual alphabetic principle.[20] The result is a schematic classification of words not unlike the original version (not the more recent, alphabetized variety) of Roget's *Thesaurus*. Domain 90, titled "Case," defines case "in terms of the relation of participants to events or states"[21] and identifies two subdomains labeled "Experiencer," and "To Cause to Experience." Not surprisingly, words listed within these domains include many of the terms familiar to the vocabulary of Pentecostal experience: *in, into, upon, fall, happen, undergo, overwhelm, enter,* and *taste.*[22] What this all adds up to is a biblical warrant for charismatic claims to the worth of personal religious experience even if the word itself does not often occur.

Corinthian Spirituality: First Century

For a century or so, biblical scholars have illuminated the letter of the Apostle Paul commonly called 1 Corinthians by discerning between its lines the weighty influence in that congregation of a particular theological outlook. At its root, the belief projects a distorted conception of human nature, of Christian human nature in particular, a valuation of spirit above matter. The view quite likely arose from the apostle's own teachings given while he served for a year and a half (Acts 18:11) as the founding pastor of the church in Corinth. Over time, by mid-second century and on to the fifth century at least, this Corinthian anthropology fed into what is commonly called Gnosticism—a diffuse and diverse movement that taught salvation by insight and that seriously rivaled early orthodox Christianity yet included people who clearly understood themselves to be Christians.

By the latter half of the twentieth century, much more had been learned of the Gnostic movement, thanks mainly to the discovery of a library of some fifty-one chiefly Gnostic texts contained in thirteen codices. These were long preserved in Egyptian sands till dug up in 1945 by a camel driver seeking fertilizer at Nag Hammadi, a site located well over three hundred miles south of Cairo.[23]

Caution censors easy generalizations about Gnosticism and first-century Christianity. It is too facile to derive second-century Gnosticism from Pauline Christianity, too myopic to define all Gnosticism as Christian, and too simplistic to view the movement as monolithic. Yet it started somewhere. The view taken here identifies certain Corinthian ideas as parallel to those that in time flowered into the larger movement called Gnosticism but holds it anachronous to thrust Gnosticism baldly on Paul's Corinth without prudent qualifiers. Better to use the term *incipient Gnosticism,* proposed by F. F. Bruce,[24] *proto-Gnosticism,* or even *embryonic Gnosticism.*[25] In any case, what follows is a reading of 1 Corinthians that presumes proto-Gnosticism at Corinth.

And what is incipient Gnosticism?[26] Fundamentally, it is a variant anthropology that assumes a body-spirit dualism for the nature of human personality, clearly distinguishing the visible from the invisible aspects of human existence. Such dualism has ample precedent in the Platonic dualism that flourished four or five centuries earlier less than a hundred miles eastward (and north a bit) in classical Athens. There is clear precedent in the sayings of Jesus for marking the difference between material goods and the life of the soul: "For what will it profit them [potential followers] to gain the whole world and forfeit their life?" (Mark 8:36).[27] Even Paul himself, in his letters to the Corinthians, could easily and often distinguish body from spirit (1 Cor. 5:3, 6:16–17, 7:34; cf. 2 Cor. 12:2–4).

But Corinthian spirituality took a fateful step beyond Jesus and Paul. An inference was drawn that the body, because it consists of matter, is inherently evil and therefore should be treated as evil, either by carefree disregard or by cultivated subjugation. These strategies for management of the perceived inferior side of human nature were quite opposite: the one libertine, the other ascetic. Both clearly existed within the Corinthian congregation.

At Corinth there flourished cliquish divisions that centered on favored ministers among those who had influenced the congregation (1 Cor. 1:11, 12, 3:5, 21–23). Some showed loyalty to Paul, founder of Christianity in Corinth.

Some preferred Apollos, whose formative culture was that of the cosmopolitan Egyptian city of Alexandria, where the Nile emptied into the Mediterranean and where Philo (ca. 15 B.C. to A.D. 45) flourished—a Jewish philosopher and biblical interpreter who was an older contemporary of Apollos. Still others favored "Cephas," keeping the Aramaic name for Peter as a symbol of their conservative Jewish interests.

But the really troublesome party at Corinth was those who fastened not on an earthly Jesus but on the risen Christ: "I belong to Christ" (1:12) must have been their ringing motto. These were individuals who valued spirit over body, the ones who—luxuriating in the language of the angels, bodiless beings they would be glad to emulate—could with consistency pronounce a charismatic curse on the physical Jesus: "Let Jesus be cursed!" (12:3). In the earthly Jesus of Nazareth, whose parents and family were known, they had no interest. But to the heavenly, post-Resurrection, nonvisible Christ, they pledged devoted allegiance.

This distinction between Jesus and Christ, hardly ever made among modern pietists, in turn yields a heretical Christology. A Christology of the Gnostic sort would deny the reality of the incarnation, since the assumption of human physical existence would require the Redeemer to take on an inherently evil body. What kind of redeemer would that be?

Exactly this sort of rejection of the materiality of the Savior, one that again reflects a charismatic spirituality, showed up at Ephesus, three or four days away by boat, across the Aegean Sea eastward from Corinth, and at the time an integral part of Greek culture. Within Johannine circles a generation after Paul (who had himself spent three years in Ephesus; see Acts 20:31), a revered elder could issue a stern warning, using *spirit* in the sense of a charismatic utterance: "Every spirit that confesses that Jesus Christ has come in the flesh is from God, and every spirit that does not confess Jesus[28] is not from God" (1 John 4:2). Charismatic denials of the truly human incarnation of Jesus Christ, in other words, cannot be permitted. They must then already have existed.

Charismatic utterance? What has speech driven by the Spirit to do with those whose Christology wedged a distinction between Jesus and Christ and readily dispensed with the material Jesus? Just this: whoever favors spirit over body will value as well the capacity to speak in the language of the angels and, to a slightly lower extent, to prophesy—that is, to use speech born and borne of the Spirit.

Such an exaggerated preference for pneumatic speech aids the assessment of the role of glossolalia at Corinth. When Paul lists a variety of spiritual gifts, he responds to a query mentioned in a letter received from the Corinthians themselves.[29] That query must have implied or stated the superiority of glossolalia among works of the Spirit, and hence Paul's response downplays that gift and surrounds it with an ad hoc list of other ways in which the Spirit works equally (1 Cor. 12:4–11). Much of 1 Corinthians 12–14 provides counsels for control (not arguments for elimination) of congregational glossolalia. A reader gets the idea that public displays of the language of the angels were frequent. If one discerns the lopsided anthropology of the Christ party, those displays also can be seen as principled.

A specially revealing manifestation of Corinthian anthropology shows up in the opposite moral extremes that coexisted there. Not only did one community member strike up an ongoing illicit sexual liaison with his stepmother (5:1–13), to the delight of certain congregational supporters (5:2), but others freely used prostitutes (6:12–20). In addition, some in the same community proposed to cease sexual relations within existing marriages (7:1, 5), and still others attempted spiritual marriages—mergers in principle not to be consummated sexually (7:25, 36–38).

What explains such surprising and novel diversity? A flawed anthropology does. By styling the human person as both body and spirit, but most importantly spirit, opposing moral extremes logically follow: libertinism and asceticism.

If the body is evil, one logic runs, it can be disregarded along with its appetites. You cannot expect more of it, for that is its nature. Sexual appetite is no more blameworthy than eating (6:13); both are normal physiological processes easily satisfied. There was a Corinthian slogan, "All things are lawful for me" (6:12; cf. 10:23), easily though wrongly inferred from Paul's own preaching about Christ as the end of the Jewish legal system. Another slogan may have run, "Every sin that a person commits is outside the body!" (6:18b), meaning that the body, inherently evil, is amoral; sin can be predicated only of what truly counts in human nature, the spirit.

A lofty spirituality, on such Corinthian terms, would be one that recognizes the insight that spirit outranks body. Truly understood, such a governing insight calls for active demonstration. Hence there appeared at Corinth incest with one's stepmother and the use of prostitutes—along with congratulatory, triumphalist, and elitist support (5:2).

But quite a different philosophy of the body can emerge from the conviction that spirit outranks body in the structure of human existence. If the body is evil, does that not call for express effort directed toward its control? Should appetites not be suppressed, desires be denied, to make room for the spirit to abound? The way to do that, some Corinthians proposed, comes from their letter to the apostle: "It is well for a man not to touch a woman" (7:1)—their words, not the apostle's.

Paul's personal sympathies did indeed run along similar lines (7:7, 20, 37, 40). But he knew that not all have the *charisma* (7:7) needed to make a success of such a venture. As for married folk, he opines, let any ascetic arrangements proceed only by mutual agreement and for temporary periods of prayer (7:3–5). And worthy as it may be to sustain a marriage never consummated sexually (7:27–28, 32–35, 37, 38, 40), if the two in such a spiritual contract find the arrangement diversionary and difficult, "Let them marry." There is no sin to that (7:36, 38).[30]

Ripples of the Corinthian anthropology affected equally their ethics and their eschatology. One evidence of a highly individualistic ethic at Corinth surrounds the controversy there over the eating of meat from animals used in ritual sacrifice in pagan temples.[31] Such foods were available both in local meat markets (procured wholesale from the same entrepreneurial clerics who collected fees from the worshipers who brought the sacrificial animals) and in restaurants attached to the temples. Some Corinthians would readily eat such meats. Others would not.

Those who *did* eat "idol meat" did so on grounds of principle. They knew there was only one God and that idols were of no religious significance (8:1, 4). They cherished the freedom of menu derived from insight: "All of us possess knowledge" (using *gnosis,* 7:1). No one should deny them the right to eat as their theological conscience may dictate: "Why should my liberty be subject to the judgment of someone else's conscience?" (10:29b, a theoretical objection raised by Paul).

At this point in the apostle's lengthy argument (8:1–11:1), he punts. "Well, whatever you do," he advises, "avoid offense whenever you can"—his own self-commended style of ministry (10:31–11:1).[32] But earlier (8:9–13) he urges deference toward the "weak," those not so theologically developed as the ones who see themselves quite mature and made so by their superior insight. There is, throughout 1 Corinthians, high frequency of a vocabulary of perspicacity. Rival Athens, a few score miles east, had the university; Corinth had the wealth. Analysis of the Corinthian congregation suggests high interest there in spiritual insight, a sort of Christianized taming of the classic Greek philosophical interests seasoned with the promise of heavenly secrets attainable through charismatic means.

Paul disparages the efficacy of the human philosophical enterprise (1:18–2:5); admits a higher wisdom yet unavailable to the feuding Corinthians (2:6–16, 3:18–20); asks—bordering on sarcasm—whether there is not one Corinthian brilliant enough to warrant dropping fraternal litigation in the pagan courts (6:5); ten times in the letter asks tauntingly, "Don't you know . . . ?" (a phrase he uses only twice elsewhere in all his writings);[33] in a shrewd concession lists wisdom and knowledge first in the table of spiritual gifts (12:8); and affirms grandly that love "rejoices in the truth" (13:6) yet cautions—in a line that sums the whole letter—that "knowledge puffs up, but love builds up" (8:1).

Clearly the Corinthian Gnostics were high on spiritual insight. And that led to elitism ("And you are arrogant!" [5:2]), to a superiority complex ("Who sees anything different in you?" [4:7]; "Are you not merely human?" [3:4]).

Finally, how should the theme of the Corinthians' denial of the Resurrection be understood (15:12)? How could a church founded by the Apostle Paul and nurtured by stellar figures such as Apollos, Luke, Timothy, and maybe Peter, along with those three influential women of Corinth, Phoebe, Priscilla, and Chloe—how could a congregation so privileged reach a conclusion so heretical, and within a half-dozen years of its birth?

It did so by expressing a flawed anthropology, coupled with notions of an esoteric sacramentalism. There was in the Corinthian church what biblical scholars have come to call a "realized eschatology," a compacted collapse of any linear sequencing of future events into a charismatically enlivened *now*. The mood there must have paralleled that which existed some years later in Ephesus: two heretics (they come in pairs in the Pastoral Epistles) named Hymenaeus and Alexander taught that "the resurrection has already taken place" (2 Tim. 2:18). "Already" is the giveaway word: "Already you have what you want!" wrote the apostle with some pain to his Corinthians. "Already you have become rich!" (1 Cor. 4:8). Who needs the future when the kingdom is here now already? The life of a missionary apostle shows a stark contrast: a spectacle to the world, weak, hungry, disreputable, poorly clothed, tired, "the rubbish of this world" (4:9–13).

Such is the stuff of ancient Corinthian spirituality.

Corinthian Spirituality: The Twentieth-Century Legacy

Ancient only, or modern as well? Corinthian spirituality threatens the Pentecostal and charismatic movements even at the dawn of the new millennium. (In what follows, prudence invites the omission of documentation to protect the guilty.)

A Pentecostal missionary tells of the havoc wreaked in a South American country when an American evangelist arrived with a message of the inferiority of the body, the inevitability of sexual temptation, the relief of accepting things as they are, and the glory of spiritual realities.

A pastor of an independent charismatic megachurch in the American South intimately explains to docile staff women how truly spiritual persons remain unscathed by sexual experimentation.

Some programs on Christian television describe material prosperity as a Christian birthright. Others give reasoned argument to convince that the kingdom is now. Both the "prosperity teaching" and "kingdom now" are fixed descriptors of identifiable subgroups within Pentecostalism, teachings that complicate the tasks of pastors and ecclesiarchs within the more established Pentecostal denominations where such beliefs are rare and not officially sanctioned.

The gospel becomes "full" when Christians are overwhelmed by a decidedly personal religious experience that yields for each one so endowed a personal language of the Spirit, the tongues of angels, one's own prayer language. Except for informed and consistent pastoral care, such a watershed spiritual experience easily generates an elitist mentality. With numbers of adherents to Pentecostal and charismatic bodies now exceeding the count of Protestants, triumphalism looms.

It is easy to point to Corinthian faults in twentieth-century Pentecostalisms. It is doubtful, however, that the many varieties of Pentecostals have any patent on spiritualities tinged with Gnosticism. Is there anything Corinthian about the mainstream—or Gnostic about Protestantism? Canadian Presbyterian pastor Philip Lee thinks so. His book *Against the Protestant Gnostics,*[34] which has little to say about Corinth or the Pentecostal or charismatic movements, makes a profound indictment: "As a Protestant, I believe I have identified the elusive modern gnostics, and they are ourselves."[35]

Such is the stuff of contemporary Corinthian spirituality.

Pauline Responses and the Pentecostal-Mainstream Intersection

What advice did the absentee apostle give to his troublesome congregation? Several items come to mind in ways that may aid analysis of the crossovers between mainstream and sidestream North American Christianity. His counsels for the congregation can be itemized readily.

As for elitism, the management of insight, the apostle pleads for the superiority of love to insight as a guide to ethical decision. Love may require the suspension, not the denial, of legitimate rights based on unquestionably true theological understandings (1 Cor. 8:1, 9, 13). He illustrates setting aside a right by appealing to his own quite exceptional practice, when in Corinth, of not accepting financial support from the church (9:4, 12b, 15, 18; cf. 2 Cor. 12:13; Acts

18:3)—even though it was authorized by apostolic practice (9:5), by the Jewish law (9:8), by a saying of Jesus (9:14), and by his more usual custom (Phil. 4:16).

Discipline emerges in 1 Corinthians as a necessary complement to community, indeed, as a facilitator of healthy togetherness. The very radical cure for the incestuous brother, Paul directed, lay in corporately executed excommunication (1 Cor. 5:2, 5, 7, 9, 13). But this stark action must be restorative, not vindictive (1 Tim. 1:20). When other directives in the New Testament are assembled, excommunication can be seen as the rare and final stage in a process that begins with one-on-one attempts at reconciliation and proceeds gradually through community-adopted patterns leading finally to enforced separation (Matt. 5:22–23, 18:15–17).

Above all, in addressing the Corinthian deviant anthropology, the apostle crafted in 1 Corinthians a doctrine of the human body, his own alternative anthropology, that restates classic Judeo-Christian conceptions. The body is a temple of the Spirit (1 Cor. 6:19), he explained to those who conducted everyday business amid the two-dozen or so temples traced over a century of archaeological explorations at Corinth. And in the next breath, in a paragraph cautioning against the use of prostitutes, he reminds them they had themselves been bought (6:20), implying they were not free to make contract with someone else. So important to God's plan is the human body, Paul taught, that it will be resurrected, an event in the needed future accredited by the only resurrection already past, that of Christ (6:14). Even so, the body will undergo an inexplicable transformation (15:42–44). The human body, in fact, furnishes a splendid analogy of the church (12:12–13), one not to be treated lightly (11:29).

Paul's fundamental point, opposite to the Corinthian libertine and ascetic alike and contrary as well to the later Gnostics, is that the body is *not* evil, that matter is *not* bad. For Paul, the grand story of the origin of the material universe arises from the opening line of the Hebrew Scriptures: "In the beginning . . . God created the heaven and the earth" (Gen. 1:1). And both were good—not evil. The Gnostics of the next century jettisoned the Old Testament and Yahweh, its God, because they brought about matter. Not so Paul.

In this larger context depicting the positive worth of the human body, the apostle gives advice about matters of sexuality. Spouses are not the lords of their own bodies: such hegemony is mutually exchanged in marriage (1 Cor. 7:4). The terror of linkage with a prostitute lies in an unintended biblical fulfillment, for the client "becomes one body with her" (6:16). The final physical duty of Christians? "Therefore glorify God in your body" (6:20). And expect resurrection, not now, but in the future (15:22).

So what has Corinthian spirituality, ancient or modern, to do with the intersection of Pentecostalisms with the mainstream North American ecclesiastical traditions? For one thing, the Pentecostalisms have been the wellspring for much Corinthian spirituality now found in the mainstream, as many ethnographic studies document. Religious television, in recent years, has been dominated by charismatic spiritualities not known for their theological substance. Such programs reach mainstream living rooms, too.

Despite its theological insufficiency, Pentecostal piety appeals particularly to persons at the edge of desperation—a considerable lot, given the state of North American culture. The radical experiential style of the Pentecostals matches the limits to which many persons, including some presently or formerly in the mainstream, have found themselves driven. Pentecostalism at times seems better at bringing people to faith than carrying them on to Christian maturity. Reliance on the Spirit couples with a biblical sentence—"the anointing that you received from him abides in you, and so you do not need anyone to teach you" (1 John 2:27)—and elitism flourishes.

After the charismatic movement emerged in the second half of the twentieth century, it took a different tack from the course of classical Pentecostalism fifty years earlier. The first Pentecostals found each other when marginalized by mainstream churches fearful of the new piety. The globalization of the world and the media revolution, however, along with steady ecumenical developments, permitted the domestication of the Pentecostal impulse within virtually every mainstream tradition. A "Charismatic Service Agency," or something similarly named, rates officially sanctioned status in virtually every mainstream denomination.[36]

"Stay in your own church" was the regular advice given to newly Pentecostalized mainstreamers by David du Plessis (1905–87), gadabout Pentecostal ambassador whose career, more than that of any other person in the twentieth century, facilitated mainstream-Pentecostal connections and deepened mutual understanding.

The charismatic movement, widely believed to have peaked, has nevertheless left a residue in the churches. The charismatic movement has tamed the Pentecostal impulse, regularized it, and absorbed it into the mainstream—thus ensuring the perpetuity of Corinthian spirituality.

I can think of no prescription for Corinthian spirituality equal to what might be called ecumenical friendliness. The apostle's advice to those who favored one cleric or one tradition over another seems apt today: "all things are yours, whether Paul or Apollos or Cephas" (1 Cor. 3:21–22). Since living waters from the sidestreams have enlivened the mainstream, the older churches in turn, having been at it awhile, might furnish theological substance and stability to the juniors. Nothing like this can happen if people do not talk to one another—hence ecumenical friendliness.

But few enterprises match in difficulty that of getting Christians to talk to one another. The leaders of established Pentecostal denominations are not mindless ecclesiocrats determined to forbid any of their own from talking across denominational lines. Nonetheless, they do have to mind the interests of their charges in distant parochial localities who only too well know the hostility and even physical assault stemming from invitations for ecumenical discussion made by representatives of the same churches. That poses a dilemma.

Matters such as what constitutes ultimate religious authority pose dilemmas as well. For evangelicalized Pentecostals, the Bible ranks as the sole and final authority for belief and practice. For the Roman Catholic Church, tradition gets that honor.

But what is a Pentecostal evangelical to say when it is learned that the Bible okays tradition as a source of authority? Just that point is made by the Apostle Paul with regard to still another episode in the Corinthian congregation. Certain Corinthian women wished to do away with some aspect of hair style or personal dress (exactly what is unclear) when they engaged in public prayer or prophecy (11:5–6). Perhaps they were asserting a right assured by an insight with which even the apostle would agree (Gal. 3:28). Unwilling to support such abrupt breach of social custom, however, the apostle marshals a stream of arguments—from Scripture, "the angels," "nature itself," and "propriety." When it seems that the arguments do not convince even the apostle himself, he appeals to tradition: "But if anyone is disposed to be contentious—we have no such custom, nor do the churches of God" (1 Cor. 11:16). The Bible supports tradition as a source of authority.

Whatever else may be said of them, mainstream churches got to be mainstream by developing substantial tradition. On the other hand, some of Jesus' fiercest words were aimed at those who regarded the human traditions more highly than the Word of God (Mark 7:9–13). Still, the practice of the churches—tradition—is clearly a standard for Paul's Corinthians (1 Cor. 4:17, 7:17, 14:33b).

The finest hope for the confluence of mainstream and sidestream may be that vitality become clothed with stability, tradition balanced with enthusiasm, and experience tempered by love.

Notes

I benefited much from critical readings of a draft of this paper made by colleagues Edith Blumhofer, Grant Wacker, and R. Stephen Warner. But they might think I did not benefit enough: although their comments guided many revisions, in the end I stayed with my own lights.

1. "We are fortunate to have more information on the early Christian church at Corinth than for any other Christian community" (Donald Engels, *Roman Corinth: An Alternative Model for the Classical City* [Chicago: University of Chicago Press, 1990], 107).

2. David B. Barrett, "Status of Global Missions, 1998, in Context of 20th and 21st Centuries," *International Bulletin for Missionary Research* 22 (Jan. 1998): 27. In his annual count of the world's Christians, Barrett reports for mid-1998 a total of 366,826,000 Protestants (not counting 55,077,000 Anglicans) and 461,000,000 Pentecostals and charismatics. Of course, many persons appear in both lists. Often maligned, these figures utilize computer extrapolations. I have not yet located any critical demolition of the statistics.

3. Bradley C. Hanson, "Introduction," in *Modern Christian Spirituality: Methodological and Historical Essays,* ed. Bradley C. Hanson, AAR Studies in Religion, no. 62 (Atlanta, Ga.: Scholars, 1990), 3; idem, "Spirituality as Spiritual Theology," in *Modern Christian Spirituality,* ed. Hanson, 45–51.

4. Sandra M. Schneiders, "Spirituality in the Academy," in *Modern Christian Spirituality,* ed. Hanson, 31.

5. Ibid., 32–33.

6. Carl G. Jung, "On the Psychology and Pathology of So-called Occult Phenomena," *Psychiatric Studies,* 2d ed., Bollingen Series 20 (Princeton, N.J.: Princeton University Press, 1970 [1902]).

7. William James, *The Varieties of Religious Experience* (New York: Longmans and Green, 1902).

8. Donald L. Gelpi, *The Turn to Experience in Contemporary Theology* (Mahwah, N.J.: Paulist, 1994). I am grateful to Professor Gelpi for a chance to see this work in manuscript form prior to its publication.

9. Ibid., 1–2.

10. Donald L. Gelpi, *Experiencing God: A Theology of Human Experience* (New York: Paulist, 1978).

11. Nelson S. T. Thayer, *Spirituality and Pastoral Care,* Theology and Pastoral Care Series (Minneapolis: Fortress, 1985): "In a cultural situation of pluralism, differing religious and philosophical positions are seen to have legitimate claims to truth. Rather than simply perceive these in opposition to each other, it makes sense to understand that every formulation is a symbolic expression ultimately grounded in experience, and to try to discern the nature of the experience so symbolized" (22–23).

12. Wayne Proudfoot, *Religious Experience* (Berkeley: University of California Press, 1985), strengthened in the same author's essay titled "From Theology to a Science of Religions: Jonathan Edwards and William James on Religious Affections," *Harvard Theological Review* 82 (1989): 149–68.

13. William P. Alston, *Perceiving God: The Epistemology of Religious Experience* (Ithaca, N.Y.: Cornell University Press, 1991).

14. A full account of the twentieth century's psychological assessment of glossolalia appears in H. Newton Malony and A. Adams Lovekin, *Glossolalia: Behavioral Science Perspectives on Speaking in Tongues* (New York: Oxford University Press, 1985).

15. These are experience, orality, spontaneity, otherwordliness, and biblical authority. See Russell Spittler, "Spirituality, Pentecostal and Charismatic," in *Dictionary of Pentecostal and Charismatic Movements,* ed. Stanley M. Burgess and Gary B. McGee (Grand Rapids, Mich.: Zondervan, 1988), 804–9.

16. This testimony may be found in the hundreds of early reports of conversions, healings, miracles, and baptisms in the Holy Spirit that filled early Pentecostal journals; in published accounts of personal charismatic renewal (such as that of Dennis J. Bennett in his book *Nine O'Clock in the Morning* [Plainfield, N.J.: Logos International, 1970]); or in collections such as the one gathering more than a dozen personal testimonies of Roman Catholic priests, edited by George W. Kosicki, *The Lord Is My Shepherd: Witnesses of Priests* [Ann Arbor: Charismatic Renewal Services, 1973]).

17. Lesslie Newbigin, *The Household of God: Lectures on the Nature of the Church,* the Kerr Lectures, 1952 (New York: Friendship, 1954).

18. Henry Pitney Van Dusen, "The Third Force in Christendom," *Life,* 8 June 1958, pp. 113–24.

19. Genesis 30:27; Ecclesiastes 1:16; Romans 5:4.

20. Johannes P. Louw and Eugene A. Nida, *Greek-English Lexicon of the New Testament Based on Semantic Domains,* 2d ed., 2 vols. (New York: United Bible Societies, 1989).

21. Ibid., 1:796.

22. These are among the English equivalents for terms taken from subdomains M and N, 90.56 to 90.97, found on pages 805–10 of Louw and Nida.

23. Authoritative English translations appear in James M. Robinson, ed., *The Nag Hammadi Library in English,* rev. ed. (San Francisco: Harper and Row, 1988). For background and synthesis, see Birger A. Pearson, *Gnosticism, Judaism, and Egyptian Christianity,* Studies in Antiquity and Christianity (Minneapolis: Fortress, 1990); and Pheme Perkins, *Gnosticism and the New Testament* (Minneapolis: Fortress, 1993).

24. F. F. Bruce, *1 and 2 Corinthians,* New Century Bible (Greenwood, S.C.: Attic, 1976).

25. Pearson displays in two ways the absence of any need for a fixed term in dealing with this outlook. He cites A. D. Nock's reference to the Corinthian situation as "a gnostic way of thinking" (Nock, "Gnosticism," *Harvard Theological Review* 57 [1964]: 278). He then expresses his own viewpoint: "I am in any case convinced that virtually everything in 1 Corinthians thought to represent a 'gnostic way of thinking' can be explained on the basis of Hellenistic Jewish speculative wisdom such as that encountered in Philo" (*Gnosticism,* 166, 171).

26. I use these terms interchangeably: "incipient Gnosticism," "proto-Gnosticism," "embryonic Gnosticism," and "Corinthian Gnosticism."

27. Unless otherwise stated, biblical quotations are taken from the New Revised Standard Version.

28. Certain ancient witnesses to the Greek text at this point read not "do not confess Jesus" but instead "destroys Jesus" or, as the NRSV note suggests, "dissolves Jesus" or "does away with Jesus." Although these readings have no serious claim to originality, they do show the persistence of disregard for the human Jesus.

29. The words usually translated as "now concerning" (*peri de*) occur in Paul's writings only at 1 Corinthians 7:11, 7:25, 8:1, 12:1, 16:1, 16:12 and 1 Thessalonians 4:9, 5:1—apparently a Pauline convention for subtopics in letters.

30. Corinth was not the last place where spiritual marriages occurred. See Peter Brown, *The Body and Society: Men, Women, and Sexual Renunciation in Early Christianity* (New York: Columbia University Press, 1988); and Dyan Elliott, *Spiritual Marriage: Sexual Abstinence in Medieval Wedlock* (Princeton, N.J.: Princeton University Press, 1993). Both volumes have extensive bibliographies.

31. Two recent studies explore this feature of 1 Corinthians: Wendel L. Willis, *Idol Meat in Corinth: The Pauline Argument in 1 Corinthians 8 and 10*, SBL Dissertation Series, 68 (Chico, Calif.: Scholars, 1985); and Peter D. Gooch, *Dangerous Food: 1 Corinthians 8–19 in Its Context,* Studies in Christianity and Judaism, 5 (Waterloo, Ont.: Wilfrid Laurier University Press, 1993).

32. This is a stylized paraphrase of my own invention.

33. 1 Corinthians 3:16, 5:6, 6:2, 3, 9, 15, 16, 19, 9:13, 24; cf. Romans 6:16, 11:2.

34. Philip J. Lee, *Against the Protestant Gnostics* (New York: Oxford University Press, 1987).

35. Ibid., preface.

36. These officially sanctioned groups are broadly described and documented by Vinson Synan in *The Twentieth-Century Pentecostal Explosion: The Exciting Growth of Pentecostal Churches and Charismatic Renewal Movements* (Altamonte Springs, Fla.: Creation House, 1987).

PART 2

Defining Boundaries: Encounters between Pentecostals and Other Protestants

2

Travail of a Broken Family: Radical Evangelical Responses to the Emergence of Pentecostalism in America, 1906–16

Grant A. Wacker

Early Pentecostals thought about themselves a great deal, and they assumed that everyone else did too—not always positively, of course, but frequently, and with secret envy. In one sense it is difficult to imagine how Pentecostals could have been more wrong. Till the 1950s most Americans had never heard of them. A handful of observers within the established churches noticed their existence, and maybe a dozen journalists and scholars took a few hours to try to figure out why a movement so manifestly backward could erupt in the sunlit Progressivism of the early twentieth century. But for the American public as a whole, that was about all there was. In another sense, however, Pentecostals' extravagant assessment of their own importance proved to be exactly right. Radical evangelicals, who were the Pentecostals' spiritual and in many cases biological parents, marshaled impressive resources to crush the menace in their midst. Abusive words flew back and forth for years, subsiding into sullen silence only in the 1930s. Things improved somewhat after World War II, but even today many on both sides of the canyon continue to eye each other with fear and suspicion.[1]

In this essay I focus on the initial decade of the confrontation, roughly 1906 to 1916, when the quarrel raged in its most ugly form. Why is this painful story worth our time? I do not claim that this fight was unprecedented in American religious history in scope, in longevity, or even in the degree of animosity it reflected. Unlike the clash between Roman Catholics and Protestants in the 1840s, or the battles between Mormons and Gentiles in the 1850s, no lives were lost. Unlike the skirmish between Unitarians and Congregationalists in the 1820s, or between Jehovah's Witnesses and mainline Protestant culture in the 1940s, no parties managed to enlist the judicial power of the state on their own behalf. Indeed, as religious fights go, this one proved to be a comparatively modest affair.[2] Only a few thousand souls were involved, large parts of the country remained unaffected, and if any individuals permanently lost faith because of it, they did not leave a record. Although it is true that a number of Pentecostal missions mysteriously caught fire in the middle of the night and that quite a number of their preachers got roughed up, most of this violence stemmed from local toughs looking for a good time or from irate neighbors trying to catch some sleep amid the din of all-night prayer meetings.

Nevertheless, I suggest that the confrontation between radical evangelicals and early Pentecostals is worth studying because it represents larger patterns of conflict in American religious history. More precisely, it exemplifies, on a scale small enough to pin down and dissect, the survival strategies that appear when some but not all the members of a family acquire a new vision of life's possibilities.

Three main themes should emerge. The first is the remarkable degree of overlap between the two factions. On all important cultural, religious, and theological questions the two groups held identical views. To outsiders their areas of disagreement appeared so small as to be laughable. Yet that was precisely the point. The fight lasted as long as it did and hurt as much as it did because the antagonists poured so much combative energy into such a tiny patch of theological space. The second theme is that both sides believed that they were grappling over matters of eternal and ultimate significance. It was not a disinterested discussion about "styles" or "options" but a brawl fought without rules, in the mud, with every rhetorical weapon available. Civility remained out of the question. Both factions knew one thing for sure: politeness was the preserve of denominational preachers who imagined that correct belief was a negotiable matter. The protagonists in this story fought for keeps because the issues were for keeps. The third theme is that scholars will have difficulty understanding any controversy, including this one, if they read only one side of the data. This point seems almost too obvious to require comment, yet historians have largely missed the emotional intensity of this quarrel because they have relied too much on Pentecostal sources alone. It is not clear why they have done so. It may be because Pentecostal materials have been more accessible, or perhaps historians have simply found them more interesting. Whatever the reason, one aim of this essay is to redress that imbalance by telling the story largely, although not exclusively, from the radical evangelical point of view. The customary portrait of Pentecostals as innocent victims of an irrational and unprovoked attack by their former brothers and sisters in the Lord simply will not do. What I hope to show, in contrast, is not that Pentecostals committed their fair share of sins too (which would get us nowhere) but that the two factions yoked themselves in a complex process of self-definition and legitimation.

One thing more should be said. Isolating and describing these three themes as I have just done is useful enough as an exercise in historical clarity and helps to suggest that what follows is both an interesting story and a laboratory study with larger implications. Yet it is important not to miss the human heart of the drama. Radical evangelicals and Pentecostals may have made a world together, but they also tore it apart together. In the end what remained was the unspeakable hurt of a broken family.

Before proceeding with the story at hand, it may be helpful to ask exactly who radical evangelicals were, who Pentecostals were, and how they differed. This is particularly important since the former fathered the latter and the family resemblance was so strong that outsiders often could not tell them apart.[3] Although variables of social class, cultural attitude, and personal temperament undoubtedly intervened, doctrinal differences more than anything else defined the lines of cleavage.

To understand this point we need to remember that at the turn of the century, the radical evangelical family itself was divided into two clans, Holiness Wesleyans on one side and higher life fundamentalists (or more precisely, prefundamentalists) on the other. The first turned up mostly in Methodist churches and in Methodist-based sects such as the Church of the Nazarene, the Church of God, and the Salvation Army. The second appeared mostly in Baptist and Presbyterian churches and in other fellowships loosely connected with the Reformed tradition, such as the Christian and Missionary Alliance. The first instinctively emphasized religious experience, buttressed by correct doctrine; the second reversed those priorities. The first stressed entire sanctification as a second, definite work of grace; the second felt more comfortable talking about a long-term process of spiritual consecration or yieldedness. It is perhaps worth noting that later on, after the years at issue in this essay, the two clans continued to follow distinct though parallel paths of institutional development. Holiness Wesleyans experienced slow but steady growth, persisting into the late twentieth century under the umbrella of the Wesleyan Holiness Association. Higher life fundamentalists, on the other hand, enjoyed rapid growth. They came to be strongly identified with the independent premillennialist movement and, eventually, with the National Association of Evangelicals. In the United States in the 1990s Holiness Wesleyans posted upward of two million adherents, whereas fundamentalists and evangelicals of higher life lineage justifiably claimed five or ten times that number.

Despite these peculiarities of emphasis and institutional history, the two traditions shared a great deal, especially during the years discussed here. Both drew from comparable trends in the British Isles. Both tended to represent God in anthropomorphic terms. Both stressed the infallibility of Scripture, the ready availability of miracles, the healing of the body, the omnipresence of demons, and the imminence of the Lord's return. More basically, the worldviews of the two proved to be virtually identical: ahistorical, supernaturalist, primitivist, apocalyptic, biblicist, and pious. In other contexts it might be useful to highlight the differences between Holiness Wesleyans and higher life fundamentalists, but in the present essay the commonalities are more important. Therefore I shall call them both radical evangelicals.

Let me turn now to consider the Pentecostals. Who were they, and how did they differ from the radical evangelicals who gave them birth? It may be clearest to begin by describing the religious impulses that ignited the Pentecostal revival and then to note the way that those impulses took institutional form. Religiously, Pentecostals distanced themselves from most Christians by their preoccupation with the gifts of the Holy Spirit described in 1 Corinthians and by their courting of miraculous signs and wonders as recounted in the Gospels and in Acts. Yet this was a difference of degree at best, for all radical evangelicals lived in a world filled with miraculous possibilities. What really set Pentecostals apart was their conviction that the order of salvation entailed, beyond conversion and sanctification, a *third* definable experience called the baptism of the Holy Spirit (a term that they cheerfully pirated from both the Holiness and the higher life traditions, which had used it to denote the second, or sanctification, phase of salvation). That innovation would not have turned into such an explosive issue if Pentecostals had said that much and no more, since the three-blessing idea had been rumbling around in the radical evangelical subculture for several decades. The dynamite in the crevice, rather, was the Pentecostals' uncompromising insistence that all who had been truly baptized by the Holy Spirit—all, in other words, who had experienced that third landmark in the order of salvation—would speak in unknown tongues as a demonstrable sign of its authenticity. When the king was home, they liked to say, the royal flag always flew from the tallest spire of the castle for all to see (or in the case of languages, for all to hear). This was a formula spoiling for a fight.

It is hard to tell exactly when this confection of doctrines and practices began to crystallize into institutional shapes. Some say the movement started in the mountains of North Carolina in the late 1890s, some trace it to Charles Fox Parham's divine healing meetings in eastern Kansas just after the turn of the century, and others attribute it to the noted Azusa Street revival in Los Angeles in the summer of 1906.[4] Whatever the real story, many radical evangelical centers soon felt the breath of fresh life. Independent chapels carrying titles such as "Full Gospel Tabernacle" and "Apostolic Faith Mission" started to spring up in all parts of the United States and other countries. Although a hefty minority of converts perennially resisted any kind of formal organization, by World War I the majority had gathered themselves into a half-dozen organized bodies. The best known included the Assemblies of God, the Church of God (not to be confused with the Wesleyan Holiness body of the same name), the Pentecostal Holiness Church, the mostly black Church of God in Christ and, after the war, the International Church of the Foursquare Gospel, made famous by its flamboyant founder, Aimee Semple McPherson. Scores of smaller bodies, many of which were non-English speaking, soon dotted the landscape.

Although it takes me beyond the period with which I am concerned in this essay, it may be helpful quickly to note that after World War I the Pentecostal movement grew to be extremely diverse. Storefront missions, opulent suburban temples, rough-tongued country preachers, and unctuous television celebrities all equally represented the sprawling revival. More important, in the 1960s an emphasis on the supernatural gifts of the Holy Spirit broke out in many of the established Protestant denominations and in the Roman Catholic church. These newer enthusiasts commonly called themselves "charismatics" rather than "Pentecostals," but the message of supernatural empowerment in the daily lives of believers proved to be similar. Whatever the label used, by the 1990s it was clear that the movement had mushroomed into one of the most powerful religious stirrings of the twentieth century, claiming perhaps ten million adherents in the United States and literally hundreds of millions in other parts of the world.[5]

To return to this essay's basic question: how did the radical evangelical movement, highly sectarian itself, respond to the eruption of an even more extremist impulse in its midst?

One of the more intriguing features of this story is how long it took for radical evangelical leaders to notice that anything was amiss in their ranks. They appeared unaware of the revival's existence until late fall 1906.[6] And even then they responded in at least three quite distinct ways. The majority, predictably, not only stayed with the tried and tested paths but seem never seriously to have considered doing otherwise. A small but vocal minority boldly stepped out in faith and cast their lot with the new movement, fearless of the future. Finally, an indeterminate number found themselves beached in the middle, earnestly pondering the alternatives. No one wanted to be deceived by the devil, yet no one dared miss a true work of the Lord either.

In the haze left by later battles, it is easy to forget that the last group, the undecideds, not only existed but persisted for a good two or three years. Clearly many leaders desired to do the right thing but simply did not know what to do. The case of A. B. Crumpler, who founded a loose fellowship called the Holiness Church of North Carolina in 1898, illustrates the dilemma. In the summer of 1906 Crumpler published a cautious editorial endorsement of the revival,[7] along with testimonials by Pentecostal enthusiasts relating their experiences of healing and speaking in tongues.[8] Through the first half of 1907 he even permitted Pentecostal firebrands to speak in Holiness churches and ran at least one wary endorsement of the movement in his paper.[9] Soon, however, Crumpler changed his mind and determined to fight the Pentecostal faction or die trying. He lost. By the end of the year practically all the ministers in the Holiness Church had embraced the Pentecostal message. The old warrior abandoned the tiny sect of his own creation and in the fall of 1908 quietly returned to the more placid waters of the Methodist Episcopal Church, South.[10] Ordinary folk too felt torn. The periodical literature brims with accounts of all-but-forgotten souls who agonized for weeks or months on end. Typical was one Miss Morrison, who converted to Pentecostalism at the East End Mission in Toronto, but only after eight months of intense spiritual and doctrinal struggle. Even then, she lamented, the decision "seemed to sever half my heart strings."[11]

Even for the first group, the stout resisters, several options short of all-out war remained. One was to minimize the severity of the threat in the hope that it would just go away. That hope prompted many to suppose that the new movement would prove to be a phantom borne on the wind. One dubbed it a "craze";[12] another, a "fad";[13] and still another, a mere "excitement."[14] A British polemicist acknowledged the revival's attractiveness to sensation-seeking souls, likening it to the glorious but passing blossoms of an apple tree.[15] In most towns, one pastor shrugged, the commotion died out almost as soon as it started.[16] The *Christian Witness and Advocate of Bible Holiness*, published in Chicago and Boston, charged that the "new fanaticism" would soon "have its run and lie a curiosity in the museum of ten thousand dead follies."[17]

Downplaying took additional forms. One was to highlight the notoriety of the revival's geographical birthplace. F. W. Pitt, a prominent nondenominational pastor in London, dismissed the stirring as a peculiarly American phenomenon, "the land of wonder-meetings and freak religions."[18] Europeans, assuming that the revival started in Los Angeles, were especially inclined to emphasize its West Coast provenance, as if by localizing the point of origin they could better contain its effects.[19] One British higher life leader red-flagged the revival as the "Californian movement."[20] Another writer explicitly affirmed what many others undoubted suspected: Los Angeles harbored more fanatics than did any other city in the United States.[21] Still another arrow in the radical evangelicals' polemical quiver was to minimize the numerical size of the menace. Phineas F. Bresee, founder of the Church of the Nazarene in Los Angeles, dismissed the revival as of "small account," exerting "about as much influence as a pebble thrown into the sea."[22] Other pastors followed Bresee's lead, variously ascribing the peril to "small sections" of the country[23] or to "small radical organizations"[24] or denying that it had impinged on other churches in any appreciable way.[25]

As the months wore on, fear eroded all semblance of restraint. By 1907 for many, and by 1908 for most, the bugle had sounded. It was time to choose sides and to expose toleration for what it really was: flirtation with the devil. Families dissolved, churches split, and denominations broke apart. The most conspicuous divisions took place within the Church of God in Christ, the Fire-Baptized Holiness Church, the Holiness Church of North Carolina, and the Christian and Missionary Alliance, all of which ruptured or suffered severe defections between 1907 and 1910. But those were only the most visible sunderings. Many, perhaps most, radical evangelical fellowships witnessed steady and painful attrition.[26] The growing alarm can be charted in the reaction of Jesse Penn-Lewis, one of the most influential voices in higher life circles in Britain, if not in the English-speaking world. At first Penn-Lewis had evinced a wary, wait-and-see attitude, calling both for an "open mind" and for honest acknowledgment of the "accompanying dangers." By November 1907, however, she had given up all pretense of impartiality, warning that the whole world was being subjected to an "onslaught of Satan upon the 'very elect.'"[27] In the face of what was turning out to be real-life nightmare, radical evangelical leaders mounted a multipronged counterattack. Space permits a brief look at only two of those prongs. The first was an assault on Pentecostals' social origins and moral character, the kind of people they were. The second was an exposé of Pentecostals' deeds, the kind of fruit they bore in daily life.[28]

Radical evangelical writers knew one thing for certain: Pentecostals came from the wrong side of the tracks. And since assumptions about social origins undoubtedly influenced all other perceptions, an examination of those notions is the logical place to begin.

From the vantage point of the 1990s, it is almost impossible to know whether radical evangelicals occupied a higher position in the social system than did their Pentecostal rivals. Although some scholars have claimed as much, the plain fact is that systematic comparisons of the two constituencies remain to be done.[29] What is clear is that the former *believed* that Pentecostals ranked beneath them in numerous respects, including economic standing. Radical evangelical critics sometimes framed class arguments in oblique ways. From the lofty perspective of her substantial English home, Jesse Penn-Lewis found American Pentecostal leaders to be "semi-educated" and possessing only a limited vocabulary of "very crude" stock expressions.[30] Others frequently linked Pentecostalism with "certain classes,"[31] with the "poorer class,"[32] or with diminished social standing in the community.[33] The Metropolitan Association's *Burning Bush* judged that just about anyone could acquire the gift of tongues—divorcées, Methodists, Mormons, and others of "crooked and ill-repute."[34] The Church of God's *Gospel Trumpet*, blowing from Anderson, Indiana, dismissed Pentecostal converts as the "very scum of sectism."[35]

Gender also served as a missile in the war of words. One writer after another stressed the disproportionate number of females in Pentecostal ranks. Baptist missionary statesman A. T. Pierson, pulling himself to his full height, judged that the revival had proved particularly attractive to "hysterical females," who were, after all, "especially excitable and prone to excesses."[36] For Plymouth Brethren speaker Harry A. Ironside, Pentecostal churches disgraced themselves by the "Scripture-defying attitude" of the women who spoke in their meetings.[37] Other writers went further, claiming that women, once infected with Pentecostal notions, grew defiant of their husbands' authority.[38] In Britain, Reader Harris, leader of the staunchly Holiness-aligned Pentecostal League (before *Pentecostal* denoted tongues speakers), underscored the kinship between the new movement and "excitable females."[39] Charles E. Cowman of the Oriental Missionary Society sniffed out numerous affinities among Pentecostals, women, and other "earnest but unstable souls."[40]

Pentecostals, then, presented themselves to their radical evangelical inspectors as typically lower class and female. But given that radical evangelicals had long perceived themselves as champions of the disinherited,[41] it was risky to make too much of anyone's humble social status. Thus it is not surprising that they turned to a different tactic, one that promised to inflict truly crippling damage. They sought to show that the upstarts represented the moral debris of modern society.

The roster of flaws that ostensibly marred the Pentecostal character was so extensive that it is hard to know where to begin. But high on everyone's list was sexual immorality. What Pentecostals did on the floor of the camp meeting, not to mention the bedroom, aroused the darkest of suspicions. Pillar of Fire leader Alma White, whose husband, Kent, left their marital bed when he joined the new sect, did not waste time with nuances. The movement had originated, she asserted, in a "pit of moral and spiritual pollution in which *free-loveism* was a dominant feature."[42] She suspected that a Pentecostal school in New Jersey served as a supply source for "white slave dens." Indeed, everyone knew that Pentecostal assemblies swarmed with "rank free lovers" prowling around seducing young girls and wives.[43] White's views, though unusually intemperate, represented those of others. When A. T. Pierson first alerted his readers to the Pentecostal menace in July 1907, he observed that their meetings involved instances of "shocking impropriety." Two months later he judged that he had erred on the side of "mildness and moderation." Accumulating evidence from reliable eyewitnesses contained "statements of facts too shocking to print."[44] Other leaders, normally reserved when it came to such matters, felt no compunctions about exposing Pentecostals' depravities. Southern Holiness evangelist W. B. Godbey detected a good deal of "hell-hatched free-loveism" in their circles, adding, for good measure, that gamblers, atheists, whores, and thieves also spoke in tongues.[45] Even the Yale-educated Reuben A. Torrey, whose preaching gave new depth to the word *stuffy*, took the bait. Pentecostal meetings, he charged, "seethed with immorality of the grossest character." No wonder. Men and women lay for hours "side by side on the ground . . . in the most unseemly and immodest way."[46]

No one actually named names, of course, but they did not have to. Everyone knew the truth. They also knew that Pentecostals' behavior did not have to be literally adulterous to be reprehensible. Critics commented on Pentecostals' reputation for foul conversation[47] or noted, with raised eyebrows, that unmarried male and female evangelists often traveled together.[48] Others alluded to male missionaries' indecent conduct with native women.[49] One observed that females "slain in the Spirit" in Holy Ghost meetings fell on the floor in "indelicate positions."[50] Other polemicists berated Pentecostals for their willingness to admit divorced and remarried followers into their assemblies.[51] The allegations of homosexual behavior that effectively destroyed the career of founder Charles Fox Parham received extended treatment in the *Burning Bush*. Although most radical evangelical periodicals rose above the temptation to publicize the episode, the *Burning Bush* gleefully noted that the "devilish 'tongues' craze" paraded hand in hand with the "sin of Sodomy."[52] Sometimes Pentecostals could not win either way. When a few advocated "marital purity" (sex only for procreation), they were excoriated for "loosening the marriage tie" and thus promoting libertinism.[53]

In radical evangelical eyes Pentecostals' spiritual pride ranked even worse than their sexual habits. Denver preacher Alma White, never the most humble soul herself, found Pentecostals to be the most "self-righteous, self-sufficient" people on earth.[54] After ticking off a long list of converts' doctrinal errors, one Church of God preacher finally trundled out the real issue: the "awful spirit that is manifested among them."[55] One Free Methodist minister left a Pentecostal meeting in Chicago shaken less by the doctrines he heard than by the "*offensive, arrogant,* and *bombastic* manner" in which they were presented.[56] A Nazarene author said that Pentecostals treated their ability to speak in tongues as a prize to be flaunted, "worn as a peacock carries its tail feathers." As far as he could see, its only purpose was "for show; and to condemn all others."[57] To Nazarene evangelist A. M. Hills, the new movement engendered smugness, transforming loving church members into "dogmatic, unteachable, schismatic and anathema-breathing souls."[58] If the movement was truly of God, charged a *Gospel Trumpet* writer, surely its adherents would manifest the fruits of the Spirit in abundance. Instead, they displayed a "proud, boastful, superior" attitude. Why, he demanded, did possession of this one gift consistently produce "such unfortunate results?"[59]

Spiritual pride spawned other worms. One was looseness with the truth. According to many radical evangelicals, Pentecostals were, to borrow Mark Twain's words, experienced, industrious, and often quite picturesque liars. They exaggerated the number of people who attended their meetings, misstated the results of their services,[60] and told outright falsehoods about miraculously speaking in foreign languages.[61] Above all, they perjured themselves when they recounted the healings that took place in their meetings. It was a question of simple fact. Were people healed or were they not? In a work symptomatically called *Faith Healing Tragedies,* F. W. Pitt claimed that he had attended many healing meetings, and yes, he had seen a few cures, but only of slight nervous conditions.[62] Other skeptics proved to be less charitable. Many insisted that they had personally visited Pentecostal gatherings and saw either nothing at all[63] or enough to know that the whole thing was a sham.[64]

Beyond all this, Pentecostals' spiritual pride seemed to breed disrespect for the wisdom of the ages. As one critic saw things, the insurgents did not "hesitate at all in disagreeing with the interpretations of deeply learned and thoroughly matured commentators."[65] Veteran Japan missionary August Youngren focused especially on the impetuousness of Pentecostal missionaries. Radical evangelical workers had toiled in Japan for decades, he pointed out, struggling to learn the language and to understand the complexities of the Buddhist religion. Then overnight these Spirit-baptized argonauts appeared on the scene, pathetically ill equipped for the task at hand. Immediately they proceeded to censure senior missionaries for failing to extirpate pagan beliefs. Worse, when things got tough, they turned tail. Unwilling to submit to the hard discipline of learning the language and the backbreaking work of planting Christianity in an alien culture, they threw up their hands and sailed home.[66]

"By their fruits you shall know them," Jesus told his followers. Taking those words to heart, Pentecostals felt confident that scoffers would be silenced if they would only look around and honestly acknowledge the immense good that the Pentecostal revival had produced. Radical evangelicals took them at their word, looked around—and found the Pentecostal fruit rotten to the core.

The bill of particulars was lengthy. To begin with, radical evangelicals charged, Pentecostal religion endangered one's physical body. Enthusiasts got hurt when they fell into trance, typically by bumping into objects or crashing to the floor, and they found themselves weak and gasping for breath when they returned to a normal state of consciousness.[67] Converts' insistence that they had been healed of one or another infirmity, even when the symptoms manifestly persisted, led to heartbreaking results. According to these critics, the records bristled with stories of devotées sprawling to the ground after discarding their crutches, fighting back tears after tossing away their eyeglasses, or even dying after stopping desperately needed medical treatments.[68] On several occasions, some said, the determination to fast until Jesus came back to earth had led to near or actual death by starvation.[69]

Yet physical harm proved to be only half the peril. Irreparable psychological damage loomed as an equally serious threat. "Good honest people," stormed Alabama educator John L. Brasher, were turned into "wild eyed fanatics . . . with love leaked out and their faith forever ruined."[70] Unhappy personality changes of that sort marked only the first step in a long downward spiral. Famed Bible teacher Harry A. Ironside knew one adolescent woman who had lost all her hair because of the "unnatural excitement" of Holy Ghost meetings. Fortunately she escaped relatively unscathed, but seven from the same Chicago mission ended up in "insane asylums."[71] Others too discerned a link between Pentecostal fervor and mental breakdown. In China, for example, China Inland Mission personnel worried that meetings of the local Pentecostal Missionary Union produced "consequences of a dangerous character," including "strain upon the brain" and occasionally "insanity."[72] Although it is not clear why they should have cared, a delegation of California ministers importuned the British government to ban Aimee Semple McPherson from preaching in Britain because of the mental ruin she might cause.[73] "One needs to know little of psychology," growled A. T. Pierson, to recognize that Pentecostal claims betokened a "heated brain, and are common with insane patients."[74] Even that was not the worst of it. The Nazarene *Herald of Holiness* alleged—without a scrap of proof, it should be said—that Pentecostal teaching stirred converts to go out and murder their enemies.[75]

At this point it is worth noting that the insanity charge may have rested on some objective foundation. By that I do not mean that early Pentecostals were more prone to mental illness than anyone else. But many recruits found themselves able to speak only in glossolalic gushings for hours or days after they had experienced the baptism of the Holy Spirit. Scattered and imprecise data in both Pentecostal and secular sources intimate that the inability to carry on a normal conversation may have given rise to the madness claims.[76]

As far as most radical evangelicals could see, the new movement seemed to inflict as much violence upon families as it did on individuals. When one member of a family changed allegiance but the others did not, passions born of genes and memory exploded into charges of betrayal and occasionally even physical violence. The situation became especially volatile when children were involved. Opponents repeatedly charged that Pentecostals went out of their way to target their offspring, especially impressionable adolescents. The case of young Ralph Herrill is instructive. Herrill was a student at Charles Fox Parham's Bethel Faith Home in Topeka. As soon as his parents read press reports about visions and speaking in tongues at the home, they wired money to Ralph and instructed a friend to hustle him out of there.[77] Presumably Herrill got out unscathed, but sometimes things took a nasty turn. Quaker Pentecostal Levi Lupton, for example, made the grave mistake of concealing one Arthur Smith at his Alliance, Ohio, camp meeting. Smith's mother sprang into action. She hired local toughs who invaded the meeting, squirted Lupton and several worshipers with sulfuric acid, and then retrieved her child.[78] Occasionally the new movement seemed so threatening that civil authorities got involved. A no-holds-barred Holy Ghost revival in 1915 in Topeka, Kansas, prompted the mayor to ask town officials to pass an ordinance forbidding minors from attending.[79]

Adults worried even about the safety of other adults. When Walter Higgins's father heard that his grown son had decided to take up preaching on the Pentecostal circuit, the elder Higgins angrily tried to break up his son's first service, arguing that the young man obviously had been "hypnotized."[80] One leader wrote to a friend in India that his "*own* brother-in-law" had been sucked into the Pentecostal net and that he had not been able to escape until he had gone though a "fearful battle" with Satan.[81] Wives and husbands experienced similar turmoil. At a 1907 Memphis revival one irate husband physically dragged his wife from the altar and then threatened to kill the speaker.[82] A few miles up the road at Aquilla, Missouri, local farmers forbade their wives and daughters from attending a Holy Ghost meeting at a vacant church building. The farmers may have foreseen more than they realized, for the service ended up in a mass fistfight between pro- and anti-Pentecostal factions.[83]

Although women constituted the majority of first-generation converts, men sometimes took the lead—and paid the price. One Arthur Watson, a Canadian, told of the rejection he suffered when he left the Salvation Army and cast his lot with Toronto's East End Mission. Both wife and children, he wrote, fought his conversion. "To have my own dear ones turn their backs on me [has] meant many tears and sorrow." Watson wavered and went back to the Salvation Army, but he knew it was not right, for when he did, his "heart turned to stone, health broke, almost died."[84] We do not know the end of the story. Like most of the figures who walked across the early Pentecostal stage, Watson made one fleeting appearance in what is now a rare periodical and then disappeared from view. But there are good reasons to believe that his experience was typical. What stuck in the mind of Pentecostal patriarch Howard Goss decades later was the number of times he had been "threatened by angry mobs or by raging individuals when some member of their family had been converted."[85]

The wrenching of families may have aroused the most intense passions, but the disruption of local churches ran a close second. "NO COMMUNITY IS SAFE from this most dangerous heresy," thundered one editor. "Whole churches have been wrecked and communities blasted."[86] A Los Angeles pastor recalled how he had begged his one-time colleagues in mission work not to deny the "faith and experience" that had wedded them in Christian love for so many years.[87] In Alabama a Holiness college president wrote to a friend that the Pentecostal eruption marked one of the saddest events of his life. It "slashed and utterly ruined . . . the work of God," he sighed. "I hope a remnant of the church will be saved from the wreck."[88] In Britain a Plymouth Brethren leader complained that the movement's main fruit was "discord, division, pride."[89] Everywhere in the world, protested Jesse Penn-Lewis, Pentecostals inflicted "*division and separation* among Christians."[90]

Rending the Body of Christ was bad enough. Rending it for no purpose beyond self-gratification seemed incomparably worse. When Pentecostals looked at themselves, they saw only a heroic willingness to surrender all personal comforts for Christ. When their radical evangelical foes stared at them, however, they saw something else: a perverse determination to spread the hoax of "signs and lying wonders."[91] "Unsettled and restless," one Holiness Church pastor snapped, Pentecostals were "filled with zeal to any extent of sacrifice."[92]

Probably we will never command enough evidence, let alone wisdom, to be able to say who was right and who was wrong in all this. But it would take determined blindness of heart not to appreciate the feelings of betrayal that turning to the new movement engendered. Religion may be a bandage for the wounded soul, but sometimes it is also the weapon that inflicts the wound.

As anger turned to bewilderment, radical evangelicals tried to figure out how all this could have happened in their very midst. In the words of one browbeaten pastor, how could trusted brothers and sisters in the Lord be so easily "beguiled from the right way"?[93] Radical evangelical stalwarts gave various answers. One was that Pentecostals frightened simple folk by raising the specter of the "Unpardonable Sin." If potential converts shunned the baptism of the Holy Spirit, Pentecostals purportedly said, they would not receive another chance, either here or in the life to come.[94] Another answer was that Pentecostals hoodwinked the gullible with promises of relief from physical suffering.[95] "Hypnotic magnetic influence" made the list,[96] along with an "unhealthy craving for 'signs and wonders.'"[97] The desire to acquire "wide influence" by flaunting the ability to speak in tongues also made the list.[98] Occasionally leaders even blamed themselves. If pastors had kept a firmer hand on the "shameful vagaries" that had arisen among the flock, one editor grumbled, none of this would have happened.[99]

All these interpretations taken together, however, paled in the face of the one master explanation that truly accounted for everything: Satan. By this reckoning Pentecostalism was—take your pick—"a gross deception of Satan,"[100] a "gigantic scheme of Satan,"[101] a "Satanic attack . . . at our Lord Himself,"[102] wholly "of the devil,"[103] "purely of the devil,"[104] or a "monstrous heresy . . . from hell."[105] Given Pentecostals' insistence that tongues represented God's Holy Spirit speaking through a human voice, it was inevitable that radical evangelicals would turn that claim inside out and insist that tongues signaled the very opposite: the devil speaking through a human voice. One combatant accordingly called tongues a mess of "Satanic manifestations."[106] Another recounted how, after much prayer, he had successfully "commanded [the] chattering devil to stop in Jesus' name."[107] Still another praised God for delivering a sister from the demons who used her mouth to speak in tongues.[108]

Yet another saw a young girl filled with demons, speaking in tongues, cursing in Latin, Italian, and French, all the while tearing and biting at her own body.[109]

The radical evangelicals' polemical tactics merit admiration for adroitness if nothing else. There is no reason to believe that their rhetoric grew from deliberate calculations about how to gain strategic advantage, but by simply inverting Pentecostal claims, the radical evangelists knifed Pentecostals where they were most vulnerable. Rightly sensing that many converts were wavering, they saw that little could be more unsettling to uncertain souls than the suspicion that their new faith was demonic precisely *because* it seemed so angelic.

Even so, how could radical evangelical leaders be so sure that Satan darkened their opponents' hearts but not their own? The proof lay in the testimonies of those who had traveled to banks of the River Styx and journeyed back to tell of it. The experience of Sister A. L. Malone of Redlands, California, was typical. After joining a full gospel band, she recalled, she found herself unable to eat, sleep, or even understand the Bible. "Awful darkness and confusion" swept over her. Tottering at the edge of insanity, Malone finally threw herself at the feet of the Savior, crying "save me or I am lost." At that point a wondrous light filled the room. The Lord revealed the error of Pentecostal teaching and left her once again in the "clear light and freedom of Heaven."[110] Others found that openly denouncing the Pentecostal snare made them stronger Christians. The Lord instructed (Wesleyan) Church of God pastor C. W. Naylor to fight the new sect without compromise. "Since I have taken a stand against it boldly," Naylor declared, "my preaching has been with more power and more souls have been saved and more sick people healed by far than at any other time." Lest anyone doubt it, Naylor added that whenever he strode forth to denounce Satan's counterfeit, "God flood[ed]" his soul with his glory.[111]

In the arena of apologetic warfare, then, Satan proved himself to be a faithful friend. Satan accounted for the breakdown of sound minds, the destruction of loving families, and the decay of healthy churches. Better still, Satan explained why the men and women who bore the greatest responsibility for proclaiming the truth, those who had personally experienced salvation, healing, and entire sanctification or the higher life, now turned their back on the genuine article in order to preach a counterfeit. W. M. Kelly, the pastor of a Los Angeles Holiness church, summed it up to the satisfaction of many. The explanation lay in 2 Thessalonians 2:11: "And for this cause God shall send them a strange delusion, that they should believe a lie."[112]

Exaggeration is always a danger. It is important to remember that some enthusiasts never felt, or at least never displayed, the kind of deep and abiding animosity we have witnessed in these pages. Many on both sides clearly were too wrapped up in daily concerns or in the work at hand to spend much time worrying about real or imagined enemies. Many others never had the stomach for fighting of any kind, especially with their erstwhile brothers and sisters in the Lord. Pentecostal evangelist Aimee McPherson, for example, perennially manifested genuinely ecumenical instincts and a profound distaste for theological polemics of any kind. Although she relished public debates, she treated them more as sporting events than as a preview of Armageddon. She went out of her way to embrace virtually anyone, literally and figuratively, who would embrace her.[113]

On the whole, however, cool heads and irenic spirits such as McPherson's were atypical. The evidence suggests that the average partisan on both sides was in fact a modern-day Zealot, ready to take up arms at the slightest provocation. Thus we are left to ask why. Why was charity so hard and anger so easy?

A number of explanations come to mind. Cultural proximity is perhaps the most obvious. Historians have always known that the radical evangelical and the Pentecostal movements were not identical twins, but to outsiders (including census takers then and pollsters now) they certainly looked the part—and with good reason. Except for the specific question of tongues, it is difficult to think of any point of doctrine or lifestyle that radical evangelicals and their Pentecostal rivals did not share wholly or in large part. That overlap surely constitutes part of the explanation. Feuds within religious families, no less than within biological families, often prove to be the bitterest of all. Still, American religious history is filled with stories of traditions that managed to divorce and amicably go their separate ways. So we are left to figure out why this one did not.

A certain amount of simple human cussedness also must be factored into the equation. When Pentecostal songwriter Herbert Buffum categorized Alma White's polemics as "turkey-buzzard vomit" splattered upon "God's elect and *select* people," it would have been something of a miracle in itself if radical evangelical polemicists had failed to respond in kind.[114] Then too we need to remember the protocols of popular theological disputation at the turn of the century. Many on both sides of the radical evangelical–Pentecostal divide were accomplished mudslingers to begin with. Provoked, radical evangelicals could turn on and attack one another as fiercely as they ever attacked Pentecostals. If Holiness guard dogs could malign the staid Keswick convention, the cornerstone of the British higher life movement, as a "snare of the devil,"[115] or if the Pillar of Fire, one Holiness sect, could disparage the Pilgrim Holiness Church, another Holiness sect, as a demonic fake,[116] it is hardly surprising that they would treat Pentecostals in like manner. For their part, Pentecostals attacked one another as viciously as they attacked any radical evangelical. To take one of countless exchanges, Texas Apostolic Faith leader E. N. Bell assailed Kansas Apostolic Faith leader Charles Fox Parham as a "heathen and a publican."[117] Parham returned the favor by calling Bell and, for good measure, all other Pentecostal leaders "driveling, spiritual idiots."[118] Clearly persons who publicly aligned themselves with any of these factions risked a good thrashing.[119]

Melvin Dieter, a historian of the American Wesleyan tradition, has offered another explanation for the intensity of the rancor. Back in the 1880s and 1890s, he notes, mainline Methodist leaders had scourged Holiness zealots for opening the floodgates to antinomian enthusiasm. That flood, once started, respected no boundaries—and the Pentecostal insurgence now seemed to prove them right. So it was hardly surprising that Holiness leaders of the following generation went out of their way to distance themselves from any hint of association with Pentecostal excess.[120] Dieter's interpretation gains cogency when we remember that many radical evangelical stalwarts—both Holiness and higher life—prided themselves not only on their spiritual rigor but also on their sober good sense. Ecstatic frenzy frightened them because they knew just how easy it was for things to get out of hand. It had happened before. Just before the turn of the century many had seemed to go off the deep end pursuing multiple baptisms of the Holy Ghost and fire, divine healing in the atonement, dispensational premillennialism, and the almost-automatic availability of miraculous signs and wonders—all in a context of wildly unrestrained worship.[121] Thus for every aspersion that radical evangelical leaders flung at the "Church of the Holy Refrigerator" on the right,[122] they hurled two more at "wild-fire religion" on the left.[123] What the Holy Spirit most wants, wrote one North Carolina pastor in 1903, was the kind of religion that accords with "reason, or common sense."[124] The *Christian Witness and Advocate of Bible Holiness* summed it all up with imperial dignity: "When the formalists consider us fanatics and the fanatics esteem us as formalists, it is safe to reckon ourselves in the right place."[125]

The careful efforts of A. B. Crumpler, founder of the Holiness Church of North Carolina, to position himself in the middle of scriptural norms is instructive. For the better part of a decade, Crumpler had occupied a spot considerably left of center on the radical evangelical playing field. In matters of doctrine and personal temperament he brushed up as close to Pentecostalism as did anyone. Even so, in the premier issue of the *Holiness Advocate,* published five years before he had even heard of Pentecostalism, Crumpler saw fit to assail fanatics on his left just as vigorously as he criticized formalists on his right.

One sentence gave away the whole plot: "There has been so much fickleness and wild-fire and backsliding among the holiness ranks that the faith of some has been greatly shaken."[126] There it was, in a line. The enemy was extremism of any kind, left or right, hot or cold.

Second-guessing anyone's motives for doing anything is risky, yet the evidence leaves us with an image of radical evangelical firebrands horrified by their movement's and perhaps their own susceptibility to excess. If we assume that Pentecostalism functioned at least to some extent as a scapegoat, as a palpable symbol of everything that might go wrong with the radical evangelical movement itself, it is easier to understand why the leaders who came closest to Pentecostalism in matters of doctrine and deportment—Crumpler, Duke M. Farson, W. B. Godbey, Reader Harris, Charles Price Jones, Reuben Torrey, Alma White, and Wilbur Glenn Voliva, among others—consistently tried to be the first to bludgeon it to death.[127]

This brings us to a more complex dimension of radical evangelical–Pentecostal interactions. Students of social movements have long recognized that such stirrings require a measure of opposition to define their boundaries and to beef up their morale. An unresisted movement soon becomes an unknown one. Since Pentecostals, like all successful sects, instinctively appreciated the value of opposition, it was almost inevitable that they would come up with some nonnegotiable doctrine or some difficult ritual, or both, that clearly distinguished them from their religious kin. The doctrine of a third work of grace, coupled with the comparatively challenging feat of speaking in tongues, met that need with admirable effectiveness.

Yet Pentecostals demanded more. The genius as well as the heartbreak of the new message was that it compelled converts to acknowledge, up front and without qualification, that their previous commitments had been not just incomplete but bogus. Herbert E. Randall's trajectory illustrates the pattern. We know almost nothing about him, like most of the figures in this story, except that by 1907 he had been a Christian for twenty-one years and "sanctified wholly" for twelve. Somehow Randall wandered into Toronto's East End Mission that summer, where he received the baptism of the Holy Spirit and joined the infant movement. It proved to be a spectacular event. Randall recorded that he "rolled around on the floor under the weight of glory." He felt a "downpour" on his head as he danced, shouted, sang, and whistled "sweet heavenly music." His very soul was "borne upon a sea of glory riding upon its billows." If Randall had said no more than this, his old friends might have raised their eyebrows and considered his new experiences a bit much, yet wished him well nonetheless. But he pressed on. "Right there," he added, "I let go my profession, which I had held until then, of having the baptism of the Holy Ghost. When I let it go I was conscious of no loss."[128] Those last six words, "I was conscious of no loss," revealed worlds. From Randall's standpoint the Pentecostal experience marked a liberation from the millstone of his past. His radical evangelical friends, on the other hand, surely took the crowing about the worthlessness of his previous affiliation as a slap in the face.

Seemingly minor incidents like these poisoned radical evangelical–Pentecostal relations for decades. If Pentecostals had been willing to say something like, "Well, yes, the second work of grace is a true work of the Holy Spirit, but it may be enriched at a later point by an additional experience, which may or may not be accompanied by tongues," then much of the friction between the two movements would have been removed. But Pentecostals did not say that because they did not want the friction removed. They needed to make clear to themselves and to all who would listen that they had put away the childish things of their past. When that intentionally invidious point became obvious, loyal soldiers of the radical evangelical cause immediately and understandably leapt to extirpate the enemy within their household.

That enemy inside the gate proved to be all the more dangerous because radical evangelicals surely knew, deep in their hearts of hearts, that Pentecostals had a powerful point. From the beginning the former had refused to countenance any finite level of spiritual achievement as sufficient. They had consistently urged believers to strive for an ever-deeper walk with Christ. And that is precisely what Pentecostals claimed to have accomplished. The plain truth is that they beat radical evangelicals at their own game, and beat them badly.

Finally, one additional possibility must be considered if we hope to understand why radical evangelicals displayed so much anger. Take them at their word. In many ways the most compelling explanation for their bitterness was the force of the theological issues involved. To outsiders it looked like the worst kind of hair-splitting, but to insiders it seemed the opposite: a life-and-death struggle over premises and goals. From the outset radical evangelical writers had consistently affirmed that the Christian's primary business was to seek not the gifts or even the fruit of the Spirit but the free, unmerited love of Jesus Christ. In these latter days, one California pastor allowed, it might well be true that the church was destined to witness an increase in miraculous gifts. But in the end such endowments held small import. For the mature Christian, a spotless character, defined by "light, purity, power, life, love and holiness," remained the main goal. If believers kept that aim clearly in focus, he suggested, all else, including miraculous signs and wonders, would fall into their proper and subordinate place.[129]

From the perspective of the late 1990s it is tempting to surmise that there might have been some room for negotiation if any of the participants in this controversy had supposed, even for a moment, that theology was a constructive rather than an exact science or that the Bible afforded more than one line of interpretation. But no one did. In their minds the New Testament, the sole and complete blueprint for Christianity, defined a single order of salvation for all times and places. Given those assumptions, the one and only truly "Unpardonable Sin" proved to be not lovelessness but deviation from orthodoxy.

Bibliographic Appendix

For a concise, perceptive overview of early Pentecostalism, see Roger G. Robins, "Pentecostal Movement," in *Dictionary of Christianity in America,* ed. Daniel G. Reid, Robert D. Linder, Bruce L. Shelley, and Harry S. Stout (Downers Grove, Ill.: InterVarsity, 1990). The best scholarly monographs on the movement's origins and early development in the United States are Robert Mapes Anderson, *Vision of the Disinherited: The Making of American Pentecostalism* (New York: Oxford University Press, 1979); and Edith L. Blumhofer, *Restoring the Faith: The Assemblies of God, Pentecostalism, and American Culture* (Urbana, Ill.: University of Illinois Press, 1993), esp. chaps. 1–4. For a glimpse of the recent worldwide growth of the movement, see Vinson Synan, *The Twentieth-Century Pentecostal Explosion: The Exciting Growth of Pentecostal Churches and Charismatic Renewal Movements* (Altamonte Springs, Fla.: Creation House, 1987.

Remarkably, no one—or at least no recent critical scholar—has surveyed the whole history of the radical evangelical tradition in America, although parts of it have been ably examined in George Marsden, *Fundamentalism and American Culture: The Shaping of Twentieth-Century Evangelicalism: 1870–1925* (New York: Oxford University Press, 1980), esp. chaps. 8 and 11; Melvin Dieter, *The Holiness Revival of the Nineteenth Century* (Metuchen, N.J.: Scarecrow, 1980), esp. chap. 5; and Donald W. Dayton, *Theological Roots of Pentecostalism* (Grand Rapids, Mich.: Zondervan, 1987), esp. chaps. 4–6. Arguably the most comprehensive, although hardly self-critical, account remains Arthur T. Pierson's classic *Forward Movements of the Last Half-century* (New York: Garland, 1984 [1905]). For a splendid bibliographical introduction to all these traditions, see Edith L. Blumhofer and Joel A. Carpenter, eds., *Twentieth-Century Evangelism: A Guide to the Sources* (New York: Garland, 1990). It is important to remember that all radical evangelicals, including their Pentecostal offspring, were conservative Protestants, but not the reverse, as the quite separate stories of Missouri Synod Lutherans, Old School Presbyterians, and the like attest.

Most of the monographs on Pentecostalism, including those by Anderson and Blumhofer noted previously, briefly address the tortured relations between Pentecostals and other Protestants, including those in the radical evangelical tradition. See also Horace S. Ward Jr., "The Anti-Pentecostal Argument," in *Aspects of Pentecostal-Charismatic Origins,* ed. Vinson Synan (Plainfield, N.J.: Logos International, 1975), 102–7, for a very short treatment of the problem from an unapologetically Pentecostal perspective. Several of the authors in the present volume examine the almost-always strained relations between Pentecostals and other Protestants from midcentury to the present. See especially the chapters by Nancy L. Eiesland, Frederick Jordan, and Albert F. Schenkel. In addition, Kurt O. Berends's chapter ably examines conflict between Pentecostals and members of fraternal orders in a northern New Hampshire town in the early twentieth century. No one, to my knowledge, has tracked the mainline Protestant culture's perception of Pentecostals before World War II or the way that secular journalists and academicians viewed them—on those rare occasions when they did. Arguably Pentecostalism was, for all practical purposes, introduced to the American public consciousness by Union Theological Seminary president Henry Pitney Van Dusen in "The Third Force in Christendom," *Life*, 9 June 1958, pp. 113–24.

Notes

This essay was originally published, in a slightly different form, in *Journal of Ecclesiastical History* 47 (July 1996): 505–28. Two grants from the Pew Charitable Trusts, one directly to me, the other administered by the Wesleyan Holiness Study Center at Asbury Theological Seminary, funded part of the research for this project. I wish to thank Professor Richard Carwardine; graduate students David McCarthy, Roger Robins, and David Zercher; and fellow members of the Institute for the Study of American Evangelicals for comments on earlier drafts.

1. I offer thumbnail historical definitions for Pentecostalism and for radical evangelicalism a little later in this essay. For secondary literature on both movements, see the bibliographical appendix. For indications that tensions persist despite ecumenical overtures of late, see Peter Hocken, *The Glory and the Shame: Reflections on the Twentieth-Century Outpouring of the Holy Spirit* (Guildford, Surrey: Eagle, 1994), chap. 3; and J. Kenneth Grider, *A Wesleyan-holiness Theology* (Kansas City, Mo.: Beacon Hill, 1994), 416–20.

2. For a focused study of some of the recurring features of religious conflict in United States history, see Robert N. Bellah and Frederick E. Greenspahn, eds., *Uncivil Religion: Interreligious Hostility in America* (New York: Crossroad, 1987), especially Bellah's concluding remarks. For a related perspective, see Albert Hirschman, *Exit, Voice, Loyalty* (Cambridge, Mass.: Harvard University Press, 1970), which discusses the cost-benefit tradeoffs, emotional and otherwise, of leaving any organized body and critiquing it from the outside versus staying in and voicing one's dissent from the inside.

3. Whether Pentecostalism stemmed primarily from the Wesleyan Holiness tradition or from the higher life fundamentalist tradition is hotly disputed by scholars. The evidence is too spotty and elusive to know for sure. My own reading of hundreds of letters to the editors in early Pentecostal periodicals (in which converts often identified their church backgrounds) suggests that a slight majority hailed from Holiness Wesleyan backgrounds. For effective statements of opposing points of view on this question, see Vinson Synan, *The Holiness-Pentecostal Movement in the United States* (Grand Rapids, Mich.: Eerdmans, 1971); and Edith L. Waldvogel [Blumhofer], "The 'Overcoming Life': A Study in the Reformed Evangelical Origins of Pentecostalism," Ph.D. diss., Harvard University, 1977.

4. The secondary literature on the origins of Pentecostalism is almost as contentious as are the controversies it describes. For a perceptive overview of the debate, see Joseph W. Creech Jr., "Visions of Glory: The Place of Azusa Street in Pentecostal History," *Church History* 65, no. 3 (1996): 405–24.

5. Adherence figures for all these traditions (that is, Holiness/Wesleyan, fundamentalist/evangelical, and Pentecostal/charismatic) are an educated guess at best. My estimates are drawn from several sources, including *The Yearbook of American and Canadian Churches, 1996*, ed. Kenneth B. Bedell (Nashville: Abingdon, 1996), 250–56; Barry A. Kosmin and Seymour P. Lachman, *One Nation under God: Religion in Contemporary American Society* (New York: Crown, 1993), esp. 15–17, 197; David B. Barrett, ed., *World Christian Encyclopedia* (New York: Oxford University Press, 1982), 711, 712, 715; and Barrett's statistical updates published annually in the January issue of the *International Bulletin of Missionary Research* (hereinafter *IBMR*). See especially *IBMR* 17 (Jan. 1993), 23; *IBMR* 18 (Jan. 1994), 24–25; and *IBMR* 19 (Jan. 1995), 25.

6. An unsigned editorial in *Christian Witness and Advocate of Bible Holiness* (15 Nov. 1906, p. 8) is the earliest clearly antagonistic reference to the "Tongues Movement" that I have unearthed. One month later the redoubtable P. F. Bresee, founder of the Church of the Nazarene in Los Angeles, similarly chose sides and came out swinging in *Nazarene Messenger,* 13 Dec. 1906, p. 6.

7. *Holiness Advocate,* June 1906, p. 4. This article was in fact a reprint from the *Way of Faith,* presumably by J. M. Pike, but since it appeared on the *Holiness Advocate*'s editorial page without comment, it undoubtedly reflected Crumpler's views as well.

8. See the testimonials by J. H. Pate and Katie Parker in *Holiness Advocate,* 1 June 1906, pp. 3, 6. Additional testimonials may have been printed in other issues, but only a half-dozen copies of this periodical seem to exist.

9. *Holiness Advocate,* 15 May 1907, p. 1. This was a reprint of Pike's editorial in the *Way of Faith,* 9 May 1907, noted previously, but Crumpler appended a note stating that it expressed his views too.

10. Vinson Synan, *The Old-Time Power: A History of the Pentecostal Holiness Church* (Franklin Springs, Ga.: Advocate, 1973), 116–18.

11. Miss Morrison, *Promise,* Feb. 1909, p. 5. *Promise* was published by the Church of God East End Mission in Toronto.

12. *Christian Witness,* reprinted without citation in *Burning Bush,* 2 May 1907, p. 5.

13. *Christian Witness and Advocate of Bible Holiness,* 15 Nov. 1906, p. 8.

14. *Free Methodist,* 6 Nov. 1906, pp. 712–13.

15. Mrs. [Jesse] Penn-Lewis, *Christian,* 13 Feb. 1908, p .11.

16. R. L. Averill, *Holiness Evangel,* 1 Jan. 1907, p. 1.

17. *Christian Witness and Advocate of Bible Holiness,* 15 Nov. 1906, p. 8. See also *Free Methodist,* 31 July 1906, p. 488, and 6 Nov. 1906, pp. 712–13.

18. F. W. Pitt, *Prophetic News and Israel's Watchman,* 7 May 1921, p. 141.

19. *Burning Bush,* 13 Sept. 1906, pp. 4–5; G. T. Neal, *Gospel Trumpet,* 31 Jan. 1907, p. 74; Alma White, *The Story of My Life and the Pillar of Fire* (Zarepath, N.J.: Pillar of Fire, 1935–43), 2:317, 3:185, and 4:225–27.

20. Mrs. [Jesse] Penn-Lewis, *Christian,* 6 Feb. 1908, p. 12.

21. *Christian Witness and Advocate of Bible Holiness,* 4 July 1907, p. 8.
22. P. F. Bresee, *Nazarene Messenger,* 13 Dec. 1906, p. 6.
23. John Norberry, *Herald of Holiness,* 30 Apr. 1919, p. 5.
24. C. H. Alger, *Herald of Holiness,* 29 Jan. 1919, p. 5.
25. I. G. Martin, *Pentecostal Herald,* 12 Dec. 1906, pp. 2–3.
26. The fracturing of the Holiness sects is well described in Synan, *Holiness-Pentecostal Movement,* chaps. 3–4; and in Melvin E. Dieter, "Wesleyan-Holiness Aspects of Pentecostal Origins," in *Aspects of Pentecostal-Charismatic Origins,* ed. Vinson Synan (Plainfield, N.J.: Logos International, 1975), 75–76. Fissures within the Christian and Missionary Alliance, which stood somewhere between the Holiness and the higher life traditions, are detailed in Robert Mapes Anderson, *Vision of the Disinherited: The Making of American Pentecostalism* (New York: Oxford University Press, 1979), 143–47; Edith L. Blumhofer, *The Assemblies of God to 1941: A Chapter in the History of American Pentecostalism* (Springfield, Mo.: Assemblies of God, 1989), 183–90; and Charles Nienkirchen, "A. B. Simpson: Forerunner and Critic of the Pentecostal Movement," in *The Birth of a Vision,* ed. David F. Harzfeld and Charles Nienkirchen (Beaverlodge, Alberta: Buena Book Services, 1986), 141–48. Breakups within individual missions are more difficult to track, but one gains a sense of the painfulness and frequency of the process in firsthand accounts such as Josephine M. Washburn, *History and Reminiscences of the Holiness Church Work in Southern California and Arizona* (New York, 1912; repr., New York: Garland, 1985), 376–90; and Frank Bartleman, *Azusa Street: The Roots of Modern-Day Pentecost,* ed. and intro. Vinson Synan (Plainfield, N.J.: Logos International, 1925; repr., 1980).
27. Mrs. [Jesse] Penn-Lewis, *Life of Faith,* 5 Mar. 1907, p. 209, and 15 Nov. 1907, p. 1037.
28. The records overflow with hints of nasty physical altercations between Pentecostals and all sorts of outsiders, occasionally including radical evangelicals. Although I will discuss two or three of those incidents, the story of physical violence in early Pentecostal culture largely falls outside the scope of this essay since the theological identity of the antagonists was irrelevant. Usually such violence stemmed from Pentecostals' real or perceived civil infractions, such as disturbing the peace, or from protocol infractions, such as the mixed assembling of blacks and whites. For representative accounts of physical violence, see the Reverend Walter J. Higgins, *Pioneering in Pentecost: My Experiences of 46 Years in the Ministry* (Bostonia, Calif.: author, 1958), 27–28, 31, 41; and A. J. Tomlinson, *Diary of A. J. Tomlinson,* 3 vols., ed. Homer A. Tomlinson (Jamaica, N.Y.: Erhardt, 1955), 1:32, 35, 57, 60, 64, 113.
29. Anderson, *Vision,* chap. 2; Walter Goldschmidt, "Class Denominationalism in Rural California Churches," *American Journal of Sociology* 41 (1944): 348–55; Donald W. Dayton, "Yet Another Layer of the Onion: Or Opening the Ecumenical Door to Let the Riffraff In," *Ecumenical Review* 40 (1988): 87–110.
30. Unsigned article, undoubtedly by Jesse Penn-Lewis, in *Overcomer,* Nov. 1909, p. 164.
31. *Free Methodist,* 6 Nov. 1906, pp. 712–13.
32. George W. Shealey, *New York Witness,* reprinted without citation in *Free Methodist,* 8 Oct. 1907, p. 649.
33. *Gospel Trumpet,* 26 Mar. 1908, p. 201.

34. *Burning Bush,* 2 May 1907, pp. 5–6.

35. C. W. Naylor, *Gospel Trumpet,* 7 May 1908, pp. 4–6. See also *Burning Bush,* 2 May 1907, pp. 5–6.

36. A. T. Pierson, "'Speaking with Tongues,'" *Missionary Review of the World,* n.s., 20 (July 1907): 488–89.

37. H. A. Ironside, *Apostolic Faith Missions and the So-called Second Pentecost* (New York: Loizeaux Brothers, n.d. [ca. 1910]), 15.

38. G. H. Lang, *The Modern Gift of Tongues* (London: Marshall Brothers, 1913), 71. See also W. E. Pietsch, *McPherson-Jeffreys: Four Square Gospel Heresy* (Runnimede, Hounslow, Middlesex, England: The Bible Witness, n.d. [probably late 1920s]), 4.

39. Reader Harris, *Tongues of Fire,* Jan. 1909, p. 6.

40. C. E. Cowman, *Tongues of Fire,* reprinted without citation in *Christian Witness and Advocate of Bible Holiness,* 1 Apr. 1909, p. 11.

41. Timothy L. Smith, "The Theology and Practices of Methodism, 1876–1919: The Holiness Crusade," in *The History of American Methodism,* 3 vols., ed. Emory Stevens Bucke (New York: Abingdon, 1964), 2:608–27, esp. 618, 625–26; and Donald W. Dayton, "The Holiness Churches: A Significant Ethical Tradition," *Christian Century,* Feb. 1975, pp. 199–200. For a less sanguine view of Holiness concern for the down-and-out, see Charles Edwin Jones, "Disinherited or Rural? A Historical Case Study in Urban Holiness Religion," *Missouri Historical Review* 46 (1972): 395–412, esp. 405–12.

42. White, *Story of My Life,* 3:145; see also 3:241. White's tortured personal life is carefully recounted in Susie Cunningham Stanley, *Feminist Pillar of Fire: The Life of Alma White* (Cleveland, Ohio: Pilgrim, 1993).

43. White, *Story of My Life,* 3:243, 242.

44. Pierson, "'Speaking with Tongues,'" 492; A. T. Pierson, "'Speaking with Tongues,'" *Missionary Review of the World,* n.s., 20 (Sept. 1907): 683.

45. W. B. Godbey, *Six Tracts by W. B. Godbey* (New York: Garland 1985), 27–28. This volume contains Godbey's *Tongue Movement, Satanic* (Zarepath, N.J.: Pillar of Fire, 1918), along with five other documents by Godbey.

46. R. A. Torrey, *Is the Present "Tongues" Movement of God?* (Los Angeles: BIOLA Book Room, n.d. [probably 1913]), 4–7.

47. H. L. Averill, *Pentecostal Advocate,* 10 Jan. 1907, p. 2.

48. H. C. Wickersham, *Gospel Trumpet,* 16 Jan. 1908, p. 45.

49. August Youngren, *Free Methodist,* 16 June 1908, p. 379.

50. See, for example, C. E. McPherson, *Life of Levi R. Lupton* (Alliance, Ohio: author, 1911), 209; and F. W. Pitt, *New Light on the Tongues Baptism* (London: West London Bible Institute, n.d. [probably 1920s]), 6.

51. *Free Methodist,* 7 May 1907, p. 296.

52. *Burning Bush,* 19 Sept. 1907, p. 7. The Parham scandal is judiciously assessed in James R. Goff Jr., *Fields White unto Harvest: Charles F. Parham and the Missionary Origins of Pentecostalism* (Fayetteville: University of Arkansas Press, 1988), 136–42, 223–25; see esp. 224 n. 41. Goff discounts the *Burning Bush*'s account as too partisan to be trusted. I disagree. However discreditable the *Burning Bush*'s motives, its rendering of the incident (or incidents) seems essentially accurate. See *San Antonio Light,* 19 July 1907, p. 1; idem, 24 July 1907, p. 2; and *Houston Chronicle,* 21 July 1907, p. 14. See also the damning data marshaled (ironically) in Parham's defense by J. G.

Campbell, *The Gospel of the Kingdom,* Apr. 1910, p. 2, reprinted in Larry Martin, *In the Beginning: Readings on the Origins of the Twentieth Century Pentecostal Revival and the Birth of the Pentecostal Church of God* (Duncan, Okla.: Christian Life, 1994), 113–15. In fairness to Goff, these items, which strengthen the *Burning Bush*'s credibility, were discovered by other researchers after his book was published.

53. *Tongues of Fire,* Nov. 1907, pp. 1–2.

54. Alma White, *Demons and Tongues* (Zarepath, N.J.: Pillar of Fire, 1919), 56.

55. G. T Neal, *Gospel Trumpet,* 31 Jan. 1907, p. 74.

56. T. J. Hoskinson *Free Methodist,* 6 Nov. 1906[?], p. 708.

57. J. L. Cox, *Herald of Holiness,* 27 June 1917, p. 4.

58. A. M. Hills, *The Tongues Movement* (Manchester, England: Star Hall, n.d. [ca. 1914]), 27.

59. *Gospel Trumpet,* 15 Mar. 1923, p. 22.

60. See, for example, Pietsch, *McPherson-Jeffreys,* 12; and John D. Goben, *"Aimee": The Gospel Gold Digger* (New York: Peoples, 1932), 12–14.

61. For one of scores of examples, see *Gospel Trumpet,* 26 Mar. 1908, p. 201.

62. F. W. Pitt, *Faith Healing Tragedies* (London: Pickering and Inglis, n.d. [probably 1920s]), 20.

63. Charles B. Ebey, *Free Methodist,* 7 May 1907, p. 296; George W. Shealey, *New York Witness,* reprinted without citation in *Free Methodist,* 8 Oct. 1907, p. 649.

64. See, for example, the extended report of a "worker" on the Pacific coast in *Christian,* 30 Jan. 1908, p. 12; and McPherson, *Lupton,* 136.

65. *Free Methodist,* 7 May 1907, p. 296.

66. August Youngren, *Free Methodist,* 16 June 1908, p. 379. See also Hills, *Tongues,* 26, for similar comments about the arrogance of Pentecostal missionaries.

67. Hills, *Tongues,* 27; G. T. Neal, *Gospel Trumpet,* 31 Jan. 1907, p. 74.

68. George W. Shealey, *New York Witness,* reprinted without citation in *Free Methodist,* 8 Oct. 1907, p. 649. The eyeglass instance comes from a Pentecostal source: Mildred Edwards, *Trust,* Feb. 1915, p. 13.

69. L. W. Dixon, comments made in 1906, printed in Washburn, *History,* 390. See also *Herald of Holiness,* 5 Apr. 1916, p. 4. One octogenarian told me how her mother, who switched from the Holiness to the Pentecostal movement about 1910, kept her locked in her bedroom for days at a stretch, dressed in white ascension robes, awaiting the Lord's return. Ms. Agnes Dooley, interview with the author, July 1988, Pasadena, Calif.

70. John L. Brasher to H. H. Glascock, 3 Sept. 1909, Brasher papers, Perkins Library, Duke University. See also J. Grant Thompson, *Gospel Trumpet,* 4 June 1908, p. 4.

71. Ironside, *Apostolic,* 10–11.

72. China Inland Mission, *Minutes,* 9 Sept. 1914, Billy Graham Center, Wheaton College, Ill.

73. David Clark, "Miracles for a Dime," *California History* (Winter 1978–79): 357.

74. Pierson, "'Speaking with Tongues,'" Sept., 683.

75. *Herald of Holiness,* 5 Apr. 1916, p. 4.

76. See, for example, "Sketch of the Life and Ministry of Mack M. Pinson," 7, Assemblies of God Archives; and *Alliance* [Ohio] *Daily Review,* 23 Dec. 1910, p. 5.

77. Goff, *Fields,* 79–81.

78. *Free Methodist,* 1 July 1907, p. 417.

79. *Word and Witness,* Oct. 1915, p. 2; Wayne E. Warner, *The Woman Evangelist: The Life and Times of Charismatic Evangelist Maria B. Woodworth-Etter* (Metuchen, N.J.: Scarecrow, 1986), 234. The evangelists were C. E. Foster and Maria Woodworth-Etter. Similarly, a London newspaper carried a lengthy letter from an unnamed observer of the meetings of Anglican-turned-Pentecostal A. A. Boddy. After describing and debunking the "manifestations" in Boddy's services, the writer warned him not to involve children (*Daily Chronicle,* Oct. 1907 tear sheet, Hannah Whitall Smith Collection, Asbury Theological Seminary).

80. Higgins, *Pioneering in Pentecost,* 16.

81. Unnamed correspondent, quoted in *A Warning,* front page of a four-page flyer published by the SPCK [Society for the Promotion of Christian Knowledge] Press, Madras, 1908, in my possession.

82. G. B. Cashwell, *Apostolic Faith* [Calif.], May 1907, p. 1.

83. Higgins, *Pioneering in Pentecost,* 48–50.

84. Arthur Watson, *Promise,* Mar. 1910, p. 7.

85. Howard Goss, as recounted in Ethel E. Goss, *The Winds of God* (New York: Comet, 1958), 87–88.

86. The quotation comes from an ad for D. F. Brooks, *The Tongues: A Critical Discussion of the Modern Tongues Movement.* The ad appeared in *Pentecostal Advocate,* 13 May 1909, p. 16.

87. L. W. Dixon in Washburn, *History,* 390.

88. Brasher to Glascock, 3 Sept. 1909. See also Bresee, *Nazarene Messenger,* 13 Dec. 1906, p. 6; Lulu B. Rogers, *Pentecostal Advocate,* 28 Mar. 1907, p. 11; and I. G. Martin, *Pentecostal Herald,* 12 Dec. 1906, pp. 2–3.

89. Lang, *Gift of Tongues,* 46.

90. Mrs. Penn-Lewis, *Christian,* 9 Jan. 1908, p. 12. The item appeared under the significant heading "An Hour of Peril."

91. White, *Story of My Life,* 3:214.

92. L. W. Dixon in Washburn, *History,* 390.

93. George W. Shealey, *Free Methodist,* 8 Oct. 1907, p. 649. See also *Christian Witness and Advocate of Bible Holiness,* 3 Oct. 1907, p. 1.

94. G. T. Neal, *Gospel Trumpet,* 31 Jan. 1907, p. 74.

95. White, *Story of My Life,* 3:116.

96. V. A. Walker, *Pentecostal Advocate,* 4 Apr. 1907, p. 11.

97. [Jesse Penn-Lewis], *The Life of Faith,* 13 Nov. 1907, p. 1037.

98. Mrs. Penn-Lewis, *Christian,* 20 Feb. 1908, p. 11.

99. Editorial, *Christian Witness and Advocate of Bible Holiness,* 15 Nov. 1906, p. 8.

100. V. A. Walker, *Pentecostal Advocate,* 4 Apr. 1907, p. 11.

101. White, *Story of My Life,* 3:139–40.

102. Reader Harris, *Tongues of Fire,* Jan. 1908, p. 7.

103. Duke M. Farson and Edwin L. Harvey, *Burning Bush,* 2 May 1907, p. 5.

104. C. W. Naylor, *Gospel Trumpet,* 7 May 1908, pp. 4–6.

105. Allie Irick, *Herald of Holiness,* 25 Aug. 1915, p. 5.

106. Editorial, *Church Advocate and Holiness Banner,* reprinted without citation in *Free Methodist,* 6 Nov. 1906, p. 713.

107. W. M. Kelly in Washburn, *History,* 383.

108. *Gospel Trumpet,* 26 Mar. 1908, p. 201.

109. Unnamed correspondent in *Overcomer,* Jan. 1910, 9–10.

110. Letter from Sister A. L. Malone to Josephine Washburn, 1 June 1908, reprinted in Washburn, *History,* 419.

111. C. W. Naylor, *Gospel Trumpet,* 7 May 1908, pp. 4–6. See also Hills, *Tongues,* 26; and L. W. Dixon in Washburn, *History,* 390: many have wept "their way back out of what they testify [was a] horrible darkness and wild, powerful delusion."

112. W. M. Kelly in Washburn, *History,* 385.

113. Edith L. Blumhofer, *Aimee Semple McPherson: Everybody's Sister* (Grand Rapids, Mich.: Eerdmans, 1993).

114. Herbert Buffum (presumably as ed.), *Gold Tried in the Fire,* Apr. 1913, pp. 6–7.

115. *Christian Witness and Advocate of Bible Holiness,* 20 May 1909, p. 6.

116. White, *Story of My Life,* 2:289.

117. E. N. Bell, *Word and Witness,* 20 Oct. 1912, p. 3.

118. Charles Fox Parham, *Apostolic Faith* [Kans.], Nov. 1912, p. 7.

119. See, for example, *Methodist Advocate Journal* [Chattanooga and Knoxville, Tenn.], 9 Aug. 1900, p. 1.

120. Melvin E. Dieter, "The Wesleyan/Holiness and Pentecostal Movements: Commonalties, Confrontation, and Dialogue," *Pneuma* 12 (1990): 10–11.

121. See, for example, C. B. Jernigan, *Pioneer Days of the Holiness Movement in the Southwest* (Kansas City, Mo.: Pentecostal Nazarene Publishing House, 1919), 151–57.

122. *Holiness Advocate,* 15 Oct. 1903, p. 7.

123. *Holiness Advocate,* 6 Dec. 1906, p. 1.

124. J. W. Hughes, *Holiness Advocate,* 1 Apr. 1903, p. 5.

125. *Christian Witness and Advocate of Bible Holiness,* 5 Aug. 1909, p. 8.

126. A. B. Crumpler and T. M. Lee, *Holiness Advocate,* 15 Apr. 1901, p. 2.

127. I owe the main point of this paragraph to Roger Robins, "From the Holiness Church of North Carolina to the Pentecostal Holiness Church," seminar paper, Department of History, University of North Carolina, 1989.

128. Herbert E. Randall, *Promise,* June 1907, pp. 1–2. For a similar narrative, also bristling with recrimination, see Arthur Watson, *Promise,* Mar. 1910, p. 7.

129. *Free Methodist,* 31 July 1906, p. 488.

3

The Protestant Missionary Establishment and the Pentecostal Movement

Daniel Bays

In the early 1900s Protestant missions had achieved an impressive presence in China while still maintaining, considering their denominational diversity, a remarkable unity. After the opening of the whole country to mission work in 1860, when there were still fewer than one hundred Protestant missionaries in only five coastal cities, the mission enterprise accelerated dynamically. Yet unity and cooperation were the rule. All missionaries enjoyed exactly the same extraterritorial and other legal rights under the "unequal treaties" between their home countries and the hapless imperial government in Beijing, and all mission societies reached amicable "comity" agreements to minimize the overlap of mission stations in the same locales—China had, after all, enough "unoccupied" territory for all. One of the reasons that comity arrangements among Protestants worked well was that they shared a common evangelical theological foundation, in addition to common assumptions about certain cultural features, such as modern education and medicine, being a natural part of the "Christian civilization" they were transmitting to China.[1] Naturally there were differences in nuance— indeed, profound disagreements over strategy, tactics, and the priority of activities such as education and social services. But the essential unity of the "force" (as many referred to the totality of missionaries in China) was clearly visible in the nationwide Shanghai conferences of 1877, 1890, and 1907. No mission society in China was not invited to, or refused to attend, any of these meetings.

Within this framework, another feature was clearly visible. From about 1880 to 1920, institution building was the hallmark of Protestant missions. Education, medicine, publishing, and journalism all developed as major foci of mission efforts, and all became more sophisticated, complex, and professionalized by the early 1900s.[2] These activities were expensive, but the resources to support them were efficiently gathered by increasingly bureaucratized mission board staff at home, especially in the United States.[3] Institutionalization, however, also drew some missionaries' energies into essentially "secular" activities even further afield from direct evangelism than education and medicine: famine relief; agitation against infanticide, polygamy, and footbinding; rehabilitation of opium addicts; and even constitutional political reform. Many younger missionaries who came to China just before or after the turn of the century in the mainline boards had a much broader view of missionary work then did their predecessors, and they shied away from "religious" work for the sake of a more "professional" calling to one of these other activities.[4] These issues caused controversy and tension, even conflicts, within the missionary community. Indeed, as we look back with the sharpened vision of hindsight, we can see many factors at work causing future fissures in the mission community: social, political, and theological time bombs waiting to explode and rend asunder Protestant unity in missions abroad as well as in the churches at home. Premonitions of the later "fundamentalist-modernist" split seem clear well before 1900: a rapid proliferation of small new missionary efforts in the 1890s and after 1900, many of them "faith missions" with no established sending body, fired by an urgent zeal to evangelize; and the sudden appearance, often in these faith missions, of many lay people or those who were products of the new Bible schools such as Moody Bible Institute or the Missionary Training Institute (Nyack, New York), whose socioeconomic status was lower than that of the ordained missionaries of earlier decades. All this was in addition to the divisive issues of "soul-winning" versus social amelioration.

We should not, however, read too much into these pre–World War I tensions. A good case can be made for the claim that what James A. Patterson calls the "Protestant missionary consensus" persisted until the 1920s.[5] Broad continuities in cultural vision, if not full agreement in theological doctrine, characterized U.S. Protestant missions until well after 1900, and even the rapid growth of faith missions from the 1890s on was at first intended not as a purposeful break with the established denominational missions but only as an accelerated version motivated by the rising strength of premillennialist urgency, a flexible evangelistic complement to the slow-moving established mission structures.[6] An excellent example of this was the Student Volunteer Movement (SVM), which, in the 1890s and early 1900s, John Mott ably built into the prime recruiting channel through which idealistic college graduates entered foreign missions. It was solidly "evangelical" in these years, in the sense of a continuing commitment to the traditional Protestant missionary consensus.[7] And yet it is also clear that few SVM recruits were millenarians, looking for the imminent return of Christ, or had an acute sense of supernatural power.

Thus, when the first Pentecostals came to China, there was as yet no consciously defined "fundamentalism" or "modernism," no unbridgeable chasm between biblical literalists and more flexible interpreters of Scripture or between social reformers and those who primarily stressed personal regeneration. But the unity of the late nineteenth century was definitely becoming frayed; its theological and social underpinnings were eroding quickly. China itself was changing, to the joy of all mission agencies. After the tragic cataclysm of the Boxer Uprising in 1900, the Chinese government and Chinese in general seemed open to ideas of reform, progress, and Christian civilization. Protestant converts increased rapidly after 1900, and so did the mission force and its institutional growth. The cheapness and ease of trans-Pacific travel, compared to just a few years before, also now made it a simple matter for new missionaries, especially the faith missionaries, to come to China, even without forethought and preparation. All these factors constituted a volatile mix of ingredients into which the arrival of Pentecostalism from North America injected one more destabilizing factor.

The First Pentecostal Missionaries to China

The first Pentecostal missionary to reach China was probably T. J. McIntosh of North Carolina, who arrived with his wife in Hong Kong in August 1907. They immediately went on to nearby Macao, where they met several missionaries and Chinese Christians. A participant in the early Hong Kong Pentecostal group later claimed that in this initial 1907 foray by McIntosh, "eleven missionaries and many Chinese received the baptism."[8] Actually, as I will show, perhaps two or three of these missionaries, enjoying cooler air at seaside Macao in the summer heat, had a Pentecostal experience.[9]

McIntosh had no known direct connection to the Los Angeles Azusa Street mission, where the great Pentecostal revival had begun in early summer 1906. But most of the other Pentecostals who came to China in 1907 and 1908 did. Alfred G. Garr, pastor of a Los Angeles church, was one of the first to receive Spirit baptism at Azusa, doing so in June 1906. In late June he heard God's call to go to India, and in July 1906 he and his wife, Lillian, headed east for New York and then passage to India.[10] After some months and many adventures in India, Garr felt led to go on to China, where he and Lillian arrived about 9 October 1907.

Here Garr's itinerary intersected precisely with the Pentecostal trajectory coming from Azusa Street across the Pacific. In the summer of 1906 Pastor M. L. Ryan of Salem, Oregon, had heard in detail of the inspiring revival in Los Angeles, and received the Spirit baptism and tongues himself.[11] Soon he moved to Spokane, where he established an "apostolic assembly" of Pentecostals. Following the common pattern of hearing a call to foreign missions soon after receiving the baptism, Ryan and a large part of his congregation sent themselves off around the world as faith missionaries. The largest group, comprising twelve people, was called to China.[12] The total of fifteen or more headed for East Asia, led by Ryan himself, set off from Seattle for Tokyo in early September 1907. Remarkably, as they waited in Seattle to embark, they met and fellowshipped for a few days with a Norwegian-American missionary, Bernt Berntsen of North China, who had heard of the Azusa Street revival in late 1906 and was now on his way to Los Angeles, arriving in Seattle in late August.[13]

Four single women were in the Ryan group, all bound for China: May Law, Rosa Pittman, Bertha Milligan, and Cora Fritsch. Law and Pittman continued straight on to Hong Kong, arriving on 12 October 1907, three days after the Garrs arrived from India; Milligan and Fritsch stayed a few months in Japan and came on to Hong Kong in 1908.[14] But for the remainder of 1907 it was just Rev. and Mrs. Alfred Garr and the Misses Law and Pittman (with Mr. and Mrs. McIntosh not far away in Macao) to try to establish a Pentecostal beachhead in Hong Kong. None of them had learned a word of Chinese, although Mrs. Garr had already become convinced back in Los Angeles the year before that she could speak both Tibetan and Chinese.

The Garrs and the two young women were all directed to the American Board of Commissioners for Foreign Missions (ABCFM) (Congregationalist) compound, where Rev. C. R. Hager was head of the Hong Kong mission. They stayed there for a time before finding their own lodgings. The board was having a property dispute over the building in which its chapel was housed, and Hager was not preaching there. He thus turned it over to Garr with his blessing. In mid-October 1907 Garr began meetings, assisted by the others, that proceeded nightly until some time in December. It is not specifically recorded whether the Americans tried to preach in Chinese, believing they had been supernaturally gifted with fluency; they probably did, because most of the first Pentecostals who felt called to foreign lands fully believed they had been or would be given instant fluency of speech. But Garr quickly began preaching in English, with a Chinese interpreter; he was fortunate to have a very able one. Garr's interpreter was Mok Lai Chi (Mo Lizhi), the proprietor of a school who spoke English fluently and who served as a deacon of the ABCFM church and as its Sunday School superintendent. The meetings seem to have been aimed at least as much at church revival as at evangelism of the unconverted. In early November Mok himself received Spirit baptism and the gift of tongues, as did several other Chinese members of the church.

In December the church took away from Garr and the growing group the right to use its premises. In his 1907 station report, Hager, referring to meetings conducted by an unnamed "American evangelist," noted that "a real blessing" and "a new spirit" had resulted from them but that the issue of tongues had eventually divided the church, and some members withdrew to form a new church.[15] Hager may have moderated his description here, because the split in the church seems to have been stormy. The January 1908 issue of the *Chinese Recorder,* the missionary journal published in Shanghai, had the following news insert that must have been written in December: "The religious world of Hong Kong has been disturbed by the advent there of representatives of the Pentecostal church, a sect recently established in California, preaching the gift of tongues and attacking the methods of other Christian missionaries. . . . Their aim seems rather to pervert Christian Chinese than to convert the heathen."[16]

Mok Lai Chi led the exodus from the American board church and became the leader of the new congregation. He and his Chinese colleagues, not Garr and the other Americans, who as yet had no Chinese ability, were in charge.[17] Moreover, in January 1908 Mok founded the first Pentecostal newspaper in China, *Pentecostal Truths* (*Wuxunjie zhenlibao*), all in Chinese except for a small section of English items at the end. This new paper, which by late 1909 was (Mok claimed) printed in six thousand copies and mailed nationwide, was a crucial transmission belt for Pentecostal ideas in China, just as diverse early publications in the United States in the years after 1906 spread Pentecostal ideas far and wide. There is ample evidence that *Pentecostal Truths* helped the networking of Pentecostal missionaries in China and also drew the attention of many Chinese. It was published until at least 1917, with thirty-nine issues appearing between January 1908 and April 1917.[18]

The American contingent of the Hong Kong group was hard hit by plague in the spring of 1908. The Garrs lost a child and returned to the United States, and May Law and Rosa Pittman had to be quarantined for several weeks. The McIntoshes by this time had left Macao for Jerusalem. But the work continued under Mok and the Chinese believers, using Mok's school as a chapel for services. Later in 1908 Law and Pittman reestablished themselves and began formal language study, and their two colleagues from the M. L. Ryan group, Bertha Milligan and Cora Fritsch, came on from Japan.[19] Other Americans came in 1909 and 1910, creating a Sino-foreign "apostolic faith" community based in Hong Kong, some of whose American members, after or while learning the language, went inland to begin schools and orphanages and to try to preach as well.

Another Pentecostal base was established in 1908 on the North China plain in southern Chihli (Hebei) province. This was the work of Bernt Berntsen, whose quest for the Pentecostal experience had begun with his reading of an early copy of Azusa's *Apostolic Faith* in late 1906. After receiving the baptism and speaking in tongues at Azusa Street, Berntsen spent the rest of 1907 on the West Coast and then gathered a group of eleven adult Pentecostals, one of them a single woman only sixteen years old, plus several children, and returned to China at the beginning of 1908 to establish a new mission in Zhengding, Hebei.[20] One of those who accompanied Berntsen back, Roy Hess, was an Azusa Street veteran of 1906.[21] Perhaps because of the disappointing revelation that, far from being fluent in Chinese, they had not a word of the language, or perhaps because of the physical difficulties of family life in a semirural area, four of the adult newcomers (Mr. and Mrs. George Hanson and seven children and Mr. and Mrs. Roy Hess with one child) moved to Shanghai, while the single persons began to study the language in Zhengding. Meanwhile, Berntsen and his wife led the mission's work of broadcasting the Pentecostal message, and Berntsen himself became one of the main Pentecostal activists in North China. He traveled to other stations to assist and encourage other missionaries in their work, and in 1912 he spearheaded the publication of a new Chinese-language paper, *Popular Gospel Truth* (*Tongchuan fuyin zhenlibao*), which unlike Mok's Hong Kong paper, did not have an English section at the end.[22] This paper highlighted graphically the millenarianism that drove Pentecostalism. On the masthead, above the title, is the Chinese phrase "Jesus will return soon." Berntsen and the Zhengding group persevered; he, his wife, and at least two others were still there in 1915.[23]

Thomas Junk and his wife were at Azusa Street early in the revival and left to evangelize further up the West Coast in September or October 1906. He passed through Oakland and Portland, finally settling in Seattle by early 1907. When and how the Junks received the call to China is unclear, but they had made it to China and settled in Caoxian, a county, in southwestern Shandong province, sometime in mid-1908. Junk and his wife were apparently the only Pentecostals in this rather isolated area, in which Junk did much traveling, using Caoxian city as a base. Mrs. Junk died in January 1909, and Junk carried on for at least two more years. He had several letters in a range of publications back in the United States, but none after 1911, and he was not listed in the nationwide mission yearbook for 1912.[24]

One other Azusa Street product was Hector and Sigrid McLean. He was Canadian; she, Swedish. They both went to China in 1901, in separate affiliations with the China Inland Mission. They were married in 1905, but sickness forced them to return home in 1907. While in the United States they went to Azusa Street and became Pentecostals. They returned to China as independent apostolic faith missionaries in 1909 and then in 1910 joined the Pentecostal Missionary Union, a British faith network organized by Cecil Polhill, himself also formerly of the China Inland Mission.[25]

All in all, the Azusa Street revival and its newspaper directly influenced the creation of permanent Pentecostal missions in several places in China to a remarkable degree. I think that the most important early sites were Hong Kong; the Berntsen mission in North China; and Shanghai, Pentecostal activity at which began with the Hanson and Hess families, who had moved there after leaving Berntsen's Zhengding mission in mid-1908. Hess's letter to the *Bridegroom's Messenger* in fall 1908 indicated that the four of them were still the only Pentecostals there at the time. But Antoinette Moomau returned to Shanghai in 1909, some other single women came that year, and late in 1910 Mrs. H. L. Lawler and her daughter arrived there to settle permanently. The Lawler family, including a son and a daughter, had been part of the M. L. Ryan expedition from Seattle in September 1907. They had stayed in Japan for some time, and Mrs. Lawler and their daughter, Beatrice, came to join the Hong Kong Pentecostal group in 1909, while Mr. Lawler and their son, Harlan, returned to the United States. At the end of 1910 Mrs. Lawler and Beatrice moved to Shanghai, and her husband and son joined them there in 1912.[26] After 1910 the number of Pentecostals nationwide steadily grew; by 1915 there were over 150, scattered over nearly thirty sites.[27]

Pentecostals and the Protestant Missionary Establishment

It is hard to know the extent to which missionaries in China may have already been familiar with the controversies surrounding early Pentecostalism even before the first Pentecostals arrived in late summer and fall 1907. Berntsen reported meeting a man at the May 1907 Shanghai conference who allegedly had visited Azusa Street and was against it. In addition, some U.S. periodicals, especially Holiness publications such as *God's Revivalist, Gospel Trumpet,* and *The Free Methodist,* had been railing against tongues and other aspects of the movement since 1906.[28] Moreover, A. G. Garr's activities in India earlier in 1907 had aroused controversy, and word of this might have reached China.

Yet the first Pentecostals in China seem to have gotten a hearing among the missionaries, at least for a time. Most established missionaries proved to be resistant, but some were attracted.

When T. J. McIntosh arrived at Macao in August 1907, he preached the Pentecostal message, including the necessity of speaking in tongues, to a large number of missionaries from the interior on vacation there. Several meetings were held, but all but two visiting Christian and Missionary Alliance missionaries, Mr. Hamill and Miss Edwards, and a local Macao U.S. missionary, Fannie Winn, rejected the message.[29] Three missionary recruits, plus several Chinese (with McIntosh using an interpreter), were a modest but tangible return on this first venture.

Garr had less luck with the Hong Kong missionary community later in 1907. After the welcome by the American Board of Commissioners church and permission to use its facilities, the Pentecostals were expelled (or withdrew) in December to go on their own, as we have seen. On 19 January 1908 Garr wrote: "It is a hard fight here at times. . . . There is not one missionary standing with us in Hong Kong. Further up in China there are a number that have received the Pentecostal blessing [referring to those in the Christian and Missionary Alliance], but in Hong Kong the Chinese are the only ones."[30]

Of course, the January 1908 Shanghai *Chinese Recorder*'s disparaging small news item about the activities of the Hong Kong Pentecostals, cited earlier, may have affected the opinion of some; this journal was read by most missionaries in China. A year later Rev. C. R. Hager was set even more in his opposition; in his annual report for 1908 he referred to the Pentecostals as a "hindrance" and a "great trial to all."[31]

Bernt Berntsen in North China also encountered considerable resistance from established missionaries. Berntsen always hoped to convince other missionaries, and in September 1908 he claimed to have made a favorable impression on a Free Methodist missionary family when he spoke in tongues while praying with them on a train journey to Shanghai. But, he admitted, "the missionaries here are not in favor of us, so many bad reports are circulated all over this country, so the poor people [i.e., the missionaries] do not know what to believe of us."[32] After an extensive discussion with Berntsen at about this time, C. F. Appleton, a Free Methodist missionary, wrote a devastating letter for *The Free Methodist*, portraying the group that had accompanied Berntsen back to China several months earlier as deluded souls who before arrival had persisted in their belief they could speak Chinese, even though Berntsen himself told them he could not recognize what they spoke, and then were pathetic in their discovery in China that they could not speak the language after all.

Appleton concluded his long report with the assertion, "I am more persuaded than ever that this whole movement is a strong delusion of the devil."[33]

The events a few years later at a small Baptist mission in Tai'an, Shandong province, give us an example of the aggressive expulsion of mission members who became Pentecostals. The Baptist Gospel Mission in Tai'an, a faith mission, was descended from a split in the U.S. Southern Baptist Shandong mission in the early 1890s and was led by the contentious T. L. Blalock. On a trip to the United States in 1909, Blalock recruited Mr. and Mrs. L. M. Anglin to join the mission as faith missionaries. The Anglins came in late 1910. In about 1912 a new missionary couple (unnamed in the records) who had just joined the mission and were staying at the Anglins' house "sprang a revival of prayer and waiting for the baptism of the Holy Spirit" at the Anglins' home. The Anglins and several Chinese church members received the baptism and spoke in tongues, and a split occurred. Blalock expelled them from the mission; as he put it, "We exercised the right and authority of every living and free Baptist—that is, to withdraw fellowship from those who had left the Baptist faith and practice, which it is clearly our duty to do." Anglin and his wife stayed in Tai'an, however, living on a shoestring for a few years, and they established contacts with the early Pentecostal information and publication network back in the United States; in 1916 they affiliated with the young Assemblies of God. Later Anglin built a community in Tai'an called the Home of Onesiphorus, with workshops and a communal lifestyle as well as schools and an orphanage.[34]

A much more favorable response to the Pentecostals took place in parts of the two major established faith missions in China, the China Inland Mission and the Christian and Missionary Alliance, especially the latter.[35] The alliance, begun in the late 1880s, had about ninety missionaries in China in 1907. It was a major Holiness organization, characterized by a strong millenarian thrust and evangelical zeal, and many of its members looked ardently toward revival and renewal in the church, as well as toward Christ's Second Coming. Thus it is not surprising that many in the alliance were attracted to the Pentecostal revival and participated in it. In 1906 and after, alliance members in the United States and Canada, including some at the Missionary Training Institute in Nyack, reported receiving Spirit baptism and speaking in tongues, and so did its missionaries overseas, apparently beginning in India.[36] When, in Macao, T. J. McIntosh tried to convince a crowd of South China missionaries from several denominations of the validity of the Pentecostal experience, it was two alliance members from South China headquarters at Wuzhou, Guangxi province, Mr. Hamill and Miss Edwards, who were practically the only ones to respond favorably. They returned to Wuzhou with their

Spirit baptism and tongues, as did some of the Wuzhou Chinese converts. Then several more alliance converts and missionaries in Wuzhou and other Guangxi stations received the baptism and tongues; six missionaries, including the writer, are mentioned by name in a 10 October 1907 letter describing these events.[37]

R. A. Jaffray was one of those alliance missionaries who received the baptism and spoke in tongues at Wuzhou in October 1907. Jaffray was an old hand, having come to China in the 1890s. In March 1909, after observing how the Pentecostal movement was developing in China, he offered some thoughtful comments and opinions in a long article, "'Speaking in Tongues'—Some Words of Kindly Counsel." Here he forcefully confirmed that the experiences of the baptism of the Holy Spirit and speaking in tongues were valid and blessed ones, producing many spiritual benefits, which he enumerated. But he denied that speaking in tongues could be considered "evidence" or a singular sign of baptism by the Holy Spirit; indeed, this teaching on evidence "has done more harm than can be estimated." Moreover, he argued powerfully that tongues are easily counterfeited; too much stress on them produces schism, not unity; and the fixation of attention and energies on gaining and using these gifts publicly detracted greatly from the real work of evangelism, education, and other mission tasks. Once received, tongues should be used mainly in private prayer and intercession. In a real slap at folks such as the Hong Kong group of Pentecostals and those who had come back to China with Berntsen, he went on to decry the "independent missionaries" of this movement who came to China or Japan planning to speak the language instantly. He said that this expectation was unscriptural, and he had never seen evidence of it really occurring. Indeed, he said, those at home that supported these independent missionaries had "given their money to a foolish cause." Overall, this was not a mean-spirited article but one evincing real concern and considered opinion.[38]

In the meantime, A. B. Simpson, head of the alliance, had come to the same view, and in 1908 he refused to link speaking in tongues normatively with Spirit baptism.[39] For a few years into the future, however, alliance missionaries would occasionally take the plunge into Pentecostalism, claiming tongues as the required evidence of the baptism; then the offender, if he or she would not recant, was expected to resign. One of the most prominent alliance missionaries, W. W. Simpson (no relation to A. B. Simpson), who had been in the West China field since 1892, was forced to resign in 1914; he later joined the Assemblies of God mission organization after it was formed and had several more years of service in China.[40] But these separations were painful for all involved and often created hard feelings and bitterness.[41]

By approximately 1915 matters had sorted themselves out sufficiently clearly so that most organizations had taken a stand on Pentecostalism. This was largely a verdict of rejection, although the Christian and Missionary Alliance continued to recognize the validity of tongues, as long as it was not seen as the litmus test of baptism by the Holy Spirit. The China Inland Mission, with over one thousand members now the largest Protestant mission body in China, for years had constant tension within its ranks in several provinces over Pentecostalism, for much the same reasons that some alliance members were attracted to it. Its ruling China Council at Shanghai finally spent much time making a definitive evaluation during 1914–15. At last, after consultation with the home councils in Britain and North America in addition to its own discussions, in April 1915 the China Council adopted a long statement firmly condemning the Pentecostal movement; in addition to committing manifold doctrinal mistakes, the movement held meetings that allegedly were "characterized by disorder and by manifestations which in some cases had led to mental derangement and maniacal ravings."[42] In the same year a Chinese-language church newspaper published by the American Presbyterian Press in Shanghai specifically warned that in quest of the "gift" of speaking in tongues, people had been know to go insane and kill themselves.[43]

What was the overall nature of the indictment that the established missions drew up against the Pentecostals? Much of it was summarized by Robert Jaffray in his 1908 article discussed previously. At the beginning, in 1907 and 1908, there was not necessarily great resistance to, and there was even some interest in, the Pentecostals' theological concepts and terminology such as the baptism or infilling of the Holy Spirit, the age of "the latter rain," elevation of the book of Acts to a normative model for the church, and so forth.[44] But the hastiness, ignorance, and poor preparation with which many of the early Pentecostals arrived, as well as the alacrity and self-assurance with which they advanced their formula for the evangelization of China, implicitly (or even explicitly) denigrating decades of work by the established missions, naturally offended many. Nothing seems to have outraged other missionaries more, however, than the newcomers' claims to be able to speak Chinese without having studied it. This was not only an insult to their long years or decades of struggle with the language, but in their opinion it made the whole mission enterprise look foolish in the eyes of the Chinese. This claim or expectation of language was a typical and general one among early Pentecostals, as far as I can tell.[45] That the disappointment that inevitably ensued did not totally discourage them all is a tribute to their adaptability and stubbornness, as well as to their strength of conviction in the new creed.

Another feature of the early Pentecostals in China was that they proselytized other missionaries and their Chinese converts at least as much as they did the unconverted. Some of this was natural. Pentecostals sincerely believed that missionaries desperately needed the baptism and tongues and the other gifts to be more effective; indeed, they believed that many of them needed to be saved in the first place. But with no language abilities, the Pentecostals found their venues for preaching limited to places where English was spoken or where an interpreter was available; moreover, interpreters familiar with key vocabulary terms had to come from the established Chinese Christian community. Thus the Pentecostals badgered the established missionaries and their churches, and even in evangelism to the unsaved they ignored long-established comity demarcations. Of course, there was no board responsible for them, with whom comity discussions could be held. They also recruited ("stole," as other missionaries saw it) valuable Chinese workers from other missions. Mok Lai Chi, who hooked up with A. G. Garr in Hong Kong in late 1907, was but one example. Over the next couple of years in South China, a Wesleyan Methodist lay leader became pastor of a new Pentecostal church near Hong Kong, and his sister, who had worked for both the Wesleyan Methodist and Baptist missions in Macao, led a new church first established in her home.[46] The fact is that capable Chinese workers, always subordinate employees in an established mission, could have much more equality and scope for their own enterprise in a new Pentecostal work, where the "missionary" had no language ability and little institutional leverage over the native participants. This was attractive to some Chinese Christians but was naturally resented by the "establishment" missions.[47]

Eventually the lines were drawn fairly sharply. After a few years of hoping for conversions among the missionaries, Pentecostals were specifically shut out of other missions and kept more to themselves, especially after they began building their own institutional structures—they had their own "mission board" under the Assemblies of God after 1914.[48] They even stopped trying to deal with the China Inland Mission or the Christian and Missionary Alliance, choosing instead simply to affiliate from the start with the Assemblies of God or the small British network or to maintain independence. Most of the other missions had made up their minds by this time, adopting the equivalent of the China Inland Mission's strong 1915 statement on the movement. So from the mid-1910s onward, there was much less interaction between Pentecostals and other missions in China. Of course, by this time many of the early Pentecostals who stayed in China had gained the language, moved out beyond the "occupied" areas where they were such an irritant to other missions, and established their own stations, which eventually took on some of the institutionalized patterns of the older missions.

Conclusion

One reason that early twentieth-century evangelicals, in the churches at home and on the mission field, were willing sometimes to at least consider Pentecostalism was that they had heightened revivalist expectations. Especially after the great Wales revival of 1904 and the worldwide publicity about it, many Christians longed for revival in their own churches. The Pentecostal movement after 1906 promised exactly that, although it also came with strings attached—a restorationist teleology and a set of "signs," tongues in particular.[49] Missionaries in China shared the revivalist hope and expectation, and some, like Jonathan Goforth, a Canadian Presbyterian, held revival meetings that in tone and enthusiasm were nearly identical to Pentecostalism.[50] As we have seen, most established missions managed eventually to distinguish between authentically revivalist wheat and Pentecostal chaff. But as was the case in the years immediately after 1906, when revivalism was mixed in with Pentecostalism, whenever revivalism accelerated in later years, Pentecostalism was never far behind.

In Weixian, Shandong, the U.S. Presbyterian mission reported unfavorably on the Pentecostal disruptions that beset the mission in 1919.[51] When we look ahead a few years, however, we observe a surprising turn of events. In the context of the "Shandong Revival," which was energizing churches in the province in the early 1930s, the Pentecostal behaviors, including tongues, that had been roundly denounced in 1919 were now at first viewed with equanimity by these same Presbyterians. Six Chinese pastors from the Weixian presbytery attended Pentecostal revival meetings elsewhere in the province in the summer of 1930 and then conducted revival meetings in the Weixian churches, with much emotion, visions, and even some speaking in tongues. The annual report noted that there was some suspicion of these "gifts of the Spirit" but that overall the churches were revitalized by the movement.[52] The U.S. Southern Baptists were also swept up in this revival and its clearly Pentecostal elements, but like the Presbyterians, they carefully avoided the term *Pentecostal* in their favorable reports of it.[53] The initial enthusiasm of these old-line missions for the movement waned over the next year or two, as its "excesses" became apparent and as the missionaries' more critical judgments outweighed the initial hopeful enthusiasm of some, especially the Chinese pastors.[54] Once again, as in the 1907–15 period, missions drew the line short of fully Pentecostal ideas and behaviors. But Pentecostalism remained available, an evangelical "alternative" to which those looking for revivals could always turn.

Another important effect of Pentecostalism on the China mission field is that it accelerated the development of indigenous churches in China. There are two aspects of this trend. The first is that, in my opinion, traditional folk religiosity in China, with its lively sense of the supernatural, made a better "fit" with Pentecostalism than with the increasingly institutionalized and "rational" mainstream missions or even with other evangelical and fundamentalist missions, which tended to be high on spiritual regeneration but a bit squeamish about the truly supernatural.[55] Indeed, most of the several indigenous Chinese Christian churches and movements of the twentieth century have been Pentecostal in explicit identity or in orientation, and a large percentage of Chinese Protestants today, especially in the rural areas, are Pentecostal.

The other aspect is that some of the implications of Pentecostalism in China, especially its egalitarian style and its provision of direct revelation to all, facilitated the emergence of Chinese independent churches. Historically Pentecostalism was among other things a revolt against hierarchy in the church. Chinese Christians who became Pentecostal sensed this and were likely drawn to it partly because of this feature. Moreover, on the practical level, Pentecostalism provided all believers with access to spiritual enlightenment and knowledge of God's will through the indwelling Holy Spirit, and it also provided for self-interpretation of this revelation via the gifts of prophecy and tongues and their interpretation. Any Chinese believer could have access to all this, and capable ones could easily claim equality with, or superiority to, any foreign missionary. A result of this situation was the strong association of Pentecostalism with several of the primary hues in the spectrum of Chinese independent churches that developed from about 1910 into the 1930s.[56] Thus the influence of those earlier Pentecostal missionaries may have been strongest in areas they had not foreseen.

Notes

For support of the research and writing at various times, I wish to thank the Henry Luce Foundation, the Pew Charitable Trusts, the Committee on Scholarly Communication with China, and the University of Kansas General Research Fund. For sharing of materials, I gratefully acknowledge Wayne Warner, Mel Robeck, and Edith L. Blumhofer.

1. William Hutchison has deftly portrayed how a consciousness of the difference between "Christ" and "culture" on the part of at least some missionary strategists in

the mid-nineteenth century (e.g., Rufus Anderson of the ABCFM) evolved into a fusing of the two in the later decades of the century and the early 1900s. See William Hutchison, *Errand to the World: American Protestant Thought and Foreign Missions* (Chicago: University of Chicago Press, 1987), chaps. 3 and 4.

2. See Irwin T. Hyatt, "Protestant Missions in China, 1877–1890: The Institutionalization of Good Works," in *American Missionaries in China: Papers from Harvard Seminars*, ed. K. C. Liu (Cambridge, Mass.: Harvard University Press, 1966), 93–126.

3. Valentin H. Rabe, *The Home Base of American China Missions, 1880–1920* (Cambridge, Mass.: Harvard University Press, 1978).

4. For concrete description of the intertwined threads of institution building, bureaucratization, and secularization during these decades, see Kenneth S. Latourette, *A History of Christian Missions in China* (London: SPCK [Society for the Promotion of Christian Knowledge], 1929), esp. 429–65, 617–72. For an example, see Shirley Garrett, *Social Reformers in Urban China: The Chinese Y.M.C.A. 1895–1926* (Cambridge, Mass.: Harvard University Press, 1970). For some impressions of the way in which these historical trends appeared in missionaries' lives, see Jane Hunter, *The Gospel of Gentility: American Women Missionaries in Turn-of-the-Century China* (New Haven, Conn.: Yale University Press, 1984); John L. Rawlinson, *Rawlinson, The Recorder, and China's Revolution: A Topical Biography of Frank Joseph Rawlinson 1871–1937, Book One* (Notre Dame, Ind.: Cross Cultural, 1990); and the fictionalized account based on a composite of China YMCA secretaries, of which his father was one, in John Hersey, *The Call: An American Missionary in China* (New York: Knopf, 1985).

5. James A. Patterson, "The Loss of a Protestant Missionary Consensus: Foreign Missions and the Fundamentalist-Modernist Conflict," in *Earthen Vessels: American Evangelicals and Foreign Missions, 1880–1980,* ed. Joel A. Carpenter and Wilbert R. Shenk (Grand Rapids, Mich.: Eerdmans, 1990), 73–91, esp. 73–77.

6. Hutchison, *Errand to the World,* chap. 4, is excellent on the conflating of Christ, culture, and moral imperialism in these years. Dana L. Robert makes a persuasive case that millenarian urgency, not separation for its own sake, drove the founding and promotion of new agencies such as the Christian and Missionary Alliance. See Dana Robert, "'The Crisis of Missions': Premillennial Mission Theology and the Origins of Independent Evangelical Missions," in *Earthen Vessels,* ed. Carpenter and Shenk, 29–46.

7. Clifton J. Phillips, "The Student Volunteer Movement and Its Role in China Missions, 1886–1920," in *The Missionary Enterprise in China and America,* ed. John K. Fairbank (Cambridge, Mass.: Harvard University Press, 1974), 91–109.

8. E. May Law, *Pentecostal Mission Work in South China* (Falcon, N.C.; Falcon, n.d.), 1. Internal evidence indicates publication in 1915.

9. McIntosh himself, in a letter of 21 Oct. 1907, claimed that seven alliance missionaries at Wuzhou had received the Spirit baptism. But he had almost certainly not gone there himself. See *Bridegroom's Messenger* [Atlanta, Ga.] 1, no. 3 (1 Dec. 1907): 1 (hereinafter *BM*). Apparently two missionaries did convert, and they then took the message back to their colleagues in Wuzhou in fall 1907. See Fannie Winn's letter, *BM* 1, no. 16 (15 June 1908): 2.

10. W. A. Ward, *The Trailblazer, Dr. A. G. Garr* (N.p., n.d.), 8–9; in the Assemblies of God Archives, Springfield, Mo.

11. He had a letter in the first issue of *The Apostolic Faith* (1, no. 1 [Sept. 1906]: 2), which was the organ of Azusa Street.

12. Others headed variously to Africa, India, South America, and Europe; see *Yearbook of Apostolic Assembly of Spokane, Washington* (Spokane, Wash.: Apostolic Assembly, 1907). The cover says "revised to July 30." Six of the China missionaries (three couples) were also called to Japan, making up six of the Japan-bound group. One was headed for Korea.

13. Bernt Berntsen, *The Apostolic Faith* 1, no. 12 (Jan. 1908): 3.

14. Law, *Pentecostal Mission Work,* 2. See also Rose Pittman Downing, transcription of 1904 interview, unpaginated, in the Assemblies of God Archives.

15. Mok Lai Chi, "Good News from the Land of Sinim," *Latter Rain Evangel,* Dec. 1909, pp. 22–23; also in *BM* 3, no. 52 (15 Dec. 1909): 4. This is an autobiographical piece by Mok. Hager's account is in "Hong Kong Record of Mission Work, 1907," *Papers of the ABCFM,* Missions to Asia 1827–1919, microfilm, Unit 3, Reel 262, South China Mission, vol. 6, p. 8. (Woodbridge, Conn.: Research Publications, 1980).

16. *Chinese Recorder* 39, no. 1 (Jan. 1908): 59. Hager, of course, had given permission for the meetings in the first place, and so his official report did not portray them as too disruptive, although it did acknowledge the split in the church.

17. In his annual report, written in early 1908, Hager made a special point that the new church was "entirely under the control of the Chinese" ("Hong Kong Record of Mission Work, 1907," 8).

18. The April 1917 issue is in my possession, along with three earlier ones.

19. See Cora Fritsch, *Letters from Cora,* comp. Homer Fritsch and Alice Fritsch (N.p., 1987), for Cora Fritsch's letters from Japan and Hong Kong until her sudden death in late 1912.

20. See *BM* 1, no. 11 (Oct. 1907–Jan. 1908): 1; *BM* 1, no. 12 (Jan. 1908): 3; *BM* 2, no. 13 (May 1908): 4. An informative report including names of all the others made soon after they settled in Zhengding is in *BM* 1, no. 14 (15 May 1908): 2. We also learn some details from a hostile report by C. F. Appleton in *The Free Methodist,* 13 Oct. 1908, p. 650.

21. Hess's letter in *BM* 2, no. 26 (15 Nov. 1908): 1.

22. Two 1912 issues are in my possession.

23. Donald MacGillivray, ed., *1915 China Mission Year Book* (Shanghai: Christian Literature Society, 1916), directory section, 78. Berntsen died in China in 1933; see *China Christian Year Book 1934–1935* (Shanghai: Christian Literature Society, 1935), 431.

24. Materials in a file on Junk collected by Mel Robeck, Fuller Theological Seminary, Pasadena, Calif.

25. Sigrid McLean, *Over Twenty Years in China* (Minneapolis: author, 1927).

26. Fritsch, *Letters from Cora,* 124.

27. This is my own count from the directory in MacGillivray, ed., *1915 China Mission Year Book,* 77–85.

28. Grant Wacker, "The Travail of a Broken Family: The Wesleyan Holiness Response to Early Pentecostalism, 1906 to 1926," *Journal of Ecclesiastical History* 47 (July 1996): 505–28.

29. Fannie Winn in *BM* 1, no. 16 (15 June 1908): 2. Also see Ethel F. Landis, letter of 10 Oct. 1907, in *BM* 1, no. 9 (1 Mar. 1908): 2.

30. A. G. Garr, *BM* 1, no. 9 (1 Mar. 1908): 4.

31. "Report of C. R. Hager, July 1908–December 31, 1908," *Papers of the ACBFM,* Missions to Asia 1827–1919, Unit 3, Reel 262, South China Mission, vol. 7, p. 3.

32. Bernt Berntsen, letter of 28 Sept. 1908, in *BM* 1, no. 26 (15 Nov. 1908): 4.

33. C. F. Appleton, *The Free Methodist,* 13 Oct. 1908, p. 650.

34. For the origins of the breakaway mission of the 1890s, see Irwin T. Hyatt Jr., *Our Ordered Lives Confess: Three Nineteenth-Century American Missionaries in East Shantung* (Cambridge, Mass.: Harvard University Press, 1976): 49–59. For Blalock's own story, see T. L. Blalock, *Experiences of a Baptist Faith Missionary for 56 Years in China* (Fort Worth, Tex.: Manney Printing, 1949) (quotations on 47 and 48, respectively). For more on Anglin's later activites, see Harry J. Albus, *Twentieth-Century Onesiphorus* (Grand Rapids, Mich.: Eerdmans, 1951); and the clipping file on Anglin in the Foreign Missions files of the Assemblies of God Archives, Springfield, Mo.

35. These were both "faith missions," but in a rather different sense than the "faith" basis of the independent missionaries such as the Pentecostals discussed in this essay. The latter had no organization sending them money; funds came directly from supporters or were sent specifically in their names to one of the publications that were willing to forward the money to them in China. The former category did have a central office that received money but divided it up among the member missionaries, although without any guarantee of a minimum stipend amount.

36. Gary B. McGee, *This Gospel Shall Be Preached: A History and Theology of Assemblies of God Foreign Missions to 1959* (Springfield, Mo.: Gospel, 1986), 57–61.

37. Ethel F. Landis, letter, in *BM* 1, no. 9 (1 Mar. 1908): 2. At the top of the item is noted "Copied from *Way of Faith.*"

38. This appeared in R. A. Jaffray, "'Speaking in Tongues'—Some Words of Kindly Counsel," *The Christian and Missionary Alliance* 31, no. 24 (13 Mar. 1909): 395–96.

39. McGee, *This Gospel,* 61.

40. See the correspondence from A. B. Simpson and J. D. Williams to R. H. Glover (head of the China mission) in Wuchang, China, 13 Apr. 1914; and W. W. Simpson's letter of resignation, 12 May 1914. Copy of typed transcript from John Sawin; original in the Assemblies of God Archives.

41. See W. W. Simpson's letter to A. B. Simpson of 17 Oct. 1916, more than two years after his separation, with various accusations of deception and other recriminations leveled at the Christian and Missionary Alliance. Attached to materials cited in note 40, original also in the Assemblies of God Archives.

42. "China Inland Mission (1915) Council Minutes," 100th session, 13–14 Apr. 1915, in the Billy Graham Center Archives, Wheaton, Ill. But Sigrid and Hector McLean, former China Inland Mission members who became Pentecostals after 1907, showed no rancor in a later memoir; see McLean, *Over Twenty Years in China.*

43. *Tongwenbao* (*The Chinese Christian Intelligencer*) 34, no. 2 (1915).

44. Of course, the idea of the baptism of the Holy Spirit had intrigued Holiness and Keswick people for many years already.

45. It figures prominently in all the criticisms of Pentecostals cited earlier. An example of the continued claim of at least one-time language competence is a little tract by Ms. Sophie Hansen, *Gift of the Chinese Language* (Oakland, Calif.: Triumphs of Faith, n.d.), written in later 1908 or after.

46. Blanche Appleby, untitled and undated manuscript inscribed on the front wih the phrase "for *With Signs Following* (by S. Frodsham), see ch. 13." In the Assemblies of God Archives.

47. Rev. C. R. Hager of the American Board of Commissioners in Hong Kong blamed the "tongues speakers" for lack of progress in his mission in 1908. Because of them and their constant meetings, he wrote, "it is not strange that we have not been able to accomplish as much as in some former years" ("Report of C. R. Hager, July 1908–December 31, 1908," 3).

48. McGee, *This Gospel,* chap. 4.

49. Edith L. Blumhofer, "Restoration as Revival: Early American Pentecostalism," in *Modern Christian Revivals,* ed. Edith L. Blumhofer and Randall Balmer (Urbana: University of Illinois Press, 1993), 145–60.

50. Daniel H. Bays, "Christian Revival in China, 1900–1937," in *Modern Christian Revivals,* ed. Blumhofer and Balmer, 161–79, esp. 162–64.

51. *The Thirty-Eighth Annual Report of Weihsien Station* (Shanghai: Presbyterian Mission Press, 1919).

52. *Forty-Nine* [*sic*] *Annual Report of the Weihsien Station, Shantung Mission* (Shanghai: Presbyterian Mission Press, 1931), 4–6.

53. Bays, "Christian Revival in China," 173–74.

54. Ibid., 174.

55. See Daniel H. Bays, "Indigenous Protestant Churches in China, 1900–1937: A Pentecostal Case Study," in *Indigenous Responses to Western Christianity,* ed. Steven Kaplan (New York: New York University Press, 1994).

56. Daniel H. Bays, "The Growth of Independent Christianity in China, 1900–1937," in *Christianity in China: From the Eighteenth Century to the Present,* ed. Daniel H. Bays (Stanford, Calif.: Stanford University Press, 1996), 307–16.

4

Social Variables and Community Response

Kurt O. Berends

In August 1908, in rural New Hampshire, the gift of tongues fell on a small Holiness movement, the First Fruit Harvesters (Harvesters). Although the group understood this experience as the culmination to their ministry, in two surrounding towns public response encompassed a whole range of opinions. In Canaan the Harvesters work continued uninterrupted by the change. The town of Jefferson, however, responded violently. On 8 December 1908, four months after the Harvesters introduced the practice of tongues to Jefferson, a mob dynamited their recently refurbished chapel. These radically different reactions were not solely based on the Harvesters' Pentecostal experience. The presence of Pentecostal features such as tongues certainly affected the communities' responses to the Harvesters, but the central issues were the Harvesters' adamant opposition to secret societies and the social standing of their communicants in Canaan and Jefferson, New Hampshire.

As the nineteenth century drew to a close, Joel Adams Wright left the Free Methodists to start an independent Holiness work. It was not the first time he had withdrawn fellowship from a denomination; four years earlier he had severed ties with the Freewill Baptists. At that time the conflict centered on the need for a second work of grace; complete deliverance (in Wright's view) from the sinful nature.[1] Wright exuberantly supported this view by faithfully proclaiming freedom from all sin, sharply attacking all forms of social evils, such as alcohol and tobacco, and proselytizing other Freewill Baptist ministers. The message proved to be too much for both his congregants and colleagues. In their view, Wright's Holiness theology demanded too much from the believer.[2] Wright, frustrated with the conflict within Freewill Baptist churches and his perceived lack of support from denominational leaders, resigned. Almost immediately he joined the denomination that first introduced him to the higher life: the Free Methodists.

New freedom brought Wright new constraints. A spiritual epiphany fostered this fettered feeling. This epiphany, a combination of spiritual vision and physical healing from a hereditary stomach problem (ulcers), forever changed his life. Twenty years after the event Wright still marked it as the changing point in his ministry.[3] First, it convinced him of the doctrine of healing in the atonement, a belief he had previously labeled "fanaticism." Second, this self-described "mighty baptism" soured his view of ecclesiastical structures. No longer would he submit to man-made organizations. The true church, the body of Jesus Christ, hearkened only to the voice of God.[4] Within months Wright, calling his decision to join the Free Methodists "the greatest mistake I have ever made in my ministry," severed the relationship.[5] Escaping the restrictive controls of a denomination would, according to Wright, free him for ministry, a ministry centered on reaching the lost souls of New England.[6] Thus, armed with a tent, a handful of sympathetic workers, and a small monthly paper called *The First-Fruit Harvester,* Wright formed the First Fruit Harvesters and began his ministry on 20 May 1897.[7]

The Harvesters grew rapidly in the early years. Six months after beginning the work, Wright purchased a house with 135 acres of forest and farmland near the town of Rumney, New Hampshire. Rumney offered an ideal site for a permanent home base for the ministry. The Baltimore and Maryland railroad steamed through the center of town and provided easy access to the towns and villages scattered throughout the nearby rugged hill country. Christened "Immanuel Home" on 1 January 1898, the house soon filled with co-workers who shared Wright's vision to reach New England with the Holiness gospel.[8] By 1902 twenty-plus workers and a renamed weekly magazine, *The Sheaf of the First Fruits* (*The Sheaf*), assisted Wright in his mission. Many of these workers purchased lots or homes near Immanuel Home, creating a small Christian community.

The message Wright proclaimed looked at once both backward and forward. It harked back to the first-century church for its prototype. The apostolic church, Wright believed, represented Christianity at its apex, pure and untarnished by the deeds of humanity over the ages. In apostolic Christianity, the period when the Holy Spirit poured out its power on the church, Wright found his answers for the problems in the church. Traits of the early church—the miraculous gifts, unity among the believers (as Wright read the Bible), and the outpouring of the Holy Spirit—all undergird the theology of the Harvesters.[9] The first edition of *The First-Fruit Harvester* summarized a "Pentecostal convention" held in Wentworth, New Hampshire. Wright, like Peter at Pentecost, preached from the second chapter of Joel. Readers were reminded that the association's past activities fit the apostolic plan and informed that the ministry would continue to follow "apostolic lines."[10] At Rumney Wright's efforts to mimic the early church led him to institute a communal pattern of living where all goods were held in common, although co-workers' dissatisfaction ended the arrangement after a year.[11] Everywhere he went Wright marshaled strong attacks on denominational churches.[12]

The Harvesters' message, while looking back to the first-century church, also looked forward to the future. A deep longing for the imminent return of Christ motivated Wright and his emissaries. As with primitivist views, this theme found a home in a number of religious groups in America.[13] From the beginning the workers used apocalyptic language and the message of premillennialism to elicit a response from their audience. Time on earth was short; now was the time for salvation. They supplied audiences with large quantities of literature, announcing the soon-to-come tribulation and millennium.[14] In addition to calling for decisions from their listeners, such apocalyptic language offered comfort to the workers. When persecution came about, which it sometimes did, they could remind themselves that it was inevitable, a sign of Christ's soon return.

The twin themes of restorationism and millennialism not only informed Wright's theology; they also shaped his method of ministry.[15] The imminent return of Christ demanded immediate action, and tent crusades provided the Harvesters the most viable means of reaching large numbers of people with the Gospel. These meetings peppered the region throughout the spring, summer, and fall months. As people responded to the calling and more workers joined the ministry, the Harvesters purchased a second tent to keep pace with expanding opportunities.[16] The New Testament example of unity led Wright to open his crusades to all ministers from any denomination. Yet Wright was convinced that denominations were human-created structures and as such destructive to the true Gospel message. As a result no convert was ever steered into a denominational church. Instead the Harvesters formed their own churches (churches they believed to be under the leadership of the Holy Spirit) wherever their message was received.[17] At times these fledging churches met in a rented schoolhouse or the town hall. More often than not, though, the home of a sympathetic follower doubled as a house of worship. Since the Holy Spirit was the giver of all gifts, training leaders for these new works was not problematic. Harvester workers waited for the gifted—usually defined as one willing to serve—to assume leadership. Once created, new works continued to receive steady support from the Harvesters. In addition to providing speakers on many occasion, the Harvesters returned two, three, or even four times a year to hold further crusades for the purpose of building up the work. By 1903 seven towns throughout New Hampshire and Vermont hosted regular or semiregular Harvester Sunday services.[18]

As the work grew in size, it also expanded its breadth. Wright, inspired by an earlier visit to the Christian and Missionary Alliance camp meetings at Old Orchard Beach in Maine, desired a place to bring together large crowds for times of outreach and worship. The result, the "World's Missionary Campground," was dedicated on 30 August 1903 and over the years evolved into the center of the Harvesters' ministry.[19] *The Sheaf* announced the creation of a ministry for women two months later and the opening of "The World's Missionary Bible Training School" at Rumney on 1 January 1904. Eventually this latter program evolved into an orphanage.[20] All were part of Wright's plan to reach New England with the message of the early church.

By the fall of 1905 news of the gift of tongues had reached Wright and his Harvesters. Reports of this new gift stirred excitement among the group, and they began to investigate the phenomenon. During the 1907 June convention, at Wright's invitation, a speaker from Wales shared information on the work of the Holy Spirit in that country.[21] In the following issue of *The Sheaf* Wright penned favorable words on this rapidly spreading gift: "My heart has rejoiced also because so many are given the wonderful gift of healing as well as also the gift of tongues and the interpretation of the same."[22] Yet with this initial endorsement he also sounded a word of caution concerning this new phenomenon. His anxiety centered on a rapidly growing dogma, the belief in "evidential tongues," which proclaimed tongues a necessary sign of Spirit baptism. The baptism with the Spirit should, according to Wright, be followed by signs, but not necessarily the gift of tongues. Despite this misgiving, the gift of tongues came the following summer to the Harvesters during their annual camp meeting at headquarters in Rumney. Harvester Alice Belie Garrigus, who later founded the Pentecostal Assemblies of Newfoundland, left the only description of the event: "The fight was fierce, but the Spirit gave the victory, and the leader of the work, Bro. J. A. Wright, went down among the pine needles, and received a precious baptism. Others quickly followed till within a short time, nearly all the saints had received."[23]

The coming of the gift of tongues did little to change the work of Wright and his Harvesters. They immediately added this feature to many of their services throughout the region. Speaking in tongues was not perceived as a radical change in direction. Neither did the gift drastically alter their style of worship. Already their meetings were characterized by loud music, shouts of joy, and exuberant body motions. Rather, Wright and his Harvesters viewed tongues speaking as the logical culmination of their efforts.[24] Ministry continued with tent meetings in the summer and Sunday services in select towns through the winter. In Canaan the community made no significant response to this added feature. In Jefferson, however, the community literally drove the Harvesters out of town within four months. Several factors other than tongues speaking proved to be significant in determining what type of reception the Harvesters received.

Rumney, home of the First Fruit Harvesters, is located in Grafton County, near the middle of New Hampshire. Roughly fifteen miles west of Rumney lies a small cluster of towns. Canaan sits in the middle of this cluster. From west to east the towns of West Canaan, Canaan Center, Cardigan, and Orange form a semicircle on the northern edge of town. Five miles to the south, Grafton, flanked on either side by East and West Grafton, completes this friendly community. Canaan is at the center of these small communities. In a similar fashion the Barney family stood at the center of life in Canaan. George Barney and his family, longtime residents of the area, were actively involved in all aspects of community life. Their involvement, more than anything or anyone else, proved to be the decisive variable in the region's open-armed welcome to the Harvesters and their message.

The Canaan district, like much of New England, had a strong religious history even though establishment religions' influence had declined by the start of the twentieth century. Congregationalism had come and gone in Canaan, and the local Freewill Baptist Society was nearing the end of its existence in both Orange and Canaan.[25] Still, at the dawn of the twentieth century, the region housed a number of thriving churches of various sorts: Baptist (two), Methodist (two), Catholic (one), and several smaller nondenominational chapels. Together these churches provided the impetus for much of the local towns' activities. A glance in the region's local weekly, the *Canaan Reporter* (the *Reporter*), revealed a wide variety of religious activity. The *Reporter* regularly informed its readers of the Baptist services, Methodist preaching activities, Sunday schools to be organized, and a wide assortment of other church-related activities in the area.[26]

The presence of numerous religious organizations never dissuaded the First Fruit Harvesters from seeing that region as a mission field. In early fall 1902 the Harvesters entered the Canaan area to proclaim their Holiness message.[27] The positive response from a number of locals to the Harvester effort, led by Rev. C. H. Bowen and S. A. White, encouraged a return trip. Over the next few years the group made repeated excursions into the neighborhood. Eventually such perseverance paid off, and they instituted regular services held in the home of lifetime residents George and Cora Barney.

Back in 1774 Jabez Bosworth Barney, one of the first settlers in the region, had carved out a farm from the hilly terrain on part of a 3,000-acre tract of land his father Aaron had purchased. As time passed the family grew and prospered, with the farm passed on to the eldest son.[28] George Barney inherited the homestead, known as Breezynook Farm, in the late 1880s. At 340 acres, it stood as one of the largest farms in the territory. Breezynook was principally a dairy farm, and the daily milk route in the town of Canaan provided the main source of income for the family. In addition, the Barneys supplemented their income with a small flock of sheep and a stand of maple trees that produced about two hundred gallons of syrup annually.[29]

The Barney name was well established in the countryside. The prominence came not so much from the family farm but from the extended family network in both the local economy and government. Over the generations most of the family had remained in the region, opened a variety of businesses, and been involved in the community. By the time George took over the farm, an elaborate network of cousins, nieces, and nephews had set deep roots in the community. One cousin, C. O. Barney, published the two local weekly newspapers, the *Canaan Reporter* and the *Mascoma Register.* Cousin Ralph T. Barney sold real estate. Still other family members owned and operated Barney Brothers, a general store that sold everything from guns and farm equipment to clothes and produce.[30] In politics George's father, Jesse, served as Grafton's representative to the General Court. From George's generation the Barney family provided the community with town clerks, treasurers, and the secretary of the Republican Caucus of Canaan. George himself dutifully served as the fire warden, while neighbors elected his son Lester to the office of selectman on several occasions.[31]

Neither the Harvesters nor the Barneys recorded their first meeting with the other. Although the date of their initial contact remains unknown, by 1905 the two were working hand in hand to reach the surrounding neighborhood with their Holiness gospel. Evidence of this relationship first comes to us from a series of articles in *The Sheaf.* Beginning with the April edition, there is a steady stream of articles by George, Cora, and their eldest son, Jesse Barney.

These reports ranged from Cora's report of her miraculous healing to her sermons exhorting the believers to live the faithful life. They also give clues to the work of the Harvesters in the Canaan region in the early years.[32]

From all accounts the work grew slowly but steadily. Initially the family assisted by opening their home to Wright and other Harvesters for speaking engagements. Soon, though, Cora assumed teaching responsibilities. For several years the Harvesters sent speakers to the Barney residence on a fairly regular schedule. By 1907 the decision was made to obtain a permanent facility for the local work. In the June 1907 edition of *The Sheaf,* the Barneys announced the beginnings of regular meetings scheduled for the first full weekend of each month. Commencing on a Friday evening and continuing through Sunday, these meetings imitated the Harvesters' semiannual Holiness conventions.[33] Five months after this initial report, a second announcement in *The Sheaf* announced the purchase of a permanent facility, an old tavern known as the Hackett Place. Purchased by the Barneys, the Hackett Place, renamed El Nathan ("God given"), was dedicated for "full gospel preaching." It soon housed both the miniconventions and weekly Sunday services during the warmer months.[34]

A large two-story structure, El Nathan stood on Razor Hill in Grafton just over a mile from the Barney homestead. Situated on the Grafton turnpike, its central location made for easy access from the surrounding region. Monthly meetings, initially from July through August and later expanded from May to November, functioned as the centerpiece for the work in the neighborhood. Cora dutifully served as hostess and, in the event a speaker from Rumney did not make the trip, doubled as speaker. With a large number of rooms available, advertisements for El Nathan promised accommodations to all who came to hear the "full gospel."[35]

With the opening of El Nathan, the community in the Canaan area embarked on a fairly consistent pattern of operation for the next eight years. During the summer months a steady interchange of workers and communication between Rumney and the Canaan satellite continued unabated. When the Spirit fell on Rumney during the annual convention in August 1908, Cora Barney was there to receive it.[36] When El Nathan held a weekend convention, the Harvesters supported it. Frequent speakers at El Nathan included Harvesters Joel Adams Wright, C. H. Bowen, Margie Bowen, Alice Belie Garrigus, Carrie Farrand, and J. Elwin Wright. In addition, a semiregular schedule of tent meetings supported the work. Well publicized, these meetings sought new converts for the ministry.[37] *The Sheaf* included El Nathan as a permanent satellite mission.[38]

Generalized information about the work at El Nathan in the early years can be found in Cora Barney's articles in *The Sheaf.* Many of her accounts reported "souls [being] saved: sanctified, filled, and healed."[39] Others were only slightly less optimistic, as in her summary of the summer meetings in the August 1909 issue of *The Sheaf,* where she declared, "Seven precious souls were baptized . . . [and] some are being led into deeper experiences and quite a lot of new ones are attending the services."[40] On occasion she even testified to a lack of response: "It has been a time of preparing for Jesus' coming. Not so much of the unsaved coming, though they have been faithfully warned, but of leading those who have started, that they may be established."[41] Almost all the articles in *The Sheaf* portray life at El Nathan during the summer months, when visitors from throughout New England often stopped by, or during the weekend conventions.

During winter harsh weather usually separated the Barneys from the Harvesters in Rumney, but this did not mean an end to their work.[42] Mabel Barney, George and Cora's daughter, kept a diary that offers a glimpse into the routine of Canaan's Pentecostal community. When weather forced the closure of El Nathan, worshipers rotated holding services in various homes throughout the region. Often they held several meetings simultaneously in two or three homes to cut down on travel distance during the bitter winter days. Unlike the warmer months, when many of the participants who attended the weekend meetings at El Nathan came from throughout New England, wintertime remained the domain of the locals. In 1915 Mabel began faithfully recording where the family attended church.[43] On many occasions the family split up and went to separate services. In one entry George and his sons worshiped in Canaan while Mabel and her mother traveled to neighboring Orange. The following week Mabel joined her father at a service in Cardigan while the rest of her family attended church in Grafton. Often the location for the morning and evening services differed.[44]

Mabel's diary also provides several clues as to the size of the church meetings. A midwinter meeting at Orange attracted twenty-three people, whereas a springtime meeting there drew thirty-two. A home in Canaan Center hosted an evening service that drew "about forty." Sunday school, often held at the Barney home, usually consisted of only three of four people besides the family in attendance.[45] Although the numbers are not large—fifty was an exceptional turnout for a Sunday service—they remained remarkably consistent over the years. The largest attendance figure on record for any event was a baptism with over two hundred people on hand.[46] Although not remarkable, the numbers remained consistent over the years, reflecting a pattern of slow growth.

By 1916 the local network of Pentecostal believers in the Canaan area decided to organize a formal church and created the Union Mission of Canaan. This decision marked the beginning of the end of their relationship with the First Fruit Harvesters. The primary factor influencing this split centered on the question of evidential tongues. Over the years Wright increasingly attacked those who centered their ministry on the gift of tongues. Although he still claimed the label "Pentecostal" for himself, many Pentecostals rejected him. What Wright moved away from the Barneys and those around them clung to, eventually leading to a formal separation of ties.[47]

The few records that remain from the early years of the Union Mission show a small but faithful congregation. Thirty people attended the initial meeting. Most of this group continued to be involved with the community on a semiregular basis through the early years.[48] In the fall of 1918 members built a chapel in Canaan Center. One year later El Nathan officially joined hands with the church, and they took the name "Mehida Pentecostal Assembly," which means "joined together."[49] In 1956 the congregation changed the name to "Canaan Assemblies of God." Today it still is a member of the Assemblies of God denomination. It is also the house of worship for several members of the Barney family.

For the most part local reaction to the work of the Harvesters in the Canaan region was positive. Although on occasion *The Sheaf* articles by Cora and George Barney mentioned being "ridiculed, misjudged and shunned," most reports paint a picture of acceptance.[50] The local newspaper, the *Reporter*, faithfully and often favorably noted the events both at tent meetings and at El Nathan. A series of reports covering an early tent meeting typifies the pattern of coverage the ministry received. Initial articles simply announced the coming of the event. As the crusade progressed however, the *Reporter* offered favorable editorial comments on both the attendance and response to the messages. By the time the Harvesters had left town, the editor concluded, "The messages were very precious and helpful to all who would receive them."[51] In later years the *Reporter* also recorded construction progress of the Union Mission chapel in Canaan Center. The building of a chapel in town would grant the Pentecostals a sense of establishment. Until then, their events had been held in homes or at El Nathan, which was located several miles from the center of either Canaan or Grafton. Now they were entering the realm of organized religion in a new way by setting their roots in the center of town within a couple of blocks of all the other mainline churches. Instead of criticizing the move, the paper praised it, noting, "The work . . . is progressing rapidly towards completion . . . for this little church which means so much for this society."[52]

When Mattie S. Crowe of Providence, Rhode Island, came to El Nathan for healing and passed away in a matter of days, the *Reporter* simply stated the facts without a trace of condemnation or sarcasm and limited its comments to those of a sympathetic nature.[53] This general acceptance of the Harvesters can be largely attributed to the Barney family. Their role in the daily life of the community led to the region's open-armed welcome to the Harvesters and their message.

At the turn of the century, Jefferson lay a good two-day's journey from Rumney. Situated roughly seventy miles directly north of Rumney, Jefferson was actually a composite of several small villages clustered within a range of a few miles. Riverton, Jefferson Center, Jefferson Highlands, and Meadows combined to form the town of Jefferson. Nestled in the heart of the White Mountains, Jefferson was surrounded with beautiful tree-covered mountains, rolling meadows, and rippling streams. With ample fishing, hunting, hiking, swimming, golf, and breathtaking scenery, Jefferson became a fashionable resort town for New England's wealthy. From the first half of the nineteenth century, summer hotels and cottages dotted the winding roads as people from throughout New England made their way by train to Jefferson for recreation and relaxation. The locals of Jefferson were also active in several thriving churches and numerous secret societies. The abundance of these two sorts of organizations, their steady memberships, and the close relationship they enjoyed with each other proved to be lethal to the Harvesters. Despite the large numbers of wealthy summer residents and active locals, the Harvesters were unable to attract prominent community members into their fold. This lack of salient community support, combined with the close association most residents maintained with the town's churches and secret societies, led to the failure of the First Fruit Harvesters' efforts to establish a permanent ministry in Jefferson.

Jefferson, like Canaan, provided its residents with an ample variety of denominations from which to choose. Church life in Jefferson, even more so than in Canaan, reflected the traditional mainstream New England religious establishment. Longtime fixtures in the center of the community included a Congregational church, an Episcopal church, a Christian Science hall and reading room, and a Methodist Episcopal church. Toward the periphery of the town stood a Freewill Baptist church. Finally, several of the villages within the borders of Jefferson also housed worship facilities: Meadows hosted a Union Mission chapel, whereas both Jefferson Highlands and Riverton supported small nondenominational chapels within their village limits.[54]

The location of the mainline establishment churches in the heart of Jefferson reflected both their prominence in the community and their longevity. They were both the busiest and largest churches, offering a wide variety of activities for the locals. Sunday morning and evening worship services, Sunday schools, concerts, church society meetings, ladies' mission circles, ladies' aid, and children's day filled the week-long ecclesiastical calendar.[55] Reflecting the growing ecumenical attitude more characteristic of many mainline churches, Jefferson's two largest churches, the Congregationalist church and Methodist Episcopal church, frequently held union services.[56]

Although the churches may have contended among themselves for the hearts of Jefferson, they also faced competition from a second social organization—secret societies. The residents of Jefferson, unlike those of Canaan, participated in numerous secret societies. In Canaan five secret societies were scattered throughout the region; Jefferson had eighteen.[57] By 1906, the year the First Fruit Harvesters first pitched a tent in Jefferson, the Freemasons possessed ten lodges in addition to their temple. Four chapters of the Orange, a farming association that required an oath of allegiance, dotted the local landscape. A single group of Odd Fellows shared space with Mount Jefferson Lodge no. 103. Finally, three assemblies adopted native American themes; the Chiefs of Metallak Council no. 21, the Jefferson Red Men, and the Daughters of Pocahontas.[58] Churches and secret societies were mutually respected by the townsfolk of Jefferson and, on occasion, even shared activities. On 29 April 1908 the *Coos County Democrat* (the *Democrat*) reported on the large attendance at a Sunday service held for the Odd Fellows in the Methodist Episcopal church.[59] Two months later an article announced a special Sunday service for the Freemasons of the region. This time the neighboring Methodist Episcopal church in Groveton hosted the event.[60] The large number of churches and secret societies did not persuade the Harvesters to avoid the area. Rather, the opposite held true. They believed the region to be ripe for harvesting souls.

During the summer of 1906, the Harvesters conducted their first series of meetings in Jefferson. Beginning in late June, at the height of tourist season, when the summer hotels and cottages filled up with guests, the Harvesters pitched a large tent in the section of town known as Meadows. Harvester E. B. Maxfield of Plainfield, Vermont, conducted the services.[61] His initial report from the field sounded a note of enthusiasm. In addition to preaching to full houses, Brother Maxfield announced three conversions. He also reminded readers of *The Sheaf* that the Harvesters demanded more than simply Gospel conversions. Maxfield informed the readers that in addition to harvesting souls, he faithfully sounded out the warnings on "the plain truth of separation from the devil and his works."[62] It was a message that the Harvesters would continue to proclaim over the coming months. It also proved to be a message that brought trouble to their work in Jefferson.

Encouraged by the response to their first crusade in Jefferson, the Harvesters immediately planned a second one. By late July they commenced a second series of meetings in the area. This time workers pitched the tent on Jefferson Hill, closer to the heart of town. Two more Harvesters from Rumney, Ralph Bailey and Frank Burdick, journeyed to Jefferson to assist Maxfield with this second crusade. Once again, reports were favorable. In fact, the second crusade looked to be even more successful than the first. Although "cold-hearted professors who are mixed up in secret orders" mounted some opposition, the Harvesters rested assured that victory was theirs. Public response encouraged this initial confidence. People came forward not just for salvation; rather, they wanted "to be saved, sanctified and healed."[63] Midway through this second effort, a ten-day suspension of activities permitted Maxfield and Burdick to leave Jefferson and attend "the Fourth Annual Missionary Camp Meeting" at Rumney. At the conference they shared the exciting news of God's work in Jefferson and the need for more workers in this great battlefield. To their delight, Joel Adams Wright and his wife, Mary, agreed to return to Jefferson for the duration of the crusade. It proved to be the turning point in the ministry at Jefferson.[64]

A captivating and dynamic speaker, Wright immediately took charge of the proceedings. Throughout much of his ministry Wright exhibited a proclivity for confrontation. Not one to avoid issues, even if they were controversial, Wright faced the situation in Jefferson head-on. Aware of the numerous secret societies in town, and always ready to attack the evils of denominationalism, he commenced his ministry in Jefferson with an acerbic barrage on both. Using a large illustrated chart to convey his points, he castigated members of secret societies and churches, alternately, as tools of the devil and harlots. Especially offensive to Wright were the articles in the local press that made known the presence of a "mixed assembly"—the joining together of church with secret society for worship services. Each day Wright chastised the townsfolk in harsh terms. Not surprisingly Wright's message evoked outrage from the local citizenry. For the duration of the crusade the Harvesters met with a vocal and boisterous opposition. Meetings were disrupted by townspeople firing guns in the air and throwing stones at the tents. Wright even received verbal threats of physical harm.[65] Undaunted by the threats and determined to remain faithful to his calling, Wright did not back down. Instead he challenged fellow Christians to "make a whip of small cords and drive [secret societies] all out or be driven out . . . in an attempt to do so."[66] Unbeknownst to Wright at the time, his words would prove to be prophetic. This early conflict was only a harbinger of things to come.

The strife of the second crusade did not keep the Harvesters from their goal of establishing a Holiness work in Jefferson. By late fall of that same year, workers embarked on a third crusade. This one lasted ten days. With a cold and snowy winter fast approaching, they held most of the meetings in the town's Freewill Baptist church. Once again reports in *The Sheaf* spoke of conversions and the sanctifying power of God in the lives of attendees. The paper also noted the commencement of regular Sunday services to be held biweekly in the Freewill Baptist church. Despite opposition, the Harvesters intended to stay in Jefferson.[67]

Little changed over the next year and a half; meetings continued and growth was slow. Articles in *The Sheaf* mentioned an occasional conversion or baptism, but nothing extraordinary. After the turmoil of the first summer, the Freewill Baptists terminated the Harvesters' plans to use the church for both their Sunday services and the fall crusade, but that proved to be more of an inconvenience than a major problem.[68] In its place, the homes of the faithful few doubled as houses of worship. Speakers from Rumney continued to lead these services on a biweekly basis. The fall of 1908 marked the initiation of two events that affected the Harvesters' ministry: the gift of tongues and the construction of a chapel in Jefferson. Only one, the erection of the chapel, contributed noticeably to the demise of their work in Jefferson. Although the introduction of the gift of tongues to the work in Jefferson created some internal dissension that the press reports later played up, it was the establishment of a permanent chapel near the center of Jefferson that brought on the wrath of the town.

For the Harvesters, the addition of tongues to the work at Jefferson occurred as elsewhere, without second thought. Once the Spirit fell at Rumney during the August 1908 camp meeting, it was inevitable that the message would be proclaimed to all their satellite missions. Excited about the presence of this new gift, they perceived tongues not as a radical change to the message they already heralded but rather as the logical outcome of the work begun. Nevertheless, some within the Harvester community in Jefferson exhibited mixed reactions. Although in Jefferson as elsewhere the Harvesters featured tongues speaking only at "tarrying meetings" held at the end of the normal services, after visitors had left, a few regular attendees viewed the activity as extreme. The already demonstrative meetings now moved beyond their level of comfort, and they left the ministry.[69]

The gift of tongues caused some minor internal tensions for the Harvesters, but it was a second "gift" that caused major trouble with the residents of Jefferson that fall. Toward the end of the summer, Jefferson native and Harvester communicant Mrs. Ellen Davis deeded a piece of land with a dilapidated house on it to the organization. The Harvesters immediately commenced to remodel the house, located in the Meadows, into a little chapel for weekly services. By the end of November workers had completed repairs on the structure and began planning for a week-long dedication service to take place in the first week of December 1908.[70]

The sight of the Harvesters building a permanent home immediately provoked public outcry. A week before the dedication of the chapel, an article appeared in the *Democrat* harshly criticizing the Harvesters' ministry. In "Holy Rollers! Jefferson Tired and Wearied of Emotional Sect Established in Town," the writer condemned Wright's constant labeling of churches and societies as "harlots and daughters of harlots." Later on the article expressed disdain over the recent "new features" introduced in worship, labeling tongues as "unintelligible gibberish." Nevertheless, that point was peripheral to the main complaint, namely, that this sect continually made "wholesale attack[s] upon Christian Churches [and] various secret fraternal organizations." In addition, although the author commended the "fair minded" character of the Jeffersonians in patiently dealing with this sect, he warned that such patience was running out.[71]

Patience was indeed wearing thin, and the article roused the town into action. Throughout the week-long dedication services, the locals bombarded the Harvesters with threats and harassment. Groups of men and boys twice interrupted services by barging into the chapel with bats and clubs in an attempt to intimidate the worshipers. Both times they failed. In the second confrontation, eleven-year-old Harvester Helen Marshall, with Bible raised high in the air, unloaded a verbal volley that halted the opponents. With shouts of praise for their deliverance, the Harvesters returned to their celebration.[72] On the night of 8 December 1908, sometime between the hours of eight and ten, a group of men estimated to be one hundred strong smashed the chapel with axes and crowbars and lit a large amount of dynamite in the chapel. News of the bombing rumbled through the region. Wright threatened civil action, but local authorities rebuffed his efforts. Later he hinted he would contact state authorities, but apparently nothing transpired.[73] Townspeople responded to the publicity by petitioning Jefferson town officers to ban the Harvesters from further ministry in the area.[74]

Although one regional newspaper carried articles on the event, the hometown *Jefferson Times* remained strangely silent on the subject. Most articles, including those in the regional *Democrat,* insinuated that the First Fruit Harvesters must shoulder most of the blame. These stories noted that the violent attacks Wright made on both denominations and secret societies encompassed almost all households in the town. After the bombing several writers intimated that townspeople were concerned about "low morals" that the tarrying meetings produced. Wright, in his rejoinder, denied that tongues had been a problem; rather, the fundamental issue was the presence of secret societies. The concern over tongues and the activities of tarrying meetings, he declared, served as a cover for the evils of the two organizations.[75] Wright declared the events to be proof of the "end times" in which they lived. He also sounded a call for Christians willing to die a martyr's death on the battlefield. The claims and charges eventually died out, and in the end the Harvesters left town for good.[76]

Studies on religious groups with conspicuous theological beliefs and practices can focus on those prominent tenets and actions and use them to explain the events around them. There is, however, a danger in such a narrow focus. Although peculiar religious features are important in creating and shaping an identity, they rarely explain the whole story. Often social elements even more than theological ones unlock the puzzle of events. Such is the case with the First Fruit Harvesters in Canaan and Jefferson. Early Pentecostalism, although shaped by a combination of convictions and behaviors, was most clearly distinguished by its profession and practice of tongues speaking.[77] Nevertheless, the introduction of tongues had minor implications for the work of the Harvesters in both Canaan and Jefferson. Instead, two nonreligious features proved to be notably influential in forming community response to their work in these respective communities.

Canaan differed from Jefferson in two ways. First, secret societies never proliferated in Canaan, and Wright offended fewer people there with his attacks on them. Although Wright consistently impugned two groups in particular—denominations and secret societies—the presence of numerous denominational churches proved to be less a problem. Ecclesiastical unity was not a driving theme at the start of the twentieth century in many areas. It was not uncommon for religious groups to launch verbal assaults on one another. In that regard Wright's attacks were accepted as "normal" religious discourse. The absence of secret societies and the tolerance of churches inevitably reduced conflict between the Canaan natives and the Harvesters.

The second fundamental difference between Canaan and Jefferson was the presence of a family institution like the Barneys only in the former town. Their social respectability and community involvement offered credibility to the fledging Pentecostal movement in Canaan. More than any other factor, the participation of George and Cora Barney granted the First Fruit Harvesters a quasi-establishment position in Canaan. Although many may have privately disagreed with the exuberant faith of the Barneys, they readily accepted them as hard-working contributors to the welfare of the community. Breezynook Farm, the primary dairy farm for Canaan, provided economic stability. George and his sons consistently involved themselves in local politics. Their extended family network provided a wide support framework. The influence of the Barneys, more than anything else, allowed the First Fruit Harvesters to enter the area and establish a ministry that would eventually attain an establishment position in the region.

The Barneys' association with the Harvesters legitimized the work of the organization. In doing so it opened the door for others within the community to affiliate with the ministry. Many of these people, like the Barneys, were also deeply ingrained into the daily life of the region both socially and economically.[78] This does not mean the Harvesters in Canaan were impervious to criticism. Yet public criticism of the group was in large part blunted by both the Barney name and the general participation of group members in the neighborhood's social and economic structure. It is not surprising, then, that public commentary in the newspaper consistently lauded the efforts of the Harvesters.

In complete contrast, coverage in Jefferson papers ranged from the early neutral reports of events to the acerbic assessments of the Harvesters' work toward the end of the group's tenure there. Resembling those from Canaan, the first reports offered basic facts about the Harvesters in language that was simple and devoid of hostile overtones.[79] Yet even such generic language did not necessarily mean acceptance by the press. All the other churches in the region received both extensive coverage and often positive endorsement. Later, when the articles on the Harvesters radiated hostility, it clearly represented an end of toleration.

After the destruction of the chapel, a number of articles appeared, both locally and throughout New England, that reviewed the chain of events and issues that led to the destruction of the facility. Although most articles noted

Wright's attacks of secret societies, some tried to pin the blame on tongues by associating the practice with "low morals." In fact, such opinions only offered the town a rationalization for the embarrassing act.[80] Wright, of course, denied such charges and pointedly identified the presence of denominations and secret societies as the cause of the attack.[81] Speaking in tongues was not the fundamental cause of rejection in Jefferson. Long before the Harvesters embraced Pentecost and introduced tongues speaking at their tarrying meetings, the town expressed agitation over the group's activities. The Harvesters' consistent attack on denominations was annoying, but the attacks on secret societies proved to be downright offensive. The large number of these societies and the close relationship they had with the established churches served only to intensify this problem. The construction of the chapel propelled the Harvesters into a permanent spotlight. Where once the activities of the group were in the public eye for only several weeks each summer during the crusades, the creation of a permanent building created the possibility of year-round attention, and most important, the unending display of the Harvesters' attitudes toward secret societies. Community status and participation in the Harvesters differed radically in Jefferson and in Canaan. At the time of the bombing of the chapel, the Jefferson Harvesters counted seven members. Only one, Truman Marshall, was male. He was joined by his wife and eleven-year-old daughter, Helen; Mrs. Joseph Davis, who donated the land; Mrs. Phil Plaisted and her daughter, Alice; and Mrs. Hosea Clough.[82] Although one article declared "they represent some of the best families in Jefferson," none of the participants ever attained a level of community importance matching that of the Barneys. Although this was a positive comment, it served the primary function of placing fault on those living outside the town, such as Wright.[83] The fact that the Harvesters in Jefferson were primarily a female society also lessened the respect it held within the town. In many ways the rejection of the Harvesters in Jefferson says as much about the status of women in the early twentieth century as the acceptance of the Harvesters in Canaan tells us of the Barney family's community influence.

The story of Pentecostalism in Canaan and Jefferson is more than just the story of a religious movement in two towns. The events of Canaan and Jefferson show the need to move beyond popular symbols, such as tongues, in explaining public response to Pentecostalism. Students of these movements must also consider the whole of theological ideologies and the community's social dynamics. Certainly tongues is an important part of Pentecostalism, even an identifying feature, but it is not necessarily the fundamental issue that elicits the public's response.

Notes

1. Joel A. Wright, "Some Things Concerning My Christian Experience and Call to the Ministry," *The Sheaf of the First Fruits* (hereinafter *The Sheaf*) 11 (Feb. 1913): 16.

2. Evans Notes, Subject 6865, Collection Number (CN) 91088, p. 6. The Evans Notes are a collection of typed notes from which Elizabeth Evans wrote *The Wright Vision* (Lanham, Md.: University Press of America, 1991); they are located in the Billy Graham Archives at Wheaton College.

3. Wright, "Some Things," 19.

4. Evans Notes, Subject 6865, CN 91088. "Jaws Testimony," n.p.

5. Joel A. Wright, "Some Things," *The Sheaf* 11 (May 1913): 14.

6. Evans, *The Wright Vision*, 2.

7. John J. Scruby, "Reports from the Field," *The First-Fruit Harvester* 1 (July 1897): 2; Evans Notes, Subject 6865, CN 91088, n.p.

8. Early information on the Harvesters draws on the Evans Notes, Subject 6865, CN 91088, as well as on Evans, *The Wright Vision.* Formally registered with the state of New Hampshire in November 1898, the First Fruit Harvesters, now known as the New England Fellowship of Evangelicals, is currently the oldest incorporated religious organization in the state.

9. For the restorationist-primitivist impulse in American religion, see Richard T. Hughes, ed., *The American Quest for the Primitive Church* (Urbana: University of Illinois Press, 1988). For restorationist themes in Pentecostalism, see Edith L. Blumhofer, *Restoring the Faith: The Assemblies of God, Pentecostalism, and American Culture* (Urbana: University of Illinois Press, 1993): esp. 11–34.

10. Scruby, "Reports from the Field," 2–3.

11. Evans Notes, Subject 6865, CN 91088, n.p.

12. For examples of Wright's attacks see the following of his articles: "Come-Outism," *The Sheaf* 1 (29 Jan. 1903): 1–2; "Midwinter Convention," *The Sheaf* 1 (5 Feb. 1903): 3–4; "Pastor's Letter," *The Sheaf* 3 (Apr. 1905): 1–2 ; "Pastor's Letter," *The Sheaf* 5 (Feb. 1907): 1–2; and "Dog in the Manger," *The Sheaf* 5 (Oct. 1907): 5–7.

13. For analysis of the modern roots of premillennialism, see Timothy Weber, *Living in the Shadow of the Second Coming: American Premillennialism, 1875–1982*, rev. ed. (Chicago: University of Chicago Press, 1987); and Emest R. Sandeen, *The Roots of Fundamentalism* (Chicago: University of Chicago Press, 1970).

14. Susie Farrand, "Reports from the Field," *The First-Fruit Harvester* 1 (July 1897): 2–4. Articles persisted throughout the publication of both *The First-Fruit Harvester* and *The Sheaf* warning of impending tribulation and the coming of Christ. For examples, see Abbie C. Merrow, "Christ's Second Coming," *The First-Fruit Harvester* 1 (23 May 1901): 4; and Susie White, "The Blessed Hope," *The Sheaf* 1 (6 Nov. 1902): 3–4.

15. Articles testifying to the premillennial hope of the Harvesters are plentiful. Examples include Merrow. "Christ's Second Coming," 4; and White, "The Blessed Hope," 3–4. In addition, numerous articles use apocalyptic language and imagery to describe the events at hand.

16. "New Gospel Tent," *The Sheaf* 1 (June 1903): 3.

17. In many ways the Harvesters are a typical example of the voluntary organization

phenomenon that so prominently shaped American religion. Wright welcomed all who agreed to abide by the organization's doctrinal statement and rule of conduct.

18. See "Appointments," *The Sheaf* 1 (21 May 1903): 4. Rumney and Maple Hill held weekly Sunday meetings. Gilford and Lakeport met on the second and fourth Sundays of each month; Manchester and Laconia, on the first and third; and Exeter, on the fourth Sunday.

19. Evans, *The Wright Vision,* 3–4. The New England Fellowship of Evangelicals still holds its annual summer Bible conference program at this campground.

20. Joel A. Wright, "The World's Missionary Bible Training School," *The Sheaf* 1 (Oct. 1903): 1–2. The name was later changed to Immanuel Bible School. For the formation of the "Door of Hope" women's center, see *The Sheaf* 1 (24 Sept. 1903): 4. The first announcement for Bethesda Home for Children appears in the July 1909 issue of *The Sheaf.*

21. S. A. White. "Rumney," *The Sheaf* 5 (June 1907): 6.

22. Joel A. Wright, "Pastor's Letter," *The Sheaf* 5 (July 1907): 7.

23. Alice B. Garrigus, "Walking in the King's Highway," *Good Tidings,* Sept. 1939, p. 11.

24. Wright, of course, saw the whole organization's conversion to tongues as inevitable. See especially Joel A. Wright, "Pastor's Letter," *The Sheaf* 10 (Aug. 1912): 4.

25. *1961 Bicentennial History of Canaan* (Canaan, N.H.: privately printed, 1961), 14–15.

26. "Local Department," *Canaan Reporter,* 23 Apr. 1902, p. 2.

27. "Grafton, N.H.," *The Sheaf* 1 (Nov. 1902): 2.

28. Kenneth Cushing, *Isinglass, Timber and Wool: A History of the Town of Grafton, N.H.* (Grafton, N.H.: author, 1992): 179–80.

29. Cushing, *Isinglass, Timber and Wool,* 182, 188.

30. Ibid., 180; federal census, Grafton County, New Hampshire, 1910; *Canaan Reporter,* 4 Sept. 1908, 13 Aug. 1909, and 30 Aug. 1909.

31. *Annual Report of the Selectmen and Other Town Officers of the Town of Grafton, New Hampshire, for the Year Ending January 31, 1918* (Canaan, N.H.: Reporter Power Print, 1918), front flyleaf, 2. See also the diary of Mabel E. Barney (hereinafter Barney Diary; photocopy in author's possession); the fifth of George and Cora's six children, Mabel kept a diary of daily family activities that included family participation in local government meetings.

32. The 1904 issues of *The Sheaf,* which might say when they first met each other, are missing. The first extant evidence for a working relationship appears in issues from the following year. Examples include the following articles by Cora Barney: "God Answers Prayer," *The Sheaf* 3 (Apr. 1905): 21; "My Dream," *The Sheaf* 4 (4 Jan. 1906): 8; "Some of God's Words," *The Sheaf* 5 (5 Feb. 1907): 6–7; "El Nathan. Razor Hill, Grafton," *The Sheaf* 7 (7 Apr. 1909): 5.

33. "Notice," *The Sheaf* 5 (June 1907): 2.

34. George Barney and Cora Barney, "Razor Hill, Grafton, N.H.," *The Sheaf* 5 (Nov. 1907): 6; "Local News," *Canaan Reporter,* 24 Apr. 1908, p. 2.

35. The opening ad for El Nathan in the 24 April 1908 issue of the *Canaan Reporter* noted, "The opening Gospel services will begin at El-Nathan, Razor Hill, Grafton. . . .

Everyone invited. A full gospel will be preached. Some workers from out of town are expected."

36. Cora actually received her Spirit baptism on the way home from the meetings while riding in a carriage. Interestingly, George never received the Spirit baptism (Reggie Barney, interview with author, 9 Nov. 1993).

37. "Local Department." *Canaan Reporter,* 23 July 1909, p. 2. A list of the speakers who came from Rumney is found in the Barney Diary, n.p.

38. *The Sheaf* 10 (July 1912): 24.

39. George Barney and Cora Barney, "Victory at Razor Hill, Grafton," *The Sheaf* 7 (Feb. 1909): 6–7.

40. Cora Barney, "Victory, Victory," *The Sheaf* 7 (Aug. 1909): 5.

41. George Barney and Cora Barney, "Razor Hill, Grafton," *The Sheaf* 7 (Dec. 1909): 2.

42. George Barney and Cora Barney, "El Nathan, Grafton," *The Sheaf* 9 (Dec. 1911): 7.

43. Mabel Barney's diary begins in 1915. I think it is safe to assume that the pattern described in the entries reflects fairly accurately the patterns of the earlier years. For a sampling of rotating services, see Barney Diary, entries for 13 Jan. 1915, 24 Jan. 1915, 31 Jan. 1915, 7 Feb. 1915, and 14 Feb. 1915.

44. A brief scanning of the Sunday entries in the diary reveals this pattern of worship.

45. Barney Diary, entries for 17 Jan. 1917, 13 Apr. 1917, and 20 May 1917.

46. The event had been advertised in the paper the previous week, and the ensuing crowd included local observers as well as members and out-of-town visitors ("Local Department," *Canaan Reporter,* 17 Sept. 1909).

47. For a more detailed account of Wright's movement away from Pentecostalism, see Kurt O. Berends, "A Divided Harvest: Alice Belie Garrigus, Joel Adams Wright, and Early New England Pentecostalism," M.A. thesis, Wheaton College, 1993, esp. 59–65, 71–73.

48. Minutes of the first annual meeting of the Union Mission, located at Canaan Assemblies of God Church, Canaan, N.H.

49. "1919 Minutes of Mehida Pentecostal Assembly," 15, located at Canaan Assemblies of God Church, Canaan, N.H.

50. George Barney and Cora Barney, "Razor Hill, Grafton," 3.

51. See "Local Department," *Canaan Reporter,* 30 July, 13 Aug., and 30 Aug. 1909.

52. "Our Street Department," *Canaan Reporter,* 8 Nov. 1918.

53. "Razor Hill," *Canaan Reporter,* 11 Sept. 1908, p. 2.

54. *Coos County Democrat,* 25 Nov. 1908, p. 7.

55. For examples, see *Coos County Democrat,* 5 June 1908, p. 4; idem, 25 Nov. 1908, p. 7; and idem, 30 Dec. 1908, p. 1.

56. See the weekly church activities announcements in *Coos County Democrat,* 25 Nov. 1908, p. 8; and 30 Dec. 1908, p. 1.

57. I reached the figure of eighteen from a combination of three sources: city directories, societies mentioned in the newspaper over a two-year period, and commentary from Joel Wright and others on the events in Jefferson.

58. "After the Hunt," *Coos County Democrat,* 25 Nov. 1908, p. 8.

59. "Jefferson," *Coos County Democrat,* 29 Apr. 1908, p. 7.

60. *Coos County Democrat,* 5 June 1908, p. 4.

61. E. B. Maxfield, "Meadows," *The Sheaf* 4 (July 1906): 6.

62. Ibid.

63. E. B. Maxfield and Frank Burdick, "Jefferson, N.H.," *The Sheaf* 4 (Sept. 1906): 8.

64. Ibid.

65. Various newspaper articles indicate the progress of the Harvesters in Jefferson; for example, see "Jefferson," *Coos County Democrat,* 29 Apr. 1908, 7. The announcement of the Jefferson convention at the Freewill Baptist Church is in *The Sheaf* 5 (Sept. 1907): 8. See also "Jefferson, NH, Rent by a Feud over the First Fruit Harvesters." A copy of this newspaper article rests in the Billy Graham Archives at Wheaton College. I have not been able to track down the source.

66. The quotation is found in Joel A. Wright, "Fellowship," *The Sheaf* 4 (Aug. 1906): 4–5. For other accounts of the events and language used at Jefferson upon Wright's arrival, see, "Preacher of Divine Healing Defies Town's Threats," *Boston American,* 27 Dec. 1908, p. 8; "Jefferson, NH, Rent by a Feud"; "Church Blown Up," *White Mountain Republican Journal,* 11 Dec. 1908, p. 1; and "Answers Back," *Coos County Democrat,* 20 Jan. 1909, p. 1.

67. "Jefferson Convention," *The Sheaf* 4 (Nov. 1906): 2.

68. "Jefferson Convention," *The Sheaf* 5 (Oct. 1907): 6.

69. How many left because of the introduction of tongues is unknown. Several news articles that appeared after the destruction of the chapel suggest the number was fairly significant. A response by Wright argues that only a few left because of tongues. See "Holy Rollers! Jefferson Tired and Wearied of Emotional Sect Established in Town,," *Coos County Democrat,* 25 Nov. 1908, p. 10. Wright's position is in "Preacher of Divine Healing."

70. Joel A. Wright, *The Sheaf* 7 (Jan. 1909): 1–4.

71. "Holy Rollers," 10.

72. The best account of this event is found in Alice Belie Garrigus's sermon "How God Delivered from a Mob," located in the archives of the Pentecostal Assemblies of Newfoundland, St. John's, Newfoundland, Canada.

73. "Briefs," *The Sheaf* 7 (Jan. 1909): 6–7.

74. "Jefferson," *Coos County Democrat,* 23 Dec. 1908, 7.

75. "Preacher of Divine Healing."

76. Wright, *The Sheaf* 7 (Jan. 1909): 1–4; "Jefferson Convention," *The Sheaf* 7 (Feb. 1909): 5–6.

77. Although tongues speaking no longer dominates the Pentecostal movement as it once did, in the early years it was the defining characteristic of who was in and who was out of the group.

78. For example, Harvester Mrs. Frank Davis supervised the "Armenia Relief Day" collection effort. Others contributed to the local economy through their labors: Hokam Nelson, carpenter; Robert VanWyck, lumberjack; R. DeLancey King, painter; C. Weld, lumberjack; Lester Barney, laborer. Data from the 1910 and 1920 federal census.

79. "Jefferson," *Coos County Democrat,* June 1907, p. 8; idem., 29 Apr. 1908, p. 7.

80. Only one article mentions tongues before the destruction of the chapel. It does not allude to low morals as a consequence of the activity. All the articles written after the bombing make that association.

81. "Preacher of Divine Healing."

82. "All Jefferson Aroused," *Coos County Democrat,* 30 Dec. 1908, p. 1.

83. Ibid.

5

Knowing the Doctrines of Pentecostals: The Scholastic Theology of the Assemblies of God, 1930–55

Douglas Jacobsen

The years 1930 to 1955 form a distinct period in the history of Pentecostal theology in general and especially within the history of the Assemblies of God church. These were the years of second-generation Pentecostalism, and the theology produced during them was decisively shaped by the particular needs of this generation and the predilections of its leaders. The most prominent characteristics of the Pentecostal theology written during this era—especially as evidenced in the works of Myer Pearlman and Ernest Williams—were its logical organization and systematic completeness. Never before had Pentecostals arranged their beliefs with such a degree of logic. Not until recent years have Pentecostals returned to the task of systematically presenting their comprehensive perspective regarding the entire range of Christian doctrines.[1]

The best way to characterize this period of Pentecostal theological history is to call it an age of Pentecostal scholasticism. The theological works written during these years were produced primarily as textbooks for "second-generation" Pentecostals and designed to school these believers into a fuller understanding of the Christian faith. The need for such books arose largely from internal developments within the Pentecostal movement. As the Pentecostal movement softened the millennial immediacy of its early leaders and settled into an expectation of continued life on this planet, second-generation Pentecostal leaders sought to domesticate, codify, and complete (and, in the process, also modify) the creative, but also varied and sometimes strange, theological legacy handed down by the movement's founders.

This history of Pentecostal theological developments can be seen to fall into a larger pattern of development for new religious movements—that is, an initial period of theological creativity followed by a relatively more pedestrian phase of consolidating scholasticism. But there is a twist here. Scholastic developments of this kind typically involve narrowing and rigidifying the religious insights achieved by the movement's founder(s). In Pentecostal scholasticism, however, a different process was at work. Rather than more strongly emphasize the distinctives of the movement and try to define all Christian theology in terms of those insights, Pentecostal scholastics sought to temper the more radical claims of the movement's varied "founders" and to reframe the distinctive beliefs of Pentecostals in the light of their compatibility with and place in the longer, larger, and broader "catholic" Christian tradition. The resultant theology was surprisingly moderate in tone and content.

The moderate, ecumenical sense of orthodoxy that pervades the Pentecostal scholasticism of this period raises the question of precisely where this theology ought to be placed on the larger map of American Protestant theology. It has often been asserted that early and midcentury Pentecostalism was theologically merely one particular version of fundamentalism. I disagree with that portrayal of Pentecostal theology if it is applied to the scholastic theology examined here. Although some Pentecostals might have been fundamentalists, this group of theologians was not. The published Pentecostal theological texts of this period were not driven by the sense of threatened orthodoxy that spawned fundamentalism. Nor did these Pentecostal scholastics spend much time denouncing the errors of others. Furthermore, Pentecostal scholastics rarely quoted from fundamentalist authors, and they certainly were not part of the fundamentalist social club. Although Pentecostal scholastics clearly intended to be orthodox in their views, and in that sense cannot by the furthest stretch of the imagination be called modernist or liberal, their orthodox orientation does not mean that they were therefore fundamentalist by default.[2]

The two most prominent theologians of this period are Myer Pearlman (1898–1943) and Ernest Swing Williams (1885–1981). Pearlman's *Knowing the Doctrines of the Bible* (1937) and Williams's *Systematic Theology* (1953) bracket this period of scholasticism like bookends. Other Pentecostal leaders were also involved in this work, however. Within the Assemblies of God other relevant works include the writings of Frank Boyd, Carl Brumback, P. C. Nelson, and Ralph Riggs. Outside the Assemblies works such as Paul Beacham's *Questions and Answers on the Scriptures and Related Subjects* and John C. Jernigan's *Doctrinal Sermon Outlines* seem to embody a similar, though less thoroughgoing, scholasticism. Although a case could thus be made that a scholastic tendency crossed Pentecostal denominational lines to some degree, the focus here will be on the Assemblies of God and more specifically on the writings of Pearlman and Williams.[3]

The Rise of Pentecostal Scholasticism

By 1930 American Pentecostalism had clearly entered its second generation. The transition of first-generation charismatic exuberance into second-generation ecclesial organization is well documented and does not need to be recounted here.[4] In the broadest sense, what was happening was the "routinization" of a new religious movement.[5] In the theological sphere, two particular "triggers" of this routinization process deserve mention. The first is a reaction against the sheer unruliness of first-generation Pentecostal leaders who were often more than willing to denounce their rivals and divide the flock. For Pentecostalism to make any constructive headway in American society, it was incumbent on the Pentecostal community to establish some kind of truce between these spiritual sparring partners—at least between those residing in the same denomination. But the routinization of Pentecostal beliefs was also demanded by more mundane reasons, such as the need to recast the radical conversionism of the first generation into a form of theology that could help establish a range of more ordinary religious instruction suited to nurture the biological second-generation children that were being born into the Pentecostal faith.

For an insider's view of this theological dimension of the transition to second-generation Pentecostalism, we can turn to the comments of a Canadian Pentecostal evangelist, A. G. Ward, in *The Whirlwind Prophet* (1927). In a chapter entitled "Qualification of Ministers," Ward lists three subjects on which ministers ought to preach: the promises of the Bible, the commands of the Bible, and the doctrines of the Bible. The first two topics were relatively unproblematic in Ward's mind. The third subject, however, raised some concerns. Ward writes:

> We must not be afraid to present the doctrines of the Bible. I know I am touching a delicate question at this point, owing to the fact that in the years that are gone, many of us carried this to the extreme. However, our people ought to be properly instructed in the doctrines which we as a movement hold, else they will be much like the man who, when asked what he believed, said, "I believe what the church believes." He was then asked what the church believed. He replied, "The church believes what I believe." This being not very satisfactory he was further asked, "Well, what do you and the church believe?" His answer was, "We both believe the same thing."[6]

In reaction to the disorderly world of first-generation Pentecostal theology, Ward sensed the need for a more reasoned, moderate, and comprehensive method of packaging and presenting Pentecostal beliefs, and he was not alone. In the 1920s and 1930s the Assemblies of God and many other Pentecostal churches established Bible institutes and correspondence courses across the country precisely for this purpose. By 1945 some forty Pentecostal Bible institutes had been organized nationwide. A number of Pentecostal churches also organized correspondence courses of one kind or another to instruct pastors and other church leaders in the faith. This new form of Pentecostal education demanded new textbooks for Pentecostal students. In the writings of those textbooks, Pentecostal scholasticism would be born.[7]

Myer Pearlman and E. S. Williams

The best-known Pentecostal scholastic textbook is Myer Pearlman's *Knowing the Doctrines of the Bible.* This work constitutes the third in a series of progressively more detailed and academic books that Pearlman wrote dealing with the Bible and theology. The first of these previous works is *Seeing the Story of the Bible* (1930); the second is Pearlman's four-volume *Through the Bible Book by Book* (1935). *Knowing the Doctrines of the Bible* (1937) is a well written and, to a moderate degree, an original treatment of most of the major themes of Christian theology. The topics he covers include the Scriptures, God, angels, man, sin, the Lord Jesus Christ, the atonement, salvation, the Holy Spirit, the church, and the last things. Pearlman states quite clearly that "the material in this book is a combination of Biblical and systematic theology." For the most part Pearlman organizes his thoughts along the more or less traditional systematic divisions of theology and then musters his supporting arguments from Scripture. Sometimes he simply lists biblical passages in proof-text form as support for his views; at other points Pearlman spends more time expounding a passage of Scripture to make his case.[8]

In terms of general style, Pearlman's doctrines book reads more like a manual of theology or a compendium of beliefs than typical systematic theology. He tends simply to define and explain what he takes to be the correct understanding of a particular doctrine without much reference to other opinions, either to refute them or to correct them. In this regard Pearlman's goal seems to be the indoctrination of students into a proper understanding of faith much more than an introduction to theological reflection in general or an argumentative defense of a particular form of orthodoxy. Pearlman as much as admits this in the introduction to the work. Echoing A. G. Ward's concern that

Pentecostals in general, and especially the members of the Assemblies of God, should understand what they believe and what the church teaches, Pearlman says his goal is to provide "an authoritative and systematically arranged answer" to the basic questions of life. Pearlman seems fairly sure that his Pentecostal peers will accept his work with respect. He asserts: "We confidently expect that theology or doctrine will find its deserved place in religious thought and education. Whatever has been said, in recent years, derogatory to this branch of study, has been ill-timed in view of the world's great need of sober and satisfying truth."[9]

Pearlman adamantly argued that Pentecostals needed to develop a coherent doctrinal understanding of their faith. Doctrine was in a certain sense more foundational to Pearlman's view of things than was either good Christian living or heart-warming Christian experience. He writes: "It has often been said, 'It does not matter what a man believes so long as he does right.' This is a way of dismissing doctrine as having no importance in relation to life. But every person has a theology whether he knows it or not; a man's actions are influenced by what he believes." He added: "Certainly it is more important to live the Christian life than to merely know Christian doctrine, but there would be no Christian experience if there were no Christian doctrine." In the light of these comments, it is interesting to note some of the things that Pearlman's *Doctrines* ignores. For example, from reading this book, one would never know that the Azusa Street revival had occurred. Accounts of the contemporary mighty acts of God (healings, worldwide revivals, etc.) that were the stock-in-trade of untold Pentecostal preachers and missionaries are also simply missing. The experiential dimension of first-generation Pentecostal faith, although essential for Pearlman as an individual, was replaced in his writings by a greater concern for doctrinal clarity.[10]

Although Pearlman could be dogmatic both in his assertions of the need for theology in general and in his presentations of various specific doctrines, he never used theology as a club against others. Theology was, in his mind, an inner support for the Christian, not a weapon for interreligious warfare. He used a physiological analogy and an old adage to explain his position: "As a good backbone is an essential part of a man's body, so a definite system of belief is an essential part of a man's religion. It has been well said that 'a man does not need to wear his backbone in front of him, but he must have a backbone and a straight one or he will be a flexible if not a humpbacked Christian.'"[11] Pearlman's advice to have a backbone but not to flaunt it is a far cry from the "intentionally scandalous" manner in which fundamentalists use dogma to attack modern infidelity. Martin Marty and Scott Appleby say: "Fundamentalists do not simply reaffirm the old doctrines; they subtly lift them from their original context, embellish and institutionalize them, and employ them as *ideological weapons against a hostile world.*"[12]

For the most part the doctrines Pearlman presents are traditional and orthodox in content. In this regard Pearlman's work reflects a general attitude that characterized Pentecostal scholasticism. Carl Brumback articulated this attitude well when in *What Meaneth This?* he wrote: "We Pentecostals owe to the Church as a whole the great body of doctrines which we have embraced as our fundamental beliefs."[13] In a sense the final goal of Pentecostal scholasticism (though it was never stated in quite this way) was to reconfigure the Pentecostal mentality so that being Christian came first and being Pentecostal came second. In this context Christian orthodoxy was understood as that body of traditional teachings that most Christians had accepted as true and faithful to the gospel throughout most of the history of the church. Nonetheless, it must be remembered that not all renderings of basic and historical Christian orthodoxy are cut from the same cloth. Generally orthodox Lutherans can look quite different from generally orthodox Wesleyans, and both of these can look quite different from generally orthodox nondenominational fundamentalists. It is important to know whether we can put any helpful adjective in front of Pearlman's generally orthodox Pentecostal scholasticism.

One way of trying to answer this question is to look at the overall configuration of sources that Pearlman uses in his text and with which he seems to be in general agreement—in essence to see what we can find out about Pearlman through the footnoted company he keeps. What we find is that Pearlman's "friends" were many and diverse. He cites about fifty authors by name—though unfortunately for the historian, he never cites the specific works from which he is quoting. There is little rhyme or reason to this list, and Pearlman seems to have no strong favorites among this diverse group of theologians. Typically he cites an individual only once or twice. The writer he cites most frequently is David S. Clarke, whom he mentions only five times. Calvin, Luther, and Wesley all appear several times. Plato and Pascal appear once. Several fundamentalists do show up among the authors cited (William Evans, three times; Lewis Sperry Chafer, twice; and the Scofield Bible, once), as do several protofundamentalists (A. J. Gordon, three times; one of the Hodges, twice; and A. T. Pierson, once). Alongside these American fundamentalists, however, a sizable group of British progressive evangelicals and moderate liberals also find their way into the text. Among these are A. B. Bruce, James Denny, Marcus Dods, George Smeaton, and H. B. Swete. The only Pentecostal writer cited by name (twice) is Donald Gee, although a single reference to "JRF" most likely means J. Roswell Flower.

What can we tell from this? The conclusion seems to be that Pearlman was not beholden to any one specific party of general orthodoxy. Rather he was an orthodox eclecticist drawing on whichever sources seemed to ring true to him and helped him to make his own doctrinal points. His purpose was to assemble a textbook of theology that would enlarge the vision of the Pentecostal faithful who studied it and that would countermand the most serious theological mistakes Pentecostals seemed prone to make. In this task he seems to have recognized that some individuals see certain items more clearly than others, and he was willing to make use of what he deemed the best and truest insights of anyone.

Ernest Williams's *Systematic Theology* was written some sixteen years after Pearlman's classic text and ten years after Pearlman's untimely death in 1943. The world of the Assemblies of God had changed during this time span, and Williams's book reflects some of these changes. In part this means that Williams's text reads more like a traditional theology text than does Pearlman's. The world of Pentecostal scholarship had matured somewhat. Rather than present his understanding of theology primarily in terms of his own interpretation of the biblical text, Williams organizes his sections and chapters on the basis of the logical presentation of the subject matter in dialogue with the ideas of a range of other theologians. But an attitudinal difference emerges as well. In particular, Williams was aware of the extent to which the Pentecostal movement had developed beyond its humble roots. Unlike some others, Williams did not lament this fact but accepted it as inevitable. He wrote in 1951: "So we have come to the place where we are today. We cannot go back. The fellow who is expecting to live forty-five years ago is doomed to disappointment, because those days are gone. . . . There is nothing to be gained by putting on a long face. We are not living forty-five years ago. We are living today."[14]

In line with this new sense of historical development, Williams also exhibits a greater degree of theological humility and allows for a greater divergence in theological opinion than does Pearlman. Despite being the general superintendent of the church for twenty years (1929–49), Williams never claimed, as did Pearlman, that his work was "authoritative" for members of the Assemblies of God. Rather, he says in the preface to his *Systematic Theology* that his goal has been humbly "to hold before the students and others who might read this book that form of doctrine which is surely believed among us, while never attempting to coerce anyone to [his] personal way of thinking." Williams did believe that "sound doctrine requires clear-cut views," but he also expressed the opinion that a certain ecumenical charity should be shown toward those who hold beliefs differing from one's own. He states: "I have noticed that some attack the beliefs of others, while they know little as to the reasons why others hold to beliefs which differ from their own. . . . Where there are differences among God's devout children, we do well, as far as we are able, to understand the nature of these differences. Such knowledge ought to lead to better understanding which, it is hoped, might provoke closer fellowship rather than separation."[15]

As it is with Pearlman, it is instructive to observe Williams's theological friends, the scholars on whom he relied heavily in his *Systematic Theology.* Four individuals stand above all others: the Methodist theologians John Miley and William Burton Pope, the Baptist theologian Augustus Strong, and Cyrus I. Scofield (most notably his *Scofield Reference Bible*). Strong and Miley were well-known late-nineteenth-century American theological centrists who sought to steer their respective churches through what they themselves saw as a critical period in the history of theology. Each was also a transition figure in the history of American theology, incorporating both progressive evangelical opinions and moderate liberal opinions into their individual works. W. B. Pope was in many ways a traditional British Wesleyan, but he, like Strong and Miley, was also progressive in many of his views. Scofield was the best-known dispensationalist in America, and in him we at last find a fundamentalist connection in Williams's *Systematic Theology.* Before we make too much of this fact, however, we need to look at how Williams employs Scofield's Bible notes in his *Systematic Theology.* For the most part, Williams tends not to emphasize Scofield's dispensational opinions (he quotes Scofield only once in his discussion of eschatology). In fact, Williams tends not to use much of Scofield's explicit theology at all. The passages quoted from Scofield's Bible are more descriptive in nature or more concerned with biblical background information than they are specifically theological. Finally, it should be noted that Williams seems more willing to criticize Scofield's views than he is the views of Miley, Pope, and Strong. In addition to citing these four individuals, Williams also often turned for help to the published works of H. R. Mackintosh (cited fourteen times), Myer Pearlman (cited eighteen times), and William Shedd (cited eighteen times). Pearlman obviously needs no introduction here. Shedd was a professor at Union Seminary in New York from 1863 to 1890; Williams quotes only from his widely used *Commentary on Romans.* H. R. Mackintosh, on whom Williams relies heavily in his discussion of Christology (over 35 percent of all quotations in that chapter come from Mackintosh's *Doctrine of the Person of Jesus Christ*), can be categorized as a moderate liberal. Mackintosh's historical and systematic evaluation of Christology is that "faith in Christ is not to be confused with adhesion to a particular Christological formula, and that the doctrine of two natures, in the rigid shape given it by tradition, is detachable from the believing estimate of our Lord." Mackintosh further rejected the notion that a proper understanding of Christology demands any "sharp rejection of heresy." Even given the fact that Williams tends to use his sources in somewhat of the same manner as Pearlman, quoting what he wants and ignoring the rest (and Williams does use his sources in a *very* loose way),[16] it is difficult to see how anyone could use Mackintosh in as positive a manner as Williams does and still be thought of as a fundamentalist in any typical sense of that word.[17]

Williams's positive use of evangelical progressives such as Miley and Strong and of moderate liberals such as Mackintosh without the need to distance himself from their "liberal" leanings is made more striking and significant given his willingness in other contexts to confront error as he sees it. This disposition is most clearly displayed in his discussion of the relative merits of the Calvinist and the Wesleyan-Arminian views regarding the nature and processes of salvation. Williams strongly opposes the traditional Calvinist view.[18] What is more, Williams is willing to use the opinions of one of his clearly nonevangelical contemporaries, Karl Barth, to support his own anti-Calvinist views.[19]

As a general rule Williams seems to strive to avoid using theological works written by his contemporaries. Most of the works he cites positively were written during the closing years of the nineteenth century, and almost all these would have been known at the time of their publication as irenic and mildly progressive in theological tone. This moderate nineteenth-century theological predilection is especially noteworthy given the fact that Williams was well connected, institutionally at least, with the burgeoning evangelical movement of the mid-twentieth century. Williams held the leadership reins of the Assemblies of God during the mid-1940s and early 1950s, when that church became associated with the National Association of Evangelicals. Despite these ties, the only "card-carrying" evangelical contemporary that Williams cites with any degree of frequency is Henry C. Thiessen (seven citations)—but Thiessen was not a central player in evangelical circles. One of the few other contemporaries from whom Williams was willing to quote was, as stated previously, "Dr. Barth" (i.e., Karl Barth). By 1953 Barth had become a bogeyman of sorts for most evangelicals, and routine denunciations of his views were part and parcel of many evangelical theological works.[20] Rather than condemn Barth, however, Williams speaks with favor of his willingness to confront "the Calvinists" on the issue of free will. (It is perhaps not insignificant to note here that many of the leading evangelicals were Calvinistic in their theology.) Whatever else he might have been, Williams was clearly not a typical midcentury evangelical theologian.

We find in the writings of both Pearlman and Williams, then, a general tendency toward broad orthodoxy. Both were concerned that Pentecostal believers understand that the longer traditions of Christian theology were not to be rejected by Pentecostals because of their own immediate experience of the Spirit. Rather, traditional Christian beliefs were to be reaffirmed and Pentecostal believers were to be taught not only by the Bible but also by the other non-Pentecostal Christian theologians. Pearlman and Williams were trying to help Pentecostals build a well-rounded and systematic understanding of the full range of Christian teachings about God, the world, and themselves. In this process they borrowed freely from the writings of a host of theologians who preceded them without ever becoming beholden to any one school of thought. The goal was to create in their textbooks a distinctive middle-of-the-road blend of theology that could be used to school Pentecostals into a more mature and ecumenically orthodox, but still clearly Pentecostal, understanding of the Christian faith.

The Evangelicalization of Pentecostal Theology

There was nothing inevitable about either the rise of Pentecostal scholasticism in general or its particular strength within the Assemblies of God. Things could have turned out differently, and if that is the case, its ultimate demise should come as no shock to us. Theological paradigms come and go. Even during its years of greatest influence at Central Bible College and in the corridors of the Assemblies of God headquarters, Pentecostal scholasticism was rejected by numerous Pentecostal believers. Perhaps the most pugnacious rejection was visible in the latter rain movement. But other, less strident alternatives to scholasticism were also available, ranging from the experiential fundamentalism of people such as Charles Price to the Pentecostal ecumenism of David du Plessis. In the light of these alternatives, the prominence and success of Pentecostal scholasticism were due to a mix of the felt theological needs of a good number of people within the Pentecostal movement and the fact that a group of people amenable to this theological vision largely controlled the denominational machinery of the Assemblies of God. As those needs changed and as new personnel came to the fore within the ecclesial structures of the Assemblies of God (i.e., as the transition to third-generation Pentecostalism was being completed), the influence of second-generation scholasticism tended naturally to wane.

Although the decline of Pentecostal scholasticism can thus be understood as part of the normal generational handing down of the faith, the particular direction in which Pentecostal theology was to be moved by third-generation Pentecostals was significantly affected by several other developments. The first development was demographic: Pentecostal churches had grown by leaps and bounds in the 1930s and 1940s, and by the 1950s the sheer numbers of Pentecostals demanded the attention of the larger American public. Symbolic of this change of status was Henry P. Van Dusen's 1958 article in *Life* magazine, where he included Pentecostals as part of what he called the emerging "third force in Christendom."[21] With this new visibility came the problem of image control, and several Pentecostal churches responded by creating departments of public relations that they hoped would be able to shape public perceptions.[22]

As part of their overall strategy for dealing with their newly found visibility, Pentecostals in the United States found themselves needing to develop new theological ways of defining themselves both to themselves and to others in terms understandable to most Americans. But in mid-twentieth-century America, the theological definitional options available to Pentecostals were limited. Americans generally thought of Protestantism as divided into two, and only two, competitive "parties" variously labeled as conservative versus liberal, fundamentalist versus modernist, or evangelical versus mainline. Given these simplistic choices, Pentecostals felt little tension in identifying themselves with the right side of the continuum and especially with the emerging neo-evangelical movement as it was embodied in the National Association of Evangelicals (NAE). Many Pentecostals seem to have felt that this alliance was almost risk free. The motto of the NAE was, after all, "cooperation without compromise." But this formal rule of association could not protect Pentecostals from being overwhelmed by the homogenizing influence of the more organized and articulate mainstream evangelical movement. Mainstream evangelicals and Pentecostals were not cultural equals in America, and in this unequal situation, Pentecostals (the culturally weaker partners) could not help but be, in a sense, colonized by the stronger. Mainstream evangelical theological ideas, attitudes, and methods were soon being imported wholesale into the Pentecostal world, and a new evangelical paradigm of Pentecostal theology quickly began to replace the waning hegemony of Pentecostal scholasticism.

Of all the Pentecostal denominations, the Assemblies of God was perhaps the most deeply affected by this process of theological evangelicalization. Stanley Horton's *Into All Truth* illustrates how this occurred. The subject of this book is distinctly Pentecostal—more distinctly Pentecostal, in fact, than many of the classic Pentecostal scholastic texts of Pearlman, Williams, and others. But the format of Horton's book is as distinctly evangelical as its message is Pentecostal. In particular, Horton adopts an evangelical "Bible only" method of theology to make his case. Rather than interact with other theologians, Horton states that he will present only "what the Bible actually teaches" and that consequently he will include "few references to books other than the Bible." The point here is not that earlier Pentecostal scholastic theologians were less attuned to the biblical text but rather that Horton displays particular fervor in rejecting the use of other theological works. This is an explicit turning away from the model embodied especially in Williams's *Systematic Theology.*[23]

But it is not just evangelical "Bible only" methodology that is at work here. Horton, and the Assemblies of God leadership with him, seems also to have adopted evangelicalism's contextual definition of the Christian faith as battle against liberalism. In the first chapter of his book Horton asks, "What is truth?" and he then proceeds to contrast truth with the empty preachments of all "liberal" and "modernistic" churches. Twenty-one years later, Horton reiterated this opinion in *What the Bible Says about the Holy Spirit.* He states: "It is worth noting that all the major denominations in America in their early days put up barriers of creeds against liberalism and against the destructive criticism of the Bible. Few succeeded in keeping this sort of unbelief out. Today the Pentecostals are in the front line of the battle against the enemy of truth who is also the enemy of our souls."[24]

Other Pentecostal churches besides the Assemblies of God were making similar moves at the same time. They too reinterpreted their histories to fit their current evangelical associations and redefined their theology in a more evangelical direction. Charles W. Conn made this shift explicit in his history of the Church of God (*Like a Mighty Army*), and Joseph Campbell similarly reinterpreted the roots and current status of the Pentecostal Holiness Church in the history of that church that he published in 1951.[25] By 1960, when Thomas Zimmerman (who was general superintendent of the Assemblies of God) was elected president of the NAE, the evangelicalization of the Assemblies of God, and most of American Pentecostalism with it, was basically complete. Edith Blumhofer summarizes these developments as follows: "In identifying with the new evangelicals, Assemblies of God leaders acted on the assumption that they were evangelicals energized by a spiritual experience, who shared both a meaningful evangelical past and a vision for the future. Some adherents disagreed, and later leaders would attempt to reemphasize Pentecostal 'distinctives,' but for the moment, at mid-century the Assemblies of God found its new identification congenial."[26]

Although many Pentecostals continued to consult the old texts of Pearlman and Williams and their other scholastic colleagues during these evangelical years, the center of gravity of Pentecostal theology had clearly shifted. For all practical purposes the age of Pentecostal scholasticism had ended by 1955.

Locating Pentecostal Scholasticism

It seems fair to say that until recent years scholars of Pentecostal history have been unwilling or unable to accord the period of Pentecostal scholasticism the kind of independent status that is required for its impartial interpretation. Rather than allow Pentecostal scholasticism to stand on its own feet, Pentecostal scholars have generally been too willing to read the history of Pentecostal theology backward and assume that the more recent alliance of Pentecostals and evangelicals must have been built on an earlier theological similarity of the two movements. I see no compelling reasons that force me to accept that teleological construction of history.

Pentecostal scholasticism did provide a bridge that allowed the theological exuberance of first-generation Pentecostalism to be transmuted during the 1930s, 1940s, and 1950s into a more rational and domesticated form of Pentecostalism that made thinkable an alliance with the evangelical movement at midcentury. But to say that Pentecostal theology evolved in this way does not require us to believe that this is the only way things could have turned out. Given different dynamics in the larger midcentury Protestant world, Pentecostal scholasticism could as easily have served as a bridge to more ecumenical developments. Historians, of course, cannot write about "what if"; they must focus on what did happen. Nonetheless, some reflection on what could have happened can helpfully free us from the tyranny of reading all historical developments as if they somehow had to happen the way they did.

In studying Pentecostal scholasticism, it must also be remembered that this was only one form of Pentecostal theology, not the whole picture. What is involved in the interpretation of this particular form of theology is neither the interpretation of Pentecostal theology in total nor the analysis of some irreducible "essence" of Pentecostal belief. The Pentecostal and charismatic communities of faith currently extend their roots and branches from the old Pentecostal denominations, to various new political neofundamentalist groups, to a variety of African American and Hispanic urban congregations, to the Roman Catholic church, and in and out of most of the "liberal" mainline churches of the country. One needs to speak, therefore, in more specific terms. What are the views of one particular Pentecostal or charismatic group, or what is the theological position of some particular Pentecostal or charismatic scholar? An analysis of one particular theological expression of Pentecostal faith, such as the one provided in this essay, may have broader application to, or reflect wider developments within, Pentecostalism or American religious faith in general. But the task of understanding Pentecostal theology must always begin with a small frame of reference and expand beyond that only as far as the evidence allows.

How then should this particular form of Pentecostal theology—Pentecostal scholasticism—be understood? I think the fairest interpretation we can make of Pentecostal scholasticism is to call it a relatively freestanding, generally orthodox, churchly theology that sought to selvage the Pentecostal faith—to sew up the edges so it would not unravel—for a second generation of Pentecostal believers and to package that theology so that it could be taught to future generations of Pentecostal believers. This selvaging activity cut off certain "loose ends" of the Pentecostal experience that some Pentecostal believers of that time thought should not have been trimmed, and it sewed into the Pentecostal worldview a range of new options that had not been present earlier. Overall, however, the work seems to have been a success. Numerous works written by Pearlman and Williams are still in print and still being used as Pentecostal theological textbooks.

Moving beyond this relatively functional description, it can be said that the general content of Pentecostal scholasticism was adapted in rough form from late nineteenth-century, prefundamentalist, progressive Wesleyan evangelical Protestantism. Pentecostal scholasticism was, accordingly, largely orthodox in the historical meaning of that term, but it was also generally irenic in tone and lacked for the most part the antimodernist fervor that has dominated much fundamentalist and evangelical scholarship.

Finally, it should be noted that these Pentecostal scholastic developments were not unique. A similar process is evident, for example, in midcentury developments in the Mennonite Church. John Christian Wenger's *Introduction to Theology* (1954) is in many ways similar to the works of Pearlman and Williams. Wenger's goal was to write a "Mennonite theology" that would be as distinctly Anabaptist as the theology of the Christian Reformed Church was Calvinist or the theology of the Church of the Nazarene was Wesleyan. His theology was clearly orthodox, but Wenger was careful to indicate that his theology was not simply one peculiar variant of fundamentalism or evangelicalism. It was something different.[27] Other works of theology written during this period that might fit the category of being generally orthodox and scholastic in nature, without being fundamentalistic in outlook, include A. M. Hills's

Fundamental Christian Theology (1931) and H. Orton Wiley's *Christian Theology* (1941), both written for the Church of the Nazarene; and Francis Pieper's *Christian Dogmatics* (German, 1917–20; English, 1950), written for the Missouri Synod Lutheran Church.[28]

It is clear today, and it has been for some time, that Pentecostal faith does not need to be wedded to one particular theological interpretation of the Bible and Christian experience. Because this is the case, the early midcentury scholasticism of the Assemblies of God church can now be allowed to stand on its own as a distinct expression of Protestant theology. The Pentecostal scholastics examined here sought to articulate a moderate and orthodox understanding of the historical Christian faith that they thought would be helpful to their particular Pentecostal church at one specific point in that church's development. There is no need either to force this round Pentecostal peg into any square fundamentalist hole or to declare the writings of Pearlman and Williams to be the canon of orthodoxy for all Pentecostal and charismatic Christians. What we have here is one particular model of Pentecostal theology that deserves to be examined on its own for whatever light it can shed on Pentecostal history and Christian faith.

Notes

1. In recent years a number of more or less systematic treatments of Christian theology have been published by different Pentecostal groups. The Assemblies of God has produced three of these: William W. Menzies, *Bible Doctrines: A Pentecostal Perspective,* revised and expanded by Stanley M. Horton (Springfield, Mo.: Logion, 1993); John R. Higgons, Michael Dusing, and Frank D. Tallman, *An Introduction to Theology: A Classical Pentecostal Perspective,* 2d ed. (Dubuque, Iowa: Kendall/Hunt, 1994); and Stanley M. Horton, ed., *Systematic Theology: A Pentecostal Perspective* (Springfield, Mo.: Logion, 1994). This last work, although it is called a "systematic" theology, is actually a collection of essays on different themes of systematic theology written as independent essays by different authors who apparently never even met. All in all, the writings of Pearlman and Williams still stand as some of the most creative systematic theological work undertaken by anyone in the Assemblies of God.

Other Pentecostal or charismatic scholars have also begun to be active in the field of systematic theology. See, for example, Raymond M. Pruitt, *Fundamentals of the Faith* (Cleveland, Tenn.: White Wing, 1981); J. Rodman Williams, *Renewal Theology,* 2 vols. (Grand Rapids, Mich.: Zondervan, 1988, 1990); and French Arrington, *Christian Doctrine: A Pentecostal Perspective,* 3 vols. (Cleveland, Tenn.: Pathway, 1992–94).

2. A great deal of contemporary scholarship dealing with American Protestantism presupposes a two-party model of Protestant divisions. This model implies that there are ultimately only two different kinds of Protestants in America, variously labeled "fundamentalist" and "modernist," "evangelical" and "mainline," or "conservative" and

"liberal." It is precisely that simple bipolar division that I want to contest here. For a more in-depth critique of the two-party paradigm, see Douglas Jacobsen and William Vance Trollinger Jr., *Re-Forming the Center: American Protestantism, 1900 to the Present* (Grand Rapids, Mich.: Eerdmanns, 1998).

3. Myer Pearlman, *Knowing the Doctrines of the Bible* (Springfield, Mo.: Gospel Publishing House, 1937); Ernest Swing Williams, *Systematic Theology,* 3 vols. (Springfield, Mo.: Gospel Publishing House, 1953); Paul F. Beacham, *Questions and Answers on the Scriptures and Related Subjects* (Franklin Springs, Ga.: Publishing House of the Pentecostal Holiness Church, 1950), which is described in the introduction as "a body of divinity, a system of sound Scriptural exposition, an encyclopedia of religious knowledge, and a course of wise counseling in spiritual and ethical problems" all rolled into one; John C. Jernigan, *Doctrinal Sermon Outlines* (Cleveland, Tenn.: author, 1940).

4. See especially the numerous histories of the Assemblies of God that describe this transition: Carl Brumback, *Suddenly . . . from Heaven* (Springfield, Mo.: Gospel Publishing House, 1961); William W. Menzies, *Anointed to Serve* (Springfield, Mo.: Gospel Publishing House, 1971); Edith L. Blumhofer, *The Assemblies of God,* 2 vols. (Springfield, Mo.: Gospel Publishing House, 1989); and idem, *Restoring the Faith* (Urbana: University of Illinois Press, 1993). For the developments in the Church of God, see Charles W. Conn, *Like a Mighty Army,* rev. ed. (Cleveland, Tenn.: Pathway, 1977); and Hickey Crews, *The Church of God: A Social History* (Knoxville: University of Tennessee Press, 1990). For an analysis of and response to these developments more contemporary to them, see Joseph E. Campbell, *The Pentecostal Holiness Church, 1898–1948* (Franklin Springs, Ga.: Publishing House of the Pentecostal Holiness Church, 1951).

5. For the concept of "routinization," see Max Weber, *The Sociology of Religion,* trans. Ephraim Fischoff (Boston: Beacon, 1963), esp. chap. 5, "The Religious Congregation, Preaching, and Pastoral Care."

6. A. G. Ward, *The Whirlwind Prophet and Other Sermons* (Springfield, Mo.: Gospel Publishing House, 1927), 81–82.

7. Concerning Pentecostal Bible colleges, see L. F. Wilson, "Bible Institutes, Colleges, Universities," in *Dictionary of Pentecostal and Charismatic Movements,* ed. Stanley Burgess and Gary McGee (Grand Rapids, Mich.: Zondervan, 1988), 61. See also Menzies, *Anointed to Serve,* 354–68; and Robert Bryant Mitchell, *Heritage and Horizons: The History of the Open Bible Standard Churches* (Des Moines, Iowa: Open Bible, 1982), 63–65. For correspondence schools, see H. Glynn Hall's dissertation, "The Development of the Workers Training Course of the Assemblies of God," Ph.D. diss., New Orleans Baptist Theological Seminary, 1973. There has been some discussion concerning whether Pentecostals adopted a fundamentalist model of Bible school education in their own educational enterprises. Virginia Lieson Brereton hints that this was so without ever explicitly arguing her case. She says: "Pentecostal Bible schools resembled Bible schools of other fundamentalist traditions in most respects, except they tended to struggle under scarcer resources and lower academic levels" (Brereton, *Training God's Army* [Indianapolis: Indiana University Press, 1990], 13). Edith Blumhofer repeats Brereton's suggestion without adding any further evidence of direct influence; see *Restoring the Faith,* 150. Even if this is the case, there is no reason

to assume that the borrowing of an educational form from fundamentalism demanded a similar and uncritical borrowing of fundamentalist theological ideas.

8. Myer Pearlman, *Seeing the Story of the Bible* (Springfield, Mo.: Gospel Publishing House, 1930); idem, *Through the Bible Book by Book,* 4 vols. (Springfield, Mo.: Gospel Publishing House, 1935); idem, *Knowing the Doctrines of the Bible* (Springfield, Mo.: Gospel Publishing House, 1937).

9. Pearlman, *Knowing the Doctrines,* 7–9.

10. Ibid., 9–10.

11. Ibid.

12. Martin E. Marty and R. Scott Appleby, "Conclusion: An Interim Report on a Hypothetical Family," in *Fundamentalisms Observed,* ed. Martin E. Marty and R. Scott Appleby (Chicago: University of Chicago Press, 1991), 818, 826.

13. Carl Brumback, *What Meaneth This?* (Springfield, Mo.: Gospel Publishing House, 1947), 30.

14. Ernest S. Williams, "Forty-Five Years of Pentecostal Revival," *Pentecostal Evangel,* 26 Aug. 1951, p. 5.

15. Williams, *Systematic Theology,* 1:vi–vii, 155.

16. Williams freely edited and altered almost all the quotations he incorporated into his manuscript. What is more, he did this while usually still placing quotation marks around these passages as if they were direct and unchanged quotations from the sources indicated. At numerous other points in his text, Williams simply borrows ideas and even direct quotations from his various sources with no indication that he is doing this. One can only assume that Williams was writing from notes he had used for lecture purposes and that he failed to check his work either for accuracy or for plagiarism.

17. H. R. Mackintosh, *The Doctrine of the Person of Jesus Christ* (New York: Scribner's, 1930), 298–99.

18. Williams, *Systematic Theology,* 1:268.

19. Ibid., 252.

20. See, for example, the way Carl F. H. Henry labels Barth a mystic who must ultimately value his own inner experiences above the historical revelation in the Bible in *The Drift of Modern Thought* (Grand Rapids, Mich.: Eerdmans, 1951), 106; or how E. J. Carnell summarily dismisses Barth as irrational in his *Introduction to Christian Apologetics* (Grand Rapids, Mich.: Eerdmans, 1948), 76–77.

21. Henry Pitney Van Dusen, "The Third Force in Christendom," *Life,* 9 June 1958, pp. 113–24.

22. The Assemblies of God established an office of public relations in 1954 (Menzies, *Anointed to Serve,* 286) and the Church of God followed suit in 1958 (Conn, *Like a Mighty Army,* 324).

23. Stanley M. Horton, *Into All Truth: A Survey of the Course and Content of Divine Revelation* (Springfield, Mo.: Gospel Publishing House, 1955), intro.

24. Stanley M. Horton, *What the Bible Says about the Holy Spirit* (Springfield, Mo.: Gospel Publishing House, 1976), 14–15.

25. Conn, *Like a Mighty Army,* xxiii–xxxvii; Campbell, *The Pentecostal Holiness Church,* 8–9.

26. Edith L. Blumhofer, *Restoring the Faith: The Assemblies of God, Pentecostalism, and American Culture* (Urbana: University of Illinois Press, 1993), 195–96.

27. John Christian Wenger, *Introduction to Theology* (Scottdale, Pa.: Herald, 1954).

28. A. M. Hills, *Fundamental Christian Theology: A Systematic Theology* (Pasadena, Calif.: Pasadena College, 1931); H. Orton Wiley, *Christian Theology*, 3 vols. (Kansas City: Beacon Hill, 1941); Francis Pieper, *Christian Dogmatics*, 3 vols. (St. Louis: Concordia Publishing House, 1950).

PART 3

Rethinking Boundaries: Encounters between the Charismatic Movement and the Protestant Mainstream

6

The Spirit-Filled Movements in Contemporary America: A Survey Perspective

Corwin E. Smidt, Lyman A. Kellstedt, John C. Green, and James L. Guth

As the twentieth century comes to a close, some systematic effort should be made to assess the significance of charismatic movements in American religious life. After all, the first such movement, American Pentecostalism, began with a series of revivals during the first days of the twentieth century. Since that time the relationship between Pentecostals and other Christians has frequently been turbulent, marked as much by disdain, skepticism, and mistrust as by charity, acceptance, and mutual understanding.

Despite these historical patterns, significant changes have occurred over the past several decades. Institutionally Pentecostalism has made important inroads within American religious life. Not only have Pentecostal denominations joined confederations such as the National Association of Evangelicals, but other charismatic movements have emerged outside the historic Pentecostal denominations, namely, the charismatic renewal movement within mainline Protestant and Roman Catholic churches and the "third wave" movement located largely within evangelical Protestant denominations and nondenominational churches.[1]

Changes have occurred at the individual level as well. Social distances between "spirit-filled" and other Christians have eroded both physically and psychologically. Religious and social interaction has increased between Pentecostals and charismatics and other Christians. Pentecostals are less often found among "the disinherited." Moreover, the intemperance displayed by many earlier Pentecostals toward other Christians is much less common today.[2] Religious radio and television, media heavily influenced by these movements, have produced a cross-fertilization of different religious traditions among listeners and viewers. Finally, changes in "styles" of worship in various religious traditions, denominations, and local churches further reveal the influence of these charismatic movements.

Despite these important changes, there has been little scholarly study of contemporary charismatic movements. Studies of Pentecostals or charismatics have been largely historical and "institutional." Thus, we know little about the size of these movements, their religious belief patterns and practices, and the similarities and differences evident within and across each movement. Likewise, little attention has been given to the effects of the particular religious context on beliefs and practices of Pentecostals and charismatics. For example, in what ways are charismatic and noncharismatic members of "mainstream" churches similar? How do they differ, if at all? Is there greater commonality between Pentecostals and charismatics than between charismatics and noncharismatics in the same denominations? These are the issues and questions that we address in this essay.

Review of the Literature

For the purposes of this study, we reserve the term *Pentecostal* for those who are either members of Pentecostal denominations or who willingly label themselves as Pentecostals, while we use *charismatic* to refer to non-Pentecostals who exhibit particular spiritual gifts (primarily speaking in tongues), subscribe to certain doctrines related to the workings of the Holy Spirit, or identify themselves as charismatics. Collectively these believers are members of charismatic movements or, as we call them for stylistic purposes, the spirit-filled movement.

What are the defining characteristics of those in the spirit-filled movement? Although scholars may know Pentecostals or charismatics when they see them, they struggle in specifying their defining nature.

Some analysts have examined the spirit-filled movement on the basis of its historical roots or in terms of those belonging to various churches and denominations associated with the Pentecostal tradition.[3] Although appropriate for certain purposes, this approach ignores charismatics and thus is insufficient for analyzing the contemporary nature of the larger spirit-filled movement.

Others have argued that the defining characteristic of the spirit-filled movement is the gift of glossolalia, or speaking in tongues.[4] Others, however, have contended that glossolalia is not an adequate defining characteristic. Many charismatics hold that although speaking in tongues is important, it is not the only authenticating gift of the Holy Spirit,[5] and growing numbers of

Pentecostals report that they do not possess the gift.[6] Not surprisingly, some scholars argue that speaking in tongues should not serve as the sole defining characteristic of the spirit-filled movement.[7]

Finally, given these definitional difficulties, some analysts have used a more psychological approach, with the defining quality being "identification" with the movement. Others have broadened this approach to encompass those who "feel close to" (proximity) the movement or simply to include those who accept certain religious gifts and experiences as "valid" indicators of the baptism and power of the Holy Spirit—not simply glossolalia but also prophecy, healing, miracles, and "other biblical paranormal phenomena."[8]

Hence, several definitional approaches have been adopted to analyze Pentecostals and charismatics. These differences set the boundaries of the phenomenon under investigation in differing ways that frequently result in different findings. Consequently, we will utilize several approaches to identifying Pentecostals and charismatics and assess the different results from each approach.

Data and Methods

We employ data from a national survey of 4,001 Americans conducted in the spring of 1992.[9] Not only was this survey based on an unusually large sample, but it contains many religious questions, including measures tapping highly specific denominational affiliation, distinct religious identifications, and the frequency of speaking in tongues.

These questions permit us to employ each analytical strategy discussed previously. First, we can analyze Pentecostalism by examining the characteristics of members of white and black Pentecostal churches scattered across the American landscape. Second, we can consider these movements behaviorally, on the basis of glossolalia. Third, we can analyze these movements as delineated by psychological measures—for example, whether respondents identified as either a Pentecostal or charismatic and whether they felt "close" to either Pentecostals or charismatics. Finally, we can use these multiple measures to examine different combinations of these characteristics and their religious consequences.

Data Analysis

We begin our analysis with the distributions of Pentecostal and charismatic Christians shown in table 1, using each of the four measurement approaches: denominational affiliation, speaking in tongues, self-identification, and proximity to Pentecostals and charismatics. Denominational affiliation is collapsed into nine religious categories: white Pentecostal, black Pentecostal, nondenominational charismatics, evangelical Protestant, mainline Protestant, black Protestant, Roman Catholic, other traditions, and seculars.[10]

The percentage of Americans who belong to classical Pentecostal denominations is at first glance relatively small, accounting for only 3.6 percent of the adult population, with "white" Pentecostals (2.5 percent) more than twice as numerous as those within historically "black" Pentecostal denominations (1.1 percent). When nondenominational charismatics are added to this mix, the numbers expand to 5.0 percent of the population. Although these numbers

Table 1. The Distribution of Pentecostals and Charismatics

Pentecostal-Charismatic Measure	Percentage	Number
Denomination		
White Pentecostal	2.5	100
Black Pentecostal	1.1	42
Nondenominational charismatics	1.4	56
Other evangelicals	21.7	868
Mainline	16.7	670
Black Protestant	6.8	273
Roman Catholic	23.2	928
Other traditions	6.8	274
Seculars	19.7	790
	100.0	4001
Speaking in tongues		
Daily or weekly	3.3	133
Monthly or less	5.4	218
Never	91.3	3650
	100.0	4001
Self-identification		
Pentecostal only[a]	4.7	187
Charismatic only[a]	6.6	266
Both	0.8	34
Neither[a]	87.9	3514
	100.0	4001
Proximity: close to		
Pentecostals only	6.3	251
Charismatics only	3.0	120
Both	5.0	201
Neither	85.7	3429
	100.0	4001

a. May include some cases that combine other identifications, such as evangelical and fundamentalist.

may seem relatively small, the only other denominational families to exceed this percentage are Baptists, Methodists, and Lutherans—with Lutherans being 0.3 percent larger (data not shown).

Clearly, denominational affiliation alone captures only a fraction of the total Pentecostal-charismatic movement. What is unclear, however, is just what fraction it does constitute. Table 1 also reports that percentage of Americans who reported having, on some occasion, spoken in tongues. When the charismatic movements are measured this way, they grow considerably, doubling to 8.7 percent. Obviously many more people exercise the gift of tongues than belong to Pentecostal denominations.

People may be psychologically tied to the spirit-filled movement without belonging to a Pentecostal denomination or speaking in tongues. Studies employing self-identification measures have generally combined "Pentecostal" and "charismatic" into a single category tapping identification "as a charismatic or Pentecostal Christian." Since many "classical Pentecostals balk at being identified with charismatics,"[11] we separated the categories, asking respondents which of a battery of religious labels—for example, *Pentecostal, charismatic, evangelical, fundamentalist,* or *mainline*—they would use to describe themselves. This approach not only enables us to assess the percentage of Americans who claim to be Pentecostals separately from the percentage who claim to be charismatics, but it also allows us to assess the percentage of Americans who choose both labels.

Approximately 5 percent (4.7 percent) chose to label themselves simply as Pentecostal, whereas a slightly higher percentage (6.6 percent) choose only charismatic. Fewer than 1 percent (0.8 percent) employed both Pentecostal and charismatic labels. Thus, when all three self-identification categories are combined, 12.1 percent can be classified as charismatic or Pentecostal Christians. This distribution of religious self-identifications reveals three important patterns: (1) the term *charismatic* is more widely adopted by Americans than *Pentecostal,* (2) few Americans employ both terms together, and (3) self-identification provides the most encompassing measure of these three measurement approaches.

Finally, the spirit-filled movement's penetration into American religious life can be analyzed by use of proximity evaluations (i.e., expressions of whether one feels close to, neutral toward, or far from Pentecostals and charismatics). Although feelings of proximity and self-identifications are likely to be related empirically, they are conceptually distinct. Given the relative ease of expressing feelings of closeness to a group, expressions of close proximity are likely to be more numerous than expressions of self-identification.

This latter expectation is evident in table 1, but not to the extent we expected. Despite the high religiosity of the American people, only 14.3 percent of the population feel close to either Pentecostals or charismatics. In fact, there were more Americans (55.3 percent) who expressed feelings of distance toward one or both groups than there were those who expressed feelings of closeness (data not shown). Thus, although proximity measures extend the parameters of the charismatic movements, they do not extend them far.

Religious Affiliation and Measures of the Spirit-Filled Movement

What are the relationships among these particular Pentecostal-charismatic markers? Table 2 reveals that slightly more than one-half of those affiliated with white Pentecostal churches report speaking in tongues, but only one-third of those affiliated with black Pentecostal churches do so. Although the gift of tongues may be visibly present within Pentecostal denominations, it is far from universal. In analysis not presented in the table, it was found that the higher

Table 2. Religious Affiliation and Measures of the Spirit-Filled Movement: Denomination, Self-Identification, Tongues, and Proximities

	Denomination							
	WPe	BPe	NC	OE	M	BPr	RC	OT
Number (*N* = 4001)	100	42	56	868	670	273	948	274
Speak in tongues								
Yes	55.6%	33.1%	74.6%	6.6%	5.9%	19.0%	9.0%	2.5%
No	44.4	66.9	25.4	93.4	94.0	81.0	91.0	97.5
Self-identification								
Pentecostal	66.9	50.9	15.3	3.0	3.0	9.5	1.7	0.7
Charismatic	12.0	7.1	54.7	6.3	5.7	9.6	9.6	2.9
Both	8.3	0.0	10.7	0.6	0.5	2.0	0.6	0.0
Neither	12.8	42.1	19.3	90.2	90.8	78.9	88.1	96.4
Proximity								
Close to:								
Pentecostals	38.0	47.0	20.1	8.5	4.0	9.5	3.8	1.8
Charismatics	3.6	0.0	11.9	3.7	1.7	2.8	4.6	1.4
Both	38.7	12.7	42.0	7.3	2.0	11.6	1.4	1.0
Far from:								
Pentecostals	2.1	3.6	6.6	8.9	11.9	10.4	16.8	7.9
Charismatics	27.0	25.4	8.4	10.9	7.9	8.7	6.1	7.4
Both	3.0	3.2	3.0	29.3	35.0	26.8	38.7	48.8

Key: WPe = white Pentecostal; BPe = black Pentecostal; NC = nondenominational charismatic; OE = other evangelical; M = mainline; BPr = black Protestant; RC = Roman Catholic; OT = other traditions the level of religious commitment (measured in terms of religious practice, belief, and salience), the greater the likelihood of the presence of the gift of tongues. Nevertheless, the fact that the gift of tongues is not universally present even in Pentecostal denominations demonstrates the inadequacy of using it as the sole criterion for defining membership in the spirit-filled movement.

On the other hand, speaking in tongues is hardly confined to Pentecostal denominations. Tongues-speakers constitute nearly three-fourths of those in nondenominational charismatic churches and about one-fifth of those black churches affiliated with non-Pentecostal denominations. Nonetheless, although the gift of tongues is diffused throughout the remaining religious categories, including other Christian traditions (e.g., the Eastern Orthodox), the gift is less commonly found there. Within these remaining categories, Catholics have the highest percentage of tongues-speakers (9.0 percent), followed by evangelical Protestants (6.6 percent) and mainline Protestants (5.9 percent).

Consequently, although fewer than 9 percent of Americans claim to speak in tongues, table 2 reveals that those with ties to four particular religious groups claim the gift of tongues at far higher rates: nondenominational charismatics, white and black Pentecostals, and black Protestants. Members of the three largest religious traditions in the United States—evangelical and mainline Protestants and Roman Catholics—claim to speak in tongues in proportions that hover around the national average of 9 percent, whereas adherents to other religious traditions rarely, if ever, claim to speak in tongues.

Turning to self-identification, we note that approximately 67 percent of those in white Pentecostal denominations classify themselves as Pentecostals, but only 12 percent identify themselves as charismatics, and another 8 percent claim both. Thus, among those in white Pentecostal congregations, nearly all (87.2 percent) use either a Pentecostal or charismatic label or both. In contrast, those in black Pentecostal denominations are less likely to do so, for a bare majority of 50.9 percent label themselves as Pentecostals, and another 7 percent classify themselves as charismatics. None, however, expresses a religious identity that incorporates both a Pentecostal and a charismatic identity. As a result, less than three-fifths in black Pentecostal denominations classify themselves as either Pentecostals or charismatic Christians.

Not surprisingly, those respondents affiliated with nondenominational "charismatic" churches frequently express a religious identification that includes a charismatic identity (54.7 percent), although some express a Pentecostal identity (15.3 percent). Even among those affiliated with these nondenominational churches, however, relatively few (10.7 percent) choose both charismatic and Pentecostal.

No other religious category reveals any sizable percentage of members who self-identify as Pentecostals or as charismatics, except that a significant portion (around 20 percent) of those with ties to non-Pentecostal black churches did so. Together, self-identified Pentecostals and charismatics constitute about 12 percent of the Roman Catholic respondents and about 9 percent of those with ties to mainline denominations. Finally, given that Pentecostal denominations and nondenominational churches have been removed from the evangelical tradition to which they belong as a result of separating Pentecostal denominations and nondenominational charismatic churches from other evangelical denominations, it is not surprising that only about 10 percent of those remaining evangelicals adopted either label.

Thus the religious bases for adopting the Pentecostal and charismatic labels are different. First, outside the historic Pentecostal denominations, *charismatic* is much more likely to be adopted than *Pentecostal*. The only exception is found within non-Pentecostal black churches, where approximately equal numbers expressed the two identities. Second, and probably more surprising, relatively few respondents expressed religious identities incorporating both the Pentecostal and charismatic labels. Of the 487 respondents claiming either a Pentecostal or charismatic religious identity, only 34 respondents (7 percent) chose both. Thus a fairly "high wall" of separation exists between Pentecostal and charismatic self-identifiers. Not only do the bases for those who adopt the Pentecostal label differ from those of the individuals who adopt the charismatic label, but relatively few respondents adopt self-identifications that combine the two.

Whether this failure to couple the two identities results from the use of different religious discourse within differing religious contexts or reflects some deeper social and psychological distance is not clear. Nevertheless, three decades after the emergence of the charismatic renewal movement,[12] the psychological linkages between the two groups still have not been deeply forged. Few charismatics and Pentecostals identify with their religious "counterparts" today.

Comparing responses to the first measures in table 2, we find that self-identification is more widespread among white and black Pentecostals and nondenominational charismatics than is speaking in tongues. Likewise, the percentage of self-identification among these groups is significantly higher than the 12 percent figure for the nation as a whole (see table 1). The greater frequency of the self-identification measure suggests that it may be a better indicator of membership in the spirit-filled movement than is glossolalia.

Finally, table 2 also analyzes feelings of proximity toward Pentecostals and charismatics expressed by respondents while controlling for religious affiliation. Not surprisingly, those in white and black Pentecostal denominations and those in nondenominational charismatic churches were the most likely to feel close to Pentecostals and charismatics. Approximately 80 percent from white Pentecostal denominations expressed close proximity toward Pentecostals or charismatics, whereas about 60 percent of those in black Pentecostal churches and 74 percent of those in nondenominational charismatic churches did so. Probably more revealing, however, is that many white and black Pentecostals reported that they felt far from charismatics (approximately one-quarter for each).[13] Obviously, the psychological distance between Pentecostals and charismatics is still great for many American Pentecostals.

Relatively few Americans from the remaining religious categories expressed feelings of closeness toward either Pentecostals or charismatics. Slightly fewer than 25 percent of those in non-Pentecostal black Protestant churches felt close to one or both groups, as did slightly fewer than 20 percent of evangelical Protestants and fewer than 10 percent of mainline Protestants and Catholics. In fact, sizable percentages of all these groups felt far from Pentecostals and charismatics. For example, in non-Pentecostal black churches, more than one-quarter (26.8 percent) felt far from both Pentecostals and charismatics. Even among evangelical Protestants, nearly one-third (29.3 percent) expressed psychological distance, not many fewer than the third of mainline Protestants and Catholics who felt the same way.

The "proximity" results also reveal that closeness to Pentecostals and charismatics is not any more extensive than is self-identification with the spirit-filled movement. Only among evangelical Protestants is closeness to the movement significantly higher than self-identification. This suggests that the greatest short-range growth potential for the spirit-filled movement is likely to come from those within evangelical Protestant denominations. Still, even among evangelical Protestants, distance from the movement is greater than proximity to it.

In sum, the results of table 2 reveal that the spirit-filled movement has made some inroads among those affiliated within non-Pentecostal black Protestant churches but less so among evangelical and mainline Protestants and Roman Catholics. The potential for further growth, however, appears most favorable among evangelical Protestants, where proximity to Pentecostals and charismatics is greatest of the three major religious traditions. Finally, the results of table 2 demonstrate the difficulty of deciding on the core dimensions of the spirit-filled movement. Clearly religious affiliations alone are not sufficient; neither is the tongues measure. The self-identification measure seems more promising. Still, no one approach seems adequate by itself. Consequently, we turn our attention to an effort that combines these different measures to better answer questions concerning the size and location of the spirit-filled movement in American society today.

Charismatic Clusters

The various measures analyzed previously were combined to cluster together respondents on the basis of the number of charismatic markers they exhibited.[14] As the four component measures (religious tradition, tongues, self-identifications, and proximities) do not overlap perfectly, this cluster approach broadens the base of these charismatic movements by incorporating into their ranks individuals who exhibit one or more of the four characteristics.

Table 3 analyzes the diffusion of Pentecostals and charismatics within American religious life when these various defining measures are clustered. Several conclusions can be drawn from the table. First, combining the "charismatic markers" increases the estimated size of the spirit-filled movement. Using this composite approach, Pentecostals and charismatics constitute 23 percent of the American public, nearly double the percentage obtained through self-identification alone (12.1 percent).

Second, most Pentecostals and charismatics seem loosely tied to the spirit-filled movement, as slightly fewer than one-half (47.1 percent) of all Pentecostals and charismatics exhibit all charismatic markers. The number of those with high charismatic scores exceeds the number in the medium category only within white and black Pentecostal denominations, in nondenominational charismatic churches, and in black Protestant churches. Thus, should the ranks of Pentecostals and charismatics be limited only to those who exhibit full charismatic markers, then the size of these movements would diminish considerably—to 10.2 percent of the total population.

Third, no one group of Pentecostals or charismatics within these traditions dominates the contemporary spirit-filled movement. As can be seen in the third column of the table, charismatics in evangelical denominations constitute a plurality of spirit-filled believers today (25.8 percent), with charismatic Catholics trailing close behind (22.1 percent). Historic Pentecostals (i.e., those within Pentecostal denominations) constitute a combined 15.5 percent of the larger movement. As a result, although the spirit-filled movement is wide in scope, it has no particular center or core.

Fourth, the charismatic renewal movement has not made the same inroads among mainline Protestants as it has among Roman Catholics. As the last column in table 3 reveals, the number who exhibit charismatic characteristics is lower among mainline Protestants (17.3 percent) than that for Roman Catholics (21.9 percent), which in turn is lower than the numbers for evangelical Protestants (27.3 percent) or black Protestants (38.8 percent). When one couples this relatively low percentage of those with charismatic traits among mainline Protestants with that tradition's small percentage of the total sample (16.8 percent), it follows that mainliners constitute a much smaller portion of the total charismatic subsample (12.7 percent) than do charismatic Catholics (22.1 percent).

Table 3. Pentecostal and Charismatic Groups in the Mass Public

	Number	Percentage of Total Sample (N = 4001)	Percentage of Charismatic Subsample (N = 917)	Percentage of Religious Tradition That Is Charismatic
White Pentecostal				
All markers	68	1.1	7.4	
Some markers	20	0.8	2.2	
Few markers[a]	12	0.6	1.3	
		2.5	10.9	100.0
Black Pentecostal				
All markers	19	0.5	2.1	
Some markers	9	0.2	1.0	
Few markers[a]	14	0.4	1.5	
		1.1	4.6	100.0
Nondenominational charismatic				
All markers	37	0.9	4.0	
Some markers	16	0.4	1.7	
Few markers[a]	3	0.1	0.3	
		1.4	6.0	100.0
Other evangelical				
Most markers	90	2.3	9.8	
Some markers	147	3.7	16.0	
Nonmember	631	15.8	—	
		21.8	25.8	27.3
Mainline				
Most markers	55	1.4	6.0	
Some markers	61	1.5	6.7	
Nonmember	554	13.9	—	
		16.8	12.7	17.3
Black Protestant				
Most markers	57	1.4	6.2	
Some markers	49	1.2	5.3	
Nonmember	167	4.2	—	
		6.8	11.5	38.8

Table 3. (cont.)

Roman Catholic				
Most markers	88	2.2	9.6	
Some markers	115	2.9	12.5	
Nonmember	725	18.1	—	
		23.2	22.1	21.9
Other traditions				
Most markers	9	0.2	1.0	
Some markers	15	0.4	1.6	
Nonmember	250	6.3	—	
		6.9	2.6	8.8
Secular				
Most markers	9	0.2	1.0	
Some markers	24	0.6	2.6	
Nonmember	749	18.7	—	
		19.5	3.6	4.2

a. Denominational affiliation but few, if any, charismatic markers.

Finally, table 3 suggests that Pentecostals and charismatics, if anything, are arranged in a "tripolar" fashion. Charismatics within evangelical denominations (25.8 percent), charismatics within the Catholic church (22.1 percent), and Pentecostals within the historic white and black Pentecostal denominations (15.5 percent combined) contribute most to the ranks of the Pentecostal-charismatic movement. Historically, of course, Pentecostals and evangelicals have exhibited fairly strong anti-Catholicism, based on theological, liturgical, and possibly nativist reasons.[15] At a minimum, such hostility is likely to contribute both to potential misunderstandings between these segments of the larger movement and to the creation of distinct social and religious structures within different religious traditions. Consequently the diffusion of charismatics across religious traditions is likely to perpetuate strains between the various charismatic movements and provide obstacles to cooperation—at least in any organized religious or political sense.

Religious Characteristics

What difference does it make religiously whether some individuals exhibit fuller charismatic traits than do others? Given that religious beliefs and commitment among individuals vary by denominational families, one would anticipate that they will also vary by location within different religious traditions. Therefore, we anticipate that those who are more fully charismatic (i.e., with higher charismatic scores) in each tradition will be more theologically "orthodox" and religiously committed than those with lower scores.

Table 4 reveals clearly that those with differing charismatic traits within the same religious tradition differ religiously as well, regardless of their particular religious affiliation. First, the most fully charismatic are the most religiously "orthodox," regardless of religious affiliation. For example, within each affiliation category, high scorers were more likely than those with lower scores to agree strongly that "miracles still occur today," that "life after death is gained only through personal faith in Jesus Christ," and that "Adam and Eve were real people." In all but one of the twenty-one comparisons (seven traditions against three questions), this pattern is evident as one moves from those who are fully charismatic to those who are less so (responses to the Adam and Eve question by mainline Protestants were the only exception).

Yet religious affiliation also influences these responses. Consider, for example, the percentage of those who believe that life after death is gained only through faith in Jesus Christ. Among white Pentecostals with *low* charismatic scores, 74 percent expressed belief in salvation through such faith. However, this percentage still exceeded the percentage expressed by those who exhibited *high* charismatic scores among mainline Protestants (71 percent) or Roman Catholics (58 percent). Thus, not only do degrees of being charismatic shape religious responses regardless of affiliation, but the religious affiliation of Pentecostals and charismatics shapes their responses as well.

These same general patterns are evident on claims that the Bible is literally true, that one is born again, or that social problems would disappear if enough people were brought to Jesus Christ. Once again, within each affiliation category, a declining percentage of respondents tend to make such claims as one moves from high scorers to those with lower scores.

Finally, table 4 reveals that those with different charismatic scores vary in religious commitment.[16] Regardless of their religious tradition, those with higher scores exhibited stronger religious commitment. Nevertheless, religious commitment is also shaped by religious tradition. Thus, both charismatic tendencies and religious tradition help to shape the respondent's religious commitment.

Several implications flow from these findings. First, although charismatic movements (as human endeavors) may be vehicles by which spiritual renewal occurs, important restraints exist on renewal within particular denominations or religious traditions. Certainly, from a theological perspective, renewal may occur through the working of the Holy Spirit. But the charismatic renewal and "third wave" movements (to the extent that they reflect simply human endeavors) are unlikely to succeed in their quest for general, uniform, spiritual renewal within American Christendom. The religious traditions through which

Table 4. Religious Beliefs and Religious Commitment by Charismatic Scores Controlling for Religious Tradition

	MIRCLE	LIFEAF	ADAMEV	BIBLE	BORNAG	SOCILL	RELCOM
White Pentecostal							
All markers	76%	91%	82%	72%	89%	55%	50%
Some markers	58	87	78	75	88	45	44
Few markers[a]	38	74	71	57	46	27	8
Black Pentecostal							
All markers	83	93	83	77	91	69	35
Some markers	40	57	74	57	84	53	24
Few markers[a]	10	43	29	0	52	20	19
Nondenominational							
All markers	82	96	90	73	89	51	64
Some markers	60	65	66	38	60	25	26
Few markers[a]	—	—	—	—	—	—	—
Other evangelical							
Most markers	69	92	78	69	87	48	49
Some markers	45	82	67	48	63	38	35
Nonmember	41	67	62	45	58	31	24
Mainline							
All markers	55	71	57	32	59	39	34
Some markers	52	60	58	35	60	30	26
Nonmember	31	48	35	14	26	19	14
Black Protestant							
All markers	66	83	82	60	85	51	46
Some markers	52	82	71	45	70	48	41
Nonmember	47	64	67	42	63	50	32
Roman Catholic							
All markers	50	58	49	23	28	24	25
Some markers	36	49	46	22	22	25	23
Nonmember	31	37	34	11	7	17	16

Key: MIRCLE = strongly agree that miracles still occur today; LIFEAF = agree that life after death is gained only through personal faith in Jesus Christ; ADAMEV = strongly agree that Adam and Eve were real people; BIBLE = agree that the Bible is literally true; BORNAG = claim to be "born again"; SOCILL = strongly agree that social ills would disappear if enough people were brought to believe in Jesus Christ; RELCOM = score high in religious commitment.

a. Denominational affiliation but few, if any, charismatic markers.

the charismatic movements flow provide a context for those touched by the movements. Thus, for example, although the charismatic renewal movement may lead to spiritual revitalization within the Roman Catholic church, any such renewal would have a distinctively Catholic flavor. Moreover, whereas the Pentecostal movement has emphasized discontinuity with the past, given the radical outpouring of the Holy Spirit in these "latter days," the choice of the word *renewal* by charismatics "implies essential links with the past and suggests a vision of historical continuity."[17] Thus, renewal movements—that is, movements that seek to make something old new again—generally seek to reappropriate their particular roots and traditions. Consequently, it would not be surprising if the Catholic renewal movement were to become more "Catholic" than "ecumenical."

Second, although unity within the spirit-filled movement may not necessarily require unity in all theological matters, the lack of a theological core nevertheless serves as an important obstacle to unity. Strains in the relationship between the Protestant and Catholic wings of the spirit-filled movement are particularly evident. Charismatic Catholics report that some Pentecostals and charismatic Protestants doubt that anyone who has received the second baptism of the Holy Spirit either would or could remain a Roman Catholic, whereas some Pentecostals and charismatic Protestants report that charismatic Catholics are interested in unity only in the sense of "us returning to the mother church."[18] Likewise, Pentecostals have been shocked to find that some charismatic Catholics claim "their baptism in the Spirit deepened their experience of the rosary and the Mass, and increased their devotion to Mary and the church."[19] Should any renewed emphasis on Mary become fairly widespread within the Catholic charismatic renewal movement, it would further erode the relationship between charismatic Protestants and Catholics.

The absence of a distinctive unifying theology erodes charismatic unity in other ways. In recent years charismatic Catholics have split among themselves over theological matters related to pastoral strategies, leadership styles, views of the end times, and views on women in leadership.[20] Obviously such theological differences among charismatics further mitigate any potential ecumenical endeavors to bridge differences between and foster good will among Pentecostals and charismatics in different religious traditions.

Finally, the "success" of the charismatic and "third wave" movements as vehicles for spiritual renewal is largely based on the assumption that charismatic Catholics, mainliners, and evangelicals will remain in their churches. However, although the charismatic renewal movement appeared to be successful in retaining "renewed" Catholics within the Catholic church during the late 1960s and 1970s, many such Catholics apparently began to defect to Protestant churches beginning in the late 1970s.[21] Obviously such religious switching militates against the charismatic renewal movement's serving as a vehicle for spiritual renewal—at least in the religious tradition that the switchers abandon.

Conclusions

Several conclusions can be drawn from our analysis. First, determining the size of the spirit-filled movement is not an easy task. The estimates vary by the measure employed to identify its members. Substantially different conclusions result from using measures of denominational affiliation, speaking in tongues, doctrinal stands, and religious self-identifications because of the relatively low overlap of these different variables. Speaking in tongues is not confined to particular denominations; many of those who identify themselves as Pentecostals or charismatics do not report the gift of tongues; and not all who speak in tongues necessarily identify themselves as Pentecostal or charismatic.

Second, we see that some important barriers exist for Pentecostals and charismatics hoping to make further inroads within American religious life. In particular, there are many more Americans who feel distant from Pentecostals and charismatics than there are those who feel close to them. Just how strong a barrier this constitutes is less clear; it is hard to tell whether distance reflects "distaste for" or "little contact with." Nonetheless, such feelings of distance from Pentecostals and charismatics are widely expressed by the American people.

Third, we have found just how different Pentecostals and charismatics are theologically. Although the absence of any theological core has probably helped the spirit-filled movement to penetrate almost all, if not all, of the different religious traditions, families, and denominations found within American society, it has at the same time hindered a high level of cohesion. What it means theologically to be a Pentecostal or charismatic varies considerably by the denominational affiliation of those who exhibit charismatic markers. Finally, because the spirit-filled movement can be absorbed by varying theological traditions and permeates vastly different segments of society, the movement's future is not likely to be confined to particular segments of American society or to particular religious traditions. Such a situation creates a context in which the potential for further growth is much greater than would exist were the movement largely confined to a much narrower theological or social base. However, this important "strength" of the spirit-filled movement is also its greatest weakness. Although the riverbed within which the charismatic currents flow is wide, it is relatively shallow. Consequently, unity within the movement is not likely to be easily achieved and must be carefully nurtured, given the tremendous diversity evident.

Appendix: Denominational Classification

White Pentecostal
Assemblies of God (N = 65)
Church of God–Cleveland, Tennessee (N = 7)
Church of God, Huntsville, Alabama (N = 7)

Church of God of Prophecy (N = 1)
Four-Square Gospel (N = 5)
Pentecostal Church of God (N = 6)
Pentecostal Holiness (N = 2)
Sectarian Pentecostal (N = 3)
Pentecostal-NFS (N = 5)

Black Pentecostal
Church of God in Christ (N = 26)
Church of God Apostolic (N = 1)
Black Pentecostal (N = 15)

Evangelical
Church of God–Seventh Day (N = 1)
Seventh-Day Adventist (N = 14)
American Baptist Association (N = 3)
American Baptist (N = 51)
Baptist General Conference (N = 3)
Baptist Missional Association (N = 19)
Conservative Baptist Association (N = 4)
Freewill Baptist (N = 6)
Regular Baptist (N = 4)
General Baptist (N = 3)
Baptist Conference-NFS (N = 3)
Primitive Baptist (N = 1)
Southern Baptist (N = 225)
Sectarian Baptist (N = 97)
General Baptist-NFS (N = 11)
Brethren in Christ (N = 1)
Brethren (N = 6)
Grace Brethren (N = 2)
Christian Church (N = 17)
Church of Christ (N = 51)
Conservative Congregational (N = 4)
Evangelical Congregational (N = 1)
Reformed Episcopal (N = 2)
Sectarian Episcopal (N = 6)
Evangelical Convenant (N = 1)
Evangelical Free (N = 5)
Moravian (N = 1)
Evangelical Friends (N = 1)
Sectarian Friends (N = 2)
Independent Fundamentalist (N = 1)
Plymouth Brethren (N = 2)
Fundamentalist-NFS (N = 2)
Christian Missionary Alliance (N = 2)
Church of God–Anderson, Ind. (N = 5)

Church of God Holiness (*N* = 5)
Nazarene (*N* = 16)
Free Methodist (*N* = 16)
Salvation Army (*N* = 2)
Wesleyan (*N* = 2)
Sectarian Holiness (*N* = 3)
General Holiness (*N* = 1)
Free Lutheran (*N* = 1)
Lutheran Brethren (*N* = 2)
Lutheran–Missouri Synod (*N* = 60)
Lutheran–Wisconsin Synod (*N* = 6)
Sectarian Lutheran (*N* = 7)
General Conference of Mennonite Churches (*N* = 1)
Mennonite Church (*N* = 2)
Sectarian Mennonite (*N* = 3)
Cumberland Presbyterian (*N* = 5)
Orthodox Presbyterian (*N* = 5)
Presbyterian Church in America (*N* = 39)
Reformed Presbyterian (*N* = 2)
United Presbyterian (*N* = 3)
Sectarian Presbyterian (*N* = 7)
Christian Reformed Church (*N* = 5)

Mainline
Disciples of Christ (*N* = 14)
United Church of Christ (*N* = 33)
General Congregational-NFS (*N* = 4)
Episcopal (*N* = 73)
General Episcopal-NFS (*N* = 3)
Society of Friends (*N* = 3)
General Friends-NFS (*N* = 2)
Evangelical Lutheran Church of America (*N* = 124)
Lutheran-NFS (*N* = 3)
United Methodist (*N* = 296)
Methodist-NFS (*N* = 9)
Presbyterian Church–USA (*N* = 57)
Presbyterian-NFS (*N* = 6)
Reformed Church in America (*N* = 8)

Black
Independent Black Baptist (*N* = 118)
National Baptist (*N* = 84)
Progressive Baptist (*N* = 15)
Black Holiness (*N* = 13)
African Methodist Episcopal (*N* = 13)
African Methodist Episcopal of Zion (*N* = 4)
Christian Methodist Episcopal (*N* = 1)

Notes

1. How to view this "third wave" is a matter of some dispute. In this essay, *third wave movement* will be used to designate the presence of the charismatic movement, whatever its form (e.g., tongues, worship style, or theology), within evangelical Protestant denominations and nondenominational churches.

2. Grant Wacker, "Playing for Keeps: The Primitive Impulse in Early Pentecostalism," in *The American Quest for the Primitive Church,* ed. Richard Hughes (Urbana: University of Illinois Press, 1988), 208; Robert Mapes Anderson, *Vision of the Disinherited: The Making of American Pentecostalism* (New York: Oxford University Press, 1979), 236.

3. John Thomas Nichol, *Pentecostalism* (New York: Harper and Row, 1966).

4. See, for example, Martin E. Marty, *A Nation of Behavers* (Chicago: University of Chicago Press, 1976), 106–25.

5. Charles Farah, "Differences within the Family," *Christianity Today* 31, no. 15 (1987): 25.

6. The Reverend Thomas Trask, the newly elected leader of the Assemblies of God, cited a report at a meeting of the Assemblies of God General Council stating that nearly 50 percent of the church's laity may not have received the infilling of the Holy Spirit. "We may be Pentecostal in doctrine, but not in experience," he said. See *National and International Religion Report* 7, no. 18 (23 Aug. 1993), 1.

7. Donald W. Dayton, "The Limit of Evangelicalism: The Pentecostal Tradition," in *The Variety of American Evangelicalism,* ed. Donald W. Dayton and Robert K. Johnson (Downers Grove, Ill.: InterVarsity, 1991), 37.

8. Margaret M. Poloma, "Pentecostals and Politics in North and Central America," in *Prophetic Religions and Politics,* ed. Jeffrey K. Hadden and Anson Shupe (New York: Paragon, 1986), 330.

9. This study was conducted by the Survey Research Center of the University of Akron and was funded, in part, by a grant from the Pew Charitable Trusts. The authors wish to thank the Pew Charitable Trusts for their help in making this study possible.

10. The particular denominations that constitute these broader religious categories and the number of respondents within each of denomination are presented in appendix A.

11. Farah, "Differences within the Family," 25.

12. The contemporary charismatic renewal movement can be traced, in large part, to 3 Apr. 1960, when Dennis Bennett, an Episcopal priest in California, announced that he had been baptized by the Holy Spirit.

13. The proximity percentages reported in table 2 do not add up to 100 percent in each column because the table reports percentages for both Pentecostals and charismatics simultaneously and because it does not include the percentage of respondents within each denominational category who report that they feel neutral toward the particular group (e.g., Pentecostals).

14. Variables were entered into the cluster analysis on the basis of their discriminatory capacity, with religious tradition being entered first, tongues second, and then proximities and identifications. Generally speaking, high scores in each religious tra-

dition include not only individuals who scored high on the tongues, proximities, and identifications measures but also individuals who scored highest on one variable and more modestly on the others.

15. Analysis of proximity scores toward Roman Catholics on the part of members of white Pentecostal denominations and other evangelical Protestant denominations reveal that these feelings of distance continue to be evident today. Among white Pentecostals as a whole, only 7 percent reported feeling close to Catholics, whereas 62 percent reported feeling far from Catholics. The comparable percentages among evangelical respondents were 11 percent and 46 percent, respectively. For further analysis of anti-Catholicism evident among evangelicals, see Lyman Kellstedt, "The Falwell Issue Core," in *Research in the Social Scientific Study of Religion: A Research Annual,* vol.1, ed. Monty Lynn and David Moberg (Greenwich, Conn.: JAI Press, 1989).

16. The respondents' level of religious commitment was obtained through the creation of an index derived from the various items. Those with high religious commitment scores met the following criteria: they expressed a religious preference, believed in life after death, prayed daily, attended church at least weekly, and stated that religion provides "a great deal of guidance."

17. Peter Hocken, "The Pentecostal-Charismatic Movement as Revival and Renewal," *Pneuma* 3 (Spring 1981): 41.

18. Julia Duin, "Catholics on the Pentecostal Trail," *Christianity Today* 36 (22 June 1992): 26.

19. Julia Duin, "Signs and Wonders in New Orleans," *Christianity Today* 30 (21 Nov. 1986): 26.

20. See, for example, "Who Are the Catholic Charismatics?" *Christianity Today* 31 (4 Sept. 1987): 47–49.

21. Duin, "Catholics on the Pentecostal Trail," 25–26.

7

A "Network of Praying Women": Women's Aglow Fellowship and Mainline American Protestantism

R. Marie Griffith

On a bitterly cold Saturday afternoon, a suburban New England hotel is filled to overflowing with women attending the 1994 Women's Aglow Fellowship regional retreat. During a break between four-hour worship services, down the corridor from the special "prayer room" complete with mechanized waterfall and plastic greenery, about half of the five hundred participants have gathered for a two-hour workshop called "Alone in the Pew," addressing anxieties over husbands who refuse to attend church with their wives. Eleanor Jacobs,[1] the workshop coordinator, begins the session by asking how many of those present attend church alone; nearly all the women in the room raise their hands and smile sympathetically at one another. Eleanor informs her audience that she too has been "unequally yoked" for the fourteen years that she has been married to her non-Christian husband and that it took ten of those years for her to learn to deal with this problem. Just over a year ago, she continues, "God spoke to me in the shower, said to me, 'Alone in the Pew,' and dropped this workshop in my lap." Although her husband and sons sometimes call her a "big wacko" because of her faith, Eleanor says, she keeps on praying for them and knows that the members of her family are slowly "coming into the kingdom," according to God's well-timed plan.

Over the next hour Eleanor teaches her listeners how to live with their common dilemma. "Give up your husband as your problem," she tells them; "begin to praise God for your husband," and "learn to submit to your husband, according to Ephesians 5:21."[2] She adds, "Go back and remember what made you fall in love with him," and she urges the women to retain hope in their marriages, because "if a woman loses hope in the marriage, you might as well count it gone; but if a man loses hope and a woman still has hope, it can be saved!" It becomes clear that what was advertised as a workshop for dealing with irreligious husbands is actually a session on coping with unhappy or even unbearable marriages and turning them into loving, affectionate, or at least endurable ones.

Even while dispensing advice on marital enrichment, Eleanor assures the women that if they have become the object of mockery and scorn in their own homes, God is their deliverer and rescuer. She chastises them for their own role in creating discord and notes: "Sometimes, despite what the churches teach, you need to stay home on Sunday mornings and lie in bed with your husband! . . . Or stay home from a special [religious] service on Friday night and cook him dinner." After giving tips on how to make husbands happy, including explicit instructions on "tradeoffs" within sexual relations, Eleanor concludes with a tearful prayer of repentance, inviting the women to pray with her for the ability to yield fully to God and their husbands, to stop blaming their husbands for personal failings, and to be cleansed from all sin within the bonds of marriage. Murmurs of assent fill the room, and the women spend the next hour praying with Eleanor and with each other, embracing and often weeping, as they seek redemptive love and solace from fellow strugglers and from the one directly addressed in prayer.[3]

The women who attended this workshop and the weekend retreat of which it was part come from a range of social, racial, and religious backgrounds, but they share a common affiliation with Women's Aglow Fellowship. Aglow was founded in 1967 as the Full Gospel Women's Fellowship, incorporating as Women's Aglow Fellowship International in 1972. The organization describes its origins in four women who gathered to pray for an interdenominational fellowship of charismatic Christian women, an organization "where those coming into the charismatic renewal could meet to pray, fellowship, and listen to the testimonies of other Christian women."[4] The first meeting was held on a Saturday morning at a hotel in the women's hometown of Seattle, Washington, and was attended by approximately 125 women. The organizers had chosen that particular hotel for its proximity to several metropolitan churches, in the hopes of drawing many mainline Protestant women to their meeting, and their plan apparently worked.[5] Monthly meetings followed, and several chapters formed throughout the Seattle area, with the group spreading rapidly across North America and much of the world. By September 1993 Aglow claimed a membership of 19,717 women in the United States and thousands more throughout the world, from Pentecostal, Roman Catholic, Eastern Orthodox, and mainline Protestant affiliations.[6]

For nearly thirty years, monthly Aglow meetings—as well as weekly Bible studies, frequent special events and weekend retreats, and annual national and international conferences—have occasioned encounters between Pentecostals of the "classical" kind and charismatics in the mainline churches. The effects of this intermingling, both on the women who participate in Aglow and on the churches with which the women are affiliated, have been complex and far-reaching, resulting in growing numbers of defections from the mainline to more conservative churches as the charismatic movement itself has become increasingly affiliated with the so-called religious right. Yet even as Aglow has participated in and contributed to the rise of the conservative Christian right in the United States and the continued decline of mainline liberal Protestantism, the organization has helped to foster and extend women's leadership roles amid the uneasy suspicions of conservative men and has in this and other ways helped to diversify gender roles within conservative Christianity more broadly.[7] The oversimplified association of the charismatic movement with what is generally termed "antifeminism" has encouraged scholars, feminist and otherwise, to overlook the dynamics of conservative women's groups such as Aglow, as well as to submit too easily to historians' functionalist interpretation of the charismatic movement as a fearful reaction against the "confusing moral relativism" of the 1960s and the fragmentation and anxiety of the modern world.[8]

Once women's participation within the charismatic movement is closely analyzed, however, the story of the charismatic movement and its relation to mainline American Protestantism becomes a more interesting and complex one, reflecting progressive and reformist impulses rather more incisive and forward-looking than a purely reactionary response to modernity. The revised story might begin in the 1950s and 1960s, a period when the charismatic movement was led almost entirely by men and its major organization, the Full Gospel Business Men's Fellowship, was directed solely toward evangelizing professional men and funding the crusades of popular revivalists. Because church pews were filled by more women than men, there seemed little need for a separate all-women's charismatic organization. However, conservative Christian women, most of them housewives, were talking to each other about feelings not unlike the sense of frustration and worthlessness—"the problem with no name"—described by Betty Friedan in *The Feminine Mystique* (1963) and echoed by vast numbers of women who joined the feminist movement.

Demands pertaining to rapidly changing gender roles and familial arrangements brought charismatic Christian women together, not in feminist consciousness-raising groups, but in small prayer groups such as those furnished by Women's Aglow Fellowship, groups wherein meanings around Christian womanhood were reshaped, reinforced, and transmitted through narrative practices, such as testimony and prayer, performed in all-female settings. Here women shared anxieties about their family lives; distributed advice, love, and solace; and gradually drifted away from the mainline Protestant churches to which most of them originally belonged, denouncing these for allegedly accommodating too easily to the ways of the world and labeling them "spiritually dead."[9] Initially friendly to the mainline denominations, Women's Aglow Fellowship began moving participants away from these and into more conservative churches, often newly formed charismatic churches such as the Vineyard Christian Fellowship and various independent congregations.[10] Although more theologically conservative and generally less friendly to women holding positions of official leadership, such churches were also places wherein public testimony, prophecy, and prayer were strongly encouraged, thus opening spaces for women to speak their stories publicly and feel them validated by the community.

To explore Aglow's complicated relation to the mainline churches, I start by examining how Women's Aglow Fellowship emerged in 1967, describing briefly the two most significant influences on its formation: the Full Gospel Business Men's Fellowship and Dennis Bennett's ministry at St. Luke's Church in Seattle. Following the story of Aglow's formation, I analyze specific narrative practices, particularly prayers that were printed in various Aglow magazines (published from 1969 until 1991), so as to highlight the ways in which Aglow women have described and prayed for the healing of fragile or broken familial relationships. Next I discuss the varied meanings pertaining to gender that have been articulated and transmitted among Aglow participants over the past twenty-five years, examining shifts as well as continuities in meanings around "Christian womanhood" over time and the ways in which such shifts embody a reformist, if not feminist, impulse among the broader sector of American charismatic/evangelical women.

My conclusion returns to Aglow's ever ambivalent relationship to mainline American Protestantism. A particular irony is evident here, in that Aglow leaders have officially encouraged women to remain within their churches (usually Protestant) even as Aglow has furnished a space for criticizing and sometimes opposing mainline pastors and denominations, influencing many women to weaken ties to their home churches and others to abandon them altogether. From one angle, the women who are drawn to Aglow describe their lives in narratives that conservative charismatic churches more than mainline ones readily accept, for the charismatic atmosphere allows them to voice and share certain felt needs (primarily domestic) in ways that they believe the mainline churches do not accommodate. From another angle, Aglow attracts female seekers who for various reasons yearn for a new narrative with which to make sense of their lives and who, finding such a coherent narrative within Aglow, are then readily transformed into conservative charismatic Christians. In any case, the largely mainline origins of Women's Aglow Fellowship have long given way to the organization's affiliations with the new religious right in the United States, as Aglow women have joined other conservatives in denouncing the perceived hypocrisy and aridity of the mainline denominations. In this and other ways that this essay will illuminate, Aglow mirrors broader social, religious, and cultural currents within the charismatic subculture in contemporary America.

The Charismatic Movement and the Emergence of Women's Aglow

In the year that Aglow emerged, 1967, the charismatic or "neo-Pentecostal" movement in mainline American churches was less than twenty years old and was still receiving mixed reviews from clergy and lay people, as well as from nonreligious observers. One of the most important Pentecostal organizations had emerged during the 1950s under the leadership of Demos Shakarian, a wealthy Armenian-born dairy farmer in California, with strong support from Oral Roberts. Having observed that at most revival meetings women outnumbered men by what appeared to be a margin of ten to one, Shakarian had lamented what he described as "a resistance of men to religion," most particularly among successful businessmen, and he organized the first Full Gospel Business Men's Fellowship meeting at a Los Angeles cafeteria in October 1951.[11] More meetings followed, often held in fine hotels, and increasingly attracted men from mainline Protestant churches who might never have attended an Oral Roberts revival.[12] The fellowship's magazine, *Full Gospel Voice,* began publication in 1953, and by 1972 the organization claimed 300,000 members and an annual operating budget of over $1,000,000.[13] What had begun as an organization of businessmen from Pentecostal churches had quickly expanded into the mainline, reaching successful middle-class non-Pentecostal men as well.[14] For many men the fellowship was a point of entry into the charismatic movement and the beginning of a new or revitalized religious life.

The Full Gospel Business Men's Fellowship was the most important parachurch organization to give some order to the charismatic revival during the 1950s and 1960s, continuing to fund independent revivalists and to provide a way for many of them to circumvent ecclesiastical regulations. Within the churches, however, changes were also taking place, though on a smaller scale. The first related event to receive wide publicity involved Dennis Bennett, rector of the wealthy St. Mark's Episcopal Church in Van Nuys, California, which at the time had 2,600 parishioners. In 1959, after talking to some lay Episcopalians and a fellow priest who claimed to have been baptized in the Holy Spirit, Bennett himself underwent this experience and began studying the Bible to learn about other gifts or "charisms" as well. When he described his experiences to his parishioners, he was met with hostility and resigned from his post. He was later assigned to a dying parish in Seattle, St. Luke's, where he became a sort of folk hero and a major leader in the charismatic movement for the next thirty years.[15] Under Bennett's leadership St. Luke's grew rapidly, attracting hundreds of men and women from various denominations who wished to receive the baptism in the Holy Spirit and participate in the charismatic renewal movement. To Bennett and other charismatics of the 1960s, the movement had emerged from a need to revitalize the staid piety of mainline American Christianity, as well as from a desire for spiritual strength in the face of a harsh world.

It was in this context that Women's Aglow emerged, its founders all having close ties to both the Full Gospel Business Men's Fellowship and Dennis Bennett's church in Seattle. All four were wives of Full Gospel Business Men members and had participated in the "women's meetings" held at annual Full Gospel Business Men conventions, and all four frequently attended charismatic prayer meetings at St. Luke's, although only one was an official member of the parish.[16] Several Aglow publications over the years have recounted the story of Aglow's founding. The official version of the story begins with the 1967 convention of the Full Gospel Business Men's Fellowship, held in late May at a hotel in Portland, Oregon. The four Seattle-area women mentioned previously joined hands after the conclusion of the convention's final session and prayed together for a fellowship in which they and other women could meet to share testimonies about the workings of God in their lives. The first meeting featured Rita Bennett—Dennis's wife—as its main speaker and was held on a Saturday morning at a Seattle hotel chosen for its proximity to "the Baptist, Presbyterian, Lutheran, Catholic, and Congregational Churches in the [University] District."[17]

More meetings of the group, which called itself the Full Gospel Women's Fellowship, followed, and over the next two years various other chapters formed in the Seattle area. One of the original four founders of the organization later wrote: "This was not a "Bless Me Club" meeting once a month: this was a group of women whose hearts were committed to introducing other women to Christ. They faithfully invited and brought women to the meetings with the goal of seeing changed lives. They prayed for their guests, shared their own personal testimonies with them while driving to and from the Hotel and were rewarded as they witnessed God's continuing blessing on our meetings."[18] Later that year one of the chapters began meeting in a furniture store, with up to 200 women in attendance. As one participant later recalled of her first meeting (in 1968), "There was absolutely no leadership, except women who felt led to do things. There was a speaker, but the meeting was pretty spontaneous. There was such an *anointing,* and I just thought to myself, 'This is home!' "[19]

The recollections of these early leaders emphasize the organization's primary purpose as evangelism, bringing their message of salvation to women who were not already Christians and urging those who were only "nominal" Christians to experience a richer religious life through the empowerment of the Holy Spirit. Between 1967 and 1969 the women brought friends not yet baptized in the Holy Spirit to the meetings with them, in the hopes that they would perceive what they were missing of God in their lives and seek his spiritual gifts. Their favorite mode of evangelization was one deeply rooted in the evangelical tradition: giving personal testimonies. Sharing stories with one another about their own spiritual struggles was from the beginning the most central feature of the women's meetings.

As more and more women flocked to Full Gospel Women's Fellowship lunches, some of the leaders began to look for ways of implementing more structure in the organization. In October 1969 a group of women met to pray about forming a newsletter for their organization. A few of them had some experience in writing or publishing and wanted to get the testimonies into print, to be used as a mission tool for reaching other women outside their fellowships. They called their new magazine *Aglow,* from the New Testament book of Romans: "Be aglow and burning with the Spirit" (Romans 12:11, RSV). The first issue, financed by the women themselves, came out in November 1969, and according to the editors, all 7,000 copies "disappeared quickly," many of them mailed to friends and relatives around the country.[20]

The organization began to develop more of a structure in 1971, when the first board was elected and the first constitution written. In 1972 the organization was incorporated as Women's Aglow Fellowship International. Subscriptions to *Aglow* magazine reached 15,000 that same year, and the first Aglow Bible study, *Creation,* was published. During the next two years new fellowships formed in Canada, New Zealand, and the Netherlands, and the first international conference was held in October 1974 at the Seattle Center, with "up to one thousand people" in attendance from twenty-five states, the Netherlands, Mexico, Canada, and Nigeria. By that year there were 197 fellowships in existence. *Aglow* magazine had a volunteer staff of twenty women and had a substantial subscription, with over 75,000 issues "going to America, Canada and fifty foreign countries." Aglow Publications had also begun to produce books and Bible studies "designed especially for charismatic women."[21]

Three years later, in 1977, there were 800 fellowships "thriving worldwide," many of them in Europe, New Zealand, and Australia, with growing numbers in Asia and Africa as well. In the United States the organization was growing rapidly, its constituency composed predominantly of white middle-class housewives but with a growing number of African American and Hispanic women also. In 1980 Jane Hansen was elected the third international president of Aglow, an office she still held in 1998. Also in 1980 Aglow sponsored its first international conference outside North America, and more than 700 women and men convened in Jerusalem for that event. By 1987 Aglow counted 1,827 fellowships in the United States, members paying ten dollars in annual dues. At that time the organization claimed to serve "more than 500,000 women" throughout the world.[22]

In September 1993 Aglow claimed a membership of 19,717 women in the United States and thousands more throughout the world, from Pentecostal, Roman Catholic, Eastern Orthodox, and mainline Protestant affiliations.[23] By this time *Aglow* magazine had folded, and increasing cutbacks at the organization's headquarters in Seattle were cause for great concern. For an organization whose magazine alone once worked with a budget of one million dollars and had 65,000 subscribers, the prognosis seemed alarming, yet new initiatives in mission work and publications suggested a stability and longevity far greater than any other evangelical women's organization since the nineteenth century. Although some early Aglow members have expressed distress toward Aglow's trajectory during the last ten to fifteen years, the thousands of women who currently attend Aglow meetings witness to its continuing importance in many women's lives. Although Aglow by no means includes all charismatic and Pentecostal Christian women, it has been the largest and most diverse charismatic women's organization in the United States and worldwide, and its constituency in this country may be viewed as broadly representative of women in contemporary charismatic movements in twentieth-century America.[24]

The vision of the original founders was one that combined evangelization of non-Christians with revitalization of those Christians perceived as starving from spiritual hunger in the "dead" mainline churches, a vision later recalled by one woman: "We were out to structure a meeting that would bring in two groups, women who were unchurched, and women who were in Denominational churches and so had no real exposure to the baptism in the Holy Spirit."[25] Aglow leaders sought to teach other women about the gifts that God would willingly give them by "witnessing," that is, telling testimonial stories of the changes they had felt in their own lives resulting from renewed Christian commitment. They emphasized the transformative possibilities of direct communion with God in prayer, and they prayed aloud with one another in the hopes of opening the way for emotional, physical, and spiritual healing. As Aglow spread throughout North America and *Aglow* magazine grew in circulation, testimony and prayer continued to work as important narrative practices for participants, who shared with one another their everyday experiences and sought to derive sacred meaning from such experiences.

Here I want to turn to these practices, focusing particularly on accounts relating to prayer as they have been printed in *Aglow* magazines or publicly articulated at meetings, retreats, and conferences, as well as in private conversations.[26] What such prayers reveal, at least partially, is what kinds of selves these women are creating together, what kinds of religious and social identities they are constructing for themselves. Practices of prayer serve well to illuminate the process through which meanings are both communally created and individually appropriated by the women of Aglow, as they seek healing, redemption, and victory beyond church walls. Careful analysis of such practices and meanings may help to answer questions concerning the effects of Aglow membership on affiliation and participation in American mainline churches.

"We Are Winning Women!": Praying for Victory

The narratives that emerge in Aglow women's spoken and written testimonies are structured around the movement from sin and suffering to redemption and healing, a transition that is initiated through the activity of prayer. Prayer is the turning point of this journey because it is through prayer that the woman surrenders her own will and submits to the will of God, imploring him for aid. Again and again the narratives describe triumphantly the victory that is to be found in such acts of surrender and supplication. This triumphant tone may be summed up in the words of the leader of an intercessory prayer workshop, who provoked cheers from her audience when she declared, "I just want to be a prayer warrior, and I'm going to pray until I win. Because God is a winner, and we are winning women!"[27]

From the prayers spoken aloud at Aglow meetings emerge various kinds of stories that, like testimonies, are meant to have a transformative effect on both the storyteller and her listeners. These stories are echoed in accounts related among Aglow women describing the effects of prayer, accounts both spoken publicly at meetings and printed in Aglow literature. Verna, whose story was printed in the second issue of *Aglow* magazine, told of being a harsh wife and mother before she surrendered her life to God. Her story began with the day the police came to her house to say that her sixteen-year-old son Bob had been caught riding in a stolen car; she had yelled at both the police and her son. Verna used this incident to suggest how poorly she handled crises before learning to "rely on God." After attending a prayer meeting "out of curiosity," Verna wrote, her whole life changed. "I turned my whole life over to Him, all the mistakes and failures, and in return He gave me His life in the Baptism of the Holy Spirit." Verna recounted in detail the differences in her life after this key event. As she became a gentler and less demanding mother, her boys grew gentler also and even began to attend church without being nagged to do so. She explained, "In these and many other ways the Holy Spirit's new and wonderful presence in my life is gradually changing what was once a miserable household into a home of peace."

Life still has its problems, Verna noted, giving as an example the fact that only the previous week the police called again to say that Bob had been arrested for shoplifting. This time, however, she responded by praying, singing, and praising God, for she knew she had nothing to fear. "I rejoiced within my heart," she writes, explaining that she felt perfect assurance and faith. In Verna's story, prayer—both private and public—works to bring her out of an old sinful life, a life of anger and harshness, into a new life of victory and peace. Praying brings transformation, not of the circumstances in which she daily lives, but in her attitude and her ability to cope with them. Praying with a friend, surrendering "all the mistakes and failures" to God, praising and praying and singing while driving her car to pick up her delinquent son: these events bring liberation to Verna by assuring her that she has indeed been transformed from a harsh and over-critical mother to a patient, loving one.[28]

In an account published a few years later, Marianne told her own story of domestic upheaval. Her narrative described her leaving her alcoholic husband, taking her two daughters with her, and moving far away to live "a life of sin." She prayed for God to take her life, she explained, because she felt so miserable. Praying in desperation after her divorce, Marianne wrote, she received two visions from God, the first of the evil and misery she was heading toward in her life of sin and the second of a beautiful life back with her ex-husband.

Knowing her life to be forever changed from this encounter with Jesus, she went back to her husband, whose drinking problem had become worse since they'd been apart, and felt "some interesting changes" from before. "I had always thought Emory was worse than I was but after our remarriage I saw he wasn't. I could see that we were both sinners! So for the first time since we had met, I could accept him exactly as he was. I no longer tried to change him, even though his drinking problem intensified during the next year and a half."

The couple joined a church and began to pray together, seeking an answer to Emory's alcoholism. The transformation, in Marianne's view, came through realizing that she needed to make a decision to love her husband unconditionally, loving him "for free."

As she became a more loving wife, loving her husband even when she did not receive love in return, her whole life began to change. "As I yielded to be a channel of God's love toward my husband and toward others, I began to experience the thrill of warm and open relationships. How simple it was! I made myself available; Jesus did the work." Marianne's final transformation occurred after she began weeping, laughing, and speaking in tongues one evening as she was driving her car. Knowing this to be a gift from God, she made a renewed commitment to a prayerful life. "The next morning I began to pray as I brushed my teeth. 'Oh God, take my life and my will today. . . .' Just then I burst into tears as I saw a vision of Jesus on the cross, and I felt the magnitude of His love for me." Finally capable and willing to love her husband fully and freely, she concluded her story rejoicing at the changes that had occurred throughout her family since "God . . . revealed Himself" to her and she surrendered herself completely to him. Although she never told whether Emory finally stopped drinking or not, her point is clear: surrender all to God to become the loving wife he wishes you to be.[29]

These stories, like countless others told by the women of Aglow, are stories of both self-transformation and transformation of one's close familial relationships. They depict the path from corruption and crisis to victory, moving from a life full of sin and pain into a life of joy and peace. This new life begins with a prayer of surrender and is nurtured by prayer, praise, and friendship with other Christian women. For all the varieties of suffering described in these stories, victory takes a similar form: relationships are healed, anger subsides, and defiant misbehavior ceases, giving way to renewed faith, piety, and obedience. Significantly, a major theme in the narratives described here is the healing of close domestic ties, either between wife and husband or between mother and child. Like the "Alone in the Pew" workshop described earlier, these stories suggest that such hearings occur not through a change in external circumstances but through changes in oneself, a transformation that comes to pass only after a complete surrender to God.

These examples broaden the context for understanding the Aglow leader's declaration cited earlier: "I just want to be a prayer warrior, and I'm going to pray until I win. Because God is a winner, and we are winning women!" Praying together in Aglow meetings creates a sense that they are indeed "winning women," with God on their side. Such meetings provide a space within which these women are able to articulate and share the domestic crises of their daily lives in a more "open" atmosphere than they believe most churches provide. The communal aspects of praying together reinforce their faith in the power of prayer and encourage them to believe that God will answer their pleas, turning crises into victories.

What constitutes a crisis for the women of Aglow has changed somewhat over the past twenty-five years, yet the continuities remain strong. The hardships of "being a woman" and living out the roles of Christian wife, mother, daughter, and friend have been themes of Aglow narratives throughout its history. The meanings of those roles have shifted significantly, as more women have pursued professional careers and as rising divorce rates have brought more single women into Aglow. Changing social, economic, and political conditions have helped to spawn historically specific tensions over the meanings of "womanhood" and "family," resulting from ambivalent feelings of desire and fear toward broadened opportunities and heightened expectations for women. But the crises of marital dissatisfaction and rebellious children, among others, remain constant themes of Aglow women's literature and their prayers, as the women surrender together their domestic tribulations to God and pray for victory.

Helpmeets and Prayer Warriors: Reconfigurations of Gender

In 1980 Aglow president Jane Hansen heard a message from God saying, "Aglow will be a network of praying, warring, interceding women, covering the face of the earth."[30] Since that time Aglow's emphasis on spiritual warfare appears to have increased dramatically, at the same time that various "intercessory prayer groups" have been formed for the purpose of engaging in spiritual warfare throughout the world.[31] Books such as *A Woman's Guide to Spiritual Warfare: A Woman's Guide for Battle* (1991), cowritten by two women with strong ties to Aglow, argue that spiritual warfare "is of special interest to women" because of women's greater "spiritual . . . sensitivity" and "loyalty in relationships," as well as women's "unique difficulties": "single parenting, the 'Super Mom' syndrome, the influence of the media, coping with addicted children and spouses, abortion, cultural pressures of a materialistic society; the list goes on."[32] What does this emphasis on women as "prayer warriors" say about the meanings of gender in Women's Aglow?[33]

Before addressing that question, it may be helpful to turn back to the early days of Aglow, to see what meanings attached to "womanhood" at that time. In 1970 an Aglow leader, a 1959 graduate of Duke University and the wife of an Episcopal priest, published an article in *Aglow* magazine entitled "My Full Inheritance as a Woman." "Two years ago the Lord pointed out to me that it was He who created us male and female, and that He was very jealous over the differences even to the point of Deuteronomy 22:5: 'The woman shall not wear that which pertaineth unto a man, neither shall a man put on a woman's garment; for all that do so are abomination unto the Lord thy God.' He showed me that to rebel against the role that one has been given in creation is to rebel against Him."[34] That female role, she writes, is "to love through adoration, reverence, and submission," submission both to Jesus as well as to "our earthly king (our husband)."[35] To the woman who may be "having a more than normal problem as a wife submitting to and reverencing [her] husband with freedom and love," the writer advocates prayer—for healing, for protection, and for acceptance.[36] The claim here, as in similar articles on women's roles in the early years of Aglow, is that an attitude of wifely submission produces the greatest freedom and harmony possible on earth, corresponding to the divine order.

The many stories centered on the theme of "rebelliousness" in *Aglow* issues throughout the years suggest that submission is not easy and that gender relations are in fact fraught with tension and conflict. Such stories often depict gender relationships as being deformed since the original sin of Adam and Eve. The "spirit of enmity" that women ought properly to have toward Satan (Genesis 3:15–16) has been displaced, in this view, so that women's hostility is often directed toward men instead of toward the real enemy. Helen, describing how she came to see her proper relationship to her husband, writes: "Women have sensed this spirit of enmity deep down inside of them. They have known that they have an enemy but they have not known exactly who he is. They have felt a sense of inferiority, a sense of being oppressed or of being treated unfairly by life." Searching for the object of this "subconscious hostility," Helen asserts, many women have "projected it on their husbands or men in general." Although women may believe it is the men who have been oppressing them, "in reality it has been the common enemy of both men and women: Satan." The necessary remedy for this sinful situation, then, is for women to "recognize their roles and relationships according to Scripture," a goal that has been part of Aglow's statement of purpose from the beginning.[37]

God made woman to be a "helpmeet" for man, which, Helen states, is not a position of inferiority but rather one of honor. "A woman finds joy in willingly being subject to her husband, for she knows this is pleasing and a 'service' to the Lord. Man takes his place as the head of the wife as an act of love, the same love as Christ had for the church. . . . So, grace is the answer for wives and love is the answer for husbands."[38] She cautions against thinking that God has called men to a higher purpose than women or that God loves men more than women, noting that this attitude leads to "horrible bondage" and unhappiness. She concludes by citing Ephesians 5:21 and asserting: "A woman must not push and strive and become a domineering female. She must walk humbly in Christ's love."[39] Through prayer and the grace of God, women will learn how to be proper "helpmeets" to their husbands, a role of reverent submission analogous to the proper human response to Christ.

The stories just recounted were written in the early 1970s. Between then and now some evident changes have taken place as gender categories have been contested on many fronts. Although not all of today's Aglow women would actively dispute these arguments regarding female submission, particularly given what they would regard as the biblical basis for such arguments, there is now little overt discussion of wifely submission in Aglow literature.[40] In its place is a revised version of the true Christian woman, an image connected to the emphasis on spiritual warfare alluded to earlier. Now, instead of urging women to be submissive to their husbands, Aglow challenges its members to be "praying, warring women," interceding in the mighty battle against Satan and the evils he has spread throughout the world. The two authors of *A Woman's Guide to Spiritual Warfare* comment approvingly on the Old Testament story of "the Israelite woman who, when she saw King Abimelech approaching her city to burn it, took immediate and decisive action." Commenting on the woman's courageous murder of the wicked king, the writers conclude: "Never let it be said that women are weak! They are still hurling stones at the enemy's plans. This unnamed woman of Thebez is one of a large company of women who continue to wreak havoc with Satan's plans."[41] The focus here is notably different from that of the Aglow articles cited previously. Here and elsewhere in recent Aglow literature are stories of women's strength, tenacity, and power over their lives.

A striking example of this theme is a book published by Aglow in 1988 entitled *Ordinary Women, Extraordinary Strength: A Biblical Perspective of Feminine Potential*. The book's back cover asks the following pointed question: "Can a woman be intelligent, think independently, fill a leadership role, be successful in business, and still be feminine?" The implicit answer, fleshed out in the book itself, is yes. In the opening chapter, "Can a Woman Be Strong?" author Barbara Cook reflects on the power that is available to the Christian woman. "If we women discover this kind of power, we will lose interest in all the destructive deadends we have pursued before. We will no longer tolerate abuse against our bodies or persons. We will gladly give up the manipulative and seductive games played in hopes of increasing our power. We will behave as adults, happily abandoning little-girl coyness and sulking, along with little-girl dependencies and resentments."[42] In language that recalls both feminism and the recovery movement, while at the same time providing a critique of both, the author concludes: "Women who hate men need this power to transform their relationships. Women who love men too much need this strength in order to give up their victimized habits. Women who desire to be godly need this strength to achieve their goal. We all need this power."[43] She tells a story about the early years of her marriage: in "an effort to be a good Christian wife . . . I had submitted myself right out of existence!"[44] Separating women's value from their "ability to adapt to male needs or [their] successes or failures in marriage, parenting, or career," Cook replaces the notion of female submission with the idea that both men and women are equally to submit to God and to accept the strength that such submission brings.[45]

In highlighting the recent emphases on spiritual warfare and women's strength, it seems easy to conclude that what has occurred has been a major shift in Aglow attitudes toward gender, from an insistence on submission and domestic responsibility to a demand that Christian women expand their horizons, break the bonds that have enchained them, and go forth battling the world. This model, however, is somewhat oversimplified, failing to account for both the continuities in Aglow's teachings on womanhood over time and the numerous possibilities that exist simultaneously at any one time. Aglow women have never held a monolithic view of "Christian womanhood"; this concept has always been rife with conflicting ideals and possibilities that have been contested and endlessly reshuffled, allowing for an unexpectedly wide array of options.

Still, it is apparent that there has been a gradual reconfiguration of the varied meanings pertaining to gender among Aglow women, a reconfiguration mirrored in the wider subculture of conservative evangelicalism and intricately connected to broader sociopolitical movements in America since the 1960s. A 1987 article on Aglow president Jane Hansen illustrates the modulation that has taken place, describing Hansen as supportive of women's equal roles in all types of religious vocations, including the ministry. Moreover, write the authors, Hansen "firmly believes that women offer a complement to men which will not replace what men do but augment it, strengthen it, bolster it." Hansen critiques the church for not properly manifesting "the kind of liberation Jesus had in mind for both male and female" yet equally critiques the feminist movement for putting women and men in competition against each other. Forging a reformist, moderately feminist position, Hansen defends her own expanded role as a woman and notes: "I love being a housewife, a mother and all that goes with that. . . . That's part of who God created me to be. But he also created me to be more than that." The authors approvingly conclude: "Where Hansen was once consumed by the role of housewife, she is now consumed by serving Jesus."[46]

Conclusion: The Relation of Women's Aglow Fellowship to Mainline American Protestantism

The stories briefly outlined here indicate the cycles of crisis and victory that pervade Aglow women's narratives about prayer, narratives patterned on various biblical stories that are transformed into explanations for the events of everyday life. These narratives illuminate the deeply felt needs and concerns of Aglow women over the domestic crises that they share, mostly crises involving familial ties. Women who attended Aglow meetings in 1967 were, like the women at the New England regional retreat in 1994, primarily concerned with healing the difficulties of their daily lives, focusing particularly on broken or distorted marital relationships. Their stories lament the failings of their husbands even as they seek to place the burden of responsibility on themselves. Such a burden notwithstanding, it is evident that these women view themselves not merely as submissive "doormats" but rather as powerful channels through which their husbands and children may receive the love and peace of God and be, in a literal sense, domesticated. It seems equally evident that the early emphasis on wifely submission has been significantly reshaped, in part because of growing opportunities for women's leadership and authority within Aglow as well as within the churches at large.

The emergence of Women's Aglow may be viewed from one angle as representing a sharp response to a perceived failure of the mainline churches, as well as male-oriented charismatic groups such as the Full Gospel Business Men's Fellowship, to deal adequately with the concerns and everyday difficulties women face in modern America. Women who join Aglow continue to come both from classical Pentecostal churches and from the mainline denominations, and in the common ground of Aglow meetings, these women stand together in an ambivalent relationship to the American churches at large. Although most claim to remain active church members, and many undoubtedly are, there is much to suggest that Aglow affiliation is more significant to them than their church membership is, certainly insofar as their daily lives are concerned. From their Aglow friends, "sisters in Christ," they receive the strength and courage to cope with everything from alcoholic husbands and domestic abuse to being ridiculed for their faith and sitting "alone in the pew."

My own ethnographic research indicates that many women have become disillusioned with mainline Protestantism after joining Aglow and have migrated to Pentecostal or nondenominational independent churches. Although statistics on church affiliation are not available for Aglow participants throughout most of the organization's history, bylines for magazine editors and authors as well as officers of the organization show strong mainline affiliations throughout the 1970s, decreasing significantly after 1980. By 1992, survey results showed that 47.4 percent of members said that they regularly attended Pentecostal or charismatic churches; 17.9 percent, nondenominational" churches; and 2.8 percent, Baptist churches. The percentage of Protestant congregants (those who specified their affiliations primarily as Episcopalian, Methodist, or Presbyterian) was only 22.7 percent, with "Catholic" adherents filling out the final 9.2 percent.[47] The shift in balance away from mainline Protestant believers has been deeply felt among some of the early members; as one of the early Aglow leaders, an Episcopalian, lamented to me, "Aglow has been taken over by the Pentecostals!"[48] Although this claim is partly true, my field research suggests that it is equally accurate to say that Aglow women themselves have defected from the mainline, transforming Aglow into more of a "Pentecostal" than a mainline organization.

Moreover, even those Aglow women who remain active mainliners articulate a strong critique of their denominations (similar to the critique made by Aglow women who are Roman Catholics). The ways in which the mainline churches may or may not have failed these women, or the measures that might be taken to prevent further defections, are issues that lie outside the scope of this essay. As I suggested earlier, there are two (at least) possible angles of interpretation here: on the one hand, perhaps women drawn to Aglow are at the same time drawn to charismatic rather than mainline churches and so easily shift their loyalties in that direction; on the other hand, perhaps the Aglow organization itself fosters dissatisfaction with mainline congregations, as the scripted critique of the "deadness" of traditional churches is transmitted and accepted. In truth, both scenarios are undoubtedly operable, and the result seems to be a real shift away from mainline Protestantism. It seems fair to speculate that Aglow's rapid movement away from the mainline theological traditions in which the majority of its founders as well as its current members were raised reflects the widespread hope that newer charismatic churches like those affiliated with the Vineyard Christian Fellowship will provide a place much like Aglow, where women may share their domestic crises and victories and where their interests may be, for now anyway, more warmly welcomed.

Notes

1. A pseudonym. Names of Aglow speakers and participants have been changed throughout this essay, except where pertaining to authorship of published texts. My data is based on two years of extensive field research; see R. Marie Griffith, *God's Daughters: Evangelical Women and the Power of Submission* (Berkeley: University of California Press, 1997).

2. Ephesians 5:21: "Submit to one another out of reverence for Christ" (NIV).

3. Author's fieldnotes, Feb. 1994.

4. "Reflections on Aglow's Twenty-Year Ministry to Women around the World," brochure (Lynnwood, Wash.: Aglow Publications, 1987), 4; "How It All Began," *Aglow* 1 (Nov. 1969): 1.

5. Ruth Gothenquist, unpublished essay received from the author, one of the original "praying women," Sept. 1993.

6. Data received from Aglow headquarters in Lynnwood, Washington. Aglow in the United States is composed primarily of women who are white and middle class. There are, however, also significant numbers of African American, Hispanic, and Asian American women involved in Aglow, particularly in urban centers. This racial mix is particularly evident at large national and international conventions; however, statistics on racial and ethnic composition are unavailable from Aglow headquarters. For more on Aglow's history and composition, see Griffith, *God's Daughters*, 46–54.

7. Other scholars have noted this diversification of gender roles and have analyzed it in various ways. Prominent examples include Judith Stacey, *Brave New Families: Stories of Domestic Upheaval in Late Twentieth Century America* (New York: Basic, 1991); and Nancy Tatom Ammerman, *Bible Believers: Fundamentalists in the Modern World* (New Brunswick, N.J.: Rutgers University Press, 1987), esp. 134–46.

8. This notion of "reaction" has dominated most traditional historical interpretations. Sydney Ahlstrom characterized those who participated in charismatic Christianity in the 1960s as fearful people, many of them students, struggling to overcome a painful feeling of "cultural and institutional alienation." Clinging to belief in Jesus, finding refuge in otherworldliness, frightened and perplexed on all fronts, according to Ahlstrom, charismatic Christians struggled to bring "the blessings of joy and love" to "grim, tormented times" (Ahlstrom, *A Religious History of the American People* [New Haven, Conn.: Yale University Press, 1972], 1086 n. 6). More recently George Marsden, arguing along similar lines, wrote that the charismatic movement in the 1960s provided many Americans "with a simple critique of the perceived failures of liberal American

culture." Noting that by the early 1980s there were approximately twenty-nine million Americans who identified themselves as charismatic Christians, Marsden explains that this form of religion "proclaimed certainty in a world of uncertainty. It offered fixed moral standards in place of confusing moral relativism. It made demands on people who did not find full satisfaction in an indulgent culture" (Marsden, *Religion and American Culture* [Orlando, Fla.: Harcourt Brace Jovanovich, 1990], 261).

9. This essay focuses on Aglow's connection to mainline Protestantism and does not discuss the large numbers of Roman Catholic women in Aglow. Most of these have not defected to independent Protestant churches but have instead remained within the Catholic church, hoping for it to become more "spirit-filled." Here a comparative study of Catholic and Protestant Aglow women would be illuminating.

10. On the Vineyard Christian Fellowship, see Paul W. Kennedy, "Sacralizing Secularization: A Sociological Analysis of the Vineyard Christian Fellowship," Ph.D. thesis, University of South California, 1993; and Donald E. Miller, *Reinventing American Protestantism: Christianity in the New Millennium* (Berkeley: University of California Press, 1997).

11. Vinson Synan, *Under His Banner: History of Full Gospel Business Men's Fellowship International* (Costa Mesa, Calif.: Gift, 1992), 32. See also John Sherrill and Elizabeth Sherrill, *The Happiest People of Earth: The Long-Awaited Personal Story of Demos Shakarian As Told to John and Elizabeth Sherrill* (Westwood, N.J.: Fleming H. Revell, 1975). For an important discussion of anxiety over unchurched men and its impact on early fundamentalism, see Margaret Lamberts Bendroth, *Fundamentalism and Gender, 1875 to the Present* (New Haven, Conn.: Yale University Pres, 1993), esp. 13–30.

12. Historian David Harrell explains, "Local chapter meetings in leading hotels put on display charismatic fervor in a dignified setting before a much broader and more sophisticated audience than the revivalists ever reached" (David Edwin Harrell Jr., *All Things Are Possible: The Healing and Charismatic Revivals in Modern America* [Bloomington: Indiana University Press, 1975], 148).

13. Harrell, 147. Vinson Synan reports that the *Full Gospel Voice* grew to reach a readership of 700,000 by 1989 (*Under His Banner,* 81).

14. Harrell, *All Things Are Possible,* 148. Of Oral Roberts's continuing ties to the Full Gospel Business Men's Fellowship International, Harrell writes: "For many years, Roberts remained the most powerful supporter of the new group and probably benefited most from its growth" (147). Roberts's own move from Pentecostal to "neo-Pentecostal" was completed when, in March 1968, he joined the wealthy Boston Avenue Methodist Church in Tulsa.

15. See Dennis J. Bennett, *Nine O'Clock in the Morning* (South Plainfield, N.J.: Bridge, 1970). This story received major coverage in national magazines; see "Rector and a Rumpus," *Newsweek,* 4 July 1960, p. 77; and "Speaking in Tongues," *Time,* 15 Aug. 1960, pp. 53, 55.

16. Early *Aglow* issues testify to the influence of Dennis and Rita Bennett in the formation of Women's Aglow; Rita herself was a frequent contributor to the magazine, and many articles were written by women who were enthusiastic members of St. Luke's.

17. Gothenquist essay.

18. Ibid. This short essay describes her remembrance of the events leading up to Aglow's founding.

19. Early Aglow participant, interview with the author, 16 Sept. 1993, Seattle, Wash.

20. Ibid. See also "Reflections"; and Pat King, "AGLOW," *Logos Journal,* May–June 1974, pp. 34–35.

21. King, "AGLOW," 35.

22. Quin Sherrer and Steve Galloway, "Jane Hansen: Waking Up from the American Dream," *Charisma and Christian Life,* Nov. 1987, p. 19; see also Galloway's postscript to that article, "What is Aglow?" 23.

23. Data received from an Aglow administrator, interview with the author, Sept. 1993, Lynnwood, Wash. The woman who gave me this information added spontaneously that this number was "just ten less than last year." In 1993 Aglow added fellowships in at least eleven countries that previously were without Aglow.

24. Indeed, Aglow also resembles a number of recently formed evangelical women's groups, such as Women of Faith, Promise Reapers, Chosen Women, and Praise Keepers. Although not charismatic, these groups are thematically quite similar to Aglow.

25. Gothenquist essay.

26. To focus on the practice of prayer, as I do here, is not to ignore the social or theological dimensions of the women's lives or to reduce their experience of Aglow to one level—to the contrary, the practice of prayer provides significant entrance into the inner workings of these women's everyday experience and to the process through which they shape their world and themselves. Prayer, like other devotional and theological practices, always emerges out of a specific social and cultural location, the specific context in which the prayer person lives and moves.

27. Author's fieldnotes taken at Aglow retreat, Feb. 1993.

28. "Police Encouter," *Aglow* 2 (Spring 1970): 14.

29. "Loving-For-Free," *Aglow* 27 (Fall 1976): 3–7.

30. "Aglow Prayer Map" (Lynnwood, Wash.: Aglow Publications, 1992); *Women of Prayer Released to the Nations: Sixteen Prayer Leaders around the Earth Reveal the Heart, Spirit, and Power of Prayer* (Lynnwood, Wash.: Women's Aglow Fellowship, 1993), 9.

31. Such groups include Elizabeth Alves's Intercessors International and Cindy Jacobs's Generals of Intercession. Both Alves and Jacobs serve as prayer leaders for Women's Aglow. See Jacobs, *Possessing the Gates of the Enemy: A Training Manual for Militant Intercession,* foreword by C. Peter Wagner (Grand Rapids, Mich.: Chosen, 1991; seventh printing, 1993).

32. Quin Sherrer and Ruthanne Garlock, *A Women's Guide to Spiritual Warfare: A Woman's Guide for Battle* (Ann Arbor, Mich.: Servant, 1991), 19–20.

33. Other ethnographers have analyzed charismatic women's self-description as "prayer warriors"; see, for instance, Susan D. Rose, "Women Warriors: The Negotiation of Gender in a Charismatic Community," *Sociological Analysis* 48, no. 3 (1987): 245–58.

34. "My Full Inheritance As a Woman," *Aglow* 4 (Winter 1970–71): 3–17, 19–20; reprinted in *Aglow* 10 (Spring–Summer 1972): 12–17; reprinted again in *Aglow* 19 (Fall 1974): 16ff. Obviously popular, this article was turned into a thirty-two-page Aglow booklet in 1974.

35. Ibid., 6.

36. Ibid., 7, 20. On the topic of women and submission, see also Eadie V. Goodboy,

"God's Daughter: A Study of Practical Christian Living for Women," in *Aglow Bible Study No. 2* (Edmonds, Wash.: Aglow Publications, 1974).

37. "Jesus Truly Set Me Free," *Aglow* 8 (Fall 1971): 9.

38. Ibid., 10.

39. Ibid., 11.

40. The exception is the current emphasis on the mutual submission of spouses to each other, invoking Ephesians 5:21. This was brought out in the Aglow workshop described at the beginning of this essay.

41. Sherrer and Garlock, *Woman's Guide,* 59–60.

42. Barbara Cook, *Ordinary Women, Extraordinary Strength: A Biblical Perspective of Feminine Potential* (Lynnwood, Wash.: Aglow Publications, 1988), 21.

43. Ibid., 21. See also Barbara Cook, "Can a Woman Be Strong?" *Aglow* 19 (Nov.–Dec. 1988): 30.

44. Ibid., 92.

45. Ibid., 66.

46. Sherrer and Galloway, "Jane Hansen," 23. For a more thorough discussion of changing gender roles in Aglow, see Griffith, *God's Daughters,* esp. 169–98.

47. "Results of the 1992 'We Are Hearing You' Survey" (unpublished, obtained at Aglow headquarters), 11.

48. Interview with early participant, Sept. 1993.

8

New Wine and Baptist Wineskins: American and Southern Baptist Denominational Responses to the Charismatic Renewal, 1960–80

Albert Frederick Schenkel

A half-dozen years before Henry P. Van Dusen identified Pentecostalism as part of a "third force" in American Christianity, Edwin S. Gaustad wrote an article entitled "Baptists and Experimental Religion" for the American Baptist Historical Society. In his article this Baptist scholar analyzed the history of the Baptist movement in search of its "basic witness." He concluded that the Baptist raison d'être was not found in such popular causes as liberty of opinion or separation of church and state—or even mode of baptism. Rather, the Baptist sect existed as a testimony to the immediate experience of divine grace; its testimony was that "the baptism by the Holy Spirit was an event . . . objective and certain." Baptists always favored the charisma of the apostle to the creed of the theologian, Gaustad observed, "and wherever and whenever special homage was paid to experimental religion, there and then Baptists prospered."[1]

If Gaustad is correct, one might have expected Baptists to welcome with open arms the charismatic renewal that swept the mainline denominations little more than a decade later. Baptists did in fact participate in the renewal, though in roughly the same percentage as other Protestants. And Baptists were less likely to practice glossolalia, one of the primary defining marks of the movement, than were Roman Catholics, Methodists, or Lutherans.[2] A study of the renewal within the American Baptist and Southern Baptist denominations yields insights both into the course of the renewal itself and into these two major bodies within modern American religion.[3]

The Charismatic Renewal and the American Baptist Convention and Churches

In the fall of 1962 Ken Pagard, a young Baptist pastor in the San Joaquin Valley, traveled south to Van Nuys to visit the Blessed Trinity Society.[4] He had been given a magazine published by the society and decided that he must visit these Episcopalians, who were experiencing a Pentecostal spiritual renewal complete with miracles of healing and speaking in tongues. Soon after Pagard was himself "baptized in the Holy Spirit," and within a few months he reported that many of the pastors in the San Joaquin Association had also received the Spirit baptism; "Our state pastors' retreats have been totally changed," he announced.[5]

The renewal within the American Baptist Convention (ABC) quickly took on national scope. At the 1963 ABC national conference in Detroit, Michigan, several dozen charismatic pastors gathered for dinner and worship. By 1968 the American Baptist Charismatic Fellowship, which continued under Pagard's perennial leadership, had been duly recognized at Valley Forge.[6]

That same year, Howard M. Ervin, an East Coast participant in the renewal, encouraged charismatic Baptists with the publication of *These Are Not Drunk As Ye Suppose,* a scholarly treatment of the New Testament texts related to the Pentecostal experience.[7] Ervin had been baptized in the Holy Spirit in 1958 while serving a Baptist church in Atlantic Highlands, New Jersey. Although he had left the Baptist pastorate to become a professor at Oral Roberts University, Ervin identified himself as a "Pentecostal Baptist," attended a Baptist church in Tulsa, and unofficially represented Baptists in the growing number of ecumenical charismatic gatherings.

At the 1971 ABC convention, 175 attended a breakfast hosted by the charismatic fellowship. The *Minneapolis Star* wrote an article on the renewal, and an Associated Press editor arranged for a visit in New York for one of its leaders.

The October issue of *The American Baptist* (*TAB*) featured an article by seminary professor and former ABC president Culbert G. Rutenber in which he announced that no denomination could any longer ignore the charismatic renewal. He cited approvingly an official report produced by a diverse panel of professionals for the United Presbyterian Church (USA) that recommended tolerance, prayerful dialogue, and openness to "new ways in which God by His Spirit may be speaking to the church." Rutenber's article closed with an assessment that would often be noted both for its humor and for its compelling logic: "My own conclusion—and appeal—is that a denomination like the ABC which, in the name of unity-in-diversity, puts up with the widest spectrum of bigots and broadminded, fundamentalists and liberals, orthodox and heretics, saints and barely-saved-if-at-all (not to mention a good sprinkling of plain kooks and crackpots) should have an honored place for some of our most sincere, committed, and grace-full pastors and laymen."[8]

During the early 1970s ABC responses to the charismatic renewal were shaped by the perception that neo-Pentecostalism was part of a larger religious revival that threatened to eclipse mainline religion. *TAB* featured an article in the summer of 1973 entitled "Will the Third Great Awakening Miss the Churches?"[9] In this article Lyle Shaller, a respected church consultant, surveyed various signs of spiritual life outside the traditional churches while encouraging the mainline churches that they too had a role to play in the building revival. Shaller praised the charismatic renewal within the churches, despite his reservations about its potential divisiveness, calling it "unquestionably the most important ecumenical development of this century." That same year, in a *TAB* article on the Jesus People movement, Terry Vaughn noted that the charismatic movement was appealing to young people with its exuberance, its emphasis on experience, and its new forms of Christian community.[10]

By 1974 Pagard was able to report to friends that the initial fear and suspicion he had felt from denominational officials had largely dissipated and that although some in leadership still felt uneasy about the movement, there seemed to be ample space for the charismatic renewal within the denomination.[11] The Charismatic Fellowship had a mailing list of 700 people, 75–80 percent of whom were pastors. The renewal was widespread geographically, a number of missionaries had become involved, and several past presidents of the ABC had "identified themselves with the renewal."[12]

Pagard was especially heartened by a positive article about his own church written by the head of the ABC's department of communication, Frank A. Sharp, and published in the March 1974 issue of *TAB*.[13] Pagard had become pastor of the First Baptist Church in Chula Vista shortly after his initial charismatic experience and had developed a model charismatic community featuring a coffeehouse outreach, common-purse households, and a growing outreach to alcoholics, drug users, and young people in trouble. Sharp was impressed by what he found in Chula Vista and suggested that perhaps the new Pentecostals had found the joyous Christianity that the ABC needed.

Despite his favorable conclusions about charismatic community, Sharp noted that many administrators were nervous about the movement because of the disruption and tension it caused within local churches and denominational associations. Sharp no doubt had in mind a report that the National Staff Council had commissioned a few months earlier on "the administrative aspects of the charismatic movement." In preparing the report, Home Missions executive Paul Madsen polled the region, state, and city secretaries, asking whether the movement represented an administrative problem within their jurisdictions. Of the thirty that responded by the time of his report, sixteen answered yes; the other fourteen answered "no, however . . ." and proceeded to point to incipient problems. The problems reported ranged from church splits—with one actual lawsuit over ownership of the property—to "hidden participation" on the part of pastors or lay people. Edginess and tension were mentioned by many respondents. One administrator reported an instance in which a pastor claimed that the denomination sanctioned the movement because of its meetings at annual conventions.[14]

Madsen's recommendations reflect the tensions felt by those American Baptist leaders who were skeptical of the charismatic movement. Madsen had handled pastoral and administrative issues for the Home Missions office for more than twenty years and was well attuned to the culture of the denomination. On the one hand, Madsen was convinced that the beliefs and practices of charismatics were not in keeping with Baptist traditions. On the other hand, he felt that the denomination's commitment to the principles of religious liberty and pluralism prevented its leaders from responding effectively to the renewal: "the pluralism of our denomination is clearly a problem for many of the administrators." Although the National Staff Council carried something like pastoral responsibility for the health of the ABC as a whole, its means of exercising that responsibility were strictly limited. The leadership might sponsor a convention resolution against the movement, but such a move would be extremely divisive and would yield little practical administrative leverage against charismatics. There was no mechanism outside the local church by which an American Baptist could be "disciplined." All Madsen could suggest was that administrators should refrain from attending charismatic meetings or making any statement that could be understood as endorsement.[15]

The next treatment of the renewal in *TAB* reflected the more guarded pastoral and administrative approach. The article, written by Connie Kirby, was the product of several months of interviews with American Baptists in all regions. It focused on the points of conflict related to the renewal, dispelling myths and counseling mutual tolerance and understanding.[16]

A sidebar to Kirby's article dealt specifically with the movement's most controversial feature: glossolalia. Although refusing to attribute to glossolalia a supernatural status, the article did imply that it could be a meaningful religious experience in which "one's relation to existence changes; one becomes part of a wholeness and realizes a kind of identification with the universe."[17] This approach to speaking in tongues echoed the approach of Episcopal priest Morton Kelsey, a disciple of Carl Jung and an early apologist for the modern occurrence of glossolalia. While many were attributing glossolalia to mental instability, Kelsey found that the practice contributed to the integration of the personality and to positive social development.

Later that summer ABC general secretary Robert C. Campbell exercised what he called the "prophetic initiative" of his office to address the phenomenon of glossolalia. Campbell cited a new study refuting theories linking glossolalia to social disorganization, economic and social deprivation, and psychological maladjustment. Addressing the charge of the movement's detractors that the only New Testament church to have experienced glossolalia was the scandalous Corinthian church, Campbell cited Harvard New Testament scholar Krister Stendahl: "The church at Corinth had many problems. It had almost all of the problems that churches have had through the ages, except the chief problem of our churches today: It was never dull." He went on to cite Emil Brunner, who had chided the churches for soft-pedaling the Spirit out of motives of "theological puritanism." Campbell expressed the hope that the ABC would "continue to be at once broad and Biblical enough to remain in fellowship with all of our brothers and sisters in Christ," unlike several Southern Baptist associations that had recently excluded charismatics. Portions of Campbell's paper appeared in *TAB* in June 1976.[18]

The renewal's most visible moment came a year later at the 1977 Conference on the Charismatic Movement in the Churches, held at Kansas City. There Baptist charismatics stood amid 40,000 participants in the renewal to celebrate their common experience in the Spirit. Basking in the ecumenical glow, American and Southern Baptists met to discuss the possibility of forming a pan-Baptist charismatic fellowship.[19]

The charismatic movement seemed to lose momentum in the late 1970s amid controversies over discipleship, authority, and community practices. The American Baptist renewal in particular was probably dampened by charges of authoritarianism in Pagard's model community in Chula Vista.[20]

By 1979 a *TAB* article on the renewal began with the question, "What ever happened to the 'Praise the Lord, Hallelujah' people?" The answer was, "They are still around, not making headlines, but in American Baptist Churches some quiet bridgebuilding is taking place."[21] Under Pagard's successor, Gary Clark, the denominational fellowship dropped the divisive term *charismatic* from its name when it incorporated in 1983 as the Holy Spirit Ministries in American

Baptist Churches, and it distanced itself from the neo-Pentecostal teaching of some early leaders that glossolalia is a necessary evidence of Holy Spirit baptism.[22] This conciliatory style has won the movement an ever more secure presence in the official life of the ABC.

The American Baptist Church, by many measures, seems to have honored the "basic witness" to the Holy Spirit suggested by Edwin Gaustad. Bolstered by cherished principles of religious liberty and pluralism, ABC leaders made a home for the charismatic renewal. In fact, a closer look at statistics bearing on Baptist participation in the renewal indicates that when American Baptists and Southern Baptists are treated separately, American Baptist participation in the renewal may actually have exceeded that of other Protestant denominations.[23]

The Charismatic Renewal and the Southern Baptist Convention

Charles Simpson was a Baptist. He'd been "born in a Baptist hospital, raised by Baptist missionaries, educated in Baptist schools, and ordained as a Baptist pastor." In the spring of 1964, however, Simpson did something that got him into trouble with the deacons of the Bay View Heights Baptist Church, where he had served for six years in his hometown, Mobile, Alabama. Through the influence of Ken Sumrall, a Southern Baptist colleague from nearby Pensacola, Florida, Simpson received a Pentecostal-style baptism in the Holy Spirit and spoke in tongues. In the course of the resulting controversy, one of the Bay View Heights deacons waved a copy of a manual entitled "What Baptists Believe and Why They Believe It" and declared, "Tongues is not in here." Simpson waved a Bible and replied, "But it's in here." Simpson won a vote of confidence from the congregation, and Bay View Heights quickly became a charismatic center for the Southeast, helping to sponsor meetings with David Wilkerson, Nicky Cruz, and other Pentecostals who were beginning to travel the developing charismatic circuit. Within a couple of years Simpson was on the circuit himself, speaking for Full Gospel Business Men's Fellowship International meetings around the country.[24]

A small number of other Southern Baptist Convention (SBC) pastors also received and began to preach about the baptism in the Holy Spirit during the late 1950s and early 1960s, including John Osteen in Houston; Howard Conatser in Dallas; Roy Stockstill in Baton Rouge; Jamie Buckingham in Melbourne, Florida; and Roy Lamberth in Louisville. Some were immediately dismissed by their congregations or chose to step down amid opposition, but others continued to pastor Southern Baptist churches.[25]

Early responses to charismatics in their midst included the predictable dispensational argument that tongues have no place in the present-day church. Herschell Hobbs, a former SBC president, produced a study of spiritual gifts in which he followed dispensationalist C. I. Scofield's gloss on 1 Corinthians 13:8 in suggesting that "in all likelihood this gift ceased with the first century."[26]

As early as 1965, however, favorable assessments of the renewal began to appear in denominational publications. The May 1965 issue of *Home Missions* magazine carried an article entitled "Speaking with Tongues," by John P. Newport, professor of the philosophy of religion at Southwestern Baptist Theological Seminary. Although challenging the Pentecostal contention that tongues is the unique sign of the Spirit's presence in the life of the believer, Newport felt that Baptists ought to be open to the practice. Citing "existentialists and phenomenologists such as Heidegger," Newport called for a renewed appreciation for the role of emotion in human life, including—within the bounds of proper order—the worship life of the church. There were, moreover, signs that charismatics such as Lutheran pastor Larry Christensen were becoming sensitive to issues of order in public worship in ways that earlier Pentecostals had not been. As was common practice among those friendly to the renewal, Newport cited Morton Kelsey's work as evidence that glossolalia might have value for personal healing. He even quoted Baptist icon Billy Graham, who confessed, "We have looked a bit askance at our brethren in Pentecostal churches," when in fact "we need to learn once again what it means to be baptized in the Holy Spirit."[27]

Conflicting opinions emerged from Southern Baptist seminaries. Faculty discussions at Southern Seminary in Louisville resulted in negative assessments from historian E. Glenn Hinton, psychologist of religion Wayne E. Gates, and New Testament scholar Frank Stagg and a positive one from professor of systematic theology Dale Moody.[28] At New Orleans Baptist Theological Seminary a course about tongue speaking resulted in a book on the subject by Fisher Humphreys and Malcolm Tolbert, who refuted claims that Pentecostals are "childish, or sick, or phony" while refusing to concede that glossolalia is proof of a baptism in the Holy Spirit or that it necessarily makes one a better Christian.[29]

Most of the popular treatments of the renewal and of glossolalia that appeared among Southern Baptists during the early 1970s adopted an irenic tone.[30] Chief among the conciliators was Watson E. Mills, a professor at Averett College in Danville, Virginia.[31] Mills's work on the renewal included a book, an edited volume of essays, and influential articles for *Home Missions* and other Southern Baptist publications. Mills's position was consistent throughout:

Baptists ought "neither to forbid nor force tongues, but rather to exercise mutual tolerance, understanding, and Christian love."[32] At a May 1974 SBC study conference on the renewal, Mills declared that divisive debate over tongues speaking was nearly ended and that the Southern Baptists were "moving toward a détente, an era of goodwill" in which both sides would be less defensive and less dogmatic than ever before.[33]

Mills was wrong; instead, the mid-1970s featured a period of open conflict over the renewal. The republication of a series of sermons critical of the movement by prominent Dallas pastor W. A. Criswell was the first sign of renewed conflict.[34] Besides firing other broadsides, Criswell claimed that no hero of the faith in all of Christian history ever spoke in tongues and that whenever the phenomenon had appeared in history, it had been treated as heresy. Broadman Press featured several negative treatments of the movement that followed similar lines of argument: modern tongues are the tongues of Corinth (pseudo-pagan ecstasies) not those of Pentecost (real languages); not just Christians but worshipers in many religions speak in tongues; and Pentecostals exalt the Holy Spirit over Christ or they exalt experience over God himself.[35]

Significantly, most opponents of the renewal who emerged in 1974 and 1975 were not academicians; they were pastors. It was in the local churches and local associations that the SBC's battle over the renewal was waged.[36]

Local associations had been dealing with the conflict over the renewal since its beginnings. Bay View Heights in Mobile had been placed on probation in 1968 and 1971. The Dallas association had questioned Howard Conatser regarding complaints about his charismatic ministry as early as 1970.[37] Five months after Mills's declaration of concord, the 1974 Dallas association meeting officially adopted an anticharismatic stance at the request of its credentials committee.[38]

Hoping to spur similar actions in other local associations, Dallas pastor Billy Weber carried his crusade against charismatics to the Baptist General Convention of Texas held two weeks later. The convention passed a resolution alerting its churches to the "potential dangers" of the movement.[39] The incident attracted the attention of Southern Baptists well beyond Texas, in part because an SBC-press reporter asked Billy Weber's father, Jaroy Weber, who happened to be the SBC president at the time, what he thought of the resolution passed by the Texas body. The elder Weber was quoted as saying, "Charismatics should get right or get out."[40] Even so, the elder Weber made it clear that he hoped the national convention would not entertain a resolution against charismatics; he saw the issue as a local one.[41]

The controversy gained momentum the following spring when Criswell treated the Dallas association's evangelism conference to a spirited diatribe against the renewal in which he branded it "near heresy." Criswell drew laughter and "amens" from the assembly when he called the charismatic renewal a "woman movement" and suggested a way to end the renewal: "You stop the women from speaking in tongues and the practice will absolutely disappear from the earth."[42] Most of those present probably missed the fact that Criswell's statement was based on a complex interpretation of 1 Corinthians 14:34 that was common in anticharismatic literature and heard it as a spirited defense of cherished southern religious tradition.

In the fall of 1975 the Southern Baptist Press Service took up the attack. Throughout the month of September, the service released to state papers a series of items entitled "Open Letters to Charismatics," by J. Terry Young. The author pilloried charismatics for spiritual pride, poor biblical exegesis, and divisiveness. The sting of the analysis was heightened by the genre, which allowed Young to address charismatics in the second person throughout: "Since you feel speaking in tongues is something of a duplication of the miracle of the coming of the Holy Spirit at Pentecost, why do you settle for only a portion . . . why not ask for the whole thing, the sound of wind, the sight of fire?"[43]

In October the service began releasing a series of twenty articles by Herschel H. Hobbs entitled "Baptist Beliefs." The articles treated 1 Corinthians 12–14 and were consistently anticharismatic.[44]

That fall a number of local associations took their cue from Criswell, Weber, and the Baptist press and moved against charismatics. In addition to the Dallas association, the Trenton and Plaquemines associations in Louisiana and those in Cincinnati, Ohio; Houston and Guadalupe County, Texas; and Oxnard, California, moved against charismatics.[45] With Southern Baptists responding pro and con to the actions of the local associations throughout the fall and winter, it was not surprising that the charismatic movement was voted the top Southern Baptist story of 1975.[46] Yet there was no action taken against charismatics in any local association in subsequent years.

The strong action taken in local associations in 1975 was never reflected in the actions of the national SBC. The 1975 national convention, meeting in Miami, rejected a resolution to denounce charismatics and chose instead to reaffirm the statement on the Holy Spirit outlined in the Baptist Faith and Message Statement of 1963. When asked about its policy toward charismatics, the Home Mission Board made public a moderate set of guidelines it had been using since 1966.[47] When 1976 convention president James L. Sullivan was asked to comment on the possibility of excluding charismatics, he affirmed the diversity of the SBC.[48] His successor, Jimmy Allen, declared that he was more open to the renewal than many of his colleagues: "There's a fresh moving of the Spirit in a great many places within our fellowship for which I'm grateful."[49] Even those who opposed the renewal, such as J. Terry Young, recommended that the national convention not act against it.[50]

State associations, with the exception of Texas, also did not move to challenge the renewal. Several actually passed resolutions defending the religious liberty of charismatics.[51] Even in Texas the 1976 convention elected a president who urged that the meeting include charismatics in 1977.[52]

Meanwhile, the renewal continued to develop. A conference for SBC charismatics held in Louisville in July 1976 was attended by 815 individuals.[53] The second such conference, held in Dallas a year later, drew more than 2,000 people from at least fifteen states. The third, in Dallas in 1977, drew 3,500 from thirty-seven states.[54]

The mood of the Baptist press moderated after 1975. *Home Mission* magazine provided its readers with a well-researched treatment of the movement in which staff writer Timothy Nicholas allowed charismatics to tell their own stories and highlighted the moderate stances of state and national conventions.[55]

According to Claude Howe, who reviewed the movement's history in a 1978 article for *Baptist History and Heritage,* the movement's influence in the SBC ceased to grow after the local association actions of 1975. Howe concluded that, based on the relatively small numbers of charismatic Southern Baptists who remained—between one and two hundred churches out of thirty-six thousand, or ten thousand members out of thirteen million—the movement appeared to have made "relatively slight impact."[56]

There is, however, evidence that the movement continued to grow in the late 1970s and throughout the 1980s.[57] The "Fullness Movement," represented by a bimonthly journal published since 1978 by Fort Worth layman Ras Robinson, sought to foster the charismatic works of the Holy Spirit within the SBC while avoiding the stumbling block of a focus on tongues speaking as an initial evidence of Spirit baptism. By 1988 it was estimated that there were as many as four hundred "fullness" churches in the SBC, and Don LeMaster, a veteran charismatic leader, was beginning to organize them into a fellowship in the context of a new round of denominational opposition.

ABC-SBC Parallels and Divergences

The stories of the renewal within the ABC and SBC follow the familiar contours of the charismatic movement: origins in an interdenominational milieu in the early 1960s, rapid spread amid controversy until the mid-1970s, and maturing and quiet growth after 1977. The later phase of the renewal has been "most difficult to describe and evaluate." According to Peter D. Hocken, although some scholars see the movement as a whole peaking in the early 1980s, most see it as "still spreading, but having moved into a new and less sensational pattern of growth."[58] This description seems to fit the SBC experience as well as that of the ABC, despite the threats and rumors of the movement's extinction in the mid-1970s within the SBC.

In both denominations the encounter between the renewal and denominational leadership changed both charismatics and those who opposed them.[59] Charismatics were forced to sort through their own principles, downplaying or discarding those—like the Pentecostal doctrine of initial evidence—that proved unacceptable. In both denominations renewal leaders eventually discarded the term *charismatic* altogether, seeking to package the spiritual essence of the movement in more palatable form. Denominational leaders in both the ABC and SBC were forced by the renewal to focus on the work of the Holy Spirit. The result was a fruitful discussion and a rich body of literature that had value beyond the various verdicts on the renewal itself.[60]

The traditional Baptist principle of religious liberty, moreover, was at work in both the ABC and the SBC. In the ABC it was wedded to concepts of pluralism and theological openness and ensured the movement a hearing despite its critics. Even those administrators who were critical of the movement felt restrained from moving against it. In the SBC it operated to restrain national and state conventions from acting to oppose the renewal.

There were, however, obvious differences in the way the renewal was received by the two denominations. The differences were due in large part to contrasts in the two denominations related to theological rigor, cultural openness, and structural development.

First, the responses of SBC leaders to the renewal tended to be more theologically rigorous that those of ABC leaders. SBC treatments, for example, took more seriously the implications of the initial evidence position, and they were more likely to appeal to biblical exegesis in articulating their opposition to the renewal. In contrast, ABC leaders tended to ignore the theological implications of the renewal and judge it on the basis of its usefulness in the life of the denomination.

SBC responses to the renewal also seem to have been influenced by negative stereotypes of Pentecostals to a greater degree than were those in the ABC. ABC leaders often explicitly removed themselves from negative judgments about Pentecostals. SBC associations listed fellowship with Pentecostals as a cause for disfellowship. SBC analyses of glossolalia more often took seriously literature that linked the practice to mental and social problems, whereas ABC leaders expressed openness to the practice in part because it appealed to those on the fringes of the core culture.

The major difference, however, was not one of attitude but one of polity; the SBC featured local associations of pastors who worked in close proximity to one another. It was these associations that moved against charismatics. Although the SBC national leaders expressed a reticence to act that paralleled that of ABC administrators, when the SBC national leaders prophesied, they set local associations free to take disciplinary action.

The association structure has recently received attention from a number of Baptist historians. The purpose of associations has been to "(1) promote fellowship among churches, (2) maintain uniformity of faith and practice among the churches, (3) give counsel and assistance to the churches, [and] (4) provide an organizational structure through which churches could cooperate in their broader ministries." The renewal ran afoul of the strong local associations in the South on all four points. The renewal was especially troubling in that it disrupted cooperative programs and changed and threatened commitments. Because the associations in the South had an autonomous mission, Southern Baptists reasoned that associations were entitled to the same privilege of self-determination as local churches. Southwestern Seminary historian Robert Baker explained that this even gave associations the right to exclude members without regard to the action or inaction of state or national bodies: exclusion "does not interfere with religious liberty or with the right of interpretation, because any structured body such as a church, association, or state convention has the right to determine its own membership; it must have that right."[61] Given the well-developed programs, theological rigor, and heated emotions that converged in many local associations, it is not surprising that some charismatics were excluded by local associations.[62]

In the final analysis, however, despite the threat the renewal presented to their programs, the structures of the ABC and SBC were flexible enough to retain large numbers of charismatic believers. Baptist wineskins did not altogether fail the charismatic vintage.

Notes

1. Edwin S. Gaustad, "Baptists and Experimental Religion," *The Chronicle: Journal of the American Baptist Historical Society* 15 (July 1952): 110, 115–16, 111.

2. Kenneth S. Kantzer, "The Charismatics among Us," *Christianity Today* 24 (22 Feb. 1980): 25. This *CT*-Gallup poll estimated that 20 percent of Baptists considered

themselves Pentecostal or charismatic Christians, a figure comparable to the percentage of Lutherans (20 percent), Roman Catholics (18 percent), and Methodists (18 percent). Roughly 1 percent of Baptists reported practicing glossolalia, whereas roughly 2 percent of Roman Catholics and Methodists and roughly 3 percent of Lutherans reported doing so.

3. The American Baptist Convention became the American Baptist Churches in the United States in 1973. The designation "ABC" is used for the denomination under both names.

4. For an account of the Pentecostal outbreak at Van Nuys, see Dennis Bennett, *Nine O'Clock in the Morning* (Plainfield, N.J.: Logos International, 1970). See also Richard Quebedeaux, *The New Charismatics: How a Christian Renewal Movement Became Part of the American Religious Mainstream* (San Francisco: Harper and Row, 1983), 61–64.

5. Kenneth Pagard, "Two Letters on Church Renewal," *New Covenant* (Nov. 1974): 15–17.

6. P. D. Hocken, "Charismatic Movement," in *Dictionary of Pentecostal and Charismatic Movements,* ed. Stanley M. Burgess and Gary B. McGee (Grand Rapids, Mich.: Zondervan, 1988), 133.

7. Howard M. Ervin, *These Are Not Drunk As Ye Suppose* (Plainfield, N.J.: Logos International, 1968); Gary Clark discussed Ervin's involvement in the denomination in an interview with the author conducted at Arcadia, California on 16 Aug. 1993.

8. Culbert G. Rutenber, "The New Charismatic Movement," *The American Baptist* 169 (Oct. 1971): 6–7; *The Work of the Holy Spirit,* a report of the Special Committee on the Work of the Spirit to the 182d General Assembly of the United Presbyterian Church in the United States of America (1970), cited in Rutenber, is included in Kilian McDonnel, ed., *Presence, Power, Praise: Documents on the Charismatic Renewal, Volume 1* (Collegeville, Minn.: Liturgical, 1980), 221–82.

9. Lyle E. Schaller, "Will the Third Great Awakening Miss the Churches?" *TAB* 171 (June 1973): 8–9.

10. Terry Vaughn, "Jumping for Jesus," *TAB* 171 (Oct. 1973): 17.

11. Pagard, "Two Letters," 16–17.

12. Paul Madsen, Memo on the Administrative Aspects of the Charismatic Movement, Nov. 1973, in "charismatic" file at American Baptist Historical Society, Valley Forge, Penn.

13. Frank A. Sharp, "An Experience of Joy," *TAB* 172 (Mar. 1974): 11–13.

14. Ibid., 13; Madsen, Memo, 1. The National Staff Council was created in 1972 on the recommendation of a study of denominational structure completed for the annual convention (See Ambrose L. Cram Jr., chair, "Report of the Study Commission on Denominational Structure of the A.B.C. for Action at the A.B.C. Convention, Denver, Colorado, May, 1972," 70–71.) The council consisted of the thirty-seven regional, state, and city executive ministers and thirty national staff persons and met three times annually in conjunction with the meetings of the General Board of the ABC.

15. Madsen, Memo, 2–7.

16. Connie Kirby, "A Look at the Charismatic Life Style," *TAB* 173 (May 1975): 8–9.

17. Nils Engleson, "Glosso-what?" *TAB* 173 (May 1975): 9–10. See Morton Kelsey,

Tongue Speaking: An Experiment in Spiritual Experience (New York: Doubleday, 1964), 194–95.

18. Robert C. Campbell, "The Phenomenon of Glossolalia, 11/11/75," in the "charismatic" file at the American Baptist Historical Society, Valley Forge, Penn. Quoted here are Krister Stendahl, "The New Testament Evidence," in *The Charismatic Movement,* ed. Michael Hamilton (Grand Rapids, Mich.: Eerdmans, 1975), 51; and Emil Brunner, *Dogmatics,* vol. 3, *The Christian Doctrines of Church, Faith, and the Consummation* (London: Lutterworth, 1962), 16. Campbell had become general secretary in 1973 and served in that office until 1987.

19. "Charismatic Unity in Kansas City," *Christianity Today* 21 (12 Aug. 1977): 37.

20. See Hocken, "Charismatic Movement," 140.

21. Wendy Ryan, "The Charismatic Movement in American Baptist Churches," *TAB* 177 (Sept. 1979): 12–13.

22. Clark interview.

23. It seems clear that participation was much higher within the ABC than within the SBC. For example, Pagard estimated that there were over five hundred pastors (out of around six thousand) on the charismatic fellowship mailing list in 1973; no estimate of the numbers of SBC pastors involved in the renewal in the 1970s exceeded two hundred (out of over thirty thousand). *Christianity Today* (21 [12 Aug. 1977]: 37) estimated that an equal number of American Baptists and Southern Baptists were charismatics—about ten thousand of each. (The ABC numbered about one and a half million at that time; the SBC, about thirteen million.) From these two comparisons one would conclude that a much higher percentage of American Baptists were charismatics. Thus, if a denominational distinction had been made in the 1980 *CT*-Gallup poll that listed "those who consider themselves Pentecostal or charismatic Christians," the American Baptist percentages would doubtless have been higher than those for all Baptists (20 percent), the general public (17 percent), Roman Catholics (18 percent), all Protestants (22 percent), Methodists (18 percent), Lutherans (20 percent), or members of small denominations (16 percent). (These were the only categories listed. It should be noted that only 17 percent of those who considered themselves Pentecostal or charismatic Christians had spoken in tongues.)

24. Charles V. Simpson, interview with the author, 19 May 1993, Mobile, Ala.

25. Synan, "Baptists Ride the Third Wave," *Charisma and Christian Life* 12, no. 5 (1986): 52–53, tells Osteen's story and mentions several others.

26. Herschel H. Hobbs, *The Holy Spirit: Believer's Guide* (Nashville, Tenn.: Broadman, 1967), 7, 132.

27. John P. Newport, "Speaking with Tongues," *Home Missions* 36 (May 1965): 7–9, 21–26 (quotation on 26). Cf. Claude Howe, "The Charismatic Movement in Southern Baptist Life," *Baptist History and Heritage* 13 (July 1978): 24. Howe lumps together the responses by SBC scholars into a single, generally negative, assessment, whereas I see significant differences.

28. Frank Stagg, E. Glenn Hinson, and Wayne E. Oates, *Glossolalia: Tongues Speaking in Biblical, Historical, and Pyschological Perspective* (Nashville, Tenn.: Abingdon, 1967), 74, 84, 96–97; Frank Stagg, *The Holy Spirit Today: Biblical Teaching Applied to Present Needs* (Nashville, Tenn.: Broadman, 1973), 57; Dale Moody, *Spirit of the Living God: The Biblical Concepts Interpreted in Context* (Philadelphia: Westminster,

1968), 10, 100–101. See also Moody, "Speaking in Tongues," *The Baptist Program,* July 1967, p. 8. *The Baptist Program* is a national magazine published by the executive committee of the SBC.

29. Fisher Humphreys and Malcolm Tolbert, *Speaking in Tongues* (Zachary, La.: Christian Lithe, 1973), vii, 79–83.

30. See C. W. Parnell, *Understanding Tongues-Speaking* (Nashville, Tenn.: Broadman, 1973); Luther B. Dyer, ed., *Tongues* (Jefferson City, Mo.: Le Roi, 1971); and Lester D. Cleveland, "Let's Demythologize Glossolalia," *The Baptist Program,* June 1967, pp. 8–9.

31. Scholars are also indebted to Mills for the volume *Charismatic Religion in Modern Research: A Bibliography* (Macon, Ga.: Mercer University Press, 1985).

32. Watson E. Mills, *Understanding Speaking in Tongues* (Grand Rapids, Mich.: Eerdmans, 1972), 76. See also Mills, ed., *Speaking in Tongues: Let's Talk about It* (Waco, Tex.: Word, 1973), 24; idem, "A New Lingo for Christendom?" *Home Missions* 41 (July 1970): 28–29; and idem, "Glossolalia: Creative Sound or Destructive Fury," *Home Missions* 43 (Aug. 1972): 13.

33. "With Glossolalia, Educator Suggests Détente," *Baptist Standard* 86 (22 May 1974).

34. W. A. Criswell, *The Baptism, Filling, and Gifts of the Holy Spirit* (Grand Rapids, Mich.: Zondervan, 1973), 123–24.

35. See Landrum P. Leavell, *God's Spirit in You* (Nashville, Tenn.: Broadman, 1974), 69–75; and Robert L. Hamblin, *The Spirit-Filled Trauma: A Candid Plea for Biblical Understanding in the Matters of the Spirit* (Nashville, Tenn.: Broadman, 1974), 88–103.

36. Minutes of the One Hundred and Twelfth Annual Session of the Mobile Baptist Association, 19–20 Oct. 1967, p. 55; Minutes of the One Hundred and Sixteenth Annual Session of the Mobile Baptist Association, 14–15 Oct. 1971, pp. 75–77.

37. Tim Nicholas, "Singing in the Spirit: A New Tune for an Old Movement?" *Home Missions* 47 (July–Aug. 1976): 38.

38. Report of the Credentials Committee, in the Minutes of the Seventy-Second Annual Meeting of the Dallas Baptist Association, 17 Oct. 1974, p. 27. The history of association dealings with Beverly Hillis and Shady Grove is in the Minutes of the Seventy-Third Annual Meeting of the Dallas Baptist Association, 16 Oct. 1975, pp. 31–32.

39. "Charismatic Dangers Voiced," *Baptist Standard* 86 (6 Nov. 1974): 5.

40. Toby Druin, "SBC President Clarifies Charismatic Position," *Baptist Standard* 87 (8 Jan. 1975): 11.

41. "Weber Views 'Divisive' Move," *Baptist Standard* 87 (18 June 1975): 7.

42. "Charismatic Movement Draws Criticism of W. A. Criswell," *Baptist Standard* 87 (23 Apr. 1975): 3.

43. J. Terry Young, "Open Letter to Charismatics," *Baptist Standard* 87 (3, 10, 17, 24 Sept. 1975); the articles were also published in *Ohio Baptist Messenger* and other state papers. There are thirty-one state Southern Baptist papers, most of them weeklies. The largest is the *Baptist Standard* [Texas], circulation 367,412 (in 1970); the *Alabama Baptist* is second largest, circulation 145,445 (1970).

44. Herschel H. Hobbs, "Baptist Beliefs," published in *Baptist Standard* and other state papers, Oct. 1975 through June 1976.

45. Minutes of the Seventy-Third Annual Meeting of the Dallas Baptist Association, 16 Oct. 1975, p. 32; "Union Association Condemns Charismatics," *Baptist Standard* 87 (29 Oct. 1975): 4; "Charismatic Warning," *Baptist Standard* 87 (12 Nov. 1975): 5; "Charismatic Church Ousted in California," *Baptist Standard* 88 (26 May 1976): 9; Nicholas, "Singing in the Spirit," 36–39.

46. Robert O'Brien, "Charismatic Issue Top Story: 1975," *Baptist Standard* 87 (Jan. 1976).

47. Nicholas, "Singing in the Spirit," 44, 46. The Home Mission Board strengthened its stance against charismatics in 1987, deciding not to "appoint, approve, or endorse" them for ministries under its oversight. See Nancy Tatom Ammerman, *Baptist Battles: Social Change and Religious Conflict in the Southern Baptist Convention* (New Brunswick, N.J.: Rutgers University Press, 1990), 224–25.

48. "Convention Presidents Sullivan, Harris View Issues," *Baptist Standard* 88 (27 Oct. 1976): 9.

49. "New President Supports Equal Rights for Women," *Biblical Recorder* [North Carolina state paper] 14 (25 June 1977): 2.

50. J. Terry Young, "Ousting Charismatic Churches," *The Theological Educator* 7 (July 1976): 8.

51. Nicholas, "Singing in the Spirit," 46–77, 44, 47.

52. "Convention Presidents Sullivan, Harris View Issues," 9.

53. Nicholas, "Singing in the Spirit," 36.

54. "Charismatic Baptists Meet," *The Baptist World* 24 (Nov. 1977), 11.

55. Nicholas, "Singing in the Spirit," 34–35.

56. Howe, "Charismatic Movement," 20.

57. Hocken, "Charismatic Movement," 141; James Allen Hewett, "Baptist Charismatics," in *Dictionary of Pentecostal and Charismatic Movements,* ed. Stanley M. Burgess and Gary B. McGee, 48–49. See also Synan, "The Third Wave," 57; "Southern Baptists Disagree over Tongues," *Charisma and Christian Life* 13 (Feb. 1983): 22.

58. Hocken, "Charismatic Movement," 139.

59. Compare, for example, Wayne E. Oates, "A Socio-Psychological Study of Glossolalia," in *Glossolalia,* 76–77 to Engleson, "Glosso-what?" 9. Simpson attested to cultural stigma attached Pentecostalism in the 19 May 1993 interview.

60. Walter B. Shurden, *Associationalism among Baptists in America: 1707–1807* (New York: Arno, 1980), 103. See also James E. Carter, "Dealing with Doctrinal Conflict in Associational History," *Baptist History and Heritage* 17 (1982): 34–35.

61. The unnamed historian is quoted in Alabama Baptist State Convention of the Southern Baptist Convention, *Annual* (Mobile, Ala., 1970), 77; Baker is quoted in idem, *Annual* (Mobile, Ala., 1978), 82.

62. Nicholas, "Singing in the Spirit," 39.

9

Irreconcilable Differences: Conflict, Schism, and Religious Restructuring in a United Methodist Church

Nancy L. Eiesland

In 1990 the Hinton Memorial United Methodist Church experienced a schism. Wracked by conflict for almost three years, the congregation finally divided along the fault lines of suburban charismatic versus small-town traditional Methodists.[1] For anyone who has spent much time examining the clashes and rapprochement of Pentecostal-mainline encounters, the story may seem familiar: a slow simmer, open factionalism, and then painful division. Behind this expected sequence of local congregational events, however, lay hints of front-line skirmishes over denominational restructuring, resulting, in part, from the influence of the charismatic movement on the mainline.

When examined in this broader context, the schism at Hinton Memorial is not primarily an example of the mainline's resistance to charismatics. Rather, the case underscores the organizational crises that accommodating them has created for mainline denominations and congregations. In particular, this local narrative illuminates the conflicts that can arise as a congregation's religious organizational context becomes increasingly complex and irreconcilably segmented. In examining changes in the religious organizational environment from the vantage point of the local congregation, we begin to see the changing institutional realities of American religion. Religious restructuring has resulted in new organizational players whose presence alters the relationships among denominational authority structures, agency networks, and local congregations.

Breaking the Tie That Binds

During my research on the effects of suburbanization on the religious institutions of a southern small town, I spent nearly two years doing participant observation at the Hinton Memorial United Methodist Church and in the Dacula area.[2] During this time I attended the typical worship, planning, and fellowship services and meetings of the congregation; I took my place on the serving line at the annual barbecue, helped with the youth car wash, cleaned the fellowship hall after potlucks, and generally participated in the formal and informal life of the church. Between April 1992 and August 1994 I conducted thirty interviews with present and past members of the congregation, in addition to interviewing key officials of the North Georgia Conference of the United Methodist Church (UMC)—the congregation's regional governing organization—key former pastors, and other individuals who were knowledgeable of or otherwise implicated in the congregational schism.

Hinton Memorial is located in Dacula, Georgia, a changing community. On the face of it, however, Dacula has changed very little in the past decade. The business district is still home to the weather-beaten country store that has been a fixture since the early 1900s, when "King Cotton" summoned local farmers to the town's gin. Yet this slow-paced small town has been at the frontier of rapid suburbanization on Atlanta's outer rim. Dacula has been slowly evolving from a rooted farming community toward an amalgamation of longtime residents, returning family members of longtime residents, and area newcomers.

Within this milieu Hinton Memorial United Methodist Church has been an enduring fixture. Its picturesque red-brick building with frosted windows and copper steeple has become a local symbol of community heritage and historical roots. Congregational life inside this and the previous building located on the same plot has often had a familial character. The sanctuary has been the site for three and four generations of baptisms, weddings, and funerals. The annual barbecue is a community family reunion as children and grandchildren, former residents, and kin return to feast on smoked pork sandwiches and vinegary coleslaw—a menu that has remained unchanged for decades.

The congregation's family feel is evident as well in the "carryin' on," as one longtime member termed the feuding that has characterized the congregation for many decades. It is impossible to say for sure whether congregants at Hinton through the years have fought more or less than the average church. But the perception of persons inside and outside the church is that Hinton earned its reputation as a fairly quarrelsome congregation. For much of its history since its founding in 1837, the congregation had been dominated by a stalwart family (for whom the church was named) whose social status in the community and regular infusions of funds guaranteed its leverage in the congregation. According to congregational tradition, however, the original Hinton family was both too controlling and too easily offended.

These qualities resulted in tense relations between the original Hintons and the North Georgia Conference as well. Judging from their actions, the conference officials felt that the church's size and budget did not warrant it the attention and special treatment, especially as regards the appointment of ministers, that the Hinton family thought was its due. In time Hinton Memorial became known in the conference as a difficult church. Through the years there were numerous congregational flare-ups about the decisions or indiscretions of pastors, use of church property, theological differences, conference slights, and so on. The significance of their reputation was not lost on the congregation when in the late 1970s, the bishop and district superintendent forced the congregation to take one of the North Georgia Conference's first "lady preachers." Convinced that the conference was conspiring to punish and humiliate them by appointing a woman to their pulpit, the offspring of the original Hinton family ceremoniously left the church, never to return.

The congregation settled into an unusually placid pattern of democratic rule for several years thereafter. The congregation's persistent shortage of funds and small size necessitated that they take part-time student pastors and young pastors fresh from seminary. For the most part, Hinton congregants were pleased with their pastoral leadership. Indeed, during the mid-1980s the congregation began to experience significant growth as young suburban families moving into the area were attracted by their young, energetic pastor, the Reverend Gerald Gerhard. Gerhard, whose appointment to Hinton was his first after completing seminary, was a talented preacher, and his family-oriented involvement and programs, such as serving on the local school advisory committee and sponsoring an alternative Halloween party, quickly earned him the allegiance of young newcomers to the area.

During the summer of 1987, as the congregation was preparing to celebrate their 150th anniversary, the old pattern of conflict and feuding returned. This time, however, after a century and a half of fighting together, the congregation experienced a schism. In 1990 their pastor of six years and nearly half of the members, approximately sixty people, left the congregation and the United Methodist Church to found an independent charismatic congregation, the Trinity Fellowship. The schism left Hinton Memorial severely crippled, financially and emotionally. In 1994 numbering approximately sixty people on Sunday mornings, Hinton Memorial began to rebound. It had not, however, experienced the growth of the schismatic group, which in 1993 exchanged their temporary quarters in the Dacula High School auditorium for a newly constructed facility for 350 worshipers. By 1996 Trinity Fellowship had approximately 225 worshipers on Sunday mornings, with several other weekday meetings drawing more than 100 participants.

The Charismatic Movement and Religious Restructuring

My exploration of the factors contributing to this congregational schism concentrates on a reconfigured religious organizational milieu and altered patterns of interaction between the congregation and denominational and extradenominational structures that fomented conflict in the congregation. The impetus for these changes in the religious organizational environment was, in part and in this case, the arrival on the United Methodist scene of the charismatic movement in the 1960s and 1970s. The history of the charismatic movement in the UMC is closely associated with other organized renewal efforts, such as the Good News and Lay Witness movements.[3] Although it is beyond the scope of this chapter to sketch the interrelationships among these populist renewal movements, it should be noted that Good News, founded in 1966, provided an important staging ground and ally for the early United Methodist charismatic movement. Like the Good News movement, charismatic Methodists presented theological and organizational challenges to the denomination.

The denomination's emphasis on theological and experiential pluralism, as well as the charismatic Methodists' explicit invocation of the denomination's early Holiness and expressivist history, led to an official UMC stance of theological tolerance for charismatic theology and worship practices.[4] At the 1976 Portland General Conference, delegates adopted a document entitled "Guidelines for the United Methodist Church and the Charismatic Movement." However, these general injunctions to, among other things, "remember that, in the history of the Church, the renewal of the church has had many forms and has come at different ages, and [that] the Charismatic renewal may have a valid contribution to make to the ecumenical Church," provided little in the way of concrete superintendence or assistance for charismatics in the denomination.[5]

This organizational vacuum was quickly filled by extradenominational charismatic agencies. In 1977 the United Methodist Renewal Service Fellowship (UMRSF), also known as Manna, was established by charismatic lay individuals. Although an autonomous agency, the UMRSF sought and received semi-official status and a liaison relationship with the denomination's Board of Discipleship. A Board of Discipleship staff member was designated to serve on the UMRSF board, and a UMRSF representative served as a member of the Board of Discipleship. The founding purposes of the UMRSF included providing an avenue for United Methodists to contribute to renewal by upholding "the teaching of Scriptural holiness in both its personal and social dimensions of the church to all constituencies of the church" and also to increase understanding of the "historical relationship between other churches in the Wesleyan tradition, including those of Holiness and Pentecostal doctrinal emphasis, and the United Methodist Church."[6]

Despite (or because of) their group's marginal status within the denomination, UMRSF leaders conceived their mission as institutional as well as theological renewal. The founding president of the UMRSF, Dr. William P. Wilson, then professor of psychiatry at Duke University Medical Center, identified the organizational implications of the charismatic movement in the UMC. In an article published in *Good News,* he proposed that many churches should he allowed to die and their property sold; that laymen and young ministers should be encouraged to establish new churches as house churches and then incorporate these congregations into the body of the church; that the denomination should consider abolishing the itinerancy of the ministry; and that the present system of church bureaucracy should be amended to make denominational boards and agencies of evangelism, education, and mission directly responsible to the membership of the church for their support.[7] Of the six proposals advanced by Wilson in this article, four regarded denominational restructuring; the other two positions taken explicitly concerned charismatic theology and practice.

In addition to the UMRSF's stated goals for institutional restructuring, its method of funding reinforced its populist stance and distanced it from the denomination's structures of authority and agencies. Unlike official UMC agencies, the UMRSF was approved but not funded. From its inception the agency has raised its funds through direct appeal to local congregations and individuals. As a result, the UMRSF has had perpetual financial strains and has often had to raise funds intensively among charismatic congregations to maintain its operations.

The UMRSF also failed in its efforts to gain acceptance among denominational leaders relatively early in its history. One former leader maintained that participation in the UMRSF was a career liability in the UMC. In recent years UMRSF leaders have spoken out against the church's rejection of their charismatic message and followers. "One of the great tragedies has been the

UM Church's failure to recognize and embrace the phenomenon of the charismatic renewal," Gary Moore, executive director of the UMRSF, stated in 1992. Because of that alienation, he believes, "tens or thousands of joyful, grace-filled Christians have wound up in other denominations and independent churches."[8]

Despite this lack of denominational inclusion, the UMRSF has had a stable and slightly increasing level of participation since its founding in 1976. Moore attributes this success to a "non-boring charismatic style of worship—worship that is exciting and full of energy, worship that lifts up and glorifies Jesus Christ. Congregations that experience that kind of worship are generally full of baby boomers, and busters, and are growing."[9] Today the UMRSF advances its charismatic agenda and cultivates relationships by conducting "Life in the Spirit" conferences and worship seminars held in local congregations, sponsoring national Aldersgate conferences that draw from 1,500 to 2,000 participants annually, holding pastoral training and enrichment gatherings, and connecting charismatic individuals with like-minded local pastors.

In addition to the UMRSF, other nondenominational charismatic special-purpose groups, such as Youth with a Mission and Women's Aglow Fellowship, have been allowed to expand their outreach within the UMC, often with the tacit approval of officials who sell them mailing lists or who invite leaders to speak at conferences. Generally, however, these groups have not had formal ties to the UMC's official bureaucratic or agency structures. They have, however, often maintained contact and provided mutual support to Methodist charismatics through the UMRSF and local congregations.

Finally, in a pattern not dissimilar to that of the Good News renewal groups, numerous other nascent specialized groups formed at the conference and regional levels to service local charismatic congregations and clergy. Many of these groups were short-lived organizations that banded together to conduct evangelistic meetings, prayer meetings, or minister training seminars. Other groups were somewhat more structured and enduring. One such organization was the Trinity Foundation. During the 1980s the Trinity Foundation was quickly becoming a clearinghouse for charismatic resources in the southeast region and a flashpoint for tensions over decentralization and diversity in the North Georgia Conference.

The Trinity Foundation was founded by the Reverend Mark Rutland, then an ordained minister in the North Georgia Conference, initially as a promotional agency for his evangelistic work. In 1987 Rutland received the "fellowship award" given by the National Association of United Methodist Evangelists. At thirty-nine, Rutland was then the youngest ever to receive the award.

Rutland traced his evangelistic success to a life-changing experience with the Holy Spirit in 1976. "Ten years ago I was sinking, going under as a Methodist pastor—involved in sin. My ministry was going bankrupt. My marriage was on the rocks. Through the ministry of David Seamands from Wilmore, Ky., and Ralph Wilkerson from California I received the Holy Spirit, and that completely revolutionized my life."[10] After his experience with the Holy Spirit, Rutland enjoyed considerable acceptance within the denomination for more than a decade. But Rutland commented that affiliation with a denomination had become less important in the contemporary religious environment. In an article published in 1986, Rutland responded to an interview question about denominational loyalty: "In my generation and in the following generation, that denominational loyalty has completely disintegrated. Methodism, per se, only means anything to anybody now as it presents a dynamic Gospel and the power of God. . . . What is needed more than anything else is for the clergy to be filled with the Holy Spirit. I think we are so rooted in climbing the corporate ladder of ecclesiastical success, of getting so involved in the church routine, that we have simply programmed power out of our own clergy."[11]

Through his Trinity Foundation, Rutland developed his own loyal following of charismatic pastors, lay persons, and missionaries. He used the foundation to further his goal of conducting conferences on the Holy Spirit in every UMC conference. In 1986 alone he reported leading more than four hundred evangelistic meetings, in addition to sponsoring pastoral training seminars and mission trips.

Restructuring Congregational Life

One of the ministers who attended a training seminar led by Rutland was Gerald Gerhard, Hinton Memorial's energetic young pastor. Gerhard, troubled by his inability to coax the Dacula congregation to take a more open stance toward the area newcomers had reached an impasse in his ministry and spiritual life. He reported that his frustration had nearly prompted him to quit the ministry before he attended Rutland's seminar. Although Gerhard did not experience the baptism in the Holy Spirit at the meeting, be did feel "a kinship in the Spirit" among the ministers that was unlike anything he had encountered in the denomination before. Within weeks Gerhard experienced the baptism of the Holy Spirit. In the months to come Gerhard became increasingly involved in the Trinity Foundation, attending seminars, reading Rutland's books, and fellowshipping with fellow charismatic pastors in Rutland's entourage.

At Hinton one longtime member who had long had "Holiness" leanings and who was instrumental in Gerhard's Holy Spirit baptism became a local ally as Gerhard made changes in the congregation's worship practices and resource procurement and allocation. But for most longtime Hinton members, Gerhard's inclusion of materials and practices gleaned from the Trinity Foundation, the UMRSF, and other extradenominational charismatic agencies was beyond the pale. Despite the protestations of Gerhard and a growing number of baby boomer charismatic congregants that Rutland was an ordained UMC minister, that the Trinity Foundation was approved by the North Georgia Conference, that the UMRSF was sanctioned by the denomination, and that charismatic theology and practices were authorized by the guidelines passed by the General Conference, traditional Methodist congregants maintained that charismatics were not Methodist. In their view, the inclusion of charismatic theological organizations and offerings within and on the margin of the denomination meant that the UMC had begun carrying a "new line" of denominationally sanctioned product—one that was often seen to be in direct competition with their "old line." Especially for small southern UMC congregations, such as Hinton Memorial, the inclusion of charismatics disrupted the southern small-town religious order, where Methodists occupied the upper echelons of social respectability and Pentecostals (all varieties) clustered near the bottom (below Baptists, both Southern Baptist Convention and independent).

Yet even this significant blow to denominational identity and small-town social order might have been sustained (the church had after all survived the "lady preacher," who also represented significant disruption of denominational identity and southern small-town order) had the congregational conflict not also become proxy for the organizational tensions within the North Georgia Conference and the denomination as a whole. During the late 1980s at Hinton, a division was emerging between the congregation's official councils—such as the administrative board and the trustees committee—which maintained the familiar but infrequent relations with the conference bishop and the district superintendent, and Gerhard and a growing group of charismatic dissidents, who related extensively to the Trinity Foundation, the UMRSF, and other extradenominational charismatic organizations. Some Hinton congregants sought continued access to the denominational Sunday school literature and mission agencies, whereas others came to employ the Sunday school literature and the mission offerings of the Trinity Foundation. Some worked to continue the United Methodist Women's Fellowship and to support the North Georgia Conference–sponsored events, whereas others attended the Gwinnett County Aglow chapter and assumed leadership roles there. As conflict within the congregation regarding group identity and resources escalated, each group called on different denominational and extradenominational religious resources.

Furthermore, these alternative denominational and extradenominational resources became symbolized in the congregation's worship and ritual practices. The charismatic faction frequently invited a fiery Trinity Foundation–funded missionary to speak at regular Sunday morning services. Several members of Hinton's administrative board, on the other hand, invited the district superintendent to their homes for "eating" meetings to get advice about the growing congregational tension. Gerhard also altered the church's longstanding liturgical practices to include numerous worship choruses projected on the cinder-block wall of the choir loft and substituted unstructured praise and prayer for the Apostles Creed and the Lord's Prayer. Additionally, he replaced the choir, composed mostly of traditional Methodists, with a worship team, including charismatic drummers and guitarists.

Disputes also erupted over religious symbols in the congregation. Several charismatic women in the congregation objected to the statue of Mary in the church's rose garden and the ceramic likeness of Jesus in the parlor, arguing that they could easily be perceived as idols. Members of the trustees' committee, however, refused to remove the figures, contending that there was "nothing in Methodism" that forbade the use of representational art. The congregation soon gained a reputation, depending on factional allegiance, as either a charismatic "safe haven" or a "ghetto."

As the traditional Methodists grew increasingly dissatisfied with the worship style and sermon content of the main worship service, they petitioned the bishop for aid in restoring Methodism to their congregation. The bishop intervened, requiring the pastor to offer a "traditional" Methodist service. Gerhard did so but scheduled the gathering for 8:00 A.M. Sundays. The bishop also ordered Hinton Memorial to sever its ties with the Trinity Foundation, although the agency continued to be a part of the North Georgia Conference and Rutland was still an ordained UMC minister in ostensibly good standing. By then the road to schism had been paved not only by the recourse to divergent denominational and extradenominational resources and structures but also by the small and large insults of face-to-face conflict. The two-service scheme lasted only four months before the bishop again intervened, at the behest of the traditional Methodist congregants. The bishop decided it was time for Gerhard to move on. Gerhard, perceiving a punitive motive in his appointment to an even smaller, more remote congregation despite the increased membership and improved financial condition of Hinton Memorial under his leadership, appealed to Mark Rutland and the Trinity Foundation for help.

By 1990 Rutland, too, had been experiencing the disadvantages of maintaining ordination and institutional ties with the denomination. Called on frequently to justify his extradenominational work—he was then serving as associate pastor at Mount Paran Church of God, an Atlanta megachurch—he had also become the focus of unflattering rumors and innuendo in the conference. Finally, after meeting with the bishop, Rutland left the denomination and made the Trinity Foundation a nondenominational agency.

Little incentive remained for Gerhard and the charismatic congregants at Hinton to maintain ties with the denomination. The charismatics left, taking with them much of the financial resources and programmatic enterprise that had fostered the church's growth. The schism at Hinton was followed within a year by schisms in five other UMC congregations in the North Georgia Conference. Each of these congregations had charismatic pastors or congregants who had maintained relations with the Trinity Foundation, the UMRSF, and other extradenominational charismatic agencies.

The Trinity Foundation had now become a loose network of congregations that combined resources for publishing efforts, training conferences, youth gatherings, and missionary and evangelistic outreach. Although Rutland had no direct authority function within the group, ministers associated with the Trinity Foundation regularly gathered with him for prayer and mutual support. Among the charismatic ministers, Rutland was clearly regarded as a spiritual leader and as a person whose advice and direction was often sought. "I'm just someone they can talk to when they need to talk," said Rutland. This minimalist organizational pattern suits these denominational defectors well.

Connecting Congregational and Denominational Restructuring

Hinton Memorial's story reveals that the outcomes of conflict in a local congregation were heavily shaped by organizations outside that congregation. In particular, the competing influence of various denominational and extradenominational organizations that provided resources and placed constraints on the congregation had much to do with the church schism examined here. Secondarily, the issues faced by this congregation are typical of the issues facing mainline Protestantism more generally. The diversity of religious identities within mainline Protestantism has led to the creation of a variety of denominational agencies and affiliation with extradenominational organizations that seek to meet the more specific needs of persons and congregations with particularistic religious identities. Thus when a single congregation incorporates people of diverse and competing identities, the outcome of conflict between these groups may well depend on the resources and constraints provided by the denominational and extradenominational organizations representing these divergent religious identities. The schism of Hinton Memorial described here would not have happened were it not for the presence of the Trinity Foundation and the UMRSF, two organizations serving the needs of charismatic ministers and congregations in the North Georgia Conference of the UMC.

Hinton Memorial's story helps us to see more clearly what the changing religious organizational environment looks like at the congregational level and to reveal the organizational factors that foment conflict and sometimes schism. A closer look at earlier research on congregational schism and religious organizational change will help us to return to the insights revealed by Hinton Memorial's narrative of conflict and schism and to address the congregational impact of the charismatic movement in particular and of the increasingly complex religious organizational environment in general.

Congregational schism and conflict can be a feature of shifting organizational patterns inside, on the margins of, and outside denominations. At present only a few studies of congregational schism exist, and even fewer deal in any detail with congregational schism in relation to the changing religious organizational nexus. The reasons for this lack of published research are many, not the least of which is the failure of denominations to compile adequate data on congregational schism. Hence sociologists lack systematic comparative data that would let them analyze, for example, the effects of church size or age as factors in conflict and schism. Terminological fuzziness around the topic of congregational schism also contributes to the inadequacy of the published research. *Schism* can refer either to secession—that is, an entire congregation's departure from its original denomination—or to intracongregational division or church splits.[12] It is this latter usage to which I refer in this essay.

Although the causes and processes of congregational secession and church splits surely overlap, the two phenomena are nonetheless quite different organizational occurrences and must be distinguished and researched separately. Research on congregational secession generally ties it to denominational conflict and schism, usually concerning disputes over doctrine or problems of governance.[13] There is a growing body of literature on this topic.[14] On church splits, however, the published literature is quite meager. This research tends to focus on the internal workings of the congregation[15] or on broad cultural changes[16] but seldom on the congregation's connections with denominational and extradenominational resources and groups. One exception to this tendency is Shin and Park's case histories of Korean American congregations.[17] Their research emphasizes the discrepancy that exists between the centrality of congregational life among Korean American immigrants and the marginality of their congregations within their various denominations. Shin and Park explain the high incidence of church splits that they found in part by the fact that local leaders and congregants who invest considerable emotional and social energy in their churches receive relatively little denominational oversight and support.

Although existing research does not aid us considerably in developing a grounded theory of congregational schism, research and theorizing about changes in the religious organizational environment does move this theoretical effort forward. This work clusters around two distinct but overlapping constellations of concerns. Some sociologists of religion have focused on denominations, examining their complex institutional histories, their multiple internal structures, and their liaison relations with special-purpose groups. Other sociologists have turned their attention to organizations, such as Calvary Chapel and the Cooperative Baptist Fellowship, that do not look like "traditional" denominations and yet are religious organizations for resourcing and supporting congregations.[18]

The changing structure and prospects of the denomination have been the topic of much social scientific speculation and research in recent years. Could it be that denominations, as we know them, are on their last leg? Some contend that the denomination "appears out of kilter, if not hopelessly obsolete."[19] Earlier theoretical approaches to denominations also appear to be somewhat antiquated. Denominations, we now know, are complex organizations whose offerings are becoming more and more diversified. They no longer "run herd" on a stable of congregations, if ever they did. Rather, congregations play a much more active role in demanding and consuming denominational and extradenominational religious and social programs and ideas.[20] Both in terms of the intellectual constructions through which denominations are analyzed and in relation to the emerging forms that these theories attempt to capture, the recurring theme is shifting power relationships and deep-seated institutional diversity.

Mark Chaves and Robert Wuthnow, in particular, have highlighted denominations' complex institutional histories, their multiple internal structures and politics, and their networks of liaison relationships with special-purpose groups. According to Chaves, treating denominations as unitary bureaucratic structures belies their historical and contemporary complexity. Distinguishing between denominational authority and agency structures, he maintains that denominations are both bureaucracies charged with maintaining religious orthodoxy and more or less loosely knit systems of religious agencies.[21] As denominations developed in the late nineteenth and early twentieth centuries, they incorporated or internally reproduced the functions of nondenominational and interdenominational voluntary societies. In so doing, denominations became organizations with parallel authority and agency structures.

Chaves notes that these structures, distinct at the national level, have interacted with congregations dissimilarly as well. Denominational authority structures have controlled goods needed by the congregation—for example, pastoral and financial resources—and represent denominational theological and ritual orthodoxy. The religious elites who constitute this structure maintain relations of relative dominance with the congregation. Authority structures differentiate through geographical segmentation, eventuating in divisions such as synods, districts, and conferences, within which quite strict hierarchical relations are maintained. Agency structures, on the other hand, are composed of those groups within denominations that service the specialized needs of congregations, including Sunday school agencies, mission groups, and charismatic service agencies. Although congregations may desire the goods offered by agencies, they are in no way constrained to accept them. Unlike the authority structure that maintains its legitimacy primarily through its constancy in identity coordination and its imposition of a strong denominational culture, agency structures must remain adaptable and responsive to changing circumstances and demands within the religious market. Emerging from common needs and niche values, agency structures often must accommodate individuals who have stronger commitment to their specialized groups than to a corporate denominational identity. Over time within denominations, agency structures adopted the bureaucratic structures that defined the authority structure, reducing their flexibility and adaptability. Although denominational agencies have undergone periods of centralization and bureaucratization, they have been regularly supplemented by other agencies whose ties with the denomination were looser and whose relations with the authority were tenuous or nonexistent.

According to Robert Wuthnow, these alternative agencies—special-purpose groups—have crowded the religious organizational environment in recent decades. As described by Wuthnow, these agencies are interdenominational or nondenominational unifocal groups, and the growth in their numbers is closely linked to increased tension within denominations between conservative and liberal factions.[22] Special-purpose groups developed by drawing on the existing religious infrastructure provided by local churches and preexistent religious groups and have employed a niche-based, single-issue marketing strategy. In the process, they have enabled denominations to "subcontract" (in fact, if not intentionally) to meet some religious needs. Noting that the number of special-purpose groups has been on the rise since the 1960s, Wuthnow contends that they constitute a significant term of restructuring of American religion. The growth of special-purpose groups has far outpaced that of denominations. During the 1960s and early 1970s special-purpose groups grew "at least a third faster than denominations," and they have continued to increase in prominence while denominations declined.[23]

In addition to the special-purpose groups identified by Wuthnow, affiliate agencies, such as the UMRSF, have become quite common. Affiliate agencies, like official denominational service agencies, provide resources exclusively within one denomination. Unlike most denominational service agencies, however, they have only semi-official status and extensive autonomy. With declining membership and budgetary strictures, denominations are resorting to affiliate agencies to provide diverse services without the necessity of funding through central budgetary allocation. These affiliate agencies must raise support directly from individuals and congregations within the denomination. This funding arrangement results in a relationship between affiliate agencies and confederate congregations that is quite sensitive to religious consumers' demands.

The past three decades have been particularly fortuitous for agency entrepreneurs. An insurgency of social and religious movements in the 1960s and 1970s resulted in the creation of numerous new service agencies within, on the margins, and outside of denominations. Increasingly denominational agency structures have evolved from relatively centralized organizations whose offerings were largely consonant with the orthodoxy promulgated by the elites of the authority structure toward diffuse, diversified networks whose services, programs, and loyalties reflect the ritual and theological diversity of the religious market. This diversity, in turn, diffuses denominational identity. Thus, a clear coincidence no longer exists between what, for example, old-timers know in their guts to be Methodism and what is tacitly or explicitly endorsed by denominational officials.

In sum, according to Chaves, tensions within denominations between agency and authority structures can foment conflict and schism within congregations, such as Hinton Memorial, whose factions maintain primary relations with elites from one or the other type of structure. In his discussion of special-purpose groups, Wuthnow sketches how their growth has resulted in the segmentation and expansion of the religious organizational environment. Furthermore, the case study of congregational conflict and schism at Hinton Memorial reveals the role of affiliate agencies, such as the UMRSF, in promoting theological, ritual, and organizational diversity within denominations.

Although they are neither denominations nor special-purpose groups, religious organizations, such as the Trinity Foundation, also provide resources, support, and connections for pastors and congregations. Several scholars see in such groups a new postmodern organizational form. In his descriptive conceptions of the Calvary Chapel, the Vineyard Christian Fellowship, and the Hope Chapel, Don Miller has maintained that these groups exhibit postmodern characteristics.[24] Although his analysis focuses on their attractiveness to "postmodern" individuals, he also highlights what he sees as their unique approach to religious leadership, which emphasizes mutuality and collegiality rather than hierarchy and direct authority.

Nancy Ammerman discusses the nature of such groups in an article suggesting that from the Baptist battles a new postmodern organization may be taking shape as the Cooperative Baptist Fellowship works to invent itself.[25] Ammerman contends that this new organizational form is distinguished by significant differences from traditional denominations in the exercise of authority and in resourcing. She detects the presence of innovative religious leaders who seek to enable effective recognition and representation of the distinct voices and perspectives of constituent groups. Groups within the Cooperative Baptist Fellowship are self-organizing to fill niches and are relating to one another to address common problems and interests, as well as to create a community of mutual identification. Ammerman notes that it is too early in its history to predict whether the Cooperative Baptist Fellowship will succeed in inventing such a postmodern denomination.

In identifying the Cooperative Baptist Fellowship as an emerging postmodern organizational form, Ammerman follows the distinctions between characteristics of modern and postmodern organizations made by Stewart Clegg in his book *Modern Organizations: Organizations in a Postmodern World.* Clegg identifies the modern organization "in terms of Weber's typifications of bureaucratised, mechanistic structures of control."[26] Rooted in an increasing functional differentiation of social phenomena, modern organizations provide the frameworks that link these differentiations and that integrate them through a formalized and codified system of rules. The modern organization is a bureaucratic regime of regulations, hierarchies, predictability, and centralization.

Clegg describes the postmodern organization in contrasting terms: "It would tend to be small or located in small subunits of larger organizations; its object is typically service or information, if not automated production; its technology is computerised; its division of labor is informal or flexible; and its management structure is functionally decentralised, eclectic and participative, overlapping in many ways with nonmanagerial functions."[27] The postmodern organization is de-differentiated, self-regulating, fluid, and flexible, held together by a communal rather than a corporate culture and by interdependent relations.

Whether or not one characterizes organizations such as Calvary Chapel and the Vineyard Christian Fellowship, as well as the smaller but ambitious Trinity Foundation, as "postmodern," these loose religious alliances now exist within the mainstream religious organizational environment. As newly recognized elements in the religious environment, they invite comparison with existent denominations by scholars, journalists, lay persons, and clergy. This relationship is particularly relevant since the popular press frequently counterposes the growth of these organizations with the decline of mainline denominations. Furthermore, these religious alliances create more options for congregations, clergy, and lay persons who are dissatisfied with their treatment, resources, or governance in their mainline denominations. Whether or not these individuals or congregations affiliate with these emerging groups, the groups' publicized success makes breaking with traditional denominations both more viable and more attractive.

Scholars interested in assessing the impact of the charismatic movement on mainline denominations and congregations must recognize that the charismatic movement has resulted in increased diversity and competition in the religious organizational environment. The charismatic movement proved to be a boon for denominational agency building similar in some ways to the missions movement of the early 1800s. In the early 1970s nearly every mainline denomination established a charismatic service agency.[28] Some of these agencies received direct denominational support, but many, such as the UMRSF, were established as affiliate agencies. In addition to nationwide charismatic agencies, regional and local organizations were organized. These organizations were often composed of several clergy members or congregations that banded together to foster and encourage charismatic theology and practice in their immediate environs. Autonomous special-purpose groups also sprang to life to support and facilitate charismatic innovation. Finally, new charismatic organizations, such as the Trinity Foundation, have created new models for religious association and programmatic cooperation that challenge existing denominational practices. This proliferation of charismatic agencies within, across, and outside denominational boundaries allowed denominations to respond to changes in the religious market by relying on a loose network of agencies many of which had little connection with the denomination's authority structure, but they did so at the expense of a unified denominational identity and denominational control of resource venues. Denominational tensions between agency networks and authority structures over identity, loyalty, and authority have been chronicled by Ammerman, Chaves, and Wuthnow.[29]

Although tensions related to organizational diversity and proliferation are evident in national denominational politics, they are also, as I have shown, very much present at the congregational level, where these organizational battles are fought by proxy. Although religious elites from the authority structure have relatively little control over the services and programs of this emergent network of agencies, they do have considerable power over the careers of denominational pastors, especially in an episcopal polity, although to a large extent in other polities as well. Hence the locus of any power struggle between the centralized authority structure attempting to maintain unified orthodoxy and the diffused network of agencies propagating theological diversity tends to be the congregation itself; in particular, such struggles are often manifested in local battles over pastoral leadership.

As an official from the UMRSF stated: "I guess we still have the biggest problems with gaining acceptance from bishops and district superintendents. They often see our pastors as a little suspect. . . . Sometimes they get moved around more than others or they get the 'difficult' churches." A charismatic pastor notes, "I was caught between [the district superintendent] who wanted to rid his area of charismatic pastors and the national guys who keep sending me stuff that told me that 'charismatic' and 'Methodist' go together."[30] Thus pastors and congregations have become the battleground as putative orthodoxies and the hierarchical power that backs them up encounter unharmonized representatives of religious variety.

Moreover, it is at the congregational level that individuals and groups must choose from this impressive array of specialized services to fashion a mission and vision. Congregations must cope, if they can, at close range with the diversity represented by groups within the congregation that may call on different and sometimes seemingly irreconcilable denominational and extradenominational offerings. Finally, with this organizational proliferation, when battles do erupt, disgruntled pastors and lay persons often have institutional options that may make denominational exit more attractive. The existence of such successful religious organizations as the Trinity Foundation, Vineyard Christian Fellowship, and Calvary Chapel has increased the legitimacy of breaking with denominations. Congregations can become "independent" and yet enjoy the benefits of shared resources, services, and support. For many charismatics in the UMC, the costs of staying have become higher than the costs of schism.

Thus, to address congregational conflict and schism, we must consider the complexity and segmentation of the religious organizational environment inhabited by most mainline congregations. In their efforts to compete in an increasingly competitive religious marketplace, denominations have sometimes created and sometimes subcontracted with agencies to meet congregational demands. The success of this arrangement has had the unintended consequence of diluting denominational identity and of vastly increasing, with at least tacit denominational sanction, the array of services, ideas, and programs available to local congregations. Denominations also have increased competition from emergent religious groups for the loyalty of congregations. Furthermore, mainline denominations are now compared, often unfavorably, to these new streamlined, innovative groups, which are relatively unencumbered bureaucratically and whose financial demands on local congregations are minimal. Participants in religious movements, such as the charismatic movement, have facilitated this segmentation and have, in turn, been caught up in the considerable controversy generated not only by theological and ritual diversity but also by the organizational changes they have helped to set in motion.

Notes

1. Pseudonyms have been used for individuals involved with Hinton Memorial, with the exception of the Reverend Mark Rutland, who is a well-known leader in the charismatic movement. Hinton Memorial was the actual name of the congregation located in Dacula, Georgia.

2. See also Nancy Eiesland, *A Particular Place: Exurbanization and Religious Response* (New Brunswick, N.J.: Rutgers University Press, forthcoming); idem, "Contending with a Giant: The Impact of a Megachurch on Exurban Religious Institutions," in *Contemporary American Religion: An Ethnographic Reader*, ed. Penny Edgell Becker and Nancy L. Eiesland, 191–219 (Walnut Creek, Calif.: AltaMira, 1997).

3. For an anecdotal history of the Good News movement by its founder, see C. W. Keyson, "The Story of Good News," *Good News* 14 (Mar.–Apr. 1980): 9–73.

4. Peter D. Hocken, "Charismatic Movement," in *Dictionary of Pentecostal and Charismatic Movements*, ed. Stanley M. Burgess and Gary B. McGee (Grand Rapids, Mich.: Zondervan, 1988).

5. Diane Knippers, "Conference Celebrates Holy Spirit," *Good News* 14 (Nov.–Dec. 1980): 50–51.

6. See General Board of Discipleship, United Methodist Church, *Guidelines for the*

United Methodist Church and the Charismatic Movement (1976), reprinted in *Good News* 9 (May–June 1976): I35–I40.

7. William P. Wilson, "A Psychiatrist Analyzes Our Church," *Good News* 11 (May–June 1978): 13–17, 76–78, 83–84.

8. "UM Charismatics Flourish," *Good News* 26 (Sept.–Oct. 1992): 41.

9. Ibid.

10. "A United Methodist Evangelist Talks about His Church," *Good News* 20 (Sept.–Oct. 1986): 35.

11. Ibid., 34–35.

12. Mary Lou Steed, "Church Schism and Secession: A Necessary Sequence," *Review of Religious Research* 27, no. 4 (1986): 344–55. See also P. E. Becker, S. Ellingson, R. Flory, W. Griswold, F. Kniss, and T. Nelson, "Straining at the Tie That Binds: Congregational Conflict in the 1980s," *Review of Religious Research* 34, no. 3 (1993): 193–209.

13. See Nancy Tatom Ammerman, *Baptist Battles: Social Change and Religious Conflict in the Southern Baptist Convention* (New Brunswick, N.J.: Rutgers University Press, 1990); and Michael I. Harrison and John K. Maniha, "Dynamics of Dissenting Movements within Established Organizations: Two Cases and a Theoretical Interpretation," *Journal for the Scientific Study of Religion* 17 (1978): 207–24.

14. See Rodney Stark and William Sims Bainbridge, "Of Churches, Sects and Cults: Preliminary Concepts for a Theory of Religious Movements," *Journal for the Scientific Study of Religion* 18 (1979): 117–33; idem, *The Future of Religion: Secularization, Revival, and Cult Formation* (Berkeley: University of California Press, 1985); J. Wilson, "The Sociology of Schism," in *A Sociology Yearbook of Religion in Britain* (N.p.: n.p., 1971), 1–20; and R. C. Liebman, J. R. Sutton, and R. Wuthnow, "Exploring the Social Sources of Denominationalism: Schisms in American Protestant Denominations, 1890–1980," *American Sociological Review* 53 (1988): 343–52.

15. Charles R. Echols, "Reuniting a Theologically Divided Church by Helping Its Charismatic and Traditional United Methodist Members Work Together as the Body of Christ," Ph.D. diss., Pittsburgh Theological Seminary, 1988.

16. Stephen Warner, *New Wine in Old Wineskins: Evangelicals and Liberals in a Small-town Church* (Berkeley: University of California Press, 1988).

17. Eui Hang Shin and Hyung Park, "An Analysis of Causes of Schism in Ethnic Churches: The Case of Korean-American Churches," *Sociological Abstracts* 49 (Fall 1988): 234–48.

18. Mark Shibley, *Resurgent Evangelicalism: Mapping Cultural Change since 1970* (Columbia: University of South Carolina Press, 1996); Donald Miller, *Reinventing American Protestantism: Christianity in the New Millenium* (Berkeley: University of California Press, 1997); R. Marie Griffith, *God's Daughters: Evangelical Women and the Power of Submission* (Berkeley: University of California Press, 1997).

19. Jackson Carroll and Wade Clark Roof, eds., *Beyond Establishment: Protestant Identity in a Post-Protestant Age* (Louisville, Ky.: Westminster/John Knox Press, 1993), 11.

20. Stephen Warner, "Work in Progress toward a New Paradigm for the Sociological Study of Religion in the United States," *American Journal of Sociology* 98, no. 5 (1993): 1044–93.

21. Mark Chaves, "Denominations as Dual Structures: An Organizational Analysis," *Sociology of Religion* 2 (1993): 147–69.

22. Robert Wuthnow, *The Restructuring of American Religion* (Princeton, N.J.: Princeton University Press, 1988).

23. Ibid., 113.

24. Miller, *Reinventing American Protestantism.*

25. Nancy Tatom Ammerman, "SBC Moderates and the Making of a Postmodern Denomination," *The Christian Century* 110 (22–29 Sept. 1993): 896–99. See also Ammerman, "Denominations: Who and What Are We Studying?" in *Reimagining Denominationalism: Interpretive Essays,* ed. R. B. Mullin and R. Richey, 111–13 (New York: Oxford University Press, 1994); and idem, *Congregation and Community* (New Brunswick, N.J.: Rutgers University Press, 1997).

26. Stewart Clegg, *Modern Organizations: Organization Studies in the Postmodern World* (London: Sage, 1990): 177.

27. Ibid., 17.

28. Hocken, "Charismatic Movement."

29. Ammerman, *Baptist Battles;* idem, *Congregation and Community;* Chaves, "Denominations as Dual Structures"; Wuthnow, *Restructuring of American Religion.*

30. Quotations from interviews conducted by the author, 1993.

10

At Arm's Length: The First Presbyterian Church, Pittsburgh, and Kathryn Kuhlman

Frederick W. Jordan

Despite her national fame at the time of her death in 1973, much of the life and ministry of Kathryn Kuhlman remains pockmarked with ambiguity. Gaps in evidence or contradictory accounts appear practically from the cradle to (beyond) the grave, from her earliest schooling to questions surrounding her will after her death.[1] The facts that do emerge paint a portrait that is anomalous in the context of explanations for the rise of neo-Pentecostalism after 1950. A faith healer, she forswore many of the manipulative devices of similar ministries.[2] She was a woman engaged in work dominated by men, uneasily passing a torch from Amiee Semple McPherson to Tammy Fay Bakker. She was one of the first televangelists, male or female. Pentecostals were not even sure she was one of them; mainline Protestants were quite sure she was not one of them. She began her ministry in an era during which Pentecostals were considered part of the lunatic fringe of Christianity, and she died just as Pentecostalism was poised to become "the second most widespread variety of Christian spiritual lifestyle" (after Roman Catholicism).[3]

Kuhlman's story is an integral part of the transition that Pentecostals made from the Azusa Street storefront mission of 1906 to Hilton ballrooms after 1970. For many years, however, hers was not a part of the development of mainline Protestantism. From the social class of her constituency (blue-collar ethnic stock) to the practices in her services to her own gender, her ministry operated on the cultural periphery of mainline churches in almost every sense of the word. How, then, did she come to hold her healing services in the sanctuary of one of the oldest and most prestigious churches in Pittsburgh from 1966 to 1976, one that stood at the center of the postwar evangelical coalition?

From the beginning of her public ministry in the 1920s until 1966, Kathryn Kuhlman's goal of a permanent base proved remarkably elusive. Various attempts to situate herself in a single place—the most notable came in Denver in the 1930s and in northwestern Pennsylvania the following decade—failed until 1952.[4] In that year, however, she began regularly holding services in Carnegie Hall, a city-owned auditorium situated in a working-class neighborhood of Pittsburgh's North Side. It met many of the needs for her ministry: it was spacious, located in a safe area, and, important to her faith-healing ministry, accessible to wheelchairs. As her stay in Pittsburgh lengthened, Kuhlman also sought to develop a sense of institutional stability, establishing the Kathryn Kuhlman Foundation in 1957. Similar to the other kinds of institution building that Pentecostals were engaged in across the country,[5] the foundation provided a means to manage and direct the large amount of money that her ministry was taking in. It also afforded her with a degree of middle-class respectability.

During the Carnegie Hall years (1952–66) Kuhlman also began assembling the building blocks for the national ministry that was to characterize the final stage of her career, beginning in 1966. She sponsored the ghostwritten *I Believe in Miracles,* a testimonial to the healings that had taken place in her ministry. It eventually sold over two million copies.[6] She also began to conduct her ministry in an increasingly wider geographic range, with regular services at the Shrine Auditorium beginning in 1965.[7]

By 1966 Kuhlman's ministry therefore appeared to be stable, entrenched, and expanding. That year, however, the city of Pittsburgh undertook an extensive urban redevelopment program on its North Side. Carnegie Hall was among the buildings slated for renovation, thus forcing Kuhlman, at least temporarily, to find other quarters.[8] Much of the North Side would be rendered impassable during the construction, imposing particular hardship on her wheelchair-bound clientele.[9] There was temporary space available elsewhere in the metropolitan area at the Soldiers and Sailors Memorial Home in nearby Oakland or perhaps at the Syna Mosque in Pittsburgh, but their small size made both locations problematic as long-term solutions.

Some options were closed to Kuhlman. One was to approach established churches. Kuhlman suffered from the fact that she walked in a theological shadow world between the Pentecostal and mainline Protestant denominations. The Pentecostals held her at arm's length. On the one hand, she did make a distinction between professing Christ and accepting the gift of the Holy Spirit, thus implying the two-stage process characteristic of classical Pentecostalism.[10] However, at least by the 1940s, she did not preach the necessity of a "second Baptism," thus denying one of Pentecostalism's central tenets. Furthermore, although she affirmed its biblical basis, she denied the necessity of speaking in tongues and often forbade its use in her healing services, preferring instead what she called a "holy hush."[11] She failed to pass their litmus test by not speaking out on her own experience of being baptized in the Spirit.[12] As time had gone on, she had increasingly restricted the use of tongues in both her services and her personal life.[13] And her almost casual use of laying hands on people gave rise to vague associations with the latter rain movement condemned by many traditional Pentecostals.[14]

Kuhlman would have had even less hope in approaching typical mainline churches, distrustful as they were of Pentecostals. Kuhlman's failure to adhere to orthodox Pentecostal practices (perhaps an oxymoronic phrase at best) makes the question of whether Kuhlman was in fact a traditional Pentecostal difficult, for she does not fit into the category easily. David Edwin Harrell categorizes her as a "fellow traveler" who was only "marginally related to the healing revival of the post–World War II era."[15] In her relationships with the established denominations, however, the determinative element was perceptions and images, not doctrine. The presence of supernatural healing in her ministry shaped the perceptions of mainliners far more than did theological statements. To them, Kuhlman looked, felt, and acted like a Pentecostal; therefore she must be considered one.

Furthermore, there were substantive issues in addition to concerns over Kuhlman's "tone." Mainliners would ignore her increasing disuse of tongues in her services and instead worry that she had spoken in tongues for years and advocated its use, for she maintained that the practice was both biblical and part of her own experience. She preached that the use of all the gifts of the Holy Spirit was normative for the church. Not only did she obviously include healing in the gifts of the Spirit, but she went a step further and held that healing is in the atonement and should therefore be an expected part of the Christian life.[16] Other factors also made her suspect. She was a woman exercising responsibilities of preaching and wielding authority.[17] The presence of Episcopalians and Roman Catholics at her services and on the platform particularly riled fundamentalists, drawing the ire of John R. Rice.[18] And then there were the goings-on in her worship services that would strike mainline Christians as odd at best. One horrified veteran of Billy Graham's Pittsburgh crusade reported the bizarre behavior of a woman in one of the crusade's counseling rooms. Mrs. Arthur Gluck reported that the woman "suddenly clenched both fists tightly and her forearms moved up and down so furiously that her whole torso vibrated. This lasted for several seconds. After a period of quiet she had another seizure." On further inquiry, Gluck was told, "If you go hear Katherine [*sic*] Kuhlman you will see that shaking all over the hall. That is the Holy Ghost coming on them."[19] The mysterious practice of "falling under the power," in which people swooned into an unconscious state, also gave mainliners pause: one woman claimed that in one service, 150 people "went under" at once.[20]

But it was not only the individual practices that bothered mainline Christians. The fact was that Pentecostal services in general, and Kuhlman's services in particular, were fundamentally different *in toto*. The stereotypical preaching, the style of praying, and the use of hand clapping all smacked of something radically different in both tone and substance. Whereas mainline churches were structured, she was spontaneous; whereas they were rational, she was emotional and even a bit mystical; whereas they often hinted at a hierarchical structure in life, her "folksy" style communicated an implicit egalitarianism.[21] Even the music in her services at times departed from traditional hymns to include early "praise choruses" such as the "Alleluia" refrain.[22] In short, to allow such practices into a mainline church would be to admit the Samaritans of twentieth-century Protestantism.

All in all, in late 1966 Kuhlman had little hope of establishing herself in a church, whether mainline or Pentecostal. Anyone suggesting that she would wind up at one of the largest and most prestigious churches in the city would have been greeted with utter derision. But at this point an extraordinary series of circumstances combined to do just that.

In 1966 the influential evangelical periodical *Christianity Today* asked the Pew Charitable Trusts to fund a worldwide conference on evangelism. With a grant of $400,000, the resulting Berlin Congress on Evangelism was broad visioned, with one stated goal being "nothing short of the evangelization of the human race in this generation, by every means God has given to the mind and will of men."[23] Billy Graham had originally formulated the idea; Carl F. H. Henry, the editor of *Christianity Today*, agreed to sponsor it as a tenth-anniversary project for the publication.[24] The congress eventually met in Berlin from 25 October to 4 November 1966.

That the congress must be an international gathering was unquestioned. A ceiling of 100 delegates from the United States was imposed, and 1,200 people from over 100 nations ultimately attended.[25] These individuals represented a wide range of church bodies, although theological liberals in the World Council of Churches declined to participate.[26] Not only were representatives from evangelical organizations, churches, and denominations there, but enormous efforts had been made to contact Christians from well outside the core of the evangelical coalition,[27] including bodies such as the Ethiopian Orthodox Church and India's Mar Thoma Church.[28] Only slightly less removed from the evangelical solar system were the Pentecostals, who were well represented at the congress. Delegates included Oral Roberts, at that time the most prominent faith healer in the United States; Thomas F. Zimmerman, general superintendent of the Assemblies of God, the largest Pentecostal denomination; and Argos Zodhiates, pastor of London's Full Gospel Tabernacle and a voice for Pentecostalism.[29] Numerous other Pentecostals attended the congress as "observers" (rather than as formal delegates), including a number of Latin American Pentecostals.[30] Before the congress even met, however, the Latin American delegation had indirectly but profoundly influenced the ministry of Kathryn Kuhlman.

Among the organizers of, and speakers at, the congress was the pastor of Pittsburgh's First Presbyterian Church, Robert Lamont.[31] A graduate of Princeton Theological Seminary, theologically conservative, and a founder and board member of *Christianity Today,* Lamont was unquestionably a part of mainstream evangelicalism.[32] So, too, was his church: it was older than the nation in which it resided, having received its charter in 1773. The current building, constructed in 1906, was an imposing Gothic structure in downtown Pittsburgh that bespoke permanence and respectability.[33] When Kuhlman arrived in 1967, only three congregations in the Pittsburgh Presbytery were larger, and none surpassed it in wealth. Furthermore, the presbytery itself was the largest in the country; with over half a million church members, it contained nearly one-sixth of the United Presbyterian Church, the largest of the Presbyterian denominations.[34]

For years the pulpit of the First Presbyterian Church had been occupied by Clarence Macartney, a bulwark of conservative Presbyterianism during the defensive years following the Scopes trial. Macartney had handpicked Lamont as his successor in 1955, but Lamont labored in his early years. Only thirty-three when appointed, Lamont had not been Macartney's first choice. Harold Ockenga of Boston's Park Street Church was, but he had turned down an offer. Lamont could not have been more different from his predecessor: whereas Macartney had made his pastoral calls in a chauffeur-driven Cadillac, Lamont arrived on the scene in an old blue Ford. Macartney was an old-line fundamentalist; Lamont was part of the effort to remake fundamentalism after World War II. Their preaching styles were quite different as well: Macartney was scholarly and theologically erudite in the pulpit, whereas Lamont was more relational. "He could pastor and shepherd like no one else," recalled an associate. "At the end his sermons, every single person in the congregation felt loved, and that they had a one-on-one relationship with Bob Lamont."[35] Lamont survived an early heresy trial orchestrated by his detractors, eventually outgrew Macartney's long shadow, and by the time of the congress, was "well established."[36] In at least one respect Lamont was similar to his predecessor: he was most definitely neither a Pentecostal nor a charismatic, nor had he had much experience with members of either movement. He cannot be said to have been actively hostile to Pentecostalism; it simply was outside of his calculations, beyond the pale. Lamont was, at least in this regard, more or less typical of what Carl Henry called "the parochialism that prevailed in the aftermath of the liberal-fundamentalist conflict."[37]

The congress—and the plane flight to Berlin—changed this. Lamont recalled:

> Among other things, Edna [my wife] and I flew over on a plane from the United States, and it was filled with Pentecostals from South and Central America. This was the first time that I had ever been in contact with people from the Pentecostal background, and we were so tremendously uplifted by their joy and . . . their praise. Those people sang almost all the way across the Atlantic Ocean. It was really quite a testimony meeting, and it was brand new to us; I had never seen it and neither had Edna because most of our careers had been in the Presbyterian denomination and related mainline organizations.[38]

Nor was this all. Once Lamont got to the congress, he met Oral Roberts, the most renowned Pentecostal in the United states at the time. Roberts had come to the congress reluctantly, bringing with him "his phobia against intruding where he was not wanted" and eating many of his initial meals in his hotel room. The congress might have turned out differently for Lamont, Roberts, and even Pentecostal-mainstream relations but for the efforts of Calvin Thielman, a Presbyterian minister and colleague of Billy Graham. Thielman went out of his way to befriend Roberts and conducted a one-man campaign to bring Roberts into the social mainstream of the congress. He introduced Roberts to people, shared cabs and meals with him, and arranged a lunch in which several delegates (including Lamont) grilled Roberts about his views and liked what they heard. Roberts also scored points in the panel that he hosted. Although it was entitled "Twentieth-Century Evangelism," the real topic was faith and healing; Roberts surprised everyone by acknowledging "some mistakes" in the past.[39] Thielman's efforts culminated when Graham, impressed both with his associate's efforts and with Roberts's reception, met with Roberts and asked him to address the plenary session of the congress.

Roberts's irenic remarks, expressing humility and a desire for conciliation, produced "an electric moment." In the midst of his remarks, Roberts thanked "Billy [Graham] and Dr. [Carl] Henry for helping to open [his] eyes to the mainstream of Christianity."[40]

Roberts was not the only one whose eyes were opened. He in turn had a profound impact on Lamont, who attended Roberts's panel on faith and healing. Lamont not only was "impressed with what he had to say and with the way he said it "but also cited his "amazing combination of authority and confidence and openness and humility." Furthermore, Roberts was not at the congress to glad-hand or play politics: "I noticed he ate almost all the time with the delegates from most of the Third World countries in the large cafeteria. He did not—at least the times I noticed him—go off on the side or to some of the restaurants with his own group or with some of the recognized leaders of all sorts of evangelical movements. That impressed me no end."[41]

By the end of the congress, Lamont's view of the church, of the Holy Spirit, and of Pentecostals had all undergone substantial revision. "I discovered that those who had the Pentecostal background, God seemed to be using in ways on the mission field through the Third World countries that he certainly was not choosing to use through the mainline denominations." The result was a significant vow:

> Finally, on the last night when everything was done, all the invitations had been made, all the commitments had been offered, and so forth, I found myself alone and just about almost the last person out of the congress hall there where we were meeting, and I simply knelt down and said to God—and I remember praying in the words of the King James version of the Scriptures—"Lord, I'm no longer going to tell the Holy Spirit how he's to move. I want to recognize what you're doing in our world and be a part of it, so give me an open mind and a willing heart." That was the prayer I made.[42]

On his return to Pittsburgh, Lamont resumed his schedule. Among the meetings that he conducted was the Tuesday Noon Men's Club, a Bible-study initiated during Macartney's tenure. Often drawing over a thousand men, it may have been the largest meeting of its type in the country.[43] There was also a comparable group for women that met on Thursdays. During the months following Lamont's return from Berlin, the news broke that Kathryn Kuhlman had lost her meeting place at Carnegie Hall.[44] Lamont was approached by several men and women after the noontime meetings who told him of her plight and asked whether First Presbyterian could offer her its facilities. Lamont later admitted that at that point he "didn't really know who Miss

Kuhlman was." After some investigation, he came to the conclusion that "she's certainly not a mainline type—a main denominational type."[45] To be sure, the Tuesday Noon club lent the weight of tradition to using its sanctuary for meetings that reached beyond the bounds of the church's membership. But if Kathryn Kuhlman were to hold her meetings there, the pastor would not be in charge.

For the next two weeks, however, the subject kept coming up, and Lamont recalled his Congress Hall vow. Reluctantly he decided to follow up on the possibility of allowing Kuhlman to hold her services in his buildings. Admitting that he was looking for an excuse to exclude her, he inquired as to when Kuhlman's "Miracle Services" were held; the time, from ten to two o'clock on Fridays, was virtually the only free block of time on the church's busy calendar.[46] The church sanctuary was physically suitable to Kuhlman's ministry as well; with broad steps, wide portals, and a large open space at the front of the sanctuary, the services would be accessible to the many people in wheelchairs who attended.

Lacking a logistical reason to reject the idea, Lamont next turned to institutional mechanisms of the Presbyterian church in search of a roadblock. He consulted his assistant pastors, thinking "surely they would turn me down and that would be that." They, however, gave their consent. Lamont therefore determined to investigate Kuhlman and her ministry further. In particular, he wanted to be convinced of Kuhlman's financial integrity. Lamont contacted the Kuhlman Foundation and informed Maggie Hartner, Kuhlman's chief aide and confidant, of his receptivity to hosting their meetings, but he demanded to see the foundation's books and interview its auditor. The interview took place the next day. Everything was "very, very much in order." Lamont was especially impressed with the money that the Kuhlman Foundation had disbursed to Christian ministries, particularly to mission work in Vietnam among both the U.S. troops and the local citizenry.[47]

At some point in the process—most likely after the meeting with the foundation's auditor—Lamont's reservations were eased, and he decided that he wanted Kuhlman to use the sanctuary. His actions prior to that were characterized by procrastination and obfuscation. After that, however, they were far more purposeful and even calculated.

And there was much to calculate. Although Lamont was unquestionably in charge, he could not ignore the existence of four basic factions within his congregation.[48] To do so would risk a split in his church over Kathryn Kuhlman. Lamont was forced to balance the urgency of his Congress Hall vow with the political realities of his church.

The two largest factions simply disagreed about primary loyalties. One group was Presbyterian first and evangelical second. Their religious loyalties lay with the denomination; they would look first at the impact of Kuhlman on the United Presbyterian Church. The second group consisted of evangelical Christians, "the Billy Graham, *Christianity Today* type."[49] Their denominational loyalties were not as strong as their commitment to evangelicalism. Simply put, a member of the first group who moved into a new city would seek out the strongest Presbyterian church in the area; a member of the second group would look for the strongest evangelical church, regardless of denomination. Together these two groups made up some three-quarters of First Presbyterian.

The other quarter was more or less evenly divided. One half consisted of those who were orthodox theologians, "the hard-line 'Tulip' type."[50] Heirs to the Westminster catechism, they represented what Gresham Machen had left behind in the denomination when he founded the rival Orthodox Presbyterian Church in the 1930s. Whereas a denomination was most important to the first group and a movement was most important to the second, doctrine was paramount to this group. Largely absent from the church today, they left for the more conservative Presbyterian Church in America in the mid-1970s.

The final group consisted of charismatics. One of Lamont's assistants, Jack Chisholm, had been converted to Christ while in the navy through the ministry of the Navigators, a parachurch ministry. His association with First Presbyterian began while he was a student at the University of Pittsburgh; after a seminary education at Pittsburgh Theological Seminary, he came onto the First Presbyterian staff as the youth minister and later became one of the associate pastors.[51] While praying in his study one day, he began to speak in tongues and thereafter began to lead an incipient charismatic group of around 200 people within the church.[52]

The issue of timing is obviously important in establishing whether Chisholm's experience was influenced by Kuhlman's arrival at First Presbyterian. Precise dates are elusive.[53] Lay members closest to the church cannot ascribe to Kuhlman any direct influence on Chisholm, but they were extremely uncomfortable with the proposition that there had been no influence whatsoever.[54] It is most likely that, in the words of the former clerk of the session, "there were parallel things going on."[55] Chisholm took the trouble to attend some of Kuhlman's meetings; Lamont did not.[56] Chisholm also met with Kuhlman periodically, further strengthening her relationship with the church.[57]

It is not necessary to establish a direct connection between Kuhlman's arrival at First Presbyterian and Chisholm's emergence as the leader of a charismatic cadre within it. Suffice it to say that the parallel developments indicate a core of support for Kuhlman within the church that would offset opposition that might arise.[58] Furthermore, this core of support did not consist merely of a dissident faction of malcontents; it was championed by a member of the pastoral staff who was "outspoken in his support of Kathryn Kuhlman."[59] They would be most supportive of Lamont's efforts to bring in Kuhlman, but that support could produce a backlash if it appeared to the anticharismatic elements that Kuhlman represented the thin end of the wedge for neo-Pentecostalism.

Even allowing for the likely support of the charismatics, under most circumstances four such disparate factions would be at each other's throats in considering something so novel as allowing Kathryn Kuhlman to hold her services in the First Presbyterian sanctuary. Lamont therefore had to move cautiously. Opposition to Kuhlman would be strongest in the first group, the denomination-first group. He also had to avoid the appearance of jeopardizing the social standing of First Presbyterian (although it is difficult to imagine his wanting to do so); there were some elders from each of the factions—with the exception of the charismatics—who held this as an extremely high priority. Nothing—especially a female, Pentecostal, lower-class healer—could be allowed to sully that reputation.

Nonetheless, it cannot be overemphasized that the most significant factor in the equation was not any one group but Robert M. Lamont. His working relationships with the session, the board of trustees, and the associate pastors was complex. Although he held sway in the church and usually got what he wanted, that did not mean that he could proceed in any way that he wanted; he moved cautiously, always making sure that his bases were covered. Memories of the early heresy trial and other lesser battles had left their scars and produced a cautious man who always guarded his flanks. "I quickly learned that when he asked for input, he didn't want insight; he just wanted to know where you stood," recalled one man. Another went even further: "He was a real operator. I'm just glad he was on the Lord's side."[60] As such, Lamont's influence was more akin to that of an extremely effective constitutional monarch than to that of an absolute one—but a monarch nonetheless. In this respect he was atypical of Presbyterian pastors of the 1960s, who as a whole seemed to "desire to purge the preaching office of authoritarianism."[61]

The decision was potentially controversial enough that Lamont had to forsake his usual practice of consulting his "kitchen cabinet" and call the full session. This was unusual, for it rarely met.[62] A pro forma body, it usually convened only to admit new members, with most of the decision-making authority on the administrative affairs of the church wielded by the board of trustees.[63] One experienced elder went so far as to advise a newly appointed man to "bring [his] rubber stamp" to the meetings.[64] The fact that Lamont would consult the session at all was indicative of the potential trouble that this decision could cause. He had to balance the urgency of his Congress Hall vow with the hostility toward the charismatic movement felt by many of the elders. This was one issue in which he could not act unilaterally.

But he did have a great deal of political capital on which to draw. It is important to remember just what Lamont's strengths were. Universally loved, the man who excelled at *caring* from the pulpit could count on support for this idea simply because he was the one proposing it. There were men who would follow him even if the decision ran counter to their basic allegiance, whether to denomination, movement, or doctrine. And they would do so particularly if the details were left sufficiently ambiguous that each could see in the arrangement precisely what he wished.

Not all the elders recall voting for the same thing when the issue was finally put to a vote in the session. Some recall voting to allow Kuhlman unconditional use of the sanctuary, whereas others recall conditions. Some thought the arrangement was temporary; others, permanent. One went so far as to accuse Lamont of duplicity. Kuhlman, he was told, would hold only her Bible studies in the sanctuary, but that "charismatic stuff" would be barred. Obviously it was a promise that was not kept.[65] The disparate recollections say much about Lamont's management style. He was a man of bedrock integrity to whom outright lying would have been utterly abhorrent. But he was determined to get his way and to do so with as much unity as possible. Strife was abhorrent to him, and civil war within First Presbyterian was unthinkable. To accomplish his goal, he would have been quite willing to plant the seed of an idea and let it run if he had known that it would achieve the desired end by having the listener believe what he wanted. Unity was the goal; the sensibilities of individuals could be soothed later. The motion did go through with a unanimous vote.[66] It is extremely doubtful, however, that all reservations were allayed or that all the elders would have agreed as to just what they had voted.

A final question remained as to whether the United Presbyterian Church would have its say: in addition to reservations at the congregational level, muted by a strong pastor, one might well expect objections to have been raised by the Pittsburgh Presbytery over Kuhlman's use of one of its buildings.

Normal protocol would have demanded that Lamont consult the presbytery and obtain its permission. To do so would have constituted some risk for Kuhlman, for there were conflicting indications as to the extent to which the

United Presbyterian Church (UPC) might be open to the "things of the Spirit" associated over the rising charismatic movement. One congregation outside Philadelphia had been the scene of a charismatic renewal for over a decade, with little friction between it and the denomination. A Presbyterian minister named James Brown had been carrying on a charismatic revival in this congregation since the mid-1950s, some years before the more widely known events in Dennis Bennett's Episcopal parish in Van Nuys, California, that most historians use to date the beginning of the neo-Pentecostal movement. Indeed, Vinson Synan notes that "the Presbyterians were at the forefront of renewal."[67] On a more official level, however, there was more overt hostility. Only three years before, a church officer had prevented a UPC minister from inviting participants at a Presbyterian Youth Assembly meeting to "repent and receive the Holy Spirit."[68] Furthermore, shortly thereafter a Presbyterian minister bluntly told a committee of the General Assembly in a formal hearing that tongues "wasn't Presbyterian" and users should be "given the left foot of fellowship."[69] Merely to aver that the denomination as a whole was pervaded by "a distinct reluctance to deal with the . . . Pentecostal and Charismatic movements" is, to say the least, a tactful assessment.[70]

However, the timing of Kuhlman's need was important. Lamont had just been through a bruising denominational battle concerning the wording of the 1967 Confession. With conservatives and liberals ready to fight over the document, Lamont carved out the middle ground and found room for compromise. Rather than being hailed for his efforts, however, he was excoriated from both sides: the liberals saw him as a thoroughgoing fundamentalist, while the conservatives felt that he had deserted the evangelical cause.[71]

As a result, Robert Lamont, the unappreciated savior of denominational unity, was not inclined to consult the presbytery. Moreover, the session held the same attitude. "We felt we were better than the presbytery," one member bluntly recalled.[72] However, the official mechanisms of the denomination would not have been able to address the matter even had anyone wished to. The United Presbyterian Church of the late 1960s was a denomination paralyzed by chaos. In 1967 it was in the first stages of an institutional restructuring that turned into a fractious brawl.[73] It was also in the midst of a longer-term debate over basic theological points and a trend away from the historical roots of the Princeton theology.[74] In such an atmosphere, molehills easily assumed the status of mountains: witness the furor over a 1971 donation to the Angela Davis defense fund.[75] At the same time, the makeup of the membership was changing, becoming more ethnically heterogeneous; the historical distinctives of the denomination, such as an educated membership, were eroding.[76] The leadership of the denomination clashed constantly with laity as it grappled with this increasing pluralism, seeking to incorporate "new voices" into its affairs.[77] For better or for worse, the UPC was in turmoil. It had far weightier matters with which to concern itself than Robert Lamont's decision to allow Kathryn Kuhlman's cultural outlanders into his building. Despite the presence of Lamont (or a substitute from First Presbyterian) at every one of its 1967 meetings, the issue was never raised.[78]

The overall result was a harmonious relationship, at least on the surface, between Kuhlman and First Presbyterian for the next ten years. During that time Kuhlman held services in the church's sanctuary as frequently as twice a week: a Monday "Bible Study" in which she spoke but made no attempt to heal maladies and the Friday "Miracle Service" of healings. Lamont had not asked for any remuneration from Kuhlman or Hartner, but shortly after her first month in the church, he received a check from the Kathryn Kuhlman Foundation for $2,800, the same amount that Kuhlman had been paying the city of Pittsburgh for the use of Carnegie Hall.[79] She continued this practice, a factor that became important when some members of the First Presbyterian congregation began complaining about the mess that Kuhlman's services frequently left behind or the damage that they caused (torn seat cushions appear to have been the most egregious problem).[80] One result of this financial gratitude was that Kuhlman's relationship with First Presbyterian was able to survive Lamont's departure in 1973.

Lamont was succeeded by the Reverend John Huffman. A graduate of Princeton Seminary, Huffman was a card-carrying evangelical whose father had been the president of Wynona Seminary. Like Lamont, Huffman was thirty-three years old when he assumed the pulpit of First Presbyterian. Also like Lamont, he succeeded a giant in that pulpit, and he fought his share of early battles. One of them was over Kathryn Kuhlman.

Without the soothing presence of Lamont, the session's subterranean resentment over Kuhlman's presence at First Presbyterian, and the means by which it had been secured, boiled to the surface. The opposition was led by one of the elders, Dr. Charles Nil, who forced the issue and demanded that the session meet to consider it. Nil was particularly upset about the mess that Kuhlman's services were causing not only in the church's sanctuary but also in the neighborhood, for many of the healer's devotees slept outside the night before each service to secure a seat the next day. Of greater concern to most of the elders was the problem of First Presbyterian's image: Kuhlman was increasingly identified with the church, to the point where Huffman was occasionally asked whether he liked working for her. Nor did she do much to dispel that notion, citing the church as her meeting place on her radio and television broadcasts. Clearly she enjoyed the prestige of using the building; equally evident was the growing disenchantment of some of the elders. Huffman, determined to be a good Presbyterian pastor and lacking the prestige simply to waive an issue aside, as Lamont could, consented to "place it on the docket."[81]

The meeting was held in early or mid-1975. "It was probably the most stately, magnificent debate we ever had there," Huffman later recalled.[82] One side pleaded that God was in Kuhlman's ministry; the other maintained that she had been allowed in for a limited time, and whether she was divinely inspired or not, it was time for her to seek other accommodations. The validity of the healings was also raised. The fact that Nil was a physician lent some weight to his doubts and some heat to the discussion when Kuhlman's supporters doubted his evaluation. Nil passionately described the litter, the defecation outside the church by people with no access to facilities, and the sleeping in the church cemetery.[83]

Huffman recommended to the evenly divided group that they delay a year and then reconsider the issue. Publicly he talked about the relative unimportance of the question and the need to preserve unity within the church. He did not voice his real reasons for his position. A native of Tulsa, Oklahoma, where Kuhlman had developed a relationship with a car dealer named Tink Wilkerson, Huffman had heard increasing rumors concerning Kuhlman's ill health.[84]

The compromise was acceptable to both sides. Obviously the issue of Kuhlman was not worth a major split in the congregation. Kuhlman's supporters were content with the fact that she was still in the building. Her detractors could point, with no small amount of satisfaction, at the openness of the debate. Most satisfying to all concerned, the session had behaved as a Presbyterian session *ought* to behave, with open debate and a chance truly to shape the policies of the church.[85] Kuhlman's services continued without further incident at First Presbyterian Church until her death in February 1976.

Neo-Pentecostalism had made great inroads into conservative evangelicalism since its beginnings in the late 1950s and early 1960s. Moving beyond its status as a movement of religious and cultural outlanders, it had penetrated churches that represented the core of the American suburban middle class. Kathryn Kuhlman had been along for much of the journey. Yet while her experience demonstrates the distance that Pentecostalism had traveled by the early 1970s, it also provides a window into the limitations still facing the movement. Mainstream acceptance was by no means complete. Despite the gains, Kuhlman and other neo-Pentecostals were still held at arm's length by the mainstream evangelicals and their churches. Although in the hallway, they were not yet accorded a seat in the parlor—or, more literally, at the dining table.

In 1972–73 two celebratory banquets were held in the city of Pittsburgh. On 27 September 1972, the Kuhlman Foundation held a dinner at the Hilton Hotel to celebrate twenty-five years of "miracle ministry" in the city.[86] Some 2,200 guests attended an evening gala of music, tributes, and gifts.[87] Kuhlman was presented with, among other things, commemorative plaques, a gold medal struck in honor of the event, and arrays of flowers that would have been the envy of a Tournament of Roses queen.[88] She made a presentation as well, to Robert M. Lamont. "At a very dramatic point in the banquet," he recalled, "she said that when she left home as a young girl to start her evangelistic career, her father gave her two five-dollar gold pieces . . . and told her to keep them as long as she lived until she found somebody that she really cared about and wanted to give them to. She said, 'I've kept them all these years,' and then she called Edna up and presented her with a bouquet of roses and then called me up and [presented them to me]."[89]

The second banquet occurred the following April and marked the two hundredth anniversary of the ministry of the First Presbyterian Church in the city of Pittsburgh.[90] Speaker of the House Carl Albert attended this banquet (he had merely sent "greetings" to Kuhlman's); other greetings were offered by civil luminaries ranging from the city's members of Congress to the mayor and the head of the Chamber of Commerce. The religious guests testified to the high position that First Presbyterian held in the evangelical constellation. Billy Graham gave the main address. Also attending were Harold Lindsell, editor of *Christianity Today,* and Harold Ockenga, president of Gordon-Conwell Seminary. Hardly missed, given such a distinguished guest list, was Miss Kathryn Kuhlman.[91]

The incidents are illuminating. Clearly even by the mid-1970s, Kuhlman needed the recognition of the evangelical mainstream. Although she may have presented material goods to Lamont in giving him the gold pieces, his acceptance of them was the true gift in the exchange: by deigning to attend the banquet and participate in the program, he was conferring on Kuhlman a degree of respectability and recognition that far exceeded the value of her gold coins.[92] Yet he, and the mainstream churches, still did not need her; she could be ignored and remain uninvited to their own banquets. As late as the mid-1970s, the cultural outlanders still had not completed their journey.

Notes

1. Kuhlman maintained that she had no formal schooling, but Wayne Warner has established that she attended Simpson Bible College in Seattle, Washington, for at least two years and may have been dismissed under disreputable circumstances. See Wayne Warner, *Kathryn Kuhlman: The Woman behind the Miracles* (Minneapolis: Fortress, 1994). Her will was disputed after a codicil was revealed that left large portions of her estate to Tink Wilkerson, an Oklahoma car dealer who had befriended her in the last six months of her life. For a biased account of the probate, see Jamie Buckingham, *Daughter of Destiny: Kathryn Kuhlman . . . Her Story* (Plainfield, N.J.: Logos International, 1976), 239–302.

2. Specifically, Kuhlman never blamed a failure to heal on the afflicted person's lack of faith. This was in stark contrast to many of her contemporaries.

3. Russell P. Spittler, "Maintaining Distinctives: The Future of Pentecostalism," in *Pentecostals from the Inside Out*, ed. Harold B. Smith (Wheaton, Ill.: Victor, 1990), 121.

4. The events surrounding the Denver Tabernacle are recounted in Buckingham, *Daughter of Destiny*, chaps. 4 and 5. Kuhlman's tenure in Franklin, Pennsylvania, ended in 1948 with a lawsuit on the part of the church that had originally hosted her meetings. See Frederick W. Jordan, "Reconcilable Differences? Kathryn Kuhlman and the Institutional Church," paper presented at the Institute for the Study of American Evangelicals Conference on Pentecostal Currents in the American Church, Fuller Seminary, 10–13 Mar. 1994, p. 17.

5. In the 1950s Gordon Lindsay, long influential in the postwar healing revival as the editor of *The Voice of Calvary* magazine, set up the Pentecostal equivalent of a Bible college, Christ for the Nations Institute in Dallas, Texas. Demos Shakarian had begun the Full Gospel Business Men's Fellowship in 1951. The following decade saw the Pentecostal movement's most ambitious undertaking, the inauguration of Oral Roberts University in Tulsa, Oklahoma, in 1967. Other examples include the Blessed Trinity Society and Christian Growth Ministries.

6. Kathryn Kuhlman, *I Believe in Miracles* (Englewood Cliffs, N.J.: Prentice-Hall, 1962). The two-million figure is from Helen Kooiman Hosier, *Kathryn Kuhlman: A Legacy* (Old Tappan, N.J.: Fleming H. Revell, 1971), 107. Data from this adulatory biography should be treated with some care.

7. *Los Angeles Herald Examiner*, 14 Aug. 1965; Buckingham, *Daughter of Destiny*, 196–203.

8. Ironically the redevelopment was an extension of the same Pittsburgh Renaissance that had originally made the city attractive to Kuhlman in the late 1940s. See Roy Lubove, *Twentieth-Century Pittsburgh: Government, Business, and Environmental Change* (New York: Wiley, 1969), chap. 6; Franklin K. Toker, "Reversing an Urban Image: New Architecture in Pittsburgh, 1890-1980," in *Pittsburgh-Sheffield: Sister Cities*, ed. Joel Tarr (Pittsburgh: Carnegie Mellon University Press, 1986), calls the Pittsburgh Renaissance "the most massive peacetime reconstruction of any city in history" (10).

9. Walter Siegfried, telephone interview with the author, 14 July 1992. Siegfried is the longtime clerk of the session, First Presbyterian Church, Pittsburgh.

10. Billy Graham Archives (hereinafter BGA), Wheaton College, Wheaton, Ill., collection 212 (hereinafter cited as "Kuhlman Papers"), video V285, *I Believe in Miracles,* 29 Feb. 1968.

11. "Healing in the Spirit," *Christianity Today* 17 (20 July 1973): 6; Tillie Szurek, interview with the author, 14 July 1992 (Szurek is a longtime associate of Kuhlman's and currently one of the five people on the Kathryn Kuhlman Foundation's board of directors); Bob Schwartz and Walt Klimko, interview with the author, 20 July 1992 (the two men are longtime veterans of Kuhlman's ministry who served as ushers and, occasionally, confidants).

12. Buckingham, *Daughter of Destiny,* 44.

13. Maggie Hartner, Kuhlman's longtime administrative assistant, claimed never to have heard her speak in tongues (Buckingham, *Daughter of Destiny,* 114). Two longtime co-workers in her services said that she did so only "two or three" times in their twenty-year association with her (Schwartz interview). Buckingham, *Daughter of Destiny,* 222–23, details her reasons and theology for the restriction.

14. For the rise of the movement, see Richard Riss, "The Latter Rain Movement of 1948," *Pneuma* 4, no. 1 (Spring 1982): "laying on of hands" conflicted with the traditional Pentecostal practice of "tarrying for the Spirit" (35).

15. David Edwin Harrell, *All Things Are Possible: The Healing and Charismatic Revivals in Modern America* (Bloomington: Indiana University Press, 1975), 188–91.

16. Buckingham, *Daughter of Destiny,* 44, 102, 104; "Healing in the Spirit," 6–9.

17. Don Basham, "Women in Ministry," *New Wine* 6, no. 9 (Oct. 1974): 21. Both mainliners and neo-Pentecostals criticized Kuhlman on this issue. She addressed it head on in the *Chistianity Today* interview by conceding the principle but pleading divine expediency: "God's first choices were men. Someplace men failed [to do God's work]. I was just stupid enough to say, Take nothing and use it. And he has been doing just that" ("Healing in the Spirit," 7).

18. John R. Rice, *The Charismatic Movement* (Murfreesboro, Tenn.: Sword of the Lord, 1976), 249.

19. Mrs. Arthur Gluck to L. Nelson Bell, 23 Feb. 1967, Bell Papers, BGA, Box 46, Folder 3.

20. Anonymous Roman Catholic woman who attended Kuhlman's service in Pittsburgh, interview with Matthew Lawson, 16 Apr. 1990; transcript in author's possession. For a description of "going under the Power" and several examples, see Buckingham, *Daughter of Destiny,* 224–31; Allen Spraggett, *Kathryn Kuhlman: The Woman Who Believes in Miracles* (Cleveland: Word, 1970), 11; Roberts Liardon, *Kathryn Kuhlman: A Spiritual Biography of God's Miracle Working Power* (Tulsa, Okla.: Harrison, 1990), 13; and *Pittsburgh Press Roto,* 3 Feb. 1974, p. 22. Bob Friedrich, the clerk of the session at First Presbyterian in 1966, described the experience occurring during a conversation with Kuhlman when she started praying for him. A 1975 film, *Dry Land, Living Waters,* results from a rare instance in which Kuhlman allowed recording equipment into one of her "Miracle Services"; it shows people "falling under the Power" (Kuhlman Papers, video V126). Another witness to the services at First Presbyterian related that "people were falling over like dominoes" (anonymous interview with a member of the First Presbyterian Church, 1993). Kuhlman maintained that the practice was biblical, likening it to the trancelike state experienced by John on

Patmos or Paul on the road to Damascus (Kuhlman Papers, video V268, *I Believe in Miracles,* 23 Apr. 1968). See also her analysis in "Healing in the Spirit," 7.

21. Robert Mapes Anderson, *Vision of the Disinherited: The Makings of American Pentecostalism* (New York: Oxford University Press, 1979), 7.

22. The refrain can be heard in *Dry Land, Living Waters* (Kuhlman papers, video 126). It is also cited as part of the twenty-fifth anniversary dinner ("Kathryn Kuhlman: 25 Years in Pittsburgh," *Logos Journal* [Nov–Dec. 1972], 33–36).

23. Letter from Jacob Stam, chairman of the Billy Graham Finance Committee, to L. Nelson Bell, Bell Papers, BGA, Box 318, Folder 51-10. Ironically, after providing the grant, J. Howard Pew declined to attend the congress because he thought it was not taking a strong enough stand against theological liberalism. See Carl F. H. Henry, *Confessions of a Theologian: An Autobiography* (Waco, Tex.: Word, 1986), 264–69.

24. Carl F. H. Henry, *Evangelicals on the Brink of Crisis: Significance of the World Congress on Evangelism* (Waco, Tex.: Word, 1967), 3.

25. Henry, *Confessions,* 252; idem, *Evangelicals,* 3.

26. The months prior to the congress were preoccupied with sniping between the congress organizers and the World Council of Churches (WCC) over the question of whether the congress's primary emphasis should be evangelism or social action. When the emphasis on evangelism won out, liberal Christians focused their energies on the WCC World Conference on Church and Society in Geneva that met 12–16 July 1996. They ignored the Berlin congress entirely; the liberal mouthpiece *Christian Century* never even mentioned it. Conservative critics included Martin Lloyd-Jones and, as usual, Carl McIntire. See Henry, *Confessions,* 253–59; and *Christian Century,* Nov–Dec 1966 issues.

27. Henry, *Evangelicals,* 3. Seventy-six church bodies were represented at the congress. Perhaps the delegation furthest removed from Western evangelicalism was that of the Auca of South America, who arrived in Berlin stomping the concrete pavement, amazed that the earth's surface could be so hard (Henry, *Confessions,* 257).

28. Ethiopian emperor Haile Selassie, a born-again Christian and the titular head of the Ethiopian Orthodox Church, spoke at the congress (Henry, *Confessions,* 257).

29. "Biographical Information of Participants, World Congress on Evangelism," Congress Papers, BGA, Collection 14, Folder 1-1.

30. Robert Lamont, interview with author, 16 July 1992. (Lamont consented to be interviewed twice, the first time on 18 Feb. 1992. The second session contained by far the greatest amount of material cited herein.) Lamont recalled Roberts as a delegate to the congress, and he is listed as such in the "Biographical Information of Participants" issued at the congress. However, L. Nelson Bell later told one critic that Roberts was merely an observer (L. Nelson Bell to Mrs. Arthur Gluck, Bell Papers, BGA, Box 46, Folder 3.

31. Lamont participated in a session entitled "Doctrinal Unbelief and Heresy" at the congress and was also a member of the sponsoring committee; See the congress program, Congress Papers, BGA, Collection 14, Box 1, Folder 6.

32. Lamont interview, 16 July 1992; Henry, *Confessions,* 152.

33. "Faith Healer Draws the Sick and Anguished," *New York Times,* 20 Oct. 1972.

34. *Minutes of the General Assembly of the United Presbyterian Church in the United States of America, Part 3, the Statistical Tables and Presbytery Rolls, Jan. 1–Dec. 31,*

1967, 7th ser., vol. 11, 1967. (Philadelphia: Office of the General Assembly, 1968), 332–36, 653. The Synod of Pennsylvania had 523,158 members, far more than the synods of California (322,119 members) or New York (514,105) had.

35. Robert B. Letsinger, interview with the author, 16 Apr. 1993, Stony Brook. Letsinger worked with a parachurch business ministry, the Pittsburgh Experiment, which was funded both by Kuhlman's foundation and by First Presbyterian; he later joined the staff of First Presbyterian, serving there from 1974 to 1979.

36. Siegfried interview; "First Presbyterian Pastor to Leave," *Pittsburgh Press*, 5 Dec. 1972; Lamont interview, 16 July 1922. In fact, his refusal to allow the board of trustees to buy him a more expensive car may have been a factor that provoked several of them to bring heresy charges against him (over doctrinal, not automotive, issues). The presbytery found for Lamont, and his persecutors left First Presbyterian. Later he did indeed switch—to a Buick (Letsinger interview).

37. Henry, *Confessions*, 261.

38. Lamont interview, 16 July 1992.

39. David Edwin Harrell, *Oral Roberts: An American Life* (Bloomington: Indiana University Press, 1985), 200–203.

40. Ibid., 204; Harrell, *All Things Are Possible*, 158.

41. Lamont interview, 16 July 1992. *Christianity Today* was also impressed, noting that "Evangelist Oral Roberts won a significant measure of new respect through the Congress. He made a host of friends among delegates who were openly impressed with his candor and humility" (*Christianity Today* 11, no. 4 [25 Nov. 1966]: 35).

42. Lamont interview, 16 July 1992.

43. Ibid.; "Presbyterian Pastor to Leave," 4. For the origins of the meeting under Macartney, see Ernest Edwin Logan, *The Church That Was Twice Born: A History of the First Presbyterian Church of Pittsburgh, Pennsylvania, 1773–1973* (Pittsburgh: Pickwick-Morecraft, 1973), 178–79; and C. Allyn Russell, *Voices of Fundamentalism: Seven Biographical Studies* (Philadelphia: Westminster, 1976), 197.

44. The exact time is uncertain. Lamont returned from Berlin in Oct. 1966; Kuhlman's first meetings in the church probably occurred no earlier than the beginning of 1967. "First Presbyterian Church" appears for the first time on Kuhlman's calendar on 4 Oct. 1968, but she undoubtedly began holding her meetings in the building long before that (Kuhlman Papers, BGA, Box 1, Folder 3).

45. Lamont interview, 16 July 1992.

46. Ibid.; Lamont interview, 18 Feb. 1992.

47. Lamont interview, 16 July 1992.

48. Interview with Rev. John Huffman Jr., 16 Apr. 1993. Huffman succeeded Lamont as pastor of First Presbyterian in 1973 when Lamont left to head the Presbyterian Ministers' Fund (now Covenant Life) in Philadelphia.

49. Huffman interview.

50. Ibid.

51. Siegfried interview.

52. Lamont interviews; Wally Dietrich, interview with the author, 3 Aug. 1992. Dietrich was a longtime member of First Presbyterian's session, including the period in which the decision was made.

53. Chisholm died in 1990.

54. Siegfried interview; Friedrich interview; anonymous First Presbyterian member, interview with the author, spring 1992. When asked about a direct connection, Siegfried noted, "I'd hesitate to say 'no.' . . . If there were, it's not as though he were a disciple sitting at her feet in her meetings." Friedrich related that the two met informally from time to time.

55. Siegfried interview.

56. Ibid.; Lamont interviews.

57. Friedrich interview.

58. At one congregational meeting, one member protested that Kuhlman meetings were "too crowded," but nothing ever came of such opposition (Siegfried interview).

59. Dietrich interview. Chisholm went on to become a member of the denominational committee that produced the 1970 "Report on the Holy Spirit," a document remarkably hospitable to the charismatic movement for a mainline denomination. Chisholm did not play a larger role than any of the other eleven members, nor did he even verbalize a direct debt to Kuhlman (Bruce M. Metzger, interview with the author, 2 Nov. 1992; Metzger was one of the eleven members of the Committee on the Holy Spirit, which produced the report).

60. Neither man wished his remarks to be attributed.

61. John McClure, "Changes in the Authority, Method and Message of Presbyterianism (UPCUSA) Preaching in the Twentieth Century," in *The Confessional Mosaic: Presbyterians and Twentieth-Century Theology,* ed. Milton J. Coalter, John M. Mulder, and Louis Weeks (Louisville, Ky.: Westminster/John Knox Press, 1990), 90.

62. Huffman interview; anonymous First Presbyterian interviews.

63. Letsinger interview.

64. Dietrich interview.

65. Lamont interview; anonymous First Presbyterian interviews.

66. Lamont interview.

67. Vinson Synan, *The Twentieth-Century Pentecostal Explosion: The Exciting Growth of Pentecostal Churches and Charismatic Renewal Movements* (Alamonte Springs, Fla.: Creation House, 1987), 161–64. Obviously this is a relative statement about a small minority within the denomination and is not meant to be indicative of the denomination as a whole.

68. Frank Ferrell, "Outburst of Tongues: The New Pentecostalism," *Christianity Today* 7, no. 24 (13 Sept. 1963): 3.

69. Metzger interview.

70. John M. Mulder and Lee A. Wyatt, "The Predicament of Pluralism: The Study of Theology in Presbyterian Seminaries since the 1920s," in *The Pluralistic Vision: Presbyterians and Mainstream Protestant Education and Leadership,* ed. Milton J. Coalter, John M. Mulder, and Louis Weeks (Louisville, Ky.: Westminster/John Knox Press, 1992), 67.

71. Letsinger interview.

72. Anonymous First Presbyterian interviews. Marianne Wolfe, the longtime stated clerk of the presbytery, also mentioned Lamont's overall disdain for the presbytery (Marianne Wolfe, interview with the author, 12 July 1992).

73. Richard Reifsnyder, "Managing the Mission: Church Restructuring in the Twen-

tieth Century," in *The Organizational Revolution: Presbyterians and American Denominationalism,* ed. Milton J. Coalter, John M. Mulder, and Louis Weeks (Louisville, Ky.: Westminster/John Knox Press, 1991), 73.

74. Mulder and Wyatt, "The Predicament of Pluralism," 67.

75. See David B. McCarthy, "The Emerging Importance of Presbyterian Polity," in *The Organizational Revolution,* 282–84.

76. Robert Wuthnow, "The Restructuring of American Presbyterianism: Turmoil in One Denomination," in *The Presbyterian Predicament: Six Perspectives,* ed. Milton J. Coalter, John M. Mulder, and Louis Weeks (Louisville, Ky.: Westminster/John Knox Press, 1991), 30–31.

77. Ironically the effort presaged a severe decline: during the next two decades, Presbyterian denominations would lose more than one quarter of their members. See Ronald H. Nash, "The Presbyterian Church," in *Evangelical Renewal in the Mainline Churches,* ed. Ronald H. Nash (Westchester, Ill.: Crossway, 1987), 87.

78. Some of the presbytery's monthly meetings were held in the very sanctuary that Kuhlman was also allowed to use (Minutes of the Pittsburgh Presbytery, 1967, copy located at the Pittsburgh Presbytery's offices).

79. Lamont interview, 16 July 1992.

80. Friedrich interview.

81. Huffman interview.

82. Ibid. Huffman was unable to recall the precise date but said that the issue did not come to a head for some time. It probably occurred within the year prior to Kuhlman's death in February 1976.

83. Letsinger interview.

84. Huffman's information came from a Presbyterian layman "of absolute integrity" whom he declined to name (Huffman interview).

85. Ibid.

86. "Kathryn Kuhlman"

87. Ibid.; *Pittsburgh Post-Gazette,* 27 Sept. 1972, p. 25; Schwartz interview; Lamont interview. The *Post* says the banquet was held at the William Penn Hotel; Schwartz, Lamont, and an anonymous source all recall it as occurring at the Hilton. A brief film clip of the banquet is in the Kuhlman Papers, BGA, video V485.

88. Buckingham, *Daughter of Destiny,* 279.

89. Lamont interview, 16 July 1992.

90. *Pittsburgh Press,* 23 March 1973, p. 12.

91. Siegfried interview; Dietrich interview; anonymous First Presbyterian interview.

92. Lamont's participation is recounted in part in "Kathryn Kuhlman."

11

Pentecostal Currents in the SBC: Divine Intervention, Prophetic Preachers, and Charismatic Worship

Helen Lee Turner

Southern Baptists have regarded the radical changes in the Southern Baptist Convention (SBC) as either a fundamentalist takeover or as a conservative recovery of a tradition being usurped by liberals. Regardless of one's perspective, however, interpreters have analyzed the changes exclusively in terms of theological, social, and political agendas; nowhere is there any suggestion that the spiritual experiences that characterize Pentecostalism might be a factor. Scholars remind us that Pentecostal practices have historically inhabited the fringes of Southern Baptist life and that Baptist attitudes toward Pentecostalism have been marked by a certain hostility. These attitudes, most would argue, have not changed during the fundamentalist rise to power. In considering these profound changes in the Southern Baptist Convention, therefore, scholars have given Pentecostal influences virtually no regard. However, despite scholarly claims that fundamentalism[1] and Pentecostalism are incompatible, Pentecostal-type influences have indeed been crucial to the sea changes in the SBC. These influences, moreover, continue to enliven the denomination.

These Pentecostal influences derive not from traditional Pentecostal practices (speaking in tongues and healing) but from an orientation toward life: the belief that the divine is both present and active in the world today. This is something more dramatic than the Baptist belief that the Holy Spirit changes lives and incites conversion and pious living. Rather, it is a belief in the power of the supernatural to intervene tangibly in history. Certainly this has been a minority perspective among twentieth-century Southern Baptists.

Social scientists have regarded this view as antagonistic to modernity, for groups with this spiritual worldview, they argue, often originate in times of social distress as a response to what are seen as the corrupt values of the modern world. It is a perspective that enables believers to find meaning in life even when the world seems to be without worthwhile values. Sociologists have called new religious movements of this sort "anthropological protest[s] against modernity."[2] Margaret Poloma, for one, contends that the rise of Pentecostalism was one such challenge to modernity.[3] So, too, is it with Southern Baptists. I have argued elsewhere that the new power structures of the SBC are a reaction to modernity manifested early on by apocalyptic concerns.[4] What I am arguing here is that these Baptist protests had a Pentecostal character.

Apocalyptic Expectation and the Remaking of a Worldview

Both Pentecostalism and SBC fundamentalism originated in apocalyptic visions. Both movements consist of believers who see the modern age as having destroyed society by its faithlessness and lack of virtue. Images of the destruction of the world give powerful voice to feelings about the status quo. But for people who, like these, experience severe social distress because of the modern world's erosion of traditional moral and social values, an expectation of the end of time also provides hope for something better—not just any hope, but the ultimate hope. Thus the eschatological vision becomes the most successful vehicle for transporting a people to another worldview. Among Christians the expectation is that Jesus will come and usher in a new age more wonderful than any heretofore imagined.[5] So the believer's life becomes oriented toward the eschaton rather than the mundane world. But the present is not forgotten; the ritual recital of the eschatological myth becomes a proleptic experience of God's divine intervention in the present.

Apocalyptic expectation, therefore, makes possible a paradigm shift that affects the day-to-day choices and experiences of believers. Encounters with the end of time through the retelling of the myth encourage people to examine their values and reorient priorities. Recitation of the eschatological myths allows people to enter into the "strong time" of the myth, empowering them both to live meaningfully in the world and to change it. This is done at the very least by forming alliances made up of people whose lives are governed by their anticipation of the apocalyptic intervention of God.[6] Eschatological expectation thus gives new direction to groups, allowing for the formation of new and powerful alliances among people who have common priorities growing out of a common vision for the future.

These new bonds—*communitas*—reinforce and re-create the divine presence felt in identification with the apocalyptic myth. Moreover, the gathering of those who are united by this belief gives new life to the vision of God's presence and ultimate conquest. Indeed, the attainment of *communitas* through such common ritual experiences is sacred, because it "breaks through the interstices of structure" and "transgresses or dissolves the norms that govern institutionalized relationships."[7] Thus, the divine breaks through the mundane not only in the eschatological vision but also in the values the vision calls forth and in the community it creates. For early Pentecostalism the apocalyptic return of Jesus was a central hope. Although it was only one of four fundamentals,[8] most interpreters claim that millennial fervor was primary. Early adherents anticipated an imminent Second Coming, and so they believed that the biblical gifts—healing, speaking in tongues, and so on—had been restored to the faithful.[9] End-time expectations led Pentecostals to practice "the same unusual psychic phenomena that characterized the early Church, and to consider them . . . the work of the Spirit." The central message was "Jesus is coming soon," and this apocalyptic hope opened the door to other experiences of divine intervention. Tongues became a means by which the message was "confirmed, legitimized, and propagated."[10] Healing, casting out demons, and other Pentecostal gifts were often interpreted in the same way.[11] Both the apocalyptic pronouncement and the Pentecostal gifts were ways of identifying with the meaning of the Parousia: "Here he is!"[12] Jesus is not merely past or future; Jesus is here changing our lives and the world *now*.

This belief in God's divine intervention was crucial. The eschatological myth provided the "disinherited" of the earth with a "pessimistic explanation of past and present that coincided with their own social experience, while at the same time it held out hope of triumph and reward in the immediate future." It was an alternative worldview, a protest against the values of modernity, and a vehicle for forming meaningful relationships based on the values of another realm. And that worldview would be confirmed and distributed through Pentecostal congregations by the Pentecostal gifts, which were a kind of eschatological fulfillment.[13] Even when the Parousia did not occur, believers maintained the conviction that the world can be changed to make it more like heaven through communities that together find life in the Pentecostal gifts.

In the SBC apocalyptic expectations also served as a mythic hope for those who saw their denomination being changed by the onslaught of a new economy, a new urbanism, and a new secularism.[14] The expectation of Christ's return, which would set the world right, became a life-giving worldview and a major catalyst for the conservative organization that took control of the SBC. As my 1986 survey of Southern Baptist ministers indicates, those who emphasized the doctrine of the Second Coming—dispensationalists—were both more dissatisfied with the modern world and more likely than any other group to vote for conservative SBC candidates.[15]

For fundamentalists, then, this eschatological intervention occurs not just in the past or future but in the present. Against Poloma, who argues that dispensationalism usually relegates divine intervention in the world to biblical times or to the future,[16] my view is that as people become convinced that the apocalypse is near and as they repeat the hope of the book of Revelation, they experience God's intervention *in the present.* People enter into this divine promise through the visionary myth, especially when they begin to see signs in their own world that Jesus might soon return. Not surprisingly, then, dispensationalists were far more likely than any other group to believe that the establishment of the state of Israel was a fulfillment of prophecy concerning the end time. Ninety percent of dispensationalists believed this, and 51 percent believed the end of time was near.[17] This group does have a place for God's intervention in the present. In addition, dispensationalists were more likely than others to believe that God gives people today specific instructions for everyday decisions—56 percent of dispensationalists held this belief, but only 49 percent of traditional premillennialists and 28 percent of nonpremillennialists did so. Perhaps most challenging to Poloma's perspective, however, is the dispensationalist belief that God controls election results. Forty-six percent of dispensationalists believed this, whereas only 20 percent of all other ministers concurred.

There were several factors in the rise of this apocalyptic myth. The earliest was the *Scofield Reference Bible,* which spread the dispensationalist form of the biblical story in the early twentieth century throughout the United States. This Bible enabled the common person to tap into the divine mysteries and combat the modern belief that truth is found only in the halls of academia. It was more influential than any other source in the formation of eschatological perspectives of SBC ministers, even in the 1980s.[18]

In the 1920s and 1930s J. Frank Norris, a renegade among Southern Baptists who preached the imminent return of Christ, probably exerted greater influence than many realized. As social stress grew, especially in rural areas of the South after World War II, the eschatological myth became more widespread, influencing first the most conservative (fundamentalists) but over time others as well. Wider belief in the imminent Parousia became evident in the early 1950s with the organization of widespread SBC premillennialist fellowships that disseminated dispensationalism, which had already made headway in the convention through the Scofield Bible.

Another significant factor in the spread of dispensationalism in the SBC was W. A. Criswell, pastor of the influential First Baptist Church of Dallas. Through the extensive dissemination of his books, sermons, and tapes on the subject, eschatological language, music, and attitudes influenced the churches and people of the SBC. The depth of this influence was evident first at the pastors' conferences during the 1970s and then later when fundamentalists began consistently winning the SBC presidency in 1979. Before long the eschatological vision propelled the fundamentalist agenda to victory after victory.[19]

The ritualistic repetition of the eschatological vision was so successful that the apocalyptic vision had turned into a kind of revolution. Even though the eschaton had not arrived, the expectation had generated a new vision—the purging of the SBC. This is the natural progress of all millennialist movements. Although the goal may be the eschaton, the real hope is a new way of understanding and experiencing the world. Social change is central to this, so such movements may take on a more worldly cast. That is what happened in the SBC.

Between the mid-1970s and early 1980s, fundamentalists interpreted their conquest of leadership positions in the SBC as a gift from God, a precursor to the eschatological promise. Their victories were often described in fantastic terms. The fundamentalist journalist Robert Tenery, for example, claimed that the conquest was "more significant than the Protestant Reformation."[20] For Tenery this was a foretaste of God's ultimate triumph, but even for those more cautious in their language, the defeat of "liberalism" was the result of God's acting among his people. It was as though the eschatological vision, repeated over and over in sermon and song, had opened the way for something else—the experience of God's intervention in the present. It was only through the eschatological vision and the fallout from it that the fundamentalists were so successful. As a group they had stood outside the traditional denominational power structures; they, like the early Pentecostals, felt themselves disinherited. As they experienced God's presence in the apocalyptic promise, however, they not only identified their priorities but also found strength in a new *communitas* and were empowered by their newfound faith in God's activity in the world. And their enthusiasm attracted others. Most Southern Baptists were not fundamentalists, but many of them were also plagued by the same concerns and were thus drawn into the fundamentalist vision. It pulled them into a fight that would not have been theirs, for the average Baptist had previously cared little about convention politics. Only through a movement built on an alternative vision of the world was the SBC so radically changed. Only through the belief in God's intervention in the world were people so fiercely loyal to their denomination and its traditions made not only to accept but also to rejoice in sweeping changes—creedalism and a new emphasis on pastoral authority—that cut to the core of Southern Baptist identity.

Great pageants of victory helped convention-goers and those who watched on cable TV to experience the full impact of what was understood as divine intervention. For those who could not appreciate changes on the convention level, the victory was brought home by identifying the successful, growing churches of the movement's leaders as signs of God's activity in a secular world. Prosperous churches, especially the megachurches, were interpreted as God's creations. These megachurches, with their vast array of programs, became a heaven on earth where the faithful could live their lives insulated from the larger society. For smaller congregations, these churches and their pastors became models and sources of inspiration.[21] In these things the power of God's intervention lived on.

On this score the SBC differs from the Assemblies of God. According to Poloma, the Assemblies of God, like other religious groups built on the experience of divine intervention, faces "the ever-present danger of the erosion of charisma." These groups can become "more intent on perpetuating the institution than the religious experiences which birthed it."[22] But the Pentecostal gifts (tongues, etc.) important to the Assemblies as its eschatological vision diminished seem less of a compromise with modernity than the SBC's church growth records. Interpreting God's intervention in terms of worldly success and growth of churches hardly reflects the gospel message. If anything, it reflects the modern world's values, with its emphasis on numbers. For Southern Baptist fundamentalists, God's intervention was supportive of their new institutional structures.

Concern for large churches and numbers did not, however, spell the end of the Pentecostal apocalyptic experience among fundamentalist Southern Baptists. They have sustained a sense of God's intervention in the world through a new kind of minister: prophetic preachers. Although few of these preachers speak in tongues or perform healings, they all reflect a Pentecostal style of ministry.

The Preacher as Prophet

Prophets are spokespersons for God who stand outside established institutions, charismatic persons who gain their status not through institutional acceptance, educational credentials, or pedigree but through divine calling. As Max Weber argues, they are crucial for new religious movements and extremely threatening to established ones. Here I will consider prophetic-type activity as well as persons who meet the sociological definition of prophet in the strict sense.

Poloma contends not only that prophetic figures are responsible for the birth of Pentecostalism but also that prophetic activity among preachers is important for the maintenance of a charismatic spirit in Assemblies of God congregations. In Poloma's study prophetic activity includes not only prophetic statements but also frequent altar calls, testimonies, and other spiritual gifts.[23] She describes the Pentecostal "prophetic preacher," who in days gone by was said to preach sermons that were the gift of "divine anointing." According to Poloma, those who today are more oriented toward prophecy regard themselves as preachers rather than teachers. In addition, the "prophets" are more likely to have traditional Pentecostal congregations.[24] At the same time, the Assemblies of God, more than some forms of Pentecostalism, has moved toward traditional institutional standards for its ministers. Educational requirements for ordination, ordered worship services, and prepared sermons are a few of the innovations. These new standards have limited the influence of more traditional prophetic preachers, especially those (e.g., women) without institutionalized ministerial standards.[25] But these institutional threats to the congregational charismatic experience of God's presence do not seem to have completely undermined the Pentecostal spirit.

Southern Baptist prophetic preachers emerged along with the fundamentalist movement in the SBC. The term "prophetic preacher" has been used before in Baptist circles, but only recently has it been used widely. To be a prophetic preacher, one need not speak in tongues or perform healings; rather, one must powerfully proclaim God's Word. Fundamentalists view this ability as a divine gift, so to be named a "prophetic preacher" gives one a great deal of power.

W. A. Criswell, the most important prophetic figure in the SBC, is the person who did the most to popularize the millennial myth in the denomination. At the same time, his explication of the eschatological hope also helped him to gain the status of prophet. Criswell has said that his most significant theological contribution is the exposition of premillennialism. He contends he was able to do this not as a result of his educational training but through the Holy Spirit's illumination. Although Criswell admits to preparing sermons and using commentaries, he says that his real insights come from his fellowship with God.[26] In the early 1960s Criswell spent three years preaching the Apocalypse during Sunday morning services in his Dallas church. Printed sermons, commentaries, and numerous speaking engagements followed. By 1968 Criswell had achieved sufficient influence to be elected president of the SBC.

This was no minor achievement, for Criswell stood well outside institutional power structures. But Criswell and his followers regarded the election as an act of God.[27]

The crowning achievement of Criswell's published works, the *Criswell Study Bible*, appeared in 1979. Several times in the "Foreward," Paige Patterson, then president of the Criswell Center for Biblical Studies, refers to Criswell by the title many had already given him—"prophet," a "Son of Thunder."[28] Criswell clearly had become, as anthropologist Kenelm Burridge says, one who is believed to have "access to a source of inspiration that transcends man's ordinary wits."[29]

Baptist ministers believed to have access to the divine are usually identified by an early and dramatic sense of God's calling. Among fundamentalists the supernatural form of such callings has achieved great significance. This is the case with Criswell. He says he knew he was called to be a preacher by the time he was six, but he encountered strong resistance from his parents, who did not want him to become a minister. But by the time he was sixteen he had his way. The First Baptist Church of Amarillo licensed the young man they believed God had called to preach.[30] All the leaders of the fundamentalist movement in the SBC—the prophetic preachers—have similar stories. Without such a divine call, the rest would be impossible.

Criswell hoped others would also take up the prophetic mantle, so in 1971 Criswell inaugurated a yearly pastors' school named the "School of the Prophets." Interestingly, this "school" was not the only Baptist institution of that era known by that name. Mid-America Seminary opened in Louisiana as the School of the Prophets in the same year that Criswell's pastors' workshop began. Although not a Southern Baptist seminary, Mid-America has traditionally been the choice for fundamentalist Southern Baptist students. Both schools teach the belief that one called by God to preach can learn to be God's spokesperson. In this regard, it should be remembered that most Pentecostals also believe that one can be prepared to receive the Pentecostal gifts.

Like traditional Pentecostal preachers, Criswell uses no written text, and he preaches "with a Bible in his hand."[31] Although he admits to sermon preparation, he still regards himself as God's inspired voice. He says that God enables him "to remember the prepared message [he] studied and prayed to deliver."[32] Prayer is crucial, and ultimately the sermon itself is regarded as a divine gift. But Criswell's philosophy and technique for sermon preparation can be taught, and the key is that "Bible in his hand."

One common technique is to use frequent cross-references, as does the Scofield Bible. The more adept a preacher is at cross-referencing his primary text with other scriptural passages, the better preacher he is,[33] and the more likely the congregations will believe that he has real access to the Sacred Word. And this, in turn, makes it more likely that he will be perceived as a "man of God," the primary criterion for prophetic leadership.[34] Kathleen Boone suggests that these practices enable preachers to "[ally] themselves with the Bible; their listeners heed both the word and the Word, without being able to determine which is which."[35] If preachers such as Criswell believe in the supernatural character of the Bible, that it *is* the inerrant Word of God, then they must conclude that a minister called of God can, with proper training and prayer, identify with that supernatural gift and become its mouthpiece. Indeed, he can become God's prophet.

One way to make obvious the preacher's prophetic status is through a ritual also found among Pentecostals: the kneeling of the pastor before the congregation prior to preaching. W. A. Criswell does this, and so did R. G. Lee, Criswell's prophetic predecessor. Lee, influential in the spread of apocalyptic hope in the SBC, was the pastor of the Bellevue Baptist Church in Memphis. In the 1950s Lee became known for his practice of kneeling beside the pulpit before he preached. With one hand on the pulpit and the Bible tucked under his arm, he knelt beneath a spotlight shining directly on him while the rest of the church was darkened. Doubtless many in the congregation sensed God's spirit coming down on their leader, blessing him with inspired words. Charles Stanley, the pastor of the Atlanta's First Baptist Church and a fundamentalist leader in the SBC, also ritually kneels occasionally. Although not a widespread practice—only about 12 percent of pastors in my survey report doing this regularly—it is important for many of the leaders of the SBC fundamentalist coalition. Indeed, this kneeling ritual adds to their influence as senior prophets of the denomination. The practice gives visual affirmation of God's spirit descending on the one who will deliver the Word.

Other elements are also important in establishing a preacher's prophetic status, and many of these elements are Pentecostal in character. W. A. Criswell has a lively, Pentecostal preaching style: he often speaks loudly and shouts at congregations; he gesticulates and paces.[36] Many have gone to his school just to hear him preach and to study his manner. Certainly Southern Baptist preaching is more animated today, sometimes even in traditionally staid pulpits. Like many Pentecostal preachers, Criswell and others who imitate his style remind their congregations occasionally that their sermons were "given by" or "laid on their hearts" by God himself.[37] Indeed, this language of legitimization was often used by fundamentalists as they took control of the SBC. At conventions they frequently spoke of each other as prophetic preachers or "men of God." Some programs, especially at the pastors' conferences, seemed designed to encourage the preachers to associate these images with themselves at home. For example, in 1970 the pastors' conference theme was "The Minister: Christ's Man for the 70's." This language of holy identification, calling preachers "God's men," was also used regularly in fundamentalist publications,[38] thus encouraging lay readers to see their own pastors in this light.

Dispensational fundamentalists, the Southern Baptists most likely to use prophetic imagery for their preachers, are also like traditional Pentecostals, the ones who in Poloma's study saw themselves as preachers rather than teachers. They were more likely to emphasize altar calls for conversion, testimonials from the congregation, and datable conversion experiences. Southern Baptist dispensationalists were also more likely than other Baptist ministers to insist on rebaptism for those who felt that their original conversion was not valid. Baptists have always emphasized conversion experiences, but rebaptism grew significantly when the fundamentalists were gaining power. By the late 1970s the practice was so widespread that it made the gathering of accurate church growth statistics difficult.

Sometimes Pentecostal-like practices have benefited fundamentalist leaders. Adrian Rogers, at the 1985 Dallas convention, reported that he once cast out a demon. While preaching in his home church, he recounted, the door burst open and a barefooted "maniacal" man charged toward him. Assured by the Lord that "the devil was about to make a fool of himself," Rogers said he stood his ground. "I kneeled beside that man," Rogers said. "I put one hand on his head and lifted the other toward heaven, and I said, 'In the Name of Jesus, Satan, I bind you.'" Forty-two persons made decisions for Christ that day at his church. "I've discovered there's power, wonder-working power in the name of Jesus," he said.[39] Although not a common type of story among SBC fundamentalists (as it is not common among many Pentecostals), it gave Rogers great influence and power.

Stories of God's direct intervention have also helped other fundamentalist leaders to gain power. Charles Stanley was made pastor of the First Baptist Church of Atlanta because of what he claimed was a word from God. According to some stories, Stanley told the pulpit committee that God had called him to that role, so he moved right into the pastor's vacant office. Despite some controversy, most agreed that God had called Stanley. The call of God was also important for several of the fundamentalists who ran for the SBC presidency. Criswell said he ran under direction from God. Adrian Rogers became a presidential candidate at the 1979 convention only at the last minute when God called him.

But charisma turns into the vehicle for new worldly standards. Those prophetic preachers, who resemble Pentecostal preachers more than they resemble local church pastors and who were on the fringes of SBC power structures, became the ones in charge during the fundamentalist rise to power. Between the early 1970s and 1987, the roles of authority became reversed; "God's men" stood before the convention as the recognized proclaimers of the "plain truth" of the Bible. The good old boy system in the academic seminary experience was now dead. The former outsiders were now *officially* the SBC leaders.[40]

Once in power, the fundamentalists used their prophetic status to institutionalize their authority, and in so doing they changed the meaning of Baptist congregationalism. The new "prophetic" pastors claimed for themselves a kind of authority that has allowed them greater influence and power than has ever been typical of Southern Baptist pastors. Although this new status is not mandatory, it has been legitimized through the passage of the extremely controversial Resolution Five ("On the Priesthood of the Believer") at the 1988 convention in San Antonio. It stated that in the local church, "structure and order is supervised through His [God's] divinely appointed authority, the pastor."[41] Surprisingly, given Southern Baptists' historical emphasis on freedom, there was little hesitation to use the word *ruler* in the debate. It was, after all, in the Bible. Furthermore, Jesus himself had given church leaders this authority, as the fundamentalists argued from Matthew 16:19. Although the pastor must be a servant-ruler, he was a ruler appointed by God. Their argument won the day.

Of course, a devout Pentecostal perspective would likely insist that as their status is institutionalized, the prophets will compromise the nature of their divine gift. But fundamentalists do not see it that way. The heightened supernaturalism associated with dispensationalism seems to be determinative of attitude here. In my own survey 62 percent of the dispensationalists said that the pastor should have the final say in church doctrinal disputes, whereas only 34 percent of the traditional premillennialists and 22 percent of the nonmillennialists agreed with that notion. Twenty-nine percent of the dispensationalists believed that they should have the final say in church business disputes, whereas only 9 percent of traditional premillennialists and a mere 3 percent of the nonmillennialists agreed.

If these attitudes about pastoral authority do indeed take hold in Southern Baptist churches, this will change the denomination more than anything else has. Southern Baptists still remain a congregational people, but ruling preachers, even if they are "God's men," certainly give a different air to those congregations. And as "God's men" become more entangled in institutional structures and all the earthly concerns that go with such responsibilities, the prophetic witness may also be tamed.

In the meantime, having "prophetic preachers" means something to many congregations. Fundamentalists are not the only people attracted to them; many traditional Southern Baptists have rallied around such preachers. Although they may not think that they themselves receive charismatic gifts from God, many congregations vicariously participate in God's gift to their preacher. They treat him almost with awe and often hang on his every word, take copious notes on what he preaches, seek his autograph, and have their photographs made with him. For some, just being a part of such a man's congregation gives a sense of power, a sense of God's presence. It is a more passive participation in the divine gifts than Pentecostal practices entail, but for many it offers something of the same experiences. Many argue that the attraction of fundamentalism is the simple answers it gives to complex questions. But the real attraction may well be the sense that one is participating in a power that is not of this world, a power that comes directly from God, a power characteristic of the Pentecostal worldview.

Pentecostal Currents Continue to Enliven the SBC

There are other Pentecostal currents in the SBC that help people to experience God's intervention vicariously through the prophetic preacher or through the sacred community (the congregation or *communitas*) that stands against the world's values. These elements certainly do not make Southern Baptists Pentecostals, but they have helped the denomination to stand out vis-à-vis mainstream Protestantism, which seems entrenched in the values of the modern world. For many, these Pentecostal-like elements are what give the denomination its liveliness, and they may account for its continued growth.

One element is church architecture, which has begun to reflect a Pentecostal style. For example, according to Dr. Gwenn McCormick, who assists congregations with their building plans through the Baptist Sunday School Board, churches with radial seating have replaced the traditional rectangular church with colonial columns as the most requested design.[42] Although no direct Pentecostal influence can be demonstrated here, radial seating is also popular among Pentecostals, and it accommodates well Pentecostal worship practices. Radial seating helps to combat the anonymity of today's society by allowing congregants to feel a greater sense of community; it is easier to feel like God's people gathered together. This, in turn, enables worshipers to experience the power of being together. For many there is a supernatural quality to that experience of community. Radial seating has other advantages for Pentecostal-type churches: there is more open space for movement, and this makes it easier to answer altar calls, something important for fundamentalists. Also, radial seating makes it easier to recognize visitors and to greet one another. Finally, radial seating brings more people closer to God's spokesperson. The new design facilitates sight lines and eye contact between pastor and congregation. If one does experience God's presence through the prophetic preacher, being able to see him means a lot.

Related to radial seating is the use of smaller or translucent pulpits that help to eliminate the distance between pastor and congregation. Some pastors have even removed the pulpit entirely, allowing themselves greater visibility and greater freedom of movement, something Pentecostal preachers also prefer.

Another new element is the larger platform area, which, as in Pentecostalism, gives more room for musical ensembles, drama, and other types of pageantry, which serve to move the spirits of worshipers. Baptists once restricted drama to the fellowship hall, but this has changed. Drama now serves to engage people in the stories acted out in the sanctuary itself. Many churches have even installed all the lighting and sound systems necessary for theater-type productions. These things help the worshiper to participate fully in the experience. The desire is that no one be a mere spectator. Church is much more than rational instruction; it is a powerful experience.

Music styles have also recently changed in the SBC, and music has become more important, often serving a purpose similar to that in Pentecostalism: reminding people of God's present involvement with them. As with Pentecostals, such experiences among fundamentalist Baptists are often identified and affirmed by the preacher's comments.[43] Music has always moved people, and for Southern Baptists traditional hymns have been a primary way of experiencing God's presence. Now, however, some churches rely on choruses, the type of music most popular in Pentecostal churches.[44] As Dan Johnson of the church music department at the Baptist Sunday School Board notes, choruses are easy to learn and sing. They require no familiarity with the denomination's musical tradition, so a newcomer can easily feel at home. These choruses reflect the Roman Catholic insight that repetition is valuable, for it helps one feel included in a tradition. Spiritual experiences become attached to the choruses, and these experiences are remembered and relived as the choruses are repeated weekly. Also, as Pentecostals have always known, choruses allow freedom from the hymnal, freedom to raise hands in praise, and freedom to join hands with one another. SBC churches that engage in this freer, more extended worship time are not numerous, but few would dispute their resemblance to Pentecostal churches.

There are also changes in worship practices that encourage worshipers to become involved, an attitude also prevalent in Pentecostal circles. In my survey Baptist ministers were asked to indicate their experience with certain practices both now and when they were young. Testimonies are now somewhat more common than they were when many of the pastors were young, and apparently applause in church is much more common. Seventy percent of the respondents reported that there was never applause in church when they were young, whereas only 36 percent reported that there is never applause in their churches today. About 25 percent report that applause is heard often or very often in their churches today, but only about 4 percent said that was true of the churches of their youth.

All these new currents in SBC worship suggest a move toward the same kind of personal experience and expression important in the Pentecostal tradition.

Conclusion

No direct influence between Pentecostalism and Southern Baptists can be demonstrated. But the Pentecostal-type worldview that upholds an alternative to the rational, modern perspective on the world is very much alive among fundamentalist Baptists. It was this alternative, Pentecostal-like worldview that made possible the fundamentalist takeover of the Southern Baptist Convention. And for many, it is those new Pentecostal elements that sustain this alternative worldview and continue to make the denomination attractive. So Pentecostals and fundamentalists may actually be more alike than scholars have assumed. They are both empowered by the vision of another world, and they both find *communitas* and the possibility of powerful individual relationships with God in this alternative worldview and in their style of worship.

The difference between the two emerges in the way this otherworldly vision has directed their relationships with the world's standards. Central to the identity of most Pentecostals is their continued separation and difference from the secular world. Although divine intervention in the form of the Pentecostal gifts may give them a sense of distinctiveness, these activities also make them unacceptable in many circles. Fundamentalist Baptists, on the other hand, may be in the back pocket of modern secularists. The belief that God has intervened to create churches may not be understood by secularists, but that they are successfully *growing* and *prosperous* churches is something that secularists could appreciate on their way to the bank. So although some may say that Pentecostal practices are a kind of crutch that enables the believer to endure modernity, others may wonder whether God's gifts to Southern Baptists have been co-opted for worldly gain. Their later understanding of divine intervention represents an accommodation with modernity and an abandonment of the Pentecostal worldview.

Notes

1. I use the term *fundamentalist* to refer to the leaders of recent changes in the SBC. Although these leaders meet the criteria for this label, some who come after them do not.

2. James Davison Hunter, "The New Religions: Demodernization and the Protest against Modernity," in *Impact of New Religious Movements,* ed. Bryan Wilson (New York: Rose of Sharon, 1981), 1–20.

3. Margaret Poloma, *The Assemblies of God at the Crossroads: Charisma and Institutional Dilemmas* (Knoxville: University of Tennessee Press, 1989).

4. For the most complete discussion of this, see Helen Lee Turner, "Fundamentalism in the Southern Baptist Convention: The Crystallization of a Millennialist Vision," Ph.D. diss., University of Virginia, 1990.

5. For a full discussion of the theories about millenarian movements and their effects in times of stress, see Kenelm Burridge, *New Heaven, New Earth: A Study of Millenarian Activities* (New York: Schocken, 1969); or Michael Barkun, *Disaster and the Millennium* (New Haven, Conn.: Yale University Press, 1974; repr., Syracuse, N.Y.: Syracuse University Press, 1986).

6. Mircea Eliade, *Myth and Reality* (New York: Harper and Row, 1963), 19.

7. Victor Turner, *Ritual Process* (Chicago: University of Chicago Press, 1969), 128.

8. The four fundamentals are salvation, healing, the baptism of the Holy Spirit, and the Second Coming of Christ. See Donald W. Dayton, *Theological Roots of Pentecostalism* (Grand Rapids, Mich.: Francis Asbury, 1987), 21.

9. See Edith L. Blumhofer, *The Assemblies of God: A Chapter in the Story of American Pentecostalism* (Springfield, Mo.: Gospel Publishing House, 1989), chaps. 1 and 2.

10. Robert Mapes Anderson, *Vision of the Disinherited: The Making of American Pentecostalism* (New York: Oxford University Press, 1979), 89, 90.

11. Ibid., 91–97.

12. Some scholars suggest that the most adequate translation of what is in many ways an untranslatable term, *parousia,* is "Here he is!" See Alexander Schmemann, *For the Life of the World* (New York: St. Vladimir's Seminary Press, 1973), 33.

13. Anderson, *Vision,* 97. Poloma also argues that Pentecostals laid hold of a "belief and experience of the paranormal as an alternative weltanschauung for our instrumental and rational modern society." She claims that for the Assemblies of God, divine intervention—the basis for an alternative to the modern worldview—is found in tongues speaking, healing, and other common Pentecostal gifts. But, as she says, apocalyptic

expectation was also important in early Pentecostalism during the early twentieth century (Poloma, *Assemblies of God,* xvii).

14. For a full discussion of the changes that swept the South and the Southern Baptist Convention and led to a sense of crisis, see Helen Lee Turner, "Societal Change and Millennialist Visions: Provocateurs of Denominational Strife," *Journal of the South Carolina Baptist Historical Society* 16 (Nov. 1990): 19–30.

15. For a more complete discussion of the role of eschatology in the recent turmoil in the SBC, see Helen Lee Turner, "Myths: Stories of This World and the World to Come," in *Southern Baptists Observed: Multiple Perspectives on a Changing Denomination,* ed. Nancy Tatom Ammerman (Knoxville: University of Tennessee Press, 1993). This survey was sent in 1986 to a random sample of 1,500 Southern Baptist ministers with a 48 percent response rate (see Turner, "Fundamentalism in the SBC"). A variety of questions about eschatology was on the survey, along with other theological questions and questions about the ministers' backgrounds, politics, and social attitudes. On this survey 71 percent of the self-proclaimed fundamentalists identified themselves as dispensationalists, and the dispensationalists were more likely than any other group to vote for the conservative agenda in the SBC. Indeed, in 1986 nearly 90 percent of the dispensationalists voted for fundamentalist Adrian Rogers rather than for his more moderate opponent.

16. Poloma, *Assemblies of God,* 60–61.

17. About 76 percent of the traditional premillennialists agreed with this idea, but only 26 percent of them believed the world would end soon. Only 27 percent of the nonpremillennialists saw the creation of the state of Israel as the fulfillment of prophecy, and a mere 4 percent of that group believed the world would end soon. In this study the group identified as "traditional premillennialists" generally gave less importance to the Second Coming and did not openly endorse the more radical tenants of dispensationalism, even though they professed belief in a premillennial return of Christ. The group identified as "nonpremillennialists" were those who placed little or no stock in eschatological doctrines.

18. In my 1987 survey of associational ministers, 41 percent said that the *Scofield Reference Bible* had the greatest influence on ministers in their area, whereas only 33.3 percent of those surveyed cited seminary education as having had the greatest influence. The response rate was a bit inflated since a number of the ministers checked more than one answer.

19. For a more complete discussion of this, see Turner, "Fundamentalism in the SBC," 285–311; or Turner, "Myths," 104–9.

20. Robert Tenery, interview with Bill Moyers, in "God and Politics: Battle for the Bible," produced by Gail Pellett, Public Affairs Television, 1987.

21. For further discussion of these ideas, see Turner, "Fundamentalism in the SBC," 436–46; or Turner, "Myths," 117–19.

22. Poloma, *Assemblies of God,* 101.

23. For a discussion of this, see ibid., 78–87.

24. Ibid., 196–98.

25. For further discussion of this, see Ibid., 101–39.

26. W. A. Criswell, *Pastor's Pen,* 2 Dec. 1960, pp. 1, 4, as quoted in Harold T. Bryson, "The Expository Preaching of W. A. Criswell in His Sermons on the Revelation," M.A.

thesis, New Orleans Baptist Theological Seminary, 1967, p. 21; Criswell, "How I Prepare Sermons," 13, cited in Bryson, "Expository Preaching," 22.

27. Criswell, like many hesitant prophets, had requested that his name not be present for nomination until six days before the election ("President Views Convention Needs," *Baptist Courier*, 13 June 1968, p. 3).

28. Paige Patterson, "Foreward," *Criswell Study Bible* (Nashville: Thomas Nelson, 1979), v, vi.

29. Burridge, *New Heaven, New Earth*, 155.

30. Dick J. Reavis, "The Politics of Armageddon," *The Texas Monthly*, Oct. 1984, p. 236.

31. Criswell, *With a Bible in My Hand* (Nashville: Broadman, 1978).

32. Ibid., 8.

33. Kathleen C. Boone, *The Bible Tells Them So: The Discourse of Protestant Fundamentalism* (Albany: State University of New York Press, 1989), 13.

34. My study indicates that Southern Baptist fundamentalists are more likely than moderates to use the *Scofield Reference Bible* in sermon preparation. My survey also reveals that fundamentalists are more likely than moderates to use a number of biblical passages in one sermon to support their main text.

35. Boone, *The Bible Tells Them So*, 109.

36. Reavis, "Politics of Armageddon," 137.

37. For Poloma's discussion of these techniques, see *Assemblies of God*, 196–203.

38. The *Southern Baptist Journal* and the *Southern Baptist Advocate*.

39. Baptist Press convention releases, 1985.

40. Beginning in the 1970s, a sign of what was coming was the regular appearance at the pastors' conference of evangelist James Robison, known for his Pentecostal style. In 1974 Bailey Smith, an often full-time evangelist, spoke on the topic of "the church's prophet." In a few years he would be president of the SBC. Another important symbol of the change was the role given vocational evangelists at the 1987 St. Louis convention. In marked contrast to their utter absence in the days of moderate control, in that year the evangelists were given the key programmatic task of theme interpretation. "Who would have thought this ten years ago?" asked career evangelist Howard Lingingfelter. "It is truly a miracle of God." See James C. Hefley, *The Truth in Crisis: The Controversy in the Southern Baptist Convention*, 3 vols. (Hannibal, Mo.: Hannibal, 1988), 3:421.

41. *Southern Baptist Advocate*, July 1988, p. 17.

42. The following information about church architecture comes from a telephone conversation with Dr. Gwenn McCormick of the Church Architecture Department of the Baptist Sunday School Board.

43. Poloma notes that worship leaders in the Pentecostal tradition often tell the congregation something like, "Don't you just feel God's presence?" This, she says, is a way to "claim a mystical experience" (*Assemblies of God*, 190).

44. The 1975 version of the Baptist hymnal contains almost no choruses. The 1991 hymnal has around forty-five, and that is not nearly enough for some churches.

Part 4:

Studying Pentecostalism: A Historiographical Overview

12

The Beginnings of American Pentecostalism: A Historiographical Overview

Augustus Cerillo

A fundamental problem with respect to the history of American Pentecostalism is the question of the movement's origins during the early decades of the twentieth century. Pioneer students of Pentecostalism, including "participant-observers" and a later generation of Pentecostal ministers and church leaders, generally saw little need to seek explanations for their movement's beginnings within the historical process, nor did they search for causal connections between Pentecostalism's emergence and a turn-of-the century American context of profound socioeconomic, political, and religious transformations. Instead these early writers, although not entirely unaware of the role of human agency in history, largely viewed Pentecostalism's arrival as a providentially generated, end-time religious revival fundamentally discontinuous with 1,900 years of Christian history.[1]

This "classical" interpretive paradigm of Pentecostal beginnings dominated the historiography of Pentecostalism until the 1950s.[2] Thereafter it was challenged and modified by a generation of academically trained historians, many of them Pentecostals themselves, who constructed what might be termed a "new" Pentecostal historiography. Practitioners of this "new" history concerned themselves with the nineteenth-century religious roots of Pentecostalism, with the larger socioeconomic and cultural context within which Pentecostalism emerged, with the social sources and theological content of Pentecostalism, with the ways in which Pentecostals viewed the world and the effects of those views on their actions, and with the processes of Pentecostal movement building. In sum, modern students of Pentecostalism want to know precisely where and why the revival emerged and how the Pentecostal movement was put together, functioned, and survived during its formative years. Undergirding these investigations is the sense that a very old yet paradoxically new religious tendency had been birthed around the turn of the century in a modernizing American society.

1961–79

Klaude Kendrick, John T. Nichol, and Vinson Synan blazed the trail of what was to become the new Pentecostal history. In 1961 Kendrick published *The Promised Fulfilled: A History of the Modern Pentecostal Movement,* an overview of the major Wesleyan and Reformed Pentecostal denominations.[3] The Assemblies of God scholar located the roots of Pentecostalism in late nineteenth-century Wesleyan-Holiness doctrinal beliefs and religious practices, among which he included the Holiness stress on experiential religion, including even a tolerance of tongues speaking; the doctrine of entire sanctification; the literal interpretation of Scripture; the use among some of the term "baptism of the Holy Spirit" to define the second blessing; and the establishment of camp meetings and Bible schools. Claiming that Charles F. Parham's formulation of the doctrine of tongues as the initial evidence of Holy Spirit baptism was the unique Pentecostal theological contribution to these existing Holiness currents, Kendrick viewed the events at Parham's Bethel Bible School in Topeka, Kansas, in 1901, and not the more well known Azusa Street revival in Los Angeles in 1906, as the start of the Pentecostal movement. Furthermore, he unequivocally declared Parham to be the "father of the modern Pentecostal Movement," almost single-handedly rescuing the enigmatic Kansas preacher from Pentecostal historiographical oblivion.[4]

Unlike Kendrick, who limited his study to American Pentecostalism, Nichol surveyed worldwide Pentecostal developments.[5] Yet he largely followed Kendrick in stressing the continuity of the Pentecostal movement with earlier Christian traditions, especially the nineteenth-century Holiness movement; in viewing the Pentecostal insistence on evidentiary tongues as the movement's defining characteristic; and in locating the birthplace of Pentecostalism in Topeka in 1901. Nichol, however, went beyond Kendrick in briefly suggesting that Pentecostalism's roots lay in evangelical theological and experiential territory much broader than just Wesleyan Methodism.

A decade after Kendrick's book initiated the modern American study of Pentecostalism, Synan's *Holiness-Pentecostal Movement* appeared.[6] Synan similarly viewed Pentecostalism as an outgrowth of the Wesleyan-inspired nineteenth-century Holiness movement, but he more tightly linked Parham's notion of a Holy Spirit baptism separate from sanctification to the prior teaching of Benjamin Hardin Irwin, founder of the Fire-Baptized Holiness Church in 1895. More than Kendrick and even Nichol had, Synan explicitly sought to broaden the socioeconomic, intellectual, and political setting of the study of American Pentecostalism. He asserted that most Pentecostals were poor farmers and small-town and urban working-class folk but did not provide an empirically based social profile of the Pentecostal constituency. He also insisted that Pentecostal groups, despite their essentially antiworldly, negative social philosophy, must be understood as part of the broad range of Gilded Age and Progressive Era reform movements that organized to confront the problems stemming from the nation's urban and industrial transformation.

There are similarities and differences among these three pioneering histories of Pentecostalism. Each originated as a dissertation for the Ph.D. in history; none utilized an explicitly providential interpretive framework; and all understood Pentecostalism as a theological movement within historical Christianity and focused primarily on the Wesleyan roots of Pentecostal religious thought and experience. Synan sought explicitly to place Pentecostalism within the broad currents of turn-of-the-century American social protest, and Nichol, anticipating a later historiographical emphasis with respect to Pentecostalism's appeal, portrayed Pentecostalism as a popular democratic religious movement whose message of Holy Spirit empowerment appealed especially to those of little status or ability. Kendrick divided his institutional history into Wesleyan and non-Wesleyan Pentecostal denominations, whereas Nichol, noting how fragmented the early Pentecostal movement was, organized his book's descriptive chapters on the development of Pentecostal denominations around chronology of origins, numerical size, and distinctive regional, ethnic, racial, and doctrinal characteristics. A Southerner and minister in the Pentecostal Holiness Church, Synan included in his book a great deal of information about Southern Holiness and Pentecostal denominational developments.

Whereas Kendrick and Synan focused exclusively on the United States as the birthplace of modern Pentecostalism, Nichol conceded that not all eruptions of Pentecostalism around the world could be causally linked to American Pentecostalism; nonetheless, he did not comment on the implications of that fact for an understanding of Pentecostal origins. Kendrick and Nichol gave the nod to Parham as the founder of Pentecostalism, but Synan forcefully argued that Parham and Seymour must share the title of founders: "Parham laid the doctrinal foundations of the movement," he wrote, "while Seymour served as the catalytic agent for its popularization."[7] Writing his book in the late 1950s, before the civil rights and other protest movements had affected American historiography, Kendrick unsurprisingly failed to comment on the socially revolutionary implications of the early Azusa Street revival's relatively egalitarian racial, ethnic, and gender practices. On the other hand, Nichol recognized the role of non-Anglos in early Pentecostalism, and Synan provided the fullest account of the interracial nature of the nascent Pentecostal movement.

A critical concern in the search for Pentecostal antecedents, as the works of Kendrick, Nichol, and Synan illustrate, is the theological relationship between Pentecostalism and nineteenth-century religious traditions. That none of the books previously cited provided a close analysis of the precise theological strands that fed into Pentecostalism prompted historical theologian Donald Dayton to focus his research at the University of Chicago on what Martin Marty, in the foreword to Dayton's *Theological Roots of Pentecostalism,* called the "prehistory" of the Pentecostal movement.[8] The key to Dayton's interpretation of the origins of Pentecostal religious thought was his premise that all of Pentecostalism could be viewed and understood through the lens of a "common theological pattern." Labeled by Dayton the "fourfold Gospel," the Pentecostal theological package consisted of the doctrines of salvation, healing, baptism in the Holy Spirit, and the Second Coming of Jesus Christ. By tracing backward to discover the source of this doctrinal pattern, Dayton was able to provide an intellectual history of these four key Pentecostal beliefs and clearly established that "nearly every wing of late nineteenth-century revivalism was teaching in one form or another all the basic themes of Pentecostalism except for the experience of glossolalia, or 'speaking in tongues.'"[9] He also skillfully and convincingly showed how within nineteenth-century Wesleyan-Holiness circles, the special doctrine of sanctification as a second work of grace was redefined and relabeled as a Pentecostal baptism in the Holy Spirit, thus further setting the stage for Pentecostalism.

Although Dayton gave greater weight to the Wesleyan-Holiness contributions to the distinctive Pentecostal theological gestalt, he did not neglect to incorporate into his doctrinal tributaries to Pentecostalism the contributions of more Reformed, evangelical, and higher life advocates of holiness who stressed the important notion of a baptism of the Spirit as an enduement of power. In fact, his richly textured analysis shows a kaleidoscopic intersection of ideas, doctrines, and religious practices among a whole range of Christians seeking more of the Holy Spirit in Gilded Age America.[10]

Despite his stress on Pentecostalism's continuity with nineteenth-century Holiness thought, Dayton also rightly warned against overemphasizing the old against the new in Pentecostalism. What was theologically new in Pentecostalism, of course, was the teaching that glossolalia is the biblical evidence of the baptism of the Holy Spirit. That belief, Dayton admitted, was "not a natural part of the currents" that fed into Pentecostalism and therefore constituted "a significant *novum* for the most part that truly does set Pentecostalism apart from the other 'higher Christian life' movements."[11] Dayton thus left open the door to a consideration of what in early Pentecostalism may have been unique and thus discontinuous with nineteenth-century evangelicalism.

At about the same time that Synan and Dayton clarified the Wesleyan Holiness roots of twentieth-century Pentecostalism, other historians, including William Menzies, Edith Blumhofer, and Robert Anderson, redirected the search for the theological roots of Pentecostalism toward Reformed and evangelical higher life currents in late nineteenth-century America.[12] They argued that these non-Wesleyan sources better accounted for the Reformed theological and political contours of the Assemblies of God and other obviously non-Wesleyan Pentecostal bodies. In her 1977 doctoral dissertation at Harvard University, Blumhofer (née Waldvogel) attributed the later Pentecostal insistence on the need for a Holy Spirit baptism separate from conversion, belief in sanctification as a progressive overcoming of sin and not an instantaneous eradication of the sinful nature, advocacy of the premillennial return of the Lord, and healing in the atonement to the teachings and ministries of non-Wesleyan evangelicals such as Reuben A. Torrey, Albert B. Simpson, Dwight L. Moody, and various British Keswick leaders.[13]

Menzies only briefly treated these non-Wesleyan sources of Pentecostalism but additionally suggested that the diverse Holiness movements were responses to liberal trends in American religious life and, like Nichol before him, noted Pentecostalism's appeal to ordinary Americans and the movement's democratic polity and character. Because *Annointed to Serve* is a history of the Assemblies of God, a Pentecostal denomination that was not founded until 1914, Menzies creatively and appropriately stretched the period of origins to include the first fifteen years of the new century, the time he noted it took for the fledging Pentecostal movement to take permanent shape. He viewed the creation of the Assemblies of God as a necessary search for order in what was a chaotically mushrooming national Pentecostalism. By doing so he was able to appreciate the importance of organization building to the movement's becoming permanent.[14]

On whatever side of the Wesleyan-Reformed Holiness divide these historians come down, they all stress the continuity of twentieth-century Pentecostalism with nineteenth-century religious and social developments. In their histories Pentecostalism came to be viewed somewhat less as a discrete doctrine, event, and moment in religious history with a unique etiology and more as the culmination of a longer-in-the-making series of Holy Spirit or otherwise precipitated theological innovations and spiritual experiences. Instead of being a sharp break in the religious flow in 1901, the Pentecostal revival was seen as part of a continuous flow of revivalistic religion that spanned the turn of the century. Whether or not they intended to do so, these accounts therefore flattened out somewhat the signal events at Topeka in 1901 and Azusa Street in 1906.

The historians of Pentecostalism discussed thus far did not entirely neglect the larger socioeconomic and cultural context within which Pentecostalism arose. In the main, however, their contextual analyses were more suggestive than substantive, more ad hoc than systematic; they lacked detailed explanations of precisely what in a modernizing America had implications, if any, for an emerging Pentecostalism. And they certainly did not locate the wellsprings of the new Pentecostal movement in secular cultural or socioeconomic change. In other words, they did not provide what might be called a social analysis of Pentecostal beginnings.

Other historians and social scientists, largely non-Pentecostal in religious affiliation, drew on theories of social disorganization, economic and social deprivation, and psychological maladjustment to explain why American Pentecostalism originated among the poor and working classes at the end of the nineteenth century.[15] Ironically, much like the providential view of origins, this sociological or contextual approach implied that Pentecostalism was in some fundamental ways discontinuous with earlier religious revivals and movements: Pentecostalism owed its existence not primarily to antecedent religious developments, as Pentecostal historians had argued, but to the historically particular context of an America in social and economic transition around the turn of the century. Of course, these sociologically informed accounts do not ignore the religious roots of Pentecostalism, but they see them as secondary elements useful for explaining who might have been attracted to Pentecostalism, the content of Pentecostal discourse, and the shape of Pentecostal religious behavior.

Robert Anderson offered the only comprehensive account of American Pentecostalism that located the movement's wellsprings in the social and cultural setting of early twentieth-century American history.[16] Unlike the majority of Pentecostal historians, Anderson insisted that Pentecostalism did not arise primarily because of the relentless inner logic of several decades of theologizing about and experiencing the Holy Spirit. It burst on the religious and social landscape, he maintained, because a group of religiously inclined social and economic losers in an industrializing America eschewed realistic secular solutions to their plight and instead sought comfort in Pentecostalism's rather unhealthy mixture of socially pessimistic millenarian thought and psychologically and socially debilitating tongues or ecstatic speech. In Pentecostal religion, Anderson insisted, "the radical social impulse inherent in the vision of the disinherited was transformed into social passivity, ecstatic escape, and finally, a most conservative conformity."[17]

On a host of specific issues central to an interpretation of Pentecostal origins, Anderson forcefully staked out his views. He argued that early Pentecostalism was characterized more by its millenarian beliefs than by its doctrine and practice of tongues speaking or divine healing and that only when the Second Coming of the Lord no longer seemed so imminent did Pentecostals elevate tongues speaking to the central motif of their movement. He noted that Pentecostalism's theological roots lay not in the Wesleyan Holiness tradition but in the Keswick branch of Holiness and that early Pentecostalism was clearly a part of the larger emerging fundamentalist movement. He constructed a collective biographical profile to show that Pentecostal leaders typically were young, poorly educated, socially marginal individuals who shared an evangelical Holiness background and an intense desire for new religious experiences; he suggested that rank-and-file Pentecostals likewise were overwhelmingly from the lower social strata. Regarding the contributions of Parham, whom he labeled a theological innovator, Anderson argued that the Kansas preacher planted the seeds of the Pentecostal movement by setting up his students at Bethel Bible College to "discover" tongues as the Bible evidence of Holy Spirit baptism, a doctrine he had previously worked out, and that Parham's religious views, even his more aberrant ones, had an affinity with other contemporary supernaturalistic religious movements and broader patterns of Progressive Era racial and social thought.

The author of *Vision of the Disinherited* also believed that only under the ministry of Seymour, an "obscure, chunky black man," was Pentecostalism transformed from "a relatively small, localized movement" to a national and even an international religious movement. He sensibly pointed out that Pentecostalism spread and institutionalized not on the wings of some disembodied religious message but through the evangelistic efforts of ambitious, hardworking men and women. He understood the many Pentecostal doctrinal conflicts to have resulted from more worldly struggles for power among leaders, rural-urban cultural differences, and class divisions. More generally, Anderson attributed the combativeness of Pentecostals to their deprived social position.[18]

Anderson's volume, arguably still the single most important history of early Pentecostalism, has been rightly criticized for its interpretive excesses and naturalistic approach to religious experience, including its patronizing assumption, as historian Grant Wacker noted some time ago, "that religious rewards were intrinsically less satisfying than rewards of a more worldly nature."[19] Anderson also failed to explain satisfactorily how people who were culturally marginal and economically deprived managed to utilize the techniques of popular culture and build a worldwide movement, to say nothing about how well these early American Pentecostals managed to achieve a decent if modest standard of living for themselves and their children. Additionally, many of his interpretations are based on an uncritical and even ahistorical imposition of questionable modern theories of social and economic deprivation and psychological maladjustment on a limited historical database; moreover, he did not recognize that the "disinherited" folk—farmers, workers, and immigrants—often were more in control of their lives and better able to cope with life's challenges than historians once believed and that a Pentecostal experience in fact may have been a source of liberation and empowerment.

Despite these and other problems with Anderson's conclusions, his book set the next decade's scholarly agenda for those working in the field of Pentecostal history. Moreover, it placed on the table of Pentecostal interpretation issues of class, power, status, and material gain.

1980–94

Since the early 1980s the study of Pentecostalism has continued to develop into a mature field of scholarship, and the historiography of Pentecostal origins has gone in a number of directions. For one, several recent "neoclassical" Pentecostal scholars, confident of their professional skills and secure in their own faith, have challenged what they consider to be secular authors' reductionist tendencies to arbitrarily dismiss the reality of the supernatural in human affair. Missiologist Paul Pomerville, for example, asserted that the Pentecostal movement was providential and spontaneous in its origins, globally diverse in terms of its manifestations, and chronologically elastic with respect to its origins, beginning as early as the mid-nineteenth century. Social ethicist Leonard Lovett and historian Vinson Synan are two scholars who also viewed this century's Pentecostal explosion, at least in part, as the "latter rain" outpouring of God's spirit promised in Scripture to precede the Lord's return. In contrast to Pomerville, they both take an "America first" view, locating the beginnings of the Pentecostal revival in the United States and suggesting that it spread from there around the globe.[20]

Of course, such a providential interpretation of Pentecostal origins must be accepted on faith. It cannot be verified by research and interpretive methods commonly accepted within the historical profession, and its persuasiveness as an explanation of origins is therefore limited and excluded from mainstream American historiography. The theory of multiple divinely caused eruptions additionally falters on the fact that, first, as church historian Cecil Mel Robeck has pointed out, most known occurrences trace back to the United States, and second, scattered glossolalic outbursts, whether in nineteenth-century America or elsewhere, have no historically specific linkages to the start of the American Pentecostal movement.[21]

A second recent historiographical trend reinterprets the central message of primitive Pentecostalism and unequivocally locates the origins of the movement within the American black community. Actually, this black interpretation of Pentecostal origins traces back to the 1970s in the writings of black scholars James Tinney and Leonard Lovett, neither of whom was a historian, and European missions scholar Walter Hollenweger.[22] These men unambiguously claimed that the Pentecostal movement began in Los Angeles in 1906 among the city's poor black Holiness folk, that Seymour unquestionably was the father of the Pentecostal movement, and that Pentecostalism, in Lovett's words, "originated from the womb of the black religious experience."[23]

Black Christianity was shaped not only by a Protestant theological mix and the experience of slavery, these scholars maintained, but also by West African folk religious customs, such as spirit possession, the sacred dance, and shout songs, many of which, Lovett explained, found their way into later Pentecostal worship practices. As a social ethicist, Lovett also theologized about the socially liberating effects of an experience of the Holy Spirit and attributed much of the success of the Azusa Street revival under Seymour's leadership to a Holy Spirit–inspired breakdown of class and racial barriers.[24] Lovett thus broadened the package of Pentecostal roots to include a unique black religious element, but he did not translate his theological insights about the socially transforming power of the Holy Spirit into a new interpretation of the meaning and origins of early Pentecostalism.

In the 1980s Douglas J. Nelson and Iain MacRobert picked up on the previous decade's work by Lovett, Tinney, and Hollenweger and expanded their ideas into a full-blown black interpretation of Pentecostalism.[25] This new interpretation can be summarized in three propositions. First, Seymour, the black pastor of the Azusa Mission, and not Parham, the white preacher from Kansas, should be regarded as the founder of the Pentecostal movement; the narrative of early Pentecostal history therefore should begin in 1906 and not 1901. Second, the central element in Pentecostal ideology was its belief in the church as a Holy Spirit–created egalitarian community in which all the walls of separation produced by racial, ethnic, gender, and class differences would be washed away in the blood of Jesus Christ. Seymour taught, Nelson and MacRobert contended, that Holy Spirit baptism expressed in "glossolalic worship" releases sufficient power in the baptized to make this vision a reality. At its root, then, these scholars insisted, the Pentecostal movement, the vision of the disinherited, was not some pie-in-the-sky socially irrelevant religious worldview, as Anderson contended, but a restoration of a New Testament–modeled social revolution that radically challenged the racist and unjust social structures of the nation. Third, the crucial source of Seymour's revolutionary new message as well as of many of the worship practices that characterized early Pentecostalism was black American Christianity, which, in turn, was a "bicultural" synthesis of Protestantism and West African folk religion. MacRobert boldly posited a direct line of continuity "between West African folk religion, black Christianity and early Pentecostalism."[26]

The work of these scholars opened up some new ways for historians to think about the meaning and origins of Pentecostalism, but to date their interpretive contentions suffer from a lack of sufficient historical evidence. Edith Blumhofer has summarized the case against what she maintains is a presentist-driven creation of "the myth of Azusa Street." Blumhofer pointed out the paucity of historical evidence informing our understanding of what actually went on at Azusa Street, questioned the representativeness of what took place at the mission, denied that there was anything "intrinsic to early Pentecostalism that fostered racial (or for that matter, gender) inclusiveness," and noted that none of the mission's members who left to form rival churches founded them on an interracial basis.[27] Additionally, the black-origins view assumes more than proves the centrality of the Azusa Street Mission to the emergence of national Pentecostalism. The racial interpretation also must satisfactorily answer the following question: would Azusa Street have happened without Topeka, or would a Pentecostal movement have emerged without the white Parham's new doctrine of initial evidence?

Still a third recent trend in Pentecostal historiography has been the attempt by scholars to move toward a synthesis of what we now know about the nineteenth-century roots of Pentecostalism; that is, to combine into a theologically holistic narrative the multiple strands of late nineteenth-century evangelical and Holiness religious thought and practice. And in yet a fourth trend, historians have sought more rigorously to understand early Pentecostalism on its own terms, as a lived religion: to understand the ideological sources and structure of its culture; to learn why and how it met the needs of those who joined the movement culture; and, following Anderson's lead, to explore more systematically how Pentecostalism intersected with and was shaped by its social and cultural setting. The publications of three historians in particular—James R. Goff, Grant Wacker, and Edith Blumhofer—stand out as examples of these newer trends in Pentecostal historiography.

Goff came at the question of origins via a biography of the controversial Charles F. Parham.[28] His book provided on the one hand the most detailed, sharply focused account of how, during the turbulent 1890s, Parham, a sickly, intelligent, restless, and religiously inquisitive young man, drew from a variety of personal, familial, and Holiness religious sources to produce many of the theological building blocks on which he would construct his historically significant Pentecostal doctrinal formulation. On the other hand, Goff's study also revealed Parham the twenty-seven-year-old theological innovator, who in the span of six months, from October 1900 to April 1901, "pieced the theological puzzle of Pentecostalism together" when he concluded that speaking in tongues—actual existing languages, or xenoglossa, he believed—was the biblical evidence of the baptism in the Holy Spirit, given to believers to expedite world evangelization in the last days before the Second Coming of Christ. Additionally, Goff points out, Parham also believed that tongues-speaking Christians were being recruited as Christ's elite "Bride" to rule with him in the millennial kingdom. With relentless logic Goff unhesitantly concluded that "Charles Parham founded the Pentecostal movement in Topeka, Kansas, early in 1901 and that the essential character of this new faith revolved around an intense millenarian-missions emphasis."[29]

Like Synan and Anderson before him, Goff also sought to embed Parham within the nation's turn-of-the-century social and cultural milieu. He plausibly suggested that Parham, much like contemporary populist leaders, "drew his formative thoughts" from the economically and culturally insecure agrarian world of the Kansas plains and found his most enthusiastic following among similarly situated people. For Goff, then, Parham was the founder of the Pentecostal movement not only because he first formulated the new religion's defining theological tenet but also because he first preached a Pentecostal full gospel message that met the social and spiritual needs of physically and psychologically hurting, politically powerless, and economically struggling poor and working-class people. Indeed, Parham was the father of "a revolution of socioreligious significance."[30] Much that Goff asserted about the functional fit between Pentecostal beliefs and the sociological identities of Pentecostals has a plausible ring. What is lacking in his account, as well as in most others that seek a sociological understanding of Pentecostalism, is enough concrete historical evidence linking Parham's followers to populism or more generally his religious message to the larger social and economic forces that were transforming America at the turn of the century.[31]

Because Parham's ministry in Missouri, Kansas, Texas, and northern Illinois, and not the entire Pentecostal movement, is the center of Goff's study, he was able to place the justly more famous West Coast Azusa Street revival in a somewhat different perspective. Goff showed that the Topeka beginnings and Parham's ministries before 1906 are not some sort of minor event or preface to the spectacular Azusa Street revival in Los Angeles under William J. Seymour's leadership. Goff did acknowledge that in the fall of 1906 Parham probably underrated the significance and dimensions of Seymour's Los Angeles revival, but he also importantly proceeded to show how, at that time, Seymour's work was strongly linked by theology, organization, and personnel to Parham's considerably larger midwestern movement, which itself was giving birth to other missions and new Pentecostal preachers who took the message across the nation. Thus on the issue of Parham's and Seymour's relative importance to the rise of Pentecostalism, Goff was clear in his view that, at least until 1909, the Pentecostal essentials preached and practiced at Azusa Street were derived from Parham, giving him priority as the father of Pentecostalism. Goff's account moreover made it clear that neither the West Coast nor Midwest branches of the Pentecostal revival, or the two combined, were growing rapidly enough to dent the national consciousness greatly. He implicitly cautioned historians not to mythologize Pentecostalism's place in the nation's past in the light of the more recent spectacular growth of the Pentecostal movement.[32]

Whereas Goff's major contribution was to provide one of the few scholarly biographies of any early Pentecostal leader, Wacker's most important contributions to the literature on Pentecostal origins lay in his opening up a fresh line of inquiry that started not with pre-1900 Pentecostal antecedents but with the fact of the movement's existence and durability, with what he early on called "the texture of Pentecostal faith." In several intellectually and conceptually creative and substantive essays, Wacker has sought to answer two questions about Pentecostalism: why did the movement survive once it had started, and who were the early converts to the movement?[33]

Initially Wacker presented a mostly positive evaluation of the structure and behavioral elements of the culture of Pentecostalism. He pointed out how Pentecostalism, with its emphasis on Jesus, supernatural beings, tongues speaking, and healings, had staying power because it met plain folk's personal needs by offering them "certitude that the supernatural claims of the gospel were really true." Additionally the new Pentecostalism offered converts friendship and security through membership in a relatively egalitarian community within which members could find help for life's problems and opportunities to develop self-respect.[34]

Wacker also suggested that the Pentecostal belief system offered members "an island of traditionalism in a sea of modernity" and as such "met the needs of ordinary people with a faith that was largely impervious to historical, rational, or empirical criticism."[35] "The movement flourished, in short," he wrote in one of his more memorable sentences, "not in spite of the fact that it was out of step with the times, but precisely because it was."[36] In later essays he more fully developed his understanding of Pentecostal antimodernism—or as he increasingly was to label it, primitivism—and elaborated on what he considered the more negative or dysfunctional consequences of the primitivistic impulse for Pentecostal belief and behavior.

Wacker defined primitivism generically "to refer to any effort to deny history, or to deny the contingencies of historical existence, by returning to the time before time, to the golden age that preceded the corruptions of life in history."[37] Starting from that general definition, he suggested that three specific patterns of primitivism largely shaped the emerging Pentecostal culture and belief system. Philosophical primitivism, the belief of Pentecostals that they could apprehend absolute truth, rendered them impervious to relativisms or antiformalistic philosophies of all sorts. This translated into a belief in a God-produced inerrant Bible whose existence and teachings transcend time and human cultures and whose timeless content should best be interpreted literally.

Historical primitivism, the Pentecostals' belief that "their movement repristinated apostolic Christianity," rendered irrelevant all church history since the second century. This ahistorical predisposition, reinforced by the latter rain theory of history, Wacker noted, translated into a Pentecostal emphasis on New Testament–like supernatural manifestations, including speaking in tongues, and an intense millenarianism. It was this belief that they were the people of the end-time latter rain, Wacker maintained, that fueled the Pentecostals' eschatological hope. "There is substantial evidence," he wrote, "that the hope of the Latter Rain came first in Pentecostal thinking, which meant that historical primitivism served as the logical and emotional foundation for dispensational premillennialism, rather than the reverse."[38] Wacker also partly attributed Pentecostalism's unconcern with public policy, politics, and societal reform, as well as its ardent missionary zeal and use of "military imagery" in religious discourse, to the movement's extreme millenarian emphasis.[39]

Wacker defined ethical primitivism as "a cluster of antimodern behavior patterns." Among pioneer Pentecostals this ethical primitivism contributed to disputes about the proper biblical pattern of church polity, a code of personal conduct characterized by a strict asceticism, hostile attitudes toward other religious traditions, and what Wacker called an "antistructuralist impulse: a determination to destroy the arbitrary conventions of denominational Christianity in order to replace them with a new order of primal simplicity and purity." Wacker suggested that this antistructuralist inclination stood behind Pentecostalism's relatively egalitarian class, gender, and ethnic social structure, as well as its stress on tongues speech, which he stated "functioned as an antistructuralist ritual." But Wacker also attributed to this same antistructuralism a more negative impulse that produced Pentecostalism's less desirable traits. The Pentecostal movement, he forebodingly wrote, "harbored a regressive strain that was, by any reasonable measure of such things, socially disruptive. Its defiance of social conventions, its bellicosity and zealotry, its ecstatic excess and deliberate scrambling of human language, surely reflected a darkly primitivist urge toward disorder."[40]

In "Character and the Modernization of North American Pentecostalism," Wacker added to the texture of Pentecostal culture a pragmatic cast of mind or impulse that, he claimed, coexisted with primitivism in dialectical tension to produce the enormous energy that permeated the entire movement. Words such as *ambitious, practical, hardheaded, independent, creative, persistent, brash,* and *tough* are among those describing the pragmatic personal character traits that Wacker culled out of the primary documents. The challenge the Duke Divinity School historian presented to students of Pentecostalism, including himself, was "to figure out why" these two character traits, primitivism and pragmatism, coexisted within the movement culture of Pentecostalism and to understand how they contributed to its origins and sustainability.[41]

Although Wacker's research has deepened our understanding of the Pentecostal mindset, it has left unclarified how Pentecostal recruits and congregations managed the contradictory primitivistic impulses toward psychological and social order and disorder so as both to prevent their communities from coming apart and to function as effectively in society as Wacker suggests they did. Nor is it certain from Wacker's analysis whether primitivistically inclined Americans were attracted to Pentecostalism because of its avowedly primitivistic message and lifestyle or whether such individuals recast the Pentecostal message in ways to suit their own needs. More generally, in Wacker's hands the concept of primitivism is stretched to cover such a wide range of contradictory values and behaviors that its heuristic value is diminished.

Goff's biography tells us much about the way one man formulated the initial evidence doctrine. Since Parham's direct institutional legacy was meager, however, his biographer did not shed much light on the way that the movement in whose beginnings Parham played a central role slowly became a group of denominations, churches, and ministries and a subculture all its own in American life. Both Anderson's and Wacker's works point us in the direction of understanding the Pentecostal subculture. In two recent books, one a history of the Assemblies of God and one a biography of Aimee Semple McPherson, Edith Blumhofer extends our knowledge of Pentecostal origins, institution building, and cultural formation, as well as of a number of other topics related to Pentecostalism's early history.[42]

Blumhofer's history of the Assemblies of God provides the most comprehensive account of the diverse late nineteenth-century religious currents that fed into Pentecostalism. Her description of the Gilded Age religious milieu is worth quoting:

> So in various settings, some late nineteenth-century evangelicals promoted an individual encounter with the Holy Spirit. Some regarded the encounter as a sanctifying event and a work of grace; others stressed its empowering and regarded it as a gift of faith. Some understood it within the experiential context of American Wesleyan thought; others saw themselves as differing significantly with Wesleyan thought on sanctification and perceived the contemporary repetition of the Pentecost event as eschatologically significant, a sign of the end times. For them, holiness and spiritual power were specifically end-times necessities. Some expressed their spiritual yearnings in Christocentric language; some dedicated themselves to the realization of restorationist hopes. But together they helped set in motion thought patterns and experiential expectations that motivated prayer for an outpouring of the Holy Spirit in a worldwide revival and influenced the development of Pentecostalism.[43]

As Blumhofer tells it, restorationism, "the attempt to recapture the presumed vitality, message, and form of the Apostolic Church," provided the ideological glue that bound these diverse theological strands into a cohesive and powerfully persuasive message. "The Pentecostal movement," she wrote, "is best understood as an expression of restorationist yearning, molded in significant ways by the hopes and dreams of late nineteenth-century restorationists."[44] She singled out four elements of restorationist thought that she believed "molded the subculture in which Pentecostalism flourished": its ahistorical, backward look to the New Testament church as the source and model of a nonevolutionary, cataclysmic view of the nature of social and religious change; its promotion of the unity of the body of Christ around the acceptance of New Testament beliefs and practices; its serious interest in eschatological issues; and its "come-outism" or anti-institutional spirit.[45]

Blumhofer used this restorationist package of ideas, especially its millenarianism, to retell the by now familiar story of Pentecostal beginnings. She cast Parham's formulation of the initial evidence doctrine in restorationist terms, but in contrast to Goff, who also stressed the millenarian context of Parham's thought, she reprioritized the Kansas preacher's motives: it was, she asserted, his craving for "assurance that he would 'go up' in the rapture" and thus escape the tribulation as part of the Holy Spirit–baptized bride of Christ that "came first and fueled Parham's determination to assert a uniform evidence for the experience." Likewise she reinterpreted Seymour's Azusa Street message and appeal. Ignoring Lovett's, Nelson's, MacRobert's, and Hollenweger's claims about the black origins of Pentecostalism, Blumhofer tightly linked Seymour's message with Parham but acknowledged that the black preacher's Los Angeles mission and its offshoots rapidly replaced Parham's ministry after 1906 as the center of Pentecostal activity and catalyzed Pentecostalism into a national and even international movement. She further stressed that Seymour's view of Holy Spirit baptism was "inextricably related to end-times evangelistic service" and that Seymour's evangelistic zeal likewise must be understood against the mission's restorationist view of history. The Azusa Street participants' view of their place in history, she maintained, was shared by other Pentecostals and is what fundamentally differentiated Pentecostals from most other Protestants.[46]

Despite Blumhofer's at times heavy-handed imposition of a restorationist gloss on almost every facet of early Pentecostalism, her history of the Assemblies of God clearly showed that the Pentecostal movement (its core values, organizational structures, programs) "didn't just happen," to borrow a phrase from Robert C. McMath Jr.'s history of populism.[47] Attuned to the institutional side of the creation of the Pentecostal movement, Blumhofer's account explained how convinced, energetic, aggressive, ambitious men and women spread the Pentecostal message, secured converts among countless Americans who shared a restorationist orientation, and built communities of solidarity—local assemblies—that constituted the infrastructure within which converts could be spiritually educated and equipped, socially enfolded into the primitive Pentecostal community, and sent out to recruit others.

As millennial restorationists, the early Pentecostals that inhabit the pages of *Restoring the Faith* are the same poor to middling folk, some recently arrived on America's shores and many recent migrants to the nation's cities, that Synan, Anderson, Goff, and Wacker have described in their writings. These

Pentecostals, or at least their leaders, added a subculture of their own to an already segmented American society. In contrast to Anderson, who viewed this Pentecostal culture as dysfunctional and reactionary, and to Wacker, who attributed both constructive and destructive character traits to the Pentecostals, Blumhofer, more in line with Goff, painted a mostly appreciative, but richly textured portrait of these primitive Pentecostal communities, which, she wrote, "functioned as exclusive total worlds, redefining reality, priorities, vocation, and relationships."[48] Pentecostal assemblies provided culturally and economically uprooted converts, strangers in their own land, a dominion of social and physical space in which to experience the supernatural, generally worship as they pleased, mutually support each other, nurture egalitarian relationships, and enhance one another's self-esteem and sense of importance in God's world. This building of a restorationist-infused culture of Pentecostalism, Blumhofer seemed to suggest, was the source of the successful rise of the Pentecostal movement.

Not quite a social history of early Pentecostalism, Blumhofer's book nonetheless sought to connect the social location, mindset, and subculture of the Pentecostals with broader cultural and social currents sweeping Progressive America. She viewed Pentecostals as a people nostalgic for an older evangelical-dominated American culture who sought solace for their cultural marginalization in the peace and hope provided by Pentecostal religion, a theme she developed more fully and successfully in her subsequent biography.

Restorationist thought explains a great deal about Pentecostal ideology and cultural patterns, especially its extreme otherworldliness and lack of social concern, and accounts for some of its institutional success. But its explanatory power stumbles a bit on the fact that so many restorationists rejected Pentecostalism and that Pentecostals were multidimensional Americans who were influenced by their inherited Protestant traditions, their rural and urban working-class cultures, and their familiarity with broader movements of social protest. Thus, despite what Blumhofer said in this book, it is not entirely clear that the restorationist dimension of the total Pentecostal message and community lifestyle was the all-consuming and dominating ideological force that drove Americans into Pentecostal missions and shaped their everyday lives. Her own well-written and insightful biography of Pentecostalism's earliest national celebrity, Aimee Semple McPherson, demonstrates that Pentecostalism's appeal was far wider than is usually assumed.

Drawing on her own prodigious research in Canadian and American archives, her earlier publications, and the work of historians Anderson, Wacker, and others who have delved into the Pentecostal mindset and culture, in *Aimee*

Semple McPherson: Everybody's Sister Blumhofer convincingly shows how at least "Sister's" variant of the Pentecostal message and lifestyle was congruent with a longstanding American-Canadian Anglo-Protestant revivalistic and pietistic tradition. She likewise provides significant evidence from McPherson's career that, as Nichol merely suggested years ago, Pentecostalism in its formative years was a doctrinally and behaviorally more fluid and diverse religious movement than was once thought to be the case: McPherson never insisted that tongues speech always manifests Holy Spirit baptism, was twice divorced, and associated with scores of the nation's civic, political, and popular cultural leaders. Moreover, she ministered in a variety of Protestant churches and was supported in her meetings by all sorts of evangelical, Pentecostal, and mainline Protestant ministers. That the Assemblies of God, the largest established classical Pentecostal denomination, was uncertain whether McPherson really belonged in an emerging "Pentecostal ministerial club" or whether her message and ministry style were authentically Pentecostal further testifies to the diversity within early Pentecostal ranks, a situation not unlike that of the contemporary charismatic movement.

The Wheaton historian's story of McPherson's life raises new interpretive possibilities about the relationship of early Pentecostalism to the larger American and Canadian Protestant tradition, and the relative unity and diversity within the young Pentecostal movement, but it also adds significantly to our understanding of the popular appeal, staying power, and cultural fit of McPherson's brand of evangelical Pentecostalism. Here Blumhofer provides a model study of the integration of Pentecostal, evangelical, mainline Protestant, and secular cultural history. She does so by surehandedly moving back and forth among the biographical facts of McPherson's life and career, the cognitive and behavioral contours of the pre–World War II Pentecostal mindset and culture, and Canadian and American social and cultural developments. The result is a lively and at times brilliant portrait of the multidimensional McPherson as the evangelist skyrocketed during the 1920s to the level of a national cultural hero among a people nostalgic for the traditional even as they experienced the rapid modernization of American life. McPherson tapped into this cultural mood by successfully blending the old biblical gospel with the new methods of mass communications and entertainment.[49]

Of course, the biography of McPherson raises questions of the extent to which the preacher's life and ministry were representative of a broader group of Pentecostal leaders and ministers and what an answer might mean for an understanding of the emergence of Pentecostalism. Blumhofer's own evidence can be read to support arguments both for Sister's typicality and for her uniqueness. Blumhofer's story of McPherson , as well as her story of the creation of the Assemblies of God, must be assessed against the other volumes discussed in this essay and ultimately against research yet to be undertaken. Nevertheless, in both books discussed here, Blumhofer has contributed immensely to our understanding of several important issues: the relationship of primitive Pentecostalism to a broader Anglo-Protestant religious world as well as to an America undergoing a major social and economic transformation; the roles and struggles of women who shaped and spread the Pentecostal message; the early Pentecostal ethos and subcultural network; the interplay of Pentecostalism and popular culture and patriotism; the close affinity of ministry and the quest for power; and how and why two very different Pentecostal denominations came into being—all topics of significance for an understanding of Pentecostalism's beginnings.

This overview of the literature on Pentecostal origins makes it abundantly clear that Pentecostal historiography has become an established subfield within the discipline of history. Over the last three decades new research in Pentecostal primary sources has given rise to new assessments of the significant events and personalities that constitute the internal history of early Pentecostalism. The use of diverse interpretive frameworks has provided insights into the broader contours that shaped the new Pentecostal movement. Each approach illuminated a slightly different set of questions and analytic concerns; each provided a slightly different angle of vision from which to view Pentecostalism's beginnings. But what of the future? I suggest six lines of inquiry that I believe need further exploration. Each arises out of the literature discussed in this essay.

First, historians need to continue exploring precisely which aspects of the nation's history in the Gilded Age and Progressive Era are most significant for helping us to understand the timing, theological and social shape, and staying power of a nascent Pentecostalism. Once those aspects have been identified, we will need an account of their roles in the movement.

Second, historians must integrate into a coherent analysis or story the elements of continuity and discontinuity between a post-1901 Pentecostalism and the nineteenth-century Holiness and evangelical movements. In doing so, they must avoid assuming that sources of influence are causes or that antecedent developments somehow inevitably had to lead to Pentecostalism. As Donald Dayton has indicated, something new did occur between 1901 and 1906 that provided the basis for the building of a religious movement distinct from the existing evangelical and Holiness groups. That newness must still be adequately explained without denying the significance of Pentecostal roots.

Third, historians must continue to refine their definitions and understandings of what constituted Pentecostalism in the early twentieth century. The histories surveyed in this essay clearly reveal that the movement was characterized both by a measure of ideological and fraternal cohesiveness and by an undeniable theological, social, and organizational diversity. They at least implicitly raised the following too infrequently asked question: should historians view the Pentecostal movement as a whole or in terms of its parts, and what are the implications of this issue for a study of origins?

Fourth, historians must more systematically address another question: who were the Pentecostals? The social location of both leaders and followers needs to be further examined, not in terms of some abstract notions of status, but in terms of the early twentieth-century American social structure. Additional biographical studies and the painstaking reconstruction of local church membership profiles would contribute to this undertaking. Until we get a more comprehensive social profile of early Pentecostals, all generalizations about the social functions and appeal of Pentecostal religion will be suspect.

Fifth, historians need to build on the work of Anderson, Wacker, and Blumhofer and continue to explore exactly how and why Pentecostals across the nation engaged in Pentecostal cultural formation and movement building. They need to address questions such as the following: Around what issues did Pentecostals form local fellowships? What was the specific role of doctrine, in contrast to other religious and social needs, in the creation of local fellowships? Did Pentecostal leaders use the rhetoric of restorationism, social criticism, traditional revivalism, or something else, along with the techniques of popular culture, to mobilize followers and resources to create Pentecostal communities and a national movement? How did American Pentecostalism actually function in society and negotiate between Pentecostals' local and social worlds and the larger, outside society? Precisely how did these two worlds intersect and shape the lives of Pentecostals? How should we define *movement* in early Pentecostalism? To what extent is it analytically helpful to view Pentecostalism, as historian Nathan Hatch suggested, as a twentieth-century mass democratic movement? On these and a host of other questions, recent studies on the populists, New Immigrants, and workers might provide insights that could be utilized to understand the world the first-generation Pentecostals made.[50]

Sixth, historians might also clarify the history of early American Pentecostalism through comparisons with other societies. Comparative analysis, such as informs Blumhofer's biography of Aimee Semple McPherson, would shed light on what was unique to the American Pentecostal experience, provide material to test the views of those who argue the movement had spontaneous global beginnings, and offer perspectives on sociological interpretations that tie Pentecostalism to the specific context of the United States in the 1890s. As scholars continue to publish notable works on Pentecostalism's history and meaning, mainstream historians will be compelled to incorporate into the general framework of twentieth-century American history the story of this nation's Pentecostals—a still largely excluded minority in the history of American life.

The Charismatic Movement, 1950s–90s

From its beginnings in 1901 Pentecostalism evolved over the course of the twentieth century into a national and international religious movement, institutionally fragmenting along racial, doctrinal, regional, and cultural lines into scores of denominations, independent churches, and parachurch organizations. Only after the mid-1950s did Pentecostal religious experiences, especially tongues speaking and other manifestations of the biblically described gifts of the Spirit, break out of their now labeled "classical" Pentecostal denominational boundaries into many mainline Protestant denominations, the Roman Catholic church, and by the 1980s, evangelical Protestant groups. Although the so-called charismatic movement has generated a substantial scholarly and popular literature, and many of the issues central to an understanding of its origins—the problem of providential versus human agency, the movement's innovative activities relative to its links to earlier religious developments, the implications of seeing the movement as a whole or in terms of its parts, its social sources and the nature of its appeal, and the movement's connection to the larger culture—parallel those raised about classical Pentecostalism, the historiography of the charismatic movement is still in its infancy and is only beginning to seriously address the questions that concern historians. A comprehensive survey of this literature is beyond the scope of this essay, but a few important works and interpretative trends will be noted here. Their significance for studying classical Pentecostal origins also will be suggested.

The earliest chroniclers of the charismatic movement were lay and clerical leaders who played crucial roles in the initiation of the charismatic renewal in their local churches and parishes, denominations, and for Roman Catholics, major universities. Much like the earliest classical Pentecostal writers, they often combined autobiography, personal testimonials, descriptive narrative, and some theological reflection, all enveloped within a providential framework, to describe why, how, and where their particular strand of Pentecostal renewal occurred, citing the help of influential classical Pentecostals when appropriate. Appearing at about the same time were works by denominational theologians that explained how the new Pentecostal spirituality in reality flowed out of or actualized particular historic church doctrines, rites, and practices. The goal was to show how the new spiritual experiences either had existed in some form earlier in church history or were at least implicit in a particular church tradition's beliefs or sacramental acts.[51]

In 1972 then Oral Roberts University professor Steve Durasoff, himself a Pentecostal, published *Bright Wind of the Spirit*, a popular history of Pentecostalism. Although in a book of thirteen chapters, based primarily on secondary sources, he devoted only one chapter each to sketching the story of the still relatively new Protestant and Roman Catholic charismatic movements, he did place these religious renewal movements in a continuum with classical Pentecostalism and earlier "spirit movements" in church history, simply labeling as Pentecostals all "spirit-filled" Christians, a conceptual approach to be later adopted by other writers.[52] Beginning in the mid-1970s a few scholars attempted to provide broad surveys and assessments of the charismatic movement. Among the more significant were works by Richard Quebedeaux, historian and outsider to the charismatic movement; Margaret Poloma, charismatic sociologist; Vinson Synan, classical Pentecostal historian; and Fr. Peter Hocken, Roman Catholic charismatic scholar and longtime secretary-treasurer of the Society for Pentecostal Studies.

Quebedeaux published *The New Charismatics* in 1976 and seven years later came out with an organizationally problematic and somewhat repetitive but very informative revised edition entitled *The New Charismatics II*. The book was not a detailed, comprehensive history of the many strands that constituted the new Pentecostalism but a historically informed conceptual "map" of the heterogeneous charismatic renewal, which ironically, Quebedeaux argued, by 1977 no longer existed as a visible religious movement. In addition to providing a brief historical sketch of the beginnings of the Protestant and Roman Catholic Pentecostal movements and including a chapter discussing the responses to the charismatic movement by mainline Protestant, evangelical Protestant, and classical Pentecostal leaders, Quebedeaux set the scholarly agenda in four areas.

First, although he viewed the new Pentecostalism as grounded in the same religious experience—baptism in the Holy Spirit—as was classical Pentecostalism, he chose to stress the contrasts between the early and later Pentecostal movements: the charismatics were theologically more moderate and nonsectarian, remained as a renewal force within their historic churches, stressed order and respectability in their meetings, integrated intellectual concerns with spirituality, and were largely white middle- and upper-class folk who comfortably embraced American culture and society. Second, Quebedeaux provided an informed and imaginative analysis of what he considered to be the main organizational, human, and spiritual components of the charismatic movement. Specifically, he outlined the decentralized structure of leadership within the charismatic movement; stressed the importance to the movement's growth and cohesion of organizational leaders, editors and publishers of charismatic literature, preachers, lecturers, and theologians; provided helpful biographical sketches of significant leaders; and described the diverse religious practices and doctrinal beliefs of a denominationally heterogeneous movement, including controversies over questions of human authority, the relationship of tongues to Spirit baptism, the relationship of Spirit baptism to church sacraments, and the charismatic movement's relationship to the larger culture and society. The thread of unity among this great diversity, Quebedeaux argued, "is the experience of baptism in the Holy Spirit, however interpreted."[53]

Third, in a rather disjointed, speculative, but suggestive chapter, Quebedeaux cited what he considered to be the movement's "reasons for success." In addition to enjoying internal strengths and aggressive leadership, the movement, according to Quebedeaux, benefited from an openness to new thinking about the Holy Spirit among ecumenical Protestant leaders and the Roman Catholic hierarchy, especially Pope John XXIII. He suggested that a favorable social setting in the 1960s encouraged historic denominations to entertain theological dissent, middle-class folk to look beyond materialism to new spiritual experiences, and young people to embrace countercultural lifestyles. In addition, he wrote, the decade was rife with other new social, ethnic, and racial movements. Fourth, Quebedeaux attributed to the charismatic movement the greater acceptance of the Pentecostal experience within the religious mainstream. He further accredited it with gaining recognition of the healthfulness of tongues speaking. And more generally, he claimed the charismatic movement restored the legitimacy of mysticism among Western middle-class Christians.[54]

A year before Quebedeaux's revised book was published, sociologist Margaret Poloma published a book-length sociological analysis of the charismatic movement. That it was a volume in Twayne's Social Movements Past and Present series suggests the extent to which secular society had taken notice of the new Pentecostal movement. Poloma provided only a brief history of the movement as a backdrop for her sociological analysis, but like Quebedeaux, she noted the distinct histories of and differences between classical Pentecostals and the new Protestant and Roman Catholic charismatics; despite this diversity, however, she too viewed all three groups as part of the same larger twentieth-century movement of Christians who emphasized a personal experience of the Holy Spirit.

Applying theoretical insights from the sociology of religion, Poloma interpreted the charismatic movement broadly; it was part, she suggested, both of a larger sacralization of society and of a religious awakening with the potential to challenge the American ethos and transform the cultural landscape. She devoted the bulk of her book to explicating the significant features of the movement, including its beliefs, organizational structures, strategies of recruitment and socialization, and use of the media. Throughout her analysis she raised questions about the negative impact on the charismatic movement of the routinization of charisma, excessive institutionalization and bureaucratization, and internal squabbles over issues of race, ethnicity, gender, ideology, and the exercise of power. Because of these issues she too considered the charismatic movement to be at a crossroads. Poloma concluded with an assessment of the movement's impact on mainstream Christian churches and contemporary politics and social action.[55]

Among classical Pentecostal historians, Vinson Synan has been in the forefront of efforts to promote spiritual unity among charismatic believers and to understand the connection between the modern charismatic movement and early twentieth-century Pentecostalism. In several writings he has viewed the development of classical Pentecostalism, the Protestant and Roman Catholic renewal movements, and the so-called third wave or evangelical practitioners of signs and wonders as phases of a singular Pentecostal movement, "variations on one Holy Spirit movement with one common factor of Spirit Baptism accompanied by glossolalia and/or other gifts of the Spirit."[56] In his popularly written *In the Latter Days: The Outpouring of the Holy Spirit in the Twentieth Century,* he viewed this century's Pentecostal explosion as the biblically implied "latter rain" outpouring of God's Spirit promised in Scripture to precede the Lord's return. Moreover, he labeled Pentecostals and charismatics collectively "The Latter-Rain People."

Provocatively, the classical Pentecostal Synan included in his short book a chapter-length sketch of the nineteenth-century Protestant and, beyond what other Pentecostal historians have suggested, Roman Catholic roots of twentieth-century Pentecostalism. "Thus, as the century came to an end," he wrote, "both Catholic and Protestant leaders were calling for a new Pentecost with a restoration of the signs and wonders that had characterized the early church. In a sense, the entire nineteenth century was like a Pentecost novena—the church waiting in the upper room praying for and expecting an outpouring of the Holy Spirit with a renewal of the gifts of the Spirit for the new century that was about to dawn."[57] Moreover, in the four chapters he devoted to telling the story of the rise of the charismatic movement, he traced in surprising detail the long spiritual preparation in the historic churches that in Synan's reconstruction made almost inevitable Pentecostalism's emergence among first mainline Protestants, then Roman Catholics, and finally evangelicals and others.[58]

Peter Hocken, a Roman Catholic theologian and an active participant in the charismatic movement, has published lengthy essays that together constitute the most comprehensive, richly detailed, and nuanced history of the entire charismatic movement.[59] Hocken, like most "participant-scholars," asserted a providential view of the origins of the movement, writing in the *Dictionary of Pentecostal and Charismatic Movements:* "Its genesis indicates that it had no one human founder, that its arrival was unexpected and unplanned, that it did not come as a set of coherent ideas or with any strategic methodology, and that it was not in its origins the product of any one Christian tradition more than others."[60] Nevertheless, in the same article he also provided the most useful introduction to the movement's story of beginnings and subsequent history, the role of key participants, and the diverse movement's organizational structures, practices, and beliefs. Perhaps his most significant interpretative contribution is his suggested chronological scaffolding for analyzing the changes in the movement's short history: "Earliest Stirrings (pre-1960)" locates the roots of the movement in religious developments in the 1940s and 1950s; "The Emergence of the Movement (1960–67)" focuses on the rise of the Protestant charismatic renewal, beginning with Episcopal priest Dennis Bennett's public announcement to his congregation in Van Nuys, California, that he spoke in tongues; "The Movement Takes Shape (1967–77)" traces the rise of the Catholic Pentecostal movement from its beginnings at Duquesne University and the University of Notre Dame and its impact on the larger charismatic movement, recounts the expansion of the renewal among mainline Protestants and nondenominational groups, and concludes with the 1977 Conference on Charismatic Renewal in Kansas City; and "Consolidation (1977–87)" treats recent trends and acknowledges that the movement, if it had not peaked by the late 1970s, as asserted by Quebedeaux, had certainly "moved into a new and less sensational pattern of growth."[61] In an article published in 1994 in *Pneuma: The Journal of the Society for Pentecostal Studies,* Hocken updated his understanding of contemporary developments and reflected on where the charismatic movement was heading.[62]

The studies by Quebedeaux, Poloma, Synan, and Hocken provide a starting point for the scholarly study of the history of the charismatic movement. They also, mostly by implication, raise interesting questions about the origins of classical Pentecostalism. If in fact one can find seeds of the later Pentecostal religious manifestations in both Protestant and Roman Catholic renewal activities in the nineteenth century, then must scholars broaden the search for the roots of classical Pentecostalism's stress on the Holy Spirit well beyond the pre-1900 Protestant Holiness and evangelical subcultures? Do the ecclesiastical diversity and separate denominational histories of the charismatic movement force historians to visit anew the question of whether there was a classical Pentecostal movement or movements? Does the middle-class composition of charismatic groups call into question the usefulness of theories of status deprivation to explain classical Pentecostalism's appeal? Might a careful sociological and organizational analysis of the ways in which the various parts of the contemporary charismatic movement came into being and developed provide insights for understanding how early twentieth-century Pentecostalism became a movement?

Notes

1. For an informative survey of this literature, see Grant A. Wacker, "Bibliography and Historiography of Pentecostalism (U.S.)," in *Dictionary of Pentecostal and Charismatic Movements,* ed. Stanley Burgess and Gary B. McGee (Grand Rapids, Mich.: Zondervan, 1988), 65–76; and idem, "Are the Golden Oldies Still Worth Playing? Reflections on History Writing among Early Pentecostals," *Pneuma* 8 (Fall 1986): 81–100.

2. Stanley Howard Frodsham, *With Signs Following: The Story of the Pentecostal Revival in the Twentieth Century,* rev. ed. (Springfield, Mo.: Gospel Publishing House, 1946); Carl Brumback, *Suddenly . . . from Heaven: A History of the Assemblies of God* (Springfield, Mo.: Gospel Publishing House, 1961); Charles Conn, *Like a Mighty Army Moves the Church of God,* rev. ed. (Cleveland, Tenn.: Pathway, 1977).

3. Klaude Kendrick, *The Promised Fulfilled: A History of the Modern Pentecostal Movement* (Springfield, Mo.: Gospel Publishing House, 1961).

4. Ibid., 31–68 (quotation on 37). Kendrick did sanitize Parham's biography by failing to discuss either the preacher's more bizarre teachings or the ultimately unproven charges of homosexuality leveled against him.

5. John T. Nichol, *The Pentecostals* (Plainfield, N.J.: Logos International, 1971). This is a revised edition of *Pentecostalism* (New York: Harper and Row, 1966).

6. Vinson Synan, *The Holiness-Pentecostal Movement in the United States* (Grand Rapids, Mich.: Eerdmans, 1971).

7. Ibid., 168.

8. Donald Dayton, *Theological Roots of Pentecostalism* (Grand Rapids, Mich.:

Zondervan, 1987). Only 7 out of 180 pages treat the emergence of Pentecostalism. Also see Dayton's earlier essay, "From 'Christian Perfection' to the 'Baptism of the Holy Ghost,'" in *Aspects of Pentecostal-Charismatic Origins*, ed. Vinson Synan (Plainfield, N.J.: Logos International, 1975), 41–54.

9. Dayton, *Theological Roots*, 167.

10. For a discussion of the broader Protestant concerns about the Holy Spirit in the Gilded Age, see Grant A. Wacker, "The Holy Spirit and the Spirit of the Age in American Protestantism, 1880–1910," *Journal of American History* 72 (June 1985): 45–62.

11. Dayton, *Theological Roots*, 176.

12. William Menzies, *Anointed to Serve: The Story of the Assemblies of God* (Springfield, Mo.: Gospel Publishing House, 1971); idem, "The Non-Wesleyan Origins of the Pentecostal Movement," in *Aspects*, ed. Synan, 83–97; Edith Waldvogel (Blumhofer), "The 'Overcoming Life': A Study in the Reformed Evangelical Origins of Pentecostalism," Ph.D. diss., Harvard University, 1977; Robert Anderson, *Vision of the Disinherited: The Making of American Pentecostalism* (New York: Oxford University Press, 1979).

13. Waldvogel, "The 'Overcoming Life,'" 1–148.

14. Menzies, *Anointed to Serve*, 40, 80–143. Because the Holiness-Pentecostal wing of the movement largely consisted of denominations that previously had been established as Holiness denominations, Synan and other historians of this branch of Pentecostalism also dealt with the institutional and organizational side of the creation of the Pentecostal movement. For example, see Vinson Synan, *The Old-Time Power*, rev. ed. (Franklin Springs, Ga.: Advocate, 1986); Joseph E. Campbell, *The Pentecostal Holiness Church, 1898–1948* (Franklin Springs, Ga.: Publishing House of the Pentecostal Holiness Church, 1951).

15. For an explanation and critique of these theories and some of the social science literature on Pentecostalism, see Kilian McDonnell, *Charismatic Renewal and the Churches* (New York: Seabury, 1976).

16. Anderson, *Vision of the Disinherited*. In a brilliantly insightful review of Anderson's book soon after it was published, historian Wacker noted Anderson's enormous contributions to the historiography of early Pentecostalism, including his book's conceptual and interpretive sophistication, breadth of coverage, and prodigiously researched database, all together making *Vision of the Disinherited* "the standard that subsequent interpreters simply shall have to come to terms with, one way or another." See Grant A. Wacker, "Taking Another Look at the *Vision of the Disinherited*," *Religious Studies Review* 8 (Jan. 1982): 15–22 (quotation on 16).

17. Anderson, *Vision of the Disinherited*, 240.

18. Ibid., 47–136; the description of Seymour is found on page 61.

19. Wacker, "Another Look," 18.

20. Paul A. Pomerville, *The Third Force in Missions* (Peabody, Mass.: Hendrickson, 1985). On the providential origins of Pentecostalism by another missiologist, see L. Grant McClung Jr., ed., *Azusa Street and Beyond* (South Plainfield, N.J.: Bridge, 1886), 3–4; Vinson Synan, *In the Latter Days: The Outpouring of the Holy Spirit in the Twentieth Century* (Ann Arbor, Mich.: Servant, 1984). Among modern scholars Leonard Lovett utilized the latter rain theory in the early 1970s to provide the overarching interpretive framework for his view of the origins of Pentecostalism. "Belief in the Lat-

ter Rain theory presupposes a 'faith' stance," he wrote. "I share and embrace such a stance unashamedly." On the basis of such a theory, Lovett dogmatically asserted that at Azusa Street "the Latter Rain poured"; earlier manifestations of the Spirit, including what took place under Charles F. Parham at Topeka, Kansas, in 1901, were only "early raindrops of the Latter Rain." See Leonard Lovett, "Black Origins of the Pentecostal Movement," in *Aspects*, ed. Synan, 125–40. For a critique of the spontaneous global origins view of Pentecostalism, see Cecil M. Robeck Jr., "Pentecostal Origins from a Global Perspective," in *All Together in One Place: Theological Papers from the Brighton Conference on World Evangelization,* ed. Harold D. Hunter and Peter D. Hocken (Sheffield, England: Sheffield Academic, 1993), 166–80.

21. Robeck, "Pentecostal Origins," 3–4. For a discussion of the problems associated with attributing events within history to God, see *A Christian View of History?* ed. George Marsden and Frank Roberts (Grand Rapids, Mich.: Eerdmans, 1975).

22. Leonard Lovett, "Perspective on the Black Origins of the Contemporary Pentecostal Movement," *Journal of the Interdenominational Theological Center* 1 (1973): 36–49 (much of this material is also contained in Lovett, "Black Origins," 125–41); James S. Tinney, "William J. Seymour: Father of Modern-Day Pentecostalism," *Journal of the Interdenominational Theological Society* 4 (Fall 1977): 34–44; idem, "Competing Theories of Historical Origins for Black Pentecostalism," paper presented at the Annual Meeting of the American Academy of Religion, Nov. 1979, New York City; idem, "Exclusivist Tendencies in Pentecostal Self-Definition," paper presented to the Society for Pentecostal Studies, Dec. 1978; Walter J. Hollenweger, "A Black Pentecostal Concept: A Forgotten Chapter of Black History: The Black Pentecostals' Contribution to the Church Universal," *Concept* 30 (June 1970): 9, 16–17.

23. Lovett, "Perspective," 42.

24. Ibid., 46; Lovett, "Black Origins," 137–40; Leonard Lovett, "Black Holiness-Pentecostalism: Implications for Ethics and Social Transformation," Ph.D. diss., Emory University, 1978. On the interracial aspects of Azusa Street also see, Cecil M. Robeck, "Azusa Street Revival," in *Dictionary of Pentecostal and Charismatic Movements,* ed. Burgess and McGee, 31–36.

25. Douglas J. Nelson, "For Such a Time As This: The Story of Bishop William J. Seymour and the Azusa Street Revival," Ph.D. diss., University of Birmingham, 1981; Iain MacRobert, *The Black Roots and White Racism of Early Pentecostalism in the USA* (New York: St. Martin's, 1988). Also see Walter J. Hollenweger, "After Twenty Years' Research on Pentecostalism," *International Review of Mission* 75 (Jan. 1986): 3–12.

26. MacRobert, *Black Roots,* 78.

27. "For Pentecostals, a Move toward Racial Reconciliation," *Christian Century,* 27 Apr. 1994, pp. 445–46.

28. James R. Goff Jr., *Fields White unto Harvest: Charles F. Parham and the Missionary Origins of Pentecostalism* (Fayetteville: University of Arkansas Press, 1988). For my extended comments on Goff's book, see Augustus Cerillo Jr., "The Origins of American Pentecostalism: A Review Essay of James R. Goff, Jr., *Fields White unto Harvest," Pneuma* 15 (Spring 1993): 77–88. Also see James R. Goff Jr., "Pentecostal Millenarianism: The Development of Premillennial Orthodoxy, 1909–1943," *Ozark Historical Review* 12 (Spring 1983), 14–24; idem, "Charles F. Parham and His Role in the Development of the Pentecostal Movement: A Reevaluation," *Kansas History* 7

(Autumn 1984): 226–37; and idem, "Initial Tongues in the Theology of Charles Fox Parham," in *Initial Evidence*, ed. Gary B. McGee (Peabody, Mass.: Hendrickson, 1991), 57–71.

29. Goff, *Fields*, 15. On the basis of his historical reconstruction, Goff also debunked as flawed both Parham's and Agnes Ozman's later conflicting accounts of the origins of the "Topeka Pentecost," especially Parham's story of the students at his recently opened (Oct. 1900) Bethel Bible College having independently concluded after studying the book of Acts that tongues are the initial evidence of the Baptism in the Holy Spirit. The historical evidence, Goff maintained, makes it clear that Parham himself, through his Bible teaching at Bethel, motivated his students to conclude that missions tongues were the New Testament evidence of Holy Spirit Baptism, which they did on 1 Jan. 1901. Also see D. William Faupel, *The Everlasting Gospel: The Significance of Eschatology in the Development of Pentecostal Thought* (Sheffield, England: Sheffield Academic, 1996); and idem, "The Function of 'Models' in the Interpretation of Pentecostal Thought," *Pneuma* 2 (Spring 1980): 51–71.

30. Goff, *Fields*, 16.

31. Mickey Crews, in his book *The Church of God: A Social History* (Knoxville, Tenn.: University of Tennessee Press, 1990), argued that the Holiness-Pentecostal Church of God had no direct connection to populism.

32. Goff, *Fields*, 87–127, 160–66.

33. Grant A. Wacker, "A Profile of American Pentecostalism," unpublished paper, 1981, pp. 17–24; idem, "The Functions of Faith in Primitive Pentecostalism," *Harvard Theological Review* 77 (1984): 353–75; idem, "Pentecostalism," in *Encyclopedia of American Religious Experience*, 3 vols., ed. Charles H. Lippy and Peter W. Williams (New York: Scribner, 1988), 2:933–45; idem, "Playing for Keeps: The Primitivist Impulse in Early Pentecostalism," in *The American Quest for the Primitive Church*, ed. Richard T. Hughes (Urbana: University of Illinois Press, 1988), 196–219; and idem, "Character and the Modernization of North American Pentecostalism," paper read at the meeting of the Society for Pentecostal Studies, 1991.

34. Wacker, "Profile," 17–24; idem, "Functions of Faith," 360–63 (quotation on 361).

35. Wacker, "Functions of Faith," 363; idem, "Profile," 35.

36. Wacker, "Functions of Faith," 374; also in idem, "Pentecostalism," 2:942.

37. Wacker, "Playing for Keeps," 197.

38. Ibid., 197–207.

39. Wacker, "Functions of Faith," 370–74.

40. Wacker, "Playing for Keeps," 207–13 (quotations, in order, on 107, 209–10, 211, and 212).

41. Wacker, "Character and Modernization," 10–22 (quotations on 10, 11); idem, "Playing for Keeps," 213.

42. Edith L. Blumhofer, *Restoring the Faith: The Assemblies of God, Pentecostalism, and American Culture* (Urbana: University of Illinois Press, 1993); *Restoring the Faith* is a slightly revised edition of *The Assemblies of God*, 2 vols. (Springfield, Mo.: Gospel Publishing House, 1989). Also see her *"Pentecost in My Soul": Explorations in the Meaning of Pentecostal Experience in the Early Assemblies of God* (Springfield, Mo.: Gospel Publishing House, 1989); idem, *Aimee Semple McPherson: Everybody's Sister* (Grand Rapids, Mich.: Eerdmans, 1993).

43. Blumhofer, *Assemblies of God,* 1:63–64.

44. Ibid., 1:18.

45. Ibid., 1:18–20, 150, 152. Also see idem, *Restoring the Faith,* 12–15.

46. Blumhofer, *Restoring the Faith,* 43–62 (quotations on 50 and 60). Also see Blumhofer, *Assemblies of God,* 1:110, 150.

47. Robert C. McMath Jr., *American Populism: A Social History 1877–1898* (New York: Hill and Wang, 1993), 153.

48. Blumhofer, *Restoring the Faith,* 88–99 (quotation on 89).

49. One cannot help noting the sociological similarities between McPherson's appeal and methods and more recent Pentecostal, charismatic, and fundamentalist radio, television, and other media "stars."

50. Nathan O. Hatch, *The Democratization of American Christianity* (New Haven, Conn: Yale University Press, 1989), 210–19; Lawrence Goodwyn, *The Populist Moment: A Short History of the Agrarian Revolt in America* (Oxford: Oxford University Press, 1978); McMath, *American Populism;* John Bodnar, *The Transplanted: A History of Immigrants in Urban America* (Bloomington: Indiana University Press, 1985); Melvyn Dubofsky, *Industrialism and the American Worker, 1865–1920,* 3d ed. (Wheeling, Ill.: Harlan Davidson, 1996).

51. Two autobiographical accounts are Dennis J. Bennett, *Nine O'clock in the Morning* (Plainfield, N.J.: Logos International, 1970); and Kevin Ranaghan and Dorothy Ranaghan, *Catholic Pentecostals* (New York: Paulist, 1969), revised as *Catholic Pentecostals Today* (South Bend, Ind.: Charismatic Renewal Services, 1983). Also see the influential book by John Sherrill, *They Speak with Other Tongues* (Westwood, N.J.: Fleming H. Revell, 1964). Some history but mostly personal reflections and theologizing are to be found in Edward D. O'Connor, *The Pentecostal Movement in the Catholic Church* (Notre Dame, Ind.: Ave Maria, 1971). Also see Ralph Martin, ed., *The Spirit and the Church* (New York: Paulist, 1976); Kilian McDonnell, ed., *The Holy Spirit and the Power: The Catholic Charismatic Renewal* (Garden City, N.Y.: Doubleday, 1975); idem, *Catholic Pentecostalism: Problems in Evaluation* (Watchung, N.J.: Charisma, 1971); Peter Hocken, "The Significance and Potential of Pentecostalism," in *New Heaven? New Earth? An Encounter with Pentecostalism,* ed. Simon Tucswell, Peter Hocken, John Orme Mills, Simon Tugwell, and George Every (Springfield, Ill.: Templegate, 1977), 15–67; J. Rodman Williams, *The Pentecostal Reality* (Plainfield, N.J.: Logos International, 1972); and, for a pioneering multidenominational view, Russell P. Spittler, ed., *Perspectives on the New Pentecostalism* (Grand Rapids, Mich.: Baker Book House, 1976). Indispensable for understanding how the various denominations responded to and sought to understand the Pentecostal phenomenon in their midst is Kilian McDonnell, ed., *Presence, Power, Praise: Documents on the Charismatic Renewal,* 3 vols. (Collegeville, Minn.: Liturgical, 1980).

52. Steve Durasoff, *Bright Wind of the Spirit: Pentecostalism Today* (Plainfield, N.J.: Logos International, 1972). Although Durasoff provided two chapters on the life and ministry of Oral Roberts and one chapter on the Full Gospel Business Men's Fellowship and frequently mentioned the ministry of David du Plessis, all these having influenced the nascent charismatic movement, he did not systematically analyze the classical Pentecostal influences on the Protestant and Roman Catholic renewal movements. On Oral Roberts's and the Full Gospel Business Mens' Fellowship Inter-

national's influence on and connection to the early charismatic movement, see David E. Harrell Jr., *All Things Are Possible: The Healing and Charismatic Revivals in Modern America* (Bloomington: Indiana University Press, 1975); idem, *Oral Roberts: An American Life* (San Francisco: Harper and Row, 1985), esp. chap. 11; and Vinson Synan, *Under His Banner* (Costa Mesa, Calif.: Gift, 1992). In 1978 Charles E. Hummel, an evangelical, published *Fire in the Fireplace: Contemporary Charismatic Renewal* (Downers Grove, Ill.: InterVarsity), a mostly theological assessment of the Pentecostal-charismatic movements; in his short historical section he suggested that the renewal movements arose spontaneously and viewed the contemporary renewal as a river fed by three sometimes merging but distinct streams: classical Pentecostalism, and what was then termed neo-Pentecostalism both in the Protestant churches and in the Roman Catholic church.

53. Richard Quebedeaux, *The New Charismatics* (Garden City, N.Y.: Doubleday, 1976); idem, *The New Charismatics II* (San Francisco: Harper and Row, 1983) (quotation on 151).

54. Quebedeaux, *The New Charismatics II,* 211–39.

55. Margaret Poloma, *The Charismatic Movement: Is There a New Pentecost?* (Boston: Twayne, 1982).

56. Synan, *In the Latter Days;* idem, *The Twentieth-Century Pentecostal Explosion: The Exciting Growth of Pentecostal Churches and Charismatic Renewal Movements* (Altamonte Springs, Fla.: Creation House, 1987); the quotation is from Synan, ed., *Aspects,* 2.

57. Synan, *In the Latter Days,* 42.

58. Ibid., 83–146. Synan's now classic work *The Holiness-Pentecostal Movement in the United States,* published in 1971 (and discussed earlier in this essay), has been reissued as *The Holiness-Pentecostal Tradition: Charismatic Movements in the Twentieth Century* (Grand Rapids, Mich.: Eerdmans, 1997). Appearing too late to be used in this essay, the book contains five new chapters treating the global expansion of Pentecostalism and the development of the charismatic movement in the mainline churches.

59. Peter Hocken, *One Lord, One Spirit, One Body: Ecumenical Grace of the Charismatic Movement* (Gaithersburg, Md.: The Word among Us, 1987); idem, "Charismatic Movement," 130–60; idem, "The Charismatic Movement in the United States," *Pneuma* 16 (Fall 1994): 191–214; and idem, "A Survey of Independent Charismatic Churches," *Pneuma* 18 (Spring 1996): 93–105. On the Catholic charismatic movement also see Francis A. Sullivan, "Catholic Charismatic Renewal," in *Dictionary of Pentecostal and Charismatic Movements,* ed. Burgess and McGee, 110–26; and idem, *Charisms and Charismatic Renewal: A Biblical and Theological Study* (Ann Arbor, Mich.: Servant, 1982).

60. Hocken, "Charismatic Movement," 158.

61. Ibid., 130–44, 155–60 (quotation on 139).

62. Hocken, "Charismatic Movement in the United States."

Contributors

DANIEL BAYS teaches modern Chinese history at the University of Kansas, Lawrence, and does research on the history of Protestantism in China. He has directed major research projects on the history of Christianity in China funded by the Henry Luce Foundation and the Pew Charitable Trusts and is the editor of *Christianity in China: The Eighteenth Century to the Present.*

KURT O. BERENDS, an adjunct assistant professor of history at Calvin College, Grand Rapids, Michigan, received his Ph.D. degree from Oxford University. He is working on a book that details the transformation of religion in the South during the Civil War.

EDITH L. BLUMHOFER is the associate director of the Public Religion Project at the University of Chicago Divinity School. The author of *Aimee Semple McPherson: Everybody's Sister* and *Restoring the Faith: The Assemblies of God, Pentecostalism, and American Culture* and the coeditor (with Randall Balmer) of *Modern Christian Revivals,* she is writing a biography of the hymnwriter Fanny J. Crosby and researching early Pentecostalism in Chicago.

AUGUSTUS CERILLO is a professor of history at California State University, Long Beach, and the director of the Lewis Wilson Institute for Pentecostal Studies at Southern California College, Costa Mesa. A former editor of *The History Teacher,* he is the book review editor for *PNEUMA: The Journal of the Society for Pentecostal Studies.* His publications, which are in the areas of urban progressivism, evangelicalism and American politics, and the Pentecostal movement, include *Reform in New York City: A Study of Urban Progressivism* and *Salt and Light: Evangelical Political Thought in Modern America* (coauthored with Murray W. Dempster).

NANCY L. EIESLAND is an assistant professor of sociology of religion at Candler School of Theology and the Graduate Division of Religion at Emory University, Atlanta, Georgia. She coedited *Contemporary American Religion: An Ethnographic Reader* and is the author of the forthcoming book *A Particular Place: Exurbanization and Religious Response.*

JOHN C. GREEN is a professor of political science and the director of the Ray C. Bliss Institute of Applied Politics at the University of Akron, Ohio. He is a coauthor of *The Bully Pulpit: The Politics of Protestant Clergy* and *Religion and the Culture Wars.*

R. MARIE GRIFFITH has held fellowships at Princeton University and at Northwestern University, where she taught in the Department of Religion. She is the author of *God's Daughters: Evangelical Women and the Power of Submission.*

JAMES L. GUTH is a professor of political science at Furman University, Greenville, South Carolina. He is a coauthor of *The Bully Pulpit: The Politics of Protestant Clergy* and *Religion and the Culture Wars.*

DOUGLAS JACOBSEN is a professor of church history and theology at Messiah College, Grantham, Pennsylvania. He is coeditor of *Re-Forming the Center: American Protestantism, 1900 to the Present* and is completing a book on the history of Pentecostal and charismatic theology in America (tentatively titled *Thinking in the Spirit*).

FREDERICK W. JORDAN is the dean of faculty and an instructor in history at Woodberry Forest School in Woodberry Forest, Virginia.

LYMAN A. KELLSTEDT is a professor of political science at Wheaton College, Wheaton, Illinois. He is a coauthor of *The Bully Pulpit: The Politics of Protestant Clergy* and *Religion and the Culture Wars.*

ALBERT FREDERICK SCHENKEL is a professor of American studies at the Uzbeck State University of Foreign Languages, Tashkent, Uzbekistan. The author of *The Rich Man and the Kingdom: John D. Rockefeller, Jr. and the Protestant Establishment* and the editor of translations of *Bukhara: An Oriental Gem* and *Khiva: The City of "A Thousand Domes,"* he is editing a translation of a book on the Muslim religious scholar Muhammad bin Ismail Al-Mughirah Al-Bukhari.

CORWIN E. SMIDT is a professor of political science at Calvin College, Grand Rapids, Michigan. He is a coauthor of *The Bully Pulpit: The Politics of Protestant Clergy* and *Religion and the Culture Wars.*

RUSSELL P. SPITTLER is provost and vice-president for academic affairs at Fuller Theological Seminary, Pasadena, California. A New Testament scholar, he was until 1995 director of Fuller Seminary's David du Plessis Center for Christian Spirituality.

HELEN LEE TURNER is an associate professor of religion at Furman University, Greenville, South Carolina. She holds M.Div. and D.Min. degrees from Vanderbilt Divinity School and a Ph.D. in religion in America from the University of Virginia. She is the author of several articles on fundamentalism in the Southern Baptist Convention and is writing an introduction to religion textbook.

GRANT A. WACKER teaches American religious history at Duke University and is senior editor of *Church History: Studies in Christianity and Culture.* He has served as president of the Society for Pentecostal Studies and as a mentor in the Young Scholars in American Religion program at Indiana University/Purdue University in Indianapolis. Most of his publications pertain to the history of the evangelical, fundamentalist, and Pentecostal traditions in North America.

Index